20-08

Video Basics

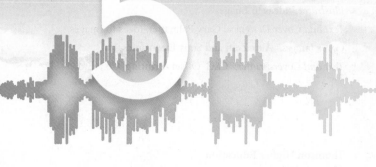

5

Herbert Zettl

San Francisco State University

THOMSON
＊
™
WADSWORTH

AUSTRALIA ■ BRAZIL ■ CANADA ■ MEXICO ■ SINGAPORE ■ SPAIN
UNITED KINGDOM ■ UNITED STATES

THOMSON

✳
™

WADSWORTH

Video Basics, **Fifth Edition**

Herbert Zettl

Publisher: Holly J. Allen

Senior Development Editor: Renee Deljon

Assistant Editor: Lucinda Bingham

Editorial Assistant: Meghan Bass

Technology Project Manager: Jeanette Wiseman

Managing Marketing Manager: Kimberly Russell

Marketing Assistant: Alexandra Tran

Senior Marketing Communications Manager: Shemika Britt

Project Manager, Editorial Production: Catherine Morris

Creative Director: Rob Hugel

Art Director: Maria Epes

Print Buyer: Judy Inouye

Permissions Editor: Bob Kauser

Production Service: Ideas to Images

Compositor: Ideas to Images

Art Editor: Gary Palmatier

Photo Researcher: Cheri Throop

Copy Editor: Elizabeth von Radics

Illustrator: Ideas to Images

Text and Cover Designer: Gary Palmatier, Ideas to Images

Cover Images: Alex Zettl and Sony Electronics, Inc.

Text and Cover Printer: C&C Offset Printing Co., Ltd.

Printed in China

3   4   5   6   7   10   09   08

ExamView® and ExamView Pro® are registered trademarks of FSCreations, Inc. Windows is a registered trademark of the Microsoft Corporation used herein under license. Macintosh and Power Macintosh are registered trademarks of Apple Computer, Inc. PixBox is a registered trademark of Dudkowski Patent Properties. Used herein under license.

Library of Congress Control Number: 2006926778

Student Edition: ISBN-13: 978-0-495-05032-2
ISBN-10: 0-495-05032-6

Thomson Higher Education
10 Davis Drive
Belmont, CA 94002-3098
USA

For more information about our products, contact us at:
Thomson Learning Academic Resource Center
1-800-423-0563

For permission to use material from this text or product, submit a request online at *http://www.thomsonrights.com*. Any additional questions about permissions can be submitted by e-mail to *thomsonrights@thomson.com*.

To Alex and Anne

Brief Contents

Contents

CHAPTER 15   Production Environment: Field and Computer-generated   316

PART VI   Production Control: Talent and Directing   337

CHAPTER 16   Talent, Clothing, and Makeup   338

About the Author

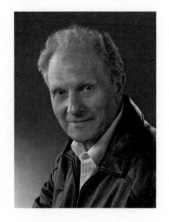

HERBERT ZETTL is a professor emeritus of the Broadcast and Electronic Communication Arts Department at San Francisco State University (SFSU). He taught there for many years in the fields of video production and media aesthetics. While at SFSU he headed the Institute of International Media Communication. For his academic contributions, he received the California State Legislature Distinguished Teaching Award and, from the Broadcast Education Association, the Distinguished Education Service Award.

Prior to joining the SFSU faculty, Zettl worked at KOVR (Stockton-Sacramento) and as a producer-director at KPIX, the CBS affiliate in San Francisco. While at KPIX he participated in a variety of CBS and NBC network television productions. Because of his outstanding contributions to the television profession, he was elected to the prestigious Silver Circle of the National Academy of Television Arts and Sciences (NATAS), Northern California Chapter. He is also a member of the Broadcast Legends of the NATAS Northern California Chapter.

In addition to this book, Zettl has authored *Video Basics Workbook, Television Production Handbook,* and *Sight Sound Motion.* All of his books have been translated into several languages and published internationally. His numerous articles on television production and media aesthetics have appeared in major media journals worldwide. He has lectured extensively on television production and media aesthetics at universities and professional broadcast institutions in the United States and abroad and has presented key papers at a variety of national and international communication conventions.

Zettl developed an interactive DVD-ROM, *Zettl's VideoLab 3.0,* published by Thomson Wadsworth. His previous CD-ROM version won several prestigious awards, among them the *Macromedia* People's Choice Award, the *New Media* Invision Gold Medal for Higher Education, and Invision Silver Medals in the categories of Continuing Education and Use of Video.

Preface

About the Author

Digital video has come of age. Today a student with a good one-chip digital consumer camcorder and a portable laptop computer with appropriate software can produce high-quality video right in his or her own home. As an unexpected benefit, the high quality of digital camcorders and projection equipment has brought traditional filmmakers and video artists closer together. This long-overdue convergence is happening not only in the big film industry but also in smaller companies and, amazingly enough, even colleges and universities.

The enthusiastic media novice will soon find out, however, that it is not necessarily the equipment that makes for a good video production: first and foremost it is having something worthwhile to say. The next step is to manage the complex and sometimes confusing production process. Even the most ingenious idea and the best available equipment are useless if the production remains incomplete.

This book is designed to help video novices learn the basics of this process and move efficiently and effectively from the idea to the finished project—to get it done.

VIDEO BASICS 5 HIGHLIGHTS

Video Basics 5 focuses on a variety of points that are especially relevant to the video production of today and tomorrow. The following summaries provide an overview of these major production points.

Video

Video is used throughout this text as a more inclusive term than *television*. Many of today's productions are done outside the traditional television station environment for nonbroadcast purposes. *Video*, then, is not meant to distinguish commercial from noncommercial, or highly artistic creations from routine programs; it encompasses the full range of today's electronically delivered moving images, from what we normally call "television" to corporate videos and productions done in media departments, to documentaries or electronic filmmaking by individuals or a group of friends, to multimedia content and streaming video on the Internet.

Basics

This book covers concepts, tools, and activities essential to getting started in video production without prior knowledge of the field. If some explanations and descriptions seem more complicated than others, it is because those specific aspects are indeed more intricate. When teaching from this text, feel free to skip certain parts that do not fit your objectives, time frame, or teaching style. The same goes for choosing the order of chapters. Although the chapters in *Video Basics 5* follow a logical progression from the idea to the various steps of image creation, you should cover the chapters in the order that you find most conducive to student learning or that is dictated by your schedule and available facilities.

Digital Equipment

The text delineates the major differences between analog and digital video processes and how they apply to production. It also clarifies the often-puzzling terminology of digital television and the various scanning systems. The scanning, sampling, and compression standards of digital television (DTV), high-definition video (HDV), and high-definition television (HDTV) are explored, and their major differences are outlined. Despite the lure of high-definition equipment, you will find that in many cases learning the actual operation of equipment and production processes is the same regardless of whether the equipment is a small consumer or a high-end HDTV one.

Aesthetics

Despite the DTV revolution, it is still the story that drives production techniques and not the other way around. And many traditional aesthetic factors of picture composition, lighting, and shot sequencing are relatively independent of technological advances and therefore form the basis of effective television production. The descriptions of basic aesthetic principles are not intended to detract from learning the major technical aspects of production equipment but rather to facilitate their optimal application. A solid foundation in the basic aesthetic principles, such as how to compose an effective shot or construct an effective sequence of close-ups, must go hand-in-hand with learning the more technical aspects of video equipment.

Production Model

The various production models introduced in chapter 1, The Production Process, are designed to make video production maximally effective and efficient. They are intended to stress the importance of preproduction and graphically show the major steps from idea to script, and from script to the actual production day. Preproduction activities are often shunned by novices of video production, who are impatient to see their ideas appear on the video screen. These models may help them realize that there is a lot of groundwork to be laid before uncapping the camera; they also provide a foundation for how to go about it. You may even find that these models suggest an approach to problem solving that goes beyond the field of video production.

Chapter Grouping

The seventeen chapters of *Video Basics 5* are grouped into six parts that follow the flow from the basic idea to the culminating experience of multicamera directing:

▶ Part I—Production: Processes and People

▶ Part II—Image Creation: Digital Video and Camera

▶ Part III—Image Creation: Sound, Light, Graphics, and Effects

▶ Part IV—Image Control: Switching, Recording, and Editing

▶ Part V—Production Environment: Studio, Field, and Synthetic

▶ Part VI—Production Control: Talent and Directing

This grouping is intended to help the reader see the logic behind the production process and to prevent reader fatigue or, worse, giving up altogether in the face of the myriad technical details.

Key Terms

Each chapter's key terms appear at the beginning of the chapter and again in the extensive glossary. They are intended to prepare the reader for each chapter's terminology and serve as a quick reference as needed. The key terms are also identified in *bold italic* in the chapter text in the context in which they are defined.

Key Concepts

The key concept margin notes emphasize each chapter's major ideas and issues and are intended primarily as a memory aid. Once the reader recalls a key concept, it should be easier for him or her to retrieve the rest of the related information.

Main Points

These summaries recap the chapter's most important points and key concepts. They do not represent a true précis—a precise and accurate abridgment of the chapter content—but are intended as a final reinforcement and contain only the essential points. Students should be reminded that simply reading the summaries is not a substitute for studying the chapters.

NEW TO *VIDEO BASICS 5*

Several new features and specific enhancements in the text should further facilitate its use for the student as well as the instructor.

New chapters and chapter order   In this edition of *Video Basics,* I again limited the text to seventeen chapters. As noted previously, chapter organization follows the logical progression from idea to image creation, but instructors should feel free to omit material that does not fit into their teaching plan.

Chapter 1 is essentially a new chapter. It stresses the importance of preproduction and demonstrates its principal activities. The former chapters 7 and 8 have been switched. Chapter 7 is now Audio and Sound Control, and chapter 8 is Light, Color, and Lighting. This switch, recommended by several of my respected colleagues, makes sense to me because it focuses right away on the importance of sound when shooting simple exercises in the field. It also acknowledges that, because of interacting with music, many students will likely come into the course with some audio experience, which is usually not the case with lighting. In no way should this switch be taken as one discipline's being more important than the other.

Chapter content   All chapters have been updated and include the most recent equipment and video production techniques. Many of the basic production techniques discussed in prior editions of this text are still valid and practical despite the shift from analog to digital. Care has been taken to point out the differences between multicamera and single-camera production whenever appropriate.

Specific Enhancements New to the Fifth Edition

These changes include the following:

▶ All screen images throughout the book are presented in color and in the 16 × 9 HDTV aspect ratio.

▶ The production model in chapter 1 has been streamlined with simpler terminology. New models stress the preproduction flow from idea to script and from script to production.

▶ The distinctions among HDV, STV, and HDTV are discussed in chapter 3.

▶ Chapter 4, The Video Camera, includes a brief discussion of tapeless recording devices and new high-quality CMOS chips.

▶ The aesthetic differences between framing for 4 × 3 and 16 × 9 aspect ratios are explained.

▶ The use of soft lights as keys is emphasized in chapter 8.

▶ Chapter 11, Video Recording, includes a more in-depth discussion of tapeless recording media.

▶ Linear editing principles are discussed before nonlinear editing because some terminology and many principles have been transferred to nonlinear editing.

▶ Whenever appropriate, clear references to the specific menu and submenu items of *Zettl's VideoLab 3.0* DVD-ROM are made throughout the book. Although not essential to the understanding of *Video Basics 5*, these references facilitate the students' use of the DVD.

SUPPORT MATERIALS

Video Basics 5 offers a wealth of support materials for both students and instructors. These thoroughly class-tested and highly praised print and electronic supplements are available to assist in making the learning—and teaching—experience as meaningful, enjoyable, and successful as possible.

For Students

The *Video Basics 5 Workbook* and *Zettl's VideoLab 3.0* DVD-ROM are intended primarily to reinforce *Video Basics 5*. They can, however, also be used independent of the text.

Video Basics 5 Workbook   The *Workbook* retains many of the successful features of the fourth edition. It can be used to test student retention and retrieval of video production basics and also serve as a primer for actual studio or fieldwork. I have also used the *Workbook* successfully as a diagnostic tool for advanced production students. Having students do various problems at the beginning of the semester (without the aid of the text) quickly reveals the strengths and weaknesses of their production knowledge and skills. Those students—who know everything even before taking the class—are usually surprised to find that there are quite a few important areas in which they have plenty to learn.

Zettl's VideoLab 3.0   The *Zettl's VideoLab 3.0* DVD-ROM (ZVL) represents a major revision of the award-winning ZVL 2.1 CD-ROM. It provides students with a truly individual, private, and nonthreatening learning experience. Combined with *Video Basics 5,* it becomes a powerful instructional ally: Students can manipulate production equipment in a virtual studio or field environment and apply numerous studio and field production techniques from the text. For example, they can mix audio, frame various shots, zoom in and out, create their own lighting effects, and have plenty of opportunity for editing.

For Instructors

Key resources for instructors also accompany *Video Basics 5.* The following class preparation, classroom activity, and assessment materials are available.

Instructor's Manual   The *Instructor's Manual with Answer Key for Video Basics 5 Workbook* includes chapter notes with teaching suggestions and activities, multiple-choice questions, essay/discussion questions, and additional teaching resources. The manual also includes the answers to the exercises in the *Workbook.*

Instructor's Web site   The password-protected instructor's Web site includes access to the online Instructor's Resource Manual. To gain access to the Web site, request a course key by opening the site's home page.

ExamView® Computerized Testing   Create, deliver, and customize tests and study guides (both print and online) in minutes using the test bank questions from the online Instructor's Resource Manual. ExamView offers both a Quick Test Wizard and an Online Test Wizard that guide you step-by-step through the process of creating tests, while its "what you see is what you get" interface allows you to see the test you are creating on-screen exactly as it will print or display online. You can build tests of up to 250 questions, using up to 12 question types. Using the complete word-processing capabilities of ExamView, you can even enter an unlimited number of new questions or edit existing ones.

These resources are available to qualified adopters, and ordering options for student supplements are flexible. Please consult your local Thomson sales representative for more information, for product demonstrations, or to evaluate examination copies of any of these instructor or student resources. You may also contact the Thomson Wadsworth Academic Resource Center at 1-800-423-0563, or visit them at *www.thomsonedu.com*. Additional information is also available at *www.thomsonedu.com/communication/zettl*.

ACKNOWLEDGMENTS

When revising this book, I always try to listen—however virtually—to the many and various questions of my former students. I also observe them struggling with a piece of video equipment or getting unexpectedly derailed by a seemingly minor procedural problem. I then write down the answers or the instructions on how to avoid such problems in the first place. So all my former students deserve a collective but heartfelt *thank-you*!

To make a book out of it all, however, I need a large team of skilled professionals. In the preparation of *Video Basics 5,* I again had ample help from my "A-team" members, who have been directly involved in the production of this book, and from many knowledgeable colleagues in the teaching profession and the media industry.

First and foremost, I am greatly indebted to Holly Allen, publisher; Renée Deljon, senior development editor; Kimberly Russell, executive marketing manager; Lucinda Bingham, assistant editor; and Meghan Bass, editorial assistant for their thoughtful guidance.

Renée Deljon was especially helpful in gathering and organizing the input from several of my respected colleagues at various colleges and universities. My sincere thanks to Anna Chen, Art Institute of Seattle; Karen Kearns, California State University, Northridge; Patrick Murphy, State University of New York, Oneonta; John Schmidt, Grand Valley State University; Ben Scholle, Lindenwood University; and Andrew H. Utterback, Ph.D., Eastern Connecticut State University for their careful analysis of the previous edition and their thoughtful recommendations for this one.

As usual, Gary Palmatier of Ideas to Images used his professional skills and creative magic to create the book you are holding. Elizabeth von Radics deserves medals not only for her deliberate and precise copy editing but also for her technical knowledge of the subject. Many thanks also to Cheri Throop, who gathered most of the new product shots for this edition.

Finally, a big thank-you to my colleagues in the Broadcast and Electronic Communication Arts Department of San Francisco State University for sharing their expertise with me—Marty Gonzales, Hamid Khani, Phil Kipper, Steve Lahey, Vinay Shrivastava, and Winston Tharp—as well as the following people and organizations: Rudolf Benzler, Plazamedia, Munich, Germany; John Beritzhoff and Greg Goddard, Snader and Associates; Ed Cosci and Jim Haman, KTVU, Oakland–San Francisco; Sonny Craven, Virginia Military Institute; Scott Fishman, Nickelodeon Studios, Orlando, Florida; Professor Manfred Muckenhaupt, University of Tuebingen; and Phil Sigmund, producer/director of BeyondPix Communications, San Francisco.

I am also indebted to the following people who appeared in this edition's photographs: Socoro Aguilar-Uriarte, Karen Austin, Ken Baird, Hoda Baydoun, Clara Benjamin, Rudolf Benzler, Gabriella Bolton, Michael Cage, William Carpenter, NeeLa Chakravartula, Christine Cornish, Ed Cosci, David Galvez, Eric Goldstein, Poleng

Hong, Michael Huston, Lauren Jones, Olivia Jungius, Akiko Kajiwara, Hamid Khani, Fawn Luu, Orcun Malkoclar, Celeste Melzer, Genevieve Melzer, Regina Melzer, Johnny Moreno, Anita Morgan, Tomoko Nakayama, Einat Nov, Tamara Perkins, Richard Piscitello, Ildiko Polony, Robaire Ream, Kerstin Riediger, Joaquin Ross, Maya Ross, Algie Salmon-Fattahian, Heather Schiffman, Alisa Shahonian, Pria Shih, Jennifer Stanonis, Mathias Stering, Heather Suzuki, Julie Tepper, Mike Vista, Andrew Wright, and Arthur Yee.

A big hug for my wife, Erika, who, once again, helped me get through this extensive revision.

Herbert Zettl

Production: Processes and People

The small digital camcorder and digital editing software have made it possible to run out and create a documentary that shakes the world and makes you rich and famous. Right? Well, there is always the possibility that you get lucky—once. But as a professional in the video business, you must be much more consistent and produce high-quality programs on a more regular basis. To achieve this goal, you must understand not only how a specific piece of equipment works but also how to get from idea to video image efficiently and effectively—the production process. Finally, you must learn to work with people—a team of experienced production experts—who must all work together to create a worthwhile program and bring it to its intended audience. This book will help you become such a professional.

Part I explores how the production process works and how to move systematically from initial idea to the finished production with confidence and minimal wasted effort. You are also introduced to the standard technical and nontechnical production team.

CHAPTER 1

KEY TERMS

angle The particular approach to a story—its central theme.

field production Production activities that take place away from the studio.

medium requirements All personnel, equipment, and facilities needed for a production, as well as budgets, schedules, and the various production phases.

multicamera production The use of two or more cameras to capture a scene simultaneously from different points of view. Each camera output can be recorded separately (iso configuration) and/or fed into a switcher for instantaneous editing.

postproduction Any production activity that occurs after the production. Usually refers to either video editing and/or audio sweetening.

preproduction Preparation of all production details.

production The actual activities in which an event is recorded and/or televised.

production model Moving from idea to the program objective and then backing up to the specific medium requirements to achieve the objective.

program objective The desired effect of the program on the viewer.

single-camera production All the video is captured by a single camera or camcorder for postproduction editing. Similar to the traditional film approach. Also called *film-style*.

studio production Production activities that take place in the studio.

The Production Process

You are ready to roll. You have got a million ideas for shows, each of which is considerably better than what you ordinarily see on television. But how exactly do you get them out of your head and onto the screen? This step—the production process—is the core of all successful programs. It cannot be done intuitively; it must be learned. But don't be dismayed. This chapter provides you with a useful guide to moving from idea to image—your prizewinning masterpiece. It also explains the various production phases and leads you through the preproduction steps. Finally, it helps you generate useful program ideas on demand and points you toward the ever-closer convergence of single- and multicamera use in studio and field productions.

▶ **THE PRODUCTION MODEL**
Organize the details for moving from original idea to finished product

▶ **THE PRODUCTION PHASES**
Preproduction, production, and postproduction

▶ **IMPORTANCE OF PREPRODUCTION**
Moving from idea to script and from script to production details

▶ **PREPRODUCTION: FROM IDEA TO SCRIPT**
Program objective, angle, evaluation, and script

▶ **PREPRODUCTION: FROM SCRIPT TO PRODUCTION**
Medium requirements and budget

▶ **GENERATING IDEAS ON DEMAND**
Brainstorming and clustering

▶ **THE CONVERGENCE OF STUDIO AND FIELD PRODUCTION**
Single- and multicamera approaches

THE PRODUCTION MODEL

Don't be dismayed. A model is not a set of absolute rules; it is strictly a suggestion of how to approach and accomplish a difficult task. In our case it is meant to help you organize the many details necessary to move from the original idea to the finished product. The production model is not a foolproof system that works every time you use it but more of a road map for how to streamline the various production phases necessary for a variety of productions.

The production model is based on the realization that the only message that counts is not necessarily the one you start with but the one that is perceived by the viewer. This process is a little bit like cooking: the final success of your undertaking is not measured by the ingredients you used (the initial idea) but whether your guests like to eat it (the message actually received). Wouldn't it make sense, then, to start with an idea of how the meal should finally look and taste and then figure out what ingredients you need to make such a meal?

This production model works on the same principle: once you have developed the initial idea, you move directly to what, ideally, you want the viewers to learn, feel, or do.[1] The ***production model*** suggests that rather than move from the initial idea to the production, you jump from the initial idea to a *program objective*—a definition of the desired effect. Then and only then do you back up and decide on the medium requirements necessary to produce the intended communication effect. The message that counts is not necessarily the one you start with but rather the one that is perceived by the viewer. **SEE 1.1**

As you can see, this model shows four distinct processes: (1) moving from the basic idea to the program objective (desired effect on the viewer) and angle; (2) determining the necessary medium requirements in preproduction; (3) generating the desired message in the production phase; and (4) distributing the message (the production) to the target audience. **ZVL3 CUE 1** ▸ PROCESS→ Effect-to-cause→ basic idea | desired effect | cause | actual effect

THE PRODUCTION PHASES

NOTE: The **ZVL3 CUE** ▸ icons point to related segments on the *Zettl's Video-Lab 3.0* DVD-ROM. You can run each module as soon as you see its cue in the text, or you may prefer to wait until you have finished reading a chapter and run all relevant modules at one time. The DVD-ROM is not an essential part of this book; it is meant to reinforce the text and to facilitate the transition from text to actual practice.

Over the years certain routines—production processes—have developed that can facilitate the complex job of the production team. These processes include a variety of chores that need to be done *before* the production, *during* the actual production activities, and *after* the production. In production lingo we call these the preproduction, production, and postproduction phases. **ZVL3 CUE 2** ▸ PROCESS→ Process introduction

Preproduction includes all the planning and coordination of details before the actual production activities.

Production starts when you open the studio doors and turn on the equipment or when you load your car or truck with equipment for a field production. In production you actually translate, or *encode*, the original program objective into a series of video segments. Production involves the medium requirements—the coordination

---

1. This concept is based on the classic instructional design by Mager. See Robert Mager, *Preparing Instructional Objectives,* 3rd ed. (Atlanta: Center for Effective Performance, 1997).

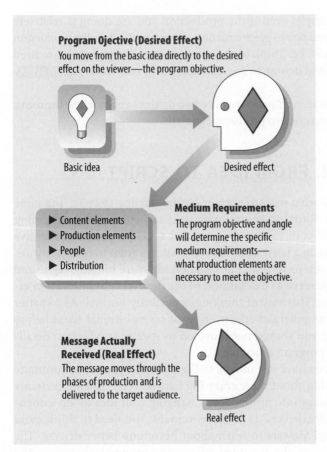

Program Ojective (Desired Effect)
You move from the basic idea directly to the desired effect on the viewer—the program objective.

Basic idea   Desired effect

Medium Requirements
The program objective and angle will determine the specific medium requirements—what production elements are necessary to meet the objective.

▶ Content elements
▶ Production elements
▶ People
▶ Distribution

Message Actually Received (Real Effect)
The message moves through the phases of production and is delivered to the target audience.

Real effect

1.1 Production Model
The production model shows how to move from the show idea to the finished program with maximum efficiency.

of production and technical people and the operation of a variety of production equipment.

In **postproduction** you select the best bits and pieces of the recorded event, enhance their picture and sound quality as necessary, correct some of the minor production mistakes, and assemble the shots and scenes into a coherent whole—the video program. For complicated programs that require a great deal of editing, the postproduction phase may take as long as the preproduction period. ZVL3 CUE 3 ▶ PROCESS→ Phases→ production | postproduction

This chapter focuses on preproduction. The details of production and postproduction take up the rest of the book.

IMPORTANCE OF PREPRODUCTION

In preproduction you develop the initial program idea, define the program objective, and select the people and the equipment necessary to translate your initial idea into effective video and audio images.

Meticulous preproduction is a key factor in maximizing your video production efficiency and effectiveness. There is a proven formula that you must not only

remember but also always apply, even if the production you are doing is relatively simple: *the more attention you pay to preproduction, the more effective the production and postproduction phases will be.* Think of this advice especially when you are tired of organizing all the details and itching to go on location and start shooting. `ZVL3 CUE 4`
PROCESS→ Phases→ preproduction

Normally, the preproduction activities require two distinct approaches: the move from idea to script and from script to production details.

PREPRODUCTION: FROM IDEA TO SCRIPT

You must have some idea of what meal to prepare before starting to cook. The same is true in video production. Running around with your camcorder before deciding on what it is you want to tell your viewers is a wasteful activity at best. An effective production process depends on a fairly clear idea of what you want to communicate. As we all experience, however, most initial production ideas are initially vague and are rarely concise enough to serve as a definition of the desired communication effect—the *program objective*. This way of thinking is perfectly normal. As a matter of fact, you should weigh the potential effectiveness of several similar ideas before settling on a single one, but you should not move on to specific production details without first having a clear program objective.

For example, suppose you have just moved to Big City, and your daily commute prompts you to "do something about these crazy Big City drivers." You are certainly not ready at this point to plunge into production. Changing your idea to "do a documentary on the crazy Big City drivers" is no improvement. You need to think more about exactly what you want viewers to learn about becoming better drivers. The more precise your definition of the intended effect—the program objective—the easier it is to decide on the appropriate production format and the necessary procedures. `ZVL3 CUE 5` PROCESS→ Effect-to-cause→ basic idea

Program Objective

Exactly what is it that you want the audience to know, feel, or do? To "do something about these crazy Big City drivers" says little about what to do and how to go about achieving that "something." What you need to do is construct a precise program objective.

Rather than tackle all the bad habits of the "crazy Big City drivers," you may want to isolate a single problem that is especially bothersome and that you consider important. As in most learning or persuasion tasks, specific objectives are usually more effective than general ones, and small steps are more easily managed and accomplished by the viewer than large ones. For instance, you may find that the misuse or nonuse of turn signals has become a serious threat to traffic safety. So, rather than address *all* the bad habits of Big City drivers, you can isolate a single objective: *Demonstrate to Big City drivers that turn signals help other drivers react to your changing directions and contribute to traffic safety.*

Now that you have a clear program objective, you can start visualizing some possible approaches. Because you are a creative person, you come up with several good approaches to this video. But which one should you choose? What you need now is an effective angle. `ZVL3 CUE 6` PROCESS→ Effect-to-cause→ desired effect

Angle

In the context of designing a show, an *angle* is a specific approach to the story—a point of view of the event. Effective video programs often have an angle that is different from the usual treatment of the same subject and are more relevant to the viewer. Although the requirement of "finding an angle" has been abused by many newspeople in their attempts to sensationalize a basically uninteresting story, it is a valuable and positive way of clarifying and intensifying an event.

In our example one of the possible angles could be to show the terrible consequences of an accident that was caused by a driver who failed to signal his lane change. Or you may show the misuse or nonuse of turn signals from a bicycler's point of view—one who has a hard time avoiding reckless drivers even during her relatively short ride to campus. You may find, however, that these drivers are not really reckless but simply absentminded or discourteous.

Isn't this now an entirely new angle on how to approach the turn signal problem? Yes, it is. Instead of telling Big City drivers that they are reckless and had better learn to use turn signals because it is the law, you may want to persuade them to be more courteous and helpful to one another and to the traffic around them. To accommodate and assist the less-than-perfect drivers, rather than accuse and attack them, may be a more effective angle for all sorts of traffic education. Instead of using threats as a means to make them use turn signals, you now appeal to their pride and self-esteem.

Unless you are the writer, you will find that scriptwriters often come up with a useful angle. Most writers will be happy to accept suggestions for an angle, even if they later discover a better one.

> ► **KEY CONCEPT**
> The angle describes the specific approach to the story.

Evaluation

Whatever angle you choose, always ask yourself: *is it doable?* Despite your good intentions and desire to rival in your production the style of an elaborate Hollywood movie, you will not succeed unless you have the Hollywood budget and the production time to match. Money and time are production factors as real as cameras and microphones.

You will find that your clients—the school board, a big corporation, or a local cable channel—are becoming more and more demanding. They expect you to come up with a superior product in an unreasonably short time for an unbelievably low budget. Give up right now? Not at all! But you may have to scale back on your grand intentions and come up with ideas that are realistic, that is, that can actually be accomplished by you and your team and that will provide the client with the promised project, on time and within budget.

Don't promise what you can't deliver. It is wise to accompany your creative leaps with the two reality factors: available time and money. You simply cannot do a million-dollar production if you have only five hundred to spend. Or, if you have only four weeks to complete a show, don't attempt a production that requires on-location shooting in different parts of the world and two months of postproduction.

1.2 Preproduction: From Idea to Script

This preproduction phase involves the major steps that lead from idea generation to script writing.

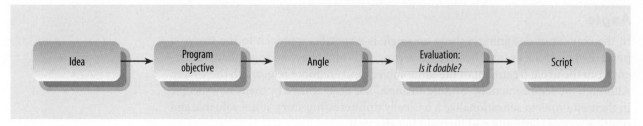

Idea → Program objective → Angle → Evaluation: Is it doable? → Script

Script

You are now ready to write the script or hire a writer. You need a script, even if all it says is "no script." The script is an essential communication device among all non-technical and technical production personnel. You will find more information on the various script formats in chapter 17. **SEE 1.2**

PREPRODUCTION: FROM SCRIPT TO PRODUCTION

In preproduction the script becomes the key for the actual production preparations. You must now translate the script into medium requirements, which includes various people and production elements.

Medium Requirements

Normally, the **medium requirements** are expressed as workflow that includes selecting talent, determining technical and nontechnical personnel, and requesting studio or field facilities and equipment. **SEE 1.3**

As you can see in figure 1.3, the script now serves as the main guide for all further technical and nontechnical production requirements. As the producer your main preproduction contact will now be the director. Under your close supervision, the director chooses the talent, assigns the art director to design a set, and discusses with the technical supervisor the necessary technical personnel, facilities (studio, location, and postproduction facilities), and specific equipment (camera, lighting, audio, and videotape recorders).

Note that who does what in preproduction in not always as clear-cut as it is in the figure. For example, you may find that sometimes the producer rather than the director will choose the talent or request a set design from the art director. This is all the more reason for you, the producer, to communicate frequently with all technical and nontechnical personnel involved in preproduction and to make sure that they all complete their assigned tasks on time—and let you know about it. A good producer triple-checks everything.

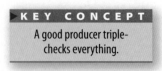

▶KEY CONCEPT

A good producer triple-checks everything.

Budget

As you determine the medium requirements, you will also have to prepare the budget. Yes, this is a typical chicken-and-egg proposition: you can determine a reasonably

1.3 Preproduction: From Script to Production

This preproduction phase involves the major steps that lead from the script to the actual production process.

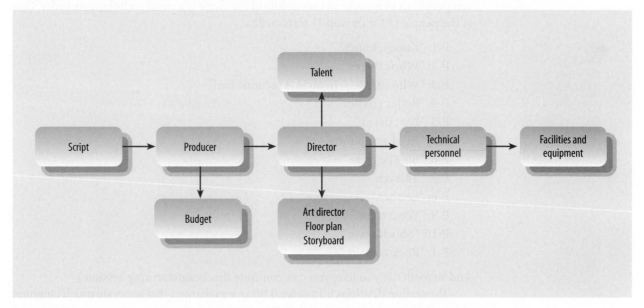

accurate budget only when you have all the information on the necessary personnel, facilities, and equipment. But you cannot really hire people or request various equipment unless you know how much money you have available.

Although budgets are extremely important, we won't worry about money just yet but rather concentrate on how to make the video production process maximally efficient and effective.

GENERATING IDEAS ON DEMAND

All good productions start with a good idea. As obvious as this sounds, you may be surprised to find that one of the more difficult demands in professional video is coming up with good ideas on a consistent basis. Often the calendar or clock dictates when to be creative. Unfortunately, tight production schedules will not tolerate your waiting for divine inspiration. You must call on techniques that help you jolt your imagination even on a down day. Two well-known and effective devices for unlocking ideas are brainstorming and clustering.

Brainstorming

Brainstorming involves freeing your mind of the restrictions you impose on it because you feel, however unconsciously, that you have to think and say something that fits the situational framework and others' expectations. It is a form of "conceptual blockbusting" that ignores or breaks down traditional barriers to creative expression.[2]

---

2. See James L. Adams, *Conceptual Blockbusting,* 4th ed. (Cambridge, Mass.: Perseus, 2001).

Picture yourself for a moment as an observer of a brainstorming session of advertising people who are supposed to come up with a new approach to a car commercial. Ten people sit in a circle; in the middle of the circle is a small audiotape recorder. One of the people (P1 = person 1) starts with:

P-1: "Knock, knock!"
P-2: "Who's there?"
P-3: "Who cares—0 to 60 in 4 seconds flat!"
P-4: "Roller coaster."
P-3: "Big curves."
P-5: "RPM symphony."
P-6: "Big speakers."
P-7: "Thieves."
P-8: "Leather."
P-9: "Watercolor."
P-10: "Shock wave."
P-1: "Rock concert."

And so forth. (If you like, you can continue this brainstorming session.)

The session develops into several bizarre exchanges that generate much laughter. Once all ideas are documented, the team reviews the comments several times and looks for relevant ideas or associations. "Quick acceleration" and "shock wave" are obvious cues. The "big curves" and "roller coaster" comments could be visualized as the car going around curves as though it were on roller-coaster tracks, and the "big speakers" could create shock waves when playing the mix of rock music and the high-rpm pitch. Or speakers and a leather interior may incite a thief to steal the car. But what about the "watercolor" remark? It's easy to declare it irrelevant, especially because it was triggered by person 9's having just sold his first painting. But after some discussion, it not only is kept but becomes the main framework for the commercial: the car racing not through an actual landscape but a watercolor-painted one. The contrast between the real image of the powerful new sports car moving through the delicate, imaginary landscape gives the commercial its creative edge.

Successful brainstorming depends on a number of conditions: (1) It is best done with several people. (2) You start out with a general idea or related image (new car) and then let everybody call out whatever springs to mind. (3) Most important, let all minds roam freely and don't pass judgment on any of the ideas. All ideas, however far-out they may seem, are equally valid (such as "thieves" and "watercolor"). (4) Document all ideas by either recording them on audiotape or writing them down. (5) Recite the list of comments several times to discover novel connections.

If necessary, you can do brainstorming all by yourself, but you'll still need to have some way of recording it or writing it down. One of the solitary brainstorming techniques is *clustering*.

Clustering

In the middle of a piece of paper, write a single word that seems somehow central to your basic program idea or program objective and circle it. Now write down and

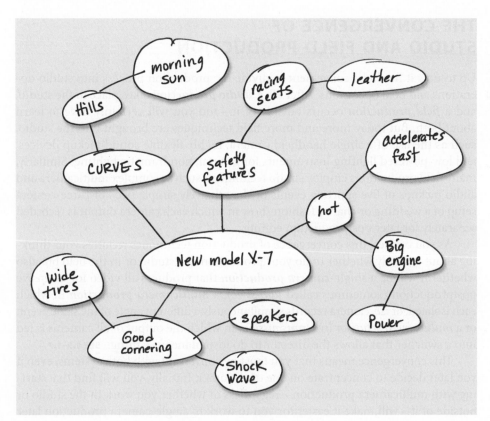

1.4 Clustering

Note that clustering starts with a central idea and then branches out in various directions. Clustering must be done quickly and uncritically; it is much like written brainstorming.

circle another word that is somehow associated with your key word and connect the two. Write down other word associations and connect them to the last one circled.

In a short time, you will have created a cluster of words or ideas. Don't try to design a cluster or be logical about it. Work fast so that you will not be tempted to ponder over your associations. Let your mind flow freely. When you feel that your ideas are exhausted, don't force yourself to find more connections or more-logical ones. The idea cluster seems to have a natural limit. You will most likely know when you have enough branches and it is time to stop. If one word or phrase is especially intriguing yet seems out of place, start a new cluster but leave the old one alone. Once you are at that point, look at the finished diagram and search for possible patterns. These patterns will inevitably reveal some novel connections and relationships that were not obvious before and can serve as springboards for the process message and the medium requirements. **SEE 1.4**

As you can see, clustering is similar to brainstorming except that during clustering you create an immediate visual pattern that yields quite readily the major interrelationships of the various ideas.[3] But it is also much more restrictive than brainstorming. **ZVL3 CUE 7** PROCESS→ Ideas

▶**KEY CONCEPT**

Successful brainstorming and clustering depend on a free, intuitive, and noncritical flow of ideas.

---

3. Clustering as an idea-unlocking technique for writing was developed by Gabriele Lusser Rico in *Writing the Natural Way,* rev. ed. (Los Angeles: J. P. Tarcher, 2000).

THE CONVERGENCE OF STUDIO AND FIELD PRODUCTION

Up to now it has been convenient to divide the production process into studio operations and field operations. After all, a **studio production** takes place in the studio, and a **field production** occurs outside of it—and you will certainly have to learn about both. But today more and more field techniques are brought into the studio, such as the use of a single handheld camera, highly flexible sound pickup devices, and low-powered lighting instruments for general, nondramatic lighting. Similarly, many field productions employ studio techniques, such as complex multicamera and audio pickups of live sporting events or the relatively simple two- or three-camera setup of a wedding or charity fashion show in which each camera output is recorded separately for later postproduction editing.

As you can see, this convergence of production techniques requires your thinking about not only whether to do your production in a studio or in the field but also whether it will be a **single-camera production** that produces all video for extensive postproduction (sometimes called *film-style*); a **multicamera production** in which each isolated, or *iso,* camera records simultaneously a different angle of the same event; or a *multicamera setup for live transmission,* in which the output of all cameras is fed into a switcher that allows the director to do instantaneous editing. **SEE 1.5–1.7**

This convergence means that you must be conversant with both systems, even if you later decide to concentrate on one or the other. Initially, you will find that starting with multicamera production—regardless of whether you work in the studio or outside of it—will make it easier for you to work in single-camera production later

1.5 Single-camera (Film-style) Approach

In this production technique, only one camera is used to record all shots for postproduction.

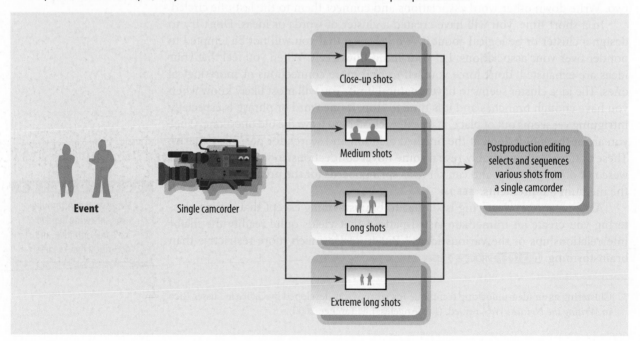

Event	Single camcorder

Close-up shots

Medium shots

Long shots

Extreme long shots

Postproduction editing selects and sequences various shots from a single camcorder

1.6 Multicamera Setup in Iso Configuration

In this setup several cameras are used to simultaneously record the same event from various viewpoints.

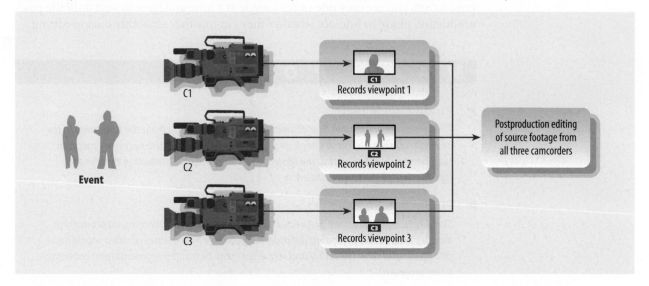

1.7 Multicamera Setup for Switching

In this setup several cameras are used to feed their output to a switcher. The switcher enables its operator to select the appropriate shots and sequence them. This is also called *instantaneous editing*.

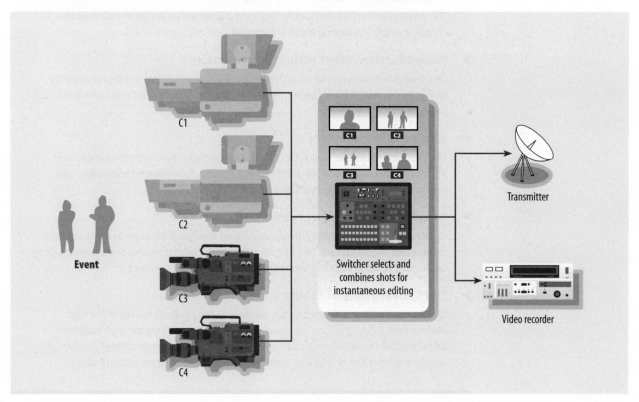

on. This is because when using two or more cameras simultaneously, you can actually see various camera angles side-by-side and how they cut together; in single-camera production, you see only one camera angle at a time and have to wait until the post-production phase to find out whether they cut together smoothly during editing.

M A I N   P O I N T S

▶ **Production Model**

This process model shows four distinct processes: (1) moving from the basic idea to the program objective (desired effect) and angle, (2) determining the necessary medium requirements, (3) generating the desired message, and (4) distributing the message (production) to the target audience.

▶ **Production Phases**

The production phases are preproduction (planning and coordinating all production details), production (encoding the program objective into a series of video segments), and postproduction (selecting and sequencing the best video segments for a coherent video program).

▶ **Importance of Preproduction**

Preproduction is a key factor in maximizing your video production efficiency and effectiveness.

▶ **Preproduction: From Idea to Script**

This preproduction step includes formulating a program objective, deciding on the encoding angle, evaluating the entire concept, and writing the script.

▶ **Preproduction: From Script to Production**

This production phase concerns all medium requirements. It requires deciding on the nontechnical and technical personnel and on the facilities and equipment for the actual production.

▶ **Medium Requirements**

The medium requirements include content elements (program objective, angle, and audience analysis), production elements (equipment, facilities, and schedules), and people (talent and nontechnical and technical personnel).

▶ **Generating Ideas on Demand**

In video production, creativity means coming up with good ideas on a consistent basis on time and within budget. Two helpful methods are brainstorming and clustering. Both techniques demand a spontaneous and noncritical delivery of ideas.

▶ **The Convergence of Studio and Field Production**

Single- and multicamera productions are done in the studio as well as in the field. Multicamera productions are sometimes instantaneously edited through switching and sometimes recorded as iso sources for postproduction. Single-camera productions usually resemble film production in shot acquisition and postproduction editing.

Z E T T L ' S   V I D E O L A B   3 . 0

 For your reference, or to track your work, the Zettl's VideoLab 3.0 program cues in this chapter are listed here with their corresponding page numbers.

CHAPTER 2

KEY TERMS

above-the-line Category for nontechnical personnel, such as producers, directors, and talent. Also used as a budget category.

below-the-line Category for technical personnel, including camera operators, floor persons, and video and audio engineers. Also used as a budget category.

EFP team Usually a three-person team, consisting of the talent; a camcorder operator; and a utility person who handles lighting, audio, and/or video recording, and, if necessary, the microwave transmission back to the studio.

postproduction team Normally consists of the director, a video editor, and, for complex productions, a sound designer who remixes the sound track.

preproduction team Comprises the people who plan the production. Normally includes the producer, writer, director, art director, and technical director. Large productions may include a composer and a choreographer. In charge: producer.

production schedule A calendar that shows the preproduction, production, and postproduction dates, and who is doing what, when, and where.

production team Consists of a variety of nontechnical and technical people, such as producer and various assistants (associate producer and production assistant), director and assistant director, and talent and production crew. In charge: director.

time line A schedule that shows the time allotments for various activities during a single production day. Often prepared by the director. Also (but erroneously) called *production schedule*.

The Production Team: Who Does What When?

If you are a painter, you can do everything yourself: come up with the idea, buy the materials, prepare the canvas, struggle with form and color, and finally sign and date the finished work. You could even do the selling without other people involved. The entire creative process is under your control.

This is not the case in video production, unless you are simply video-recording your vacation adventures or working for a news department that has its *VJs* (video journalists) not only determine the best way to report a story but also do the camera work, the editing, and the voice-over narration. Although this is technically possible, it rarely results in a high-quality product.

Most professional video productions involve a group of people—a *production team*—with each member performing a clearly defined function.

This chapter focuses on the many roles in video production: what the people do and how they work together.

▶ **PRODUCTION TEAMS**
   The preproduction, production, and postproduction teams

▶ **PASSING THE BUCK**
   What happens when production people do not work as a team

▶ **TAKING AND SHARING RESPONSIBILITY**
   What happens when production people know their functions and work as a team

▶ **PRODUCTION SCHEDULE AND TIME LINE**
   How to set up a production schedule and develop a realistic time line

You may best understand who does what by dividing the team into people involved in the preproduction, production, and postproduction phases. The *preproduction* team includes the people primarily involved with planning the production; the *production* team comprises the people who translate the ideas into actual video pictures and sound; and the *postproduction* people put together all the selected videotape pieces, which contain the optimum video and audio segments, and give the whole production the final polish.

Some production people are involved in only one of these phases; others may be involved in all three. As you can readily see, no single individual has complete control over the entire creative process. Unlike the painter, you must learn to work as an effective team member, which means that you know exactly what is expected of you when assigned to a specific production position and also what everybody else is supposed to be doing. Once you know who is supposed to do what, when, and where, you can establish effective communication among the team members and let them know when specific things need to be done. A *production schedule* and a *time line* are essential in coordinating the different production steps and the efforts of all team members.

Regardless of whether you are a member of the preproduction, production, or postproduction team, you will find that some team members are more engaged and interested in what they are doing than others, or that even the most conscientious team members have an off-day. But it is usually the weakest link in a chain that needs attention, not the strongest one. Rather than complain about the weak performance of some team members, help them improve their performance. You must also get used to the idea that, in such a complex and high-pressure job as video production, occasional mistakes are inevitable. Fixing blame should then be done not to vindicate the other team members but to define the problem so that it can be avoided the next time.

Primary requisites for any kind of a team are that all members respect one another and work for a common goal. A famous football coach and television commentator was once asked how to improve a team's sagging spirit and attitude. His answer: "By winning!" *Winning* in video production means enabling each team member to do his or her best to produce exceptionally good shows on a consistent basis.

PRODUCTION TEAMS

The size and the makeup of the production team depend on the scope of the production. *Electronic news gathering (ENG)* for simple stories could be done by a single person, who simultaneously acts as reporter, camcorder operator, and editor/narrator. While financially profitable for the news operation, this one-person-band approach is very hard on the person who is doing it. Even relatively simple *electronic field productions (EFPs)* are usually done with three people. The *EFP team* consists of talent, camcorder operator, and a utility person who takes care of the lighting, audio, and, if necessary, additional video-recording devices. A big-remote telecast, such as a live sporting event, may keep thirty or more people very busy (see chapter 15).

The accompanying tables summarize the major nontechnical and technical personnel and their principal functions. **SEE 2.1 AND 2.2**

Sometimes the production people are divided into *above-the-line* and *below-the-line* personnel. These designations are not clear-cut and have more to do with who pays whom than who does what. In general, **above-the-line** personnel are preproduction and supervisory people; **below-the-line** personnel are involved in production and postproduction. **SEE 2.3** ZVL3 CUE 1 ▶ PROCESS→ People→ nontechnical | technical

2.1 Nontechnical Production Personnel

PERSONNEL	FUNCTION
A B O V E - T H E - L I N E	
Executive producer	In charge of one or several programs or program series. Coordinates with client, station or corporate management, advertising agencies, investors, and talent and writer's agents. Approves and manages budget.
Producer	In charge of an individual production. Is responsible for all personnel working on the production and for coordinating technical and non-technical production elements. Often doubles as writer and director.
Line producer	Supervises daily production activities on the set.
Studio and field producers	In large operations, studio and field producers are assigned different producing responsibilities: the studio producer takes care of all studio productions, and the field producer handles all field productions.
Associate producer (AP)	Assists producer in all production matters. Often does the actual production coordination jobs, such as telephoning talent and making sure that deadlines are met.
Production assistant (PA)	Assists producer and director during the actual production. Takes notes of comments made by the producer or the director during rehearsals, which serve as a guide for the crew to fix minor production flaws before the final recording.
Director	In charge of directing talent and technical operations. Is ultimately responsible for transforming a script into effective video and audio messages. In smaller operations also assumes the producer's responsibilities.
Associate, or assistant, director (AD)	Assists director during the actual production. Often does timing for director. In complex multicamera productions, helps to "ready" various operations (such as presetting specific camera shots or calling for a graphic effect).
Talent	Refers, not always accurately, to all performers and actors who regularly appear on video.
Actor	Someone who portrays someone else on-camera.
Performer	Someone who appears on-camera in nondramatic activities. Always portrays himself or herself.
Announcer	Reads narration but does not appear on-camera. If on-camera, the announcer moves into the talent category.
Writer	Writes video scripts. In smaller-station operations or in corporate video, the writer's function is often assumed by the director or the producer or by somebody hired on a freelance basis.
Art director	In charge of the creative design aspects of show (set design, location, and graphics).
Music director/conductor	Responsible for music group in large productions, such as the band that plays in variety shows. Can also be the person who picks all the recorded music for a specific show or series.
Choreographer	Determines all movements of dancers.

2.1 **Nontechnical Production Personnel** *(continued)*

PERSONNEL	FUNCTION
BELOW-THE-LINE	
Floor manager	Also called *floor director* or *stage manager*. In charge of all activities on the studio floor, such as setting up scenery, getting talent into place, and relaying all director's cues to talent. In the field the floor manager is basically responsible for preparing the location for the shoot and for cueing all talent.
Floor persons	Also called *grips, stagehands,* or *facilities persons*. Set up and dress sets. Operate cue cards or other prompting devices. Sometimes operate microphone booms. Assist camera operators in moving camera dollies and pulling camera cables. In small operations also act as wardrobe and makeup people. Set up and ready all nontechnical facilities in the field.
Makeup artist	Does the makeup for all talent (in large productions only).
Costume designer	Designs and sometimes constructs various costumes for dramas, dance numbers, and children's shows (in large productions only). Sometimes classified as above-the-line personnel.
Property manager	Maintains and manages use of various set and hand properties, such as tables, chairs, and office furniture (set properties), and telephones, coffee cups, and flashlights (hand properties)—for large productions only. In smaller operations props are managed by the floor manager.

Let's find out who is normally involved in the three primary production stages: preproduction, production, and postproduction.

Preproduction Team

The primary responsibility of the *preproduction team* is to develop the idea for the video and plan its production so that the translation of idea to pictures and sound is as efficient as possible. For most standard EFPs, the preproduction team consists of the producer, the director, and sometimes the talent. But in larger field or studio productions, the people involved in this initial idea-generating phase include the producer, writer, director, and scene designer or art director and sometimes the technical supervisor or technical director.

The original idea may come from the corporate manager ("Do a 10-minute videotape showing that the customer is our most precious commodity") or the producer ("Do a piece on your campus food service"), or it may come from a concerned citizen ("I would like to do a show on the pros and cons of timber clear-cutting"). Often specific show ideas are the product of several people's brainstorming.

Producer   Once the general idea is born, it is nurtured through all preproduction stages by the *producer,* who states the specific purpose of the show—the program objective—and prepares a budget for the entire production.

2.2 Technical Production Personnel

This category includes engineers who are actually engaged in engineering functions, such as installing and maintaining new electronic equipment; it also includes people who operate such equipment. Because operating much of the electronic equipment, such as cameras, switchers, character generators, and video-tape-editing machines, does not require engineering knowledge, most of the operation of television equipment is performed by nonengineering personnel.

PERSONNEL	FUNCTION
ABOVE-THE-LINE	
Chief engineer	In charge of all technical personnel, budgets, and equipment. Designs electronic systems, including signal transmission facilities, and overseas installations, day-to-day operations, and all maintenance.
Assistant chief engineer or technical supervisor	Assists the chief engineer in all technical matters and operations. Is often involved in preproduction activities of large productions. Schedules crews and participates in big-remote surveys.
BELOW-THE-LINE	
Technical director (TD)	In charge of all technical setups and operations during a production. Does the actual switching in a studio production. Often acts as technical crew chief.
Lighting director (LD)	In charge of studio and field lighting; normally for large productions only.
Director of photography (DP)	Carryover from film production. Takes care of lighting and camera operation in single-camera productions.
Camera operators	Also called *videographers* or *shooters*. Operate studio and field cameras. Sometimes also do lighting.
Video operator (VO)	Also called *video engineer* or *shader*. Adjusts the camera controls for optimal camera pictures (also called *shading*). Sometimes doubles as maintenance engineer.
Video-recording, or videotape, operator	Operates videotape recorders during the production. In small field productions, the audio technician doubles as VTR (videotape recorder) operator.
Video, or videotape, editor	Operates videotape-editing equipment. Often makes creative editing decisions as well.
Sound designer	In charge of "designing" the sound track of a complex production, such as a drama, commercial, or large corporate assignment. Sometimes listed as above-the-line nontechnical personnel.
Audio engineer	Often called *audio technician*. In charge of all audio operations in production and, in the absence of a sound designer, in postproduction. Sets up microphones and operates audio console during the show.
Maintenance engineer	A true engineering position. Maintains all technical equipment and troubleshoots during productions.

2.3 Above-the-line and Below-the-line Personnel

ABOVE-THE-LINE

Production people	Executive producer
	Producer and associates
	Director and associates
	Chief engineer and associates
	Technical supervisor
Idea people	Writer
	Art director
	Composer
	Choreographer
Talent	Performers
	Actors

BELOW-THE-LINE

Technical people	Technical director
	Director of photography
	Lighting director
	Maintenance engineers
Production — technical	Camera operator
	Video operator
	Audio engineer
	Video-recording, or videotape, operator
	Video, or videotape, editor
Production—nontechnical	Floor manager
	Floor persons
	Grips
	Property manager
	C.G. operator
	Makeup and wardrobe people

As soon as the budget has been approved, you, as producer, need to hire and/or coordinate all additional personnel, equipment, and production activities. You or your associate producer will then have to devise a production schedule that indicates specifically who is supposed to do what and the times when the assigned tasks should be completed. This calendar is essential for coordinating the activities of all the people involved in the production.

Writer   The next step is writing the script. The *writer* interprets the program objective into a video production and writes down what he or she wants the viewers to see and hear. This production step is obviously crucial. It often determines the production format, such as instructional show, interactive multimedia show, or documentary, and the style and the quality of the production. Like the production schedule, the *script* serves as the guide for all production activities.

Scripts are almost always revised several times. Sometimes the original content isn't accurate and needs some corrections. At other times the words sound too stilted and academic when actually spoken, or there may be some shots that are unnecessary or too difficult to produce. For all these reasons, good video writers do not come cheaply. Settle on a fee before the delivery of the script. (There are various script samples in chapter 17.)

Director   The *director* translates the script into specific video and audio images and selects the necessary production crew and equipment. The sooner the director is brought onboard in preproduction, the better. The director may work with the writer early on, for example, to ensure the most effective interpretation of the program objective. He or she may even help the writer with the basic approach, such as changing the original idea of producing a brief instructional tape into an interactive multimedia experience, or a documentary into a dramatic format, or a company president's address into a town hall–type forum. The director can also define or change the angle or help with ideas about the specific environment in which the event is to take place.

When directing an electronic field production or a big remote, the director is part of the survey team (see chapter 15).

Art director   The *art director* uses the script and the director's comments for the set design or the specific location for the show. He or she is also in charge of decorating the set and designing the various graphics, such as titles and charts. The art director must create an environment that fits the overall style of the show and that facilitates the anticipated production procedures. Even the most beautifully designed set is useless if there is not enough room for camera movement and microphones or if it cannot be properly lighted.

The art director prepares a *floor plan,* which is a diagram of scenery, stage properties (tables and chairs), and set dressings (wall hangings, lamps, and plants) drawn on a grid. (See chapter 14 for a more detailed discussion of the floor plan.) The floor plan is an important preproduction guide for the director, and, for large productions, the lighting director (LD), the audio engineer, and the floor manager. With a good floor plan, these people can visualize the major shots and place the cameras, lights, and microphones accordingly. The floor manager needs the floor plan to set up and dress the studio set.

Technical director   The preproduction team may also include a *technical director* (*TD*), or a technical supervisor, especially if the production is a live telecast of a special event, such as a parade or the dedication of a new building. The TD can determine ahead of time the major technical facilities necessary for the proposed production.

Small production companies or television stations often combine the various roles. The functions of the producer and the director, and even the writer, might be carried out by a single person—the producer-director; and the floor manager might also act as art director and property manager.

Large productions, however, may include on the preproduction team a graphic artist, a costume designer, a sound designer, and a choreographer. **ZVL3 CUE 2** PROCESS→ Phases→ preproduction

Production Team

As mentioned before, even if some news organizations send out a single person to do the reporting, camera operation, and postproduction, most routine EFPs are accomplished by a three-person **production team**: the talent, the camcorder operator, and a utility person who takes care of audio, lighting, recording, and/or transmission. If you use two cameras for a multicamera shoot, you have to add a second camcorder operator. In more-ambitious, single-camera EFPs, the camera operator may also take care of the lighting; this dual job is carried out by the *director of photography* (*DP*)—a carryover from film production.

In most multicamera productions, the production team is considerably larger. The nontechnical members include the producer and various assistants—*associate producer* (*AP*) and *production assistant* (*PA*)—the director, the *associate* or *assistant director* (*AD*) if it is a complex show, and the *talent*. Whereas the major part of the producer's job is in preproduction, the director is totally involved in the actual production phase. Sometimes there are several producers for a show series: a producer who arranges the budget and negotiates with talent, and a *line producer,* who supervises the daily activities on the set or in the studio. Sometimes there is a *studio producer* who is responsible for the studio segments of a show, and a *field producer* who takes care of the segments videotaped outside the studio.

The production crew, which is made up of technical and nontechnical personnel, normally includes the floor manager and *floor persons* (*grips* or *utility persons*), the technical director, camera operators, the lighting director, video and audio engineers, the videotape operator, the *C.G. (character generator) operator,* and the *video operator* (*VO*), who adjusts the cameras during the production for optimal video output. Large productions add an engineering supervisor as well as various costume people, a property manager, makeup artists, and hairdressers. **ZVL3 CUE 3** PROCESS→ Phases→ production

Postproduction Team

The **postproduction team** is relatively small and normally consists of a video editor and the director. The editor will try to make sense of the various video-recorded segments and put them in the order indicated by the script. The director will guide the editor in the selection and the sequencing of shots. If you, as the director, have a good editor and a detailed script, you will have relatively little to do. You may want to see a *rough-cut,* or an "off-line" editing version, before you give the editor the go-ahead to prepare the final "on-line" videotape. If the project requires more-complex editing, you may have to sit with the editor throughout the process to select most of the shots and determine their sequence.

Complex postproduction may also include extensive manipulation of sound, called *audio sweetening.* It consists of remixing, adding, or replacing small or large portions of the original sound track and can take more time and effort than editing pictures. Major sound postproduction is done by a *sound designer.*

Most producers do not get involved in postproduction, at least not until the first rough-cut is done. Some producers cannot stay away from the editing room, however, and get intimately involved in every decision. Such fervor is, despite all good intentions, not always appreciated by the editor and the director. **ZVL3 CUE 4** PROCESS→ Phases→ postproduction

PASSING THE BUCK

Let's visit a television studio to watch the video recording of a visiting rock group.

When you arrive at the studio well before the scheduled start time, the production is already in the wrap-up stage. Neither the musicians nor the production people look too happy. The PA tells you that the recording session had been pushed ahead three hours because of the band's tight schedule. It becomes obvious that the session did not go as planned. There are small groups of people on the studio floor engaged in rather lively discussions. Let's listen in on what they are saying.

In one group, the band manager is complaining about poor scheduling and the "static look" of the show, and the lead singer is kvetching about the "bad sound." The executive producer tries to appease the band members, while the producer accuses everybody of not communicating with him. The director defends his overall visual concept and personal style and accuses the musicians of not understanding the "true nature of video." The band manager mutters something about the sloppy contract and the lack of coffee during rehearsals.

Some crew and band members vent their frustrations about technical problems. They argue about which microphones should have been used and where they should have been placed and about light levels that were much too uneven for good pictures. The LD counters by saying that she had practically no time for adequate lighting, mainly because she lost three hours of setup time. The musicians complain that the sound levels were too low, while the camera operators say that the music was too loud for them to hear the director's instructions in their headsets. They felt lost, especially because the director had not briefed them ahead of time on what shots to get.

The floor manager and his crew wonder aloud why they had no floor plan. It would have saved them from having to move the heavy platform on which the band performed from place to place until the director was finally satisfied with its location.

Everyone seems to be passing the buck and blaming everybody else for the various production problems. What could have been done to minimize or avoid these problems? Before reading on, write down the major complaints of the band and the production members and, by referring to figures 2.1 and 2.2, try to figure out who should have done what.

Ready? Now compare your notes with the following recommendations.

Situation: The video-recording session was pushed ahead by three hours because of the band's tight schedule.

Responsibility: Producer. He should have coordinated the band's schedule more carefully with his production schedule. Moving up a shooting schedule by three hours forces the crew to work unreasonably fast, causing stress and inviting serious production mistakes.

Situation: The band's manager complains about poor scheduling and the "static look" of the show. The lead singer is unhappy with the sound as recorded.

Responsibility: Again, the producer is responsible for scheduling and should have double-checked with the band manager about exactly when the band would be available for the studio production. The "static look" complaint is aimed at the show's director; and the "bad sound" is directed at the audio engineer, who chose the type and the position of microphones and did the sound mixing. Ultimately, the TD is responsible for all technical processes, including the sound pickup and mixing. The producer should have brought together the lead singer, band manager, and audio engineer in the preproduction phase to discuss the sound requirements. The producer should also have arranged for the band manager to meet with the director to discuss the visual requirements and the overall look of the performance. The director could then have discussed his ideas about the "true nature of video" with the band manager. Even if the initiative did not come from the producer, the director and the audio engineer should have pressed for such a meeting. Obviously, there was little communication among the members of the production team. The blame for the sloppy contract goes to the band manager and the executive producer, and the PA should have arranged for coffee.

Situation: The choice of microphones and their placement is being challenged. The band members complain that sound levels of the foldback—during which the sound as mixed is played back to the band members—were too low. The camera operators could not hear the director's instructions because of the music's high volume and were without direction.

Responsibility: The type of microphones used and their placement is clearly the responsibility of the audio engineer. Again, despite the drastically reduced setup time, a preproduction meeting with the key members of the band could have prevented most of the sound problems, including the low playback levels. The director or the TD should have anticipated the intercommunication problems between the director and the camera operators. Even the best intercom headsets will not function when used close to high-volume sound sources such as the speakers of a rock band. The director could have minimized this problem by meeting with the camera operators ahead of time to discuss the principal shots for each camera.

Situation: The light levels were too uneven for good pictures.

Responsibility: The LD is responsible for the uneven light levels. Her excuse is that she lost three full hours of setup time and that she had no floor plan with which to do even the most rudimentary preproduction planning. She could have contacted the director during the preproduction stage, however, or at least two days before the production, and asked about the floor plan and the lighting requirements for the show. In addition, when time is tight it is more sensible to illuminate the set with a generous amount of overall light rather than with highly specific light beams in limited areas. This would have made the lighting more even. (See chapter 7 for more-detailed lighting techniques.)

Situation: The floor manager and his crew lacked a floor plan, which resulted in needlessly moving a heavy platform.

Responsibility: A floor plan would have told the floor crew the exact location of the platform on which the musicians perform. It would also have helped the LD decide on the basic lighting setup and the director on the basic camera positions. The lack of a floor plan is a direct result of poor communication among the preproduction team and, therefore, the ultimate responsibility of the producer. The director should have consulted the art director about the set and the floor plan during preproduction and then asked the art director why the floor plan was not done according to schedule. The TD, LD, and floor manager should have asked the director for the floor plan before the actual production date.

As you can see, a production team can operate successfully only when each team member knows his or her assignment and all members are in constant communication with one another during the preproduction and production phases. Just like with team sports, if a single member of the production team makes a major mistake, the show goes down despite the superior performance of everyone else. More-thorough preproduction could have averted many of these problems.

> **▶ KEY CONCEPT**
>
> Know the functions and the responsibilities of each member of the nontechnical and technical production staffs.

TAKING AND SHARING RESPONSIBILITY

Fortunately, a subsequent visit to an elaborate multicamera EFP of an MTV segment turns out to be a much happier experience than our studio encounter.

When you get to the location of the MTV shoot, you find a whole section of the street already blocked off by local police, and you have to show your pass. You see action everywhere. The audio engineer and his assistants are adjusting the loudspeakers, and the camera operators are checking out some shots. You are greeted by the floor manager and introduced to the producer and the director. Despite the bustling activity, the producer seems amazingly calm and takes time out to explain the concept of the MTV segment: the lead singer drives an old Cadillac convertible down the street to a stop sign, where the dancers mob his car.

Some of the dancers are already practicing their routine, while others are coming out of a large trailer that serves as the talent's makeup and dressing facility. Everybody seems relaxed, and you sense purpose and competence in what each team member is doing.

The director checks the time line, posted by the trailer, and asks the floor manager to call for a run-through. There is instant activity: the dancers take their positions, the car is moved to the starting point, the camera operators get their opening shots, and the audio people start the sound track playback. So far as you can tell, the run-through goes very smoothly; the crew and the talent also seem happy with the outcome. Nevertheless, the director calls for a brief meeting of crew and talent to discuss some production problems.

The PA reads the notes that were dictated to him by the producer and the director during the run-through:

▶ "Dancers in the back can't hear the music."

▶ "Johnny [the lead singer driving the Cadillac] can't see the mark."

▶ "Shadows on him are too harsh when the car stops."

▶ "Need a tighter shot of Johnny."

▶ "We should be looking up at Johnny, not down on him."

▶ "Johnny is sweating too much. Light reflects off his nose."

▶ "Lots of dirt in the dancing area."

▶ "We can see audio cables in the background."

▶ "Some dancers are blocking Johnny on a close-up."

Which people would you ask to take care of these minor production problems? Let's look at the notes again.

"Dancers in the back can't hear the music."

Correction by the audio engineer.

"Johnny can't see the mark."

This means that Johnny can't see the mark on the curb that tells him exactly where to stop the car. The mark has to be moved to the stop sign.

Correction by the floor manager.

"Shadows on him are too harsh when the car stops."

Correction by the grips, under the direction of the LD.

"Need a tighter shot of Johnny."

Correction by the director and, ultimately, the camera operator.

"We should be looking up at Johnny, not down on him."

The producer looks at the director. She turns to the specific camera operator.

Correction by the director and, ultimately, the camera operator.

"Johnny is sweating too much. Light reflects off his nose."

The director looks at the makeup artist. This problem has nothing to do with lighting.

Correction by the makeup artist.

"Lots of dirt in the dancing area."

Correction by the floor manager and the floor crew.

"We can see audio cables in the background."

The audio engineer says that he will take care of it.

Correction by the audio assistant and the floor persons.

"Some dancers are blocking Johnny on a close-up."

Correction by the director and the choreographer.

After this brief meeting, the director calls for a 15-minute *reset* break during which the production crewmembers go about correcting the various problems. After the reset the director checks the time line and calls for another run-through. The following three hours are taken up by more rehearsals, two more such brief production meetings (often called *notes*), and several *takes*. The floor manager calls for a *wrap* (the completion of all production activities) a half-hour ahead of schedule.

Unlike the studio show of the rock band, this MTV field production was obviously well prepared in preproduction. During production the members of the technical and nontechnical staffs knew what they had to do, how to communicate constructively, and how to share responsibilities. The various notes meetings were an effective and efficient way to identify major and minor production problems and to ensure that the appropriate people took care of them. Some directors in complex productions schedule as much as one-third of the total rehearsal time for notes and resets.

> **► KEY CONCEPT**
>
> Establish and maintain effective communication among all production personnel.

PRODUCTION SCHEDULE AND TIME LINE

Like the script, a production schedule is essential to proper production coordination. It shows the specific dates for preproduction, production, and broadcast. Although the terms *production schedule* and *time line* are sometimes used interchangeably, they are quite different from each other and fulfill different functions. The **production schedule,** compiled by the producer, is the overall calendar for a production, which can span weeks. The **time line,** on the other hand, is usually drawn up by the director and shows the allotted time segments for a single production day.

Here is an example of a production schedule for a 15-minute studio interview with the president of City College.

INTERVIEW PRODUCTION SCHEDULE

March 1	Confirmation by college president.
March 2	First preproduction meeting. Interview format ready.
March 4	Second preproduction meeting. Script ready. Floor plan ready.
March 5	All facilities requests due, including set and prop requests.
March 9	Production. Studio 1.
March 10	Postproduction, if any.
March 14	Air date (broadcast).

Note the four-day lead-time from the due date for all facilities requests (March 5) to the actual production date (March 9). This lead-time is necessary to ensure that the studio and all facilities requested are available.

The time line for the actual production is much more detailed and breaks a single production day into blocks of time for certain activities. As you recall from the MTV field production, the director, floor manager, and PA periodically checked the time line to see whether the production was on schedule. Following is the director's time line for the interview of March 9, as indicated on the producer's production schedule.

TIME LINE: MARCH 9—INTERVIEW (STUDIO 1)

8:00 a.m.	Crew call
8:30–9:00 a.m.	Technical meeting
9:00–11:00 a.m.	Setup and lighting
11:00 a.m.–12:00 p.m.	Meal
12:00–12:15 p.m.	Notes and reset
12:15–12:30 p.m.	Briefing of guest in Green Room
12:30–12:45 p.m.	Run-through and camera rehearsal
12:45–12:55 p.m.	Notes
12:55–1:10 p.m.	Reset
1:10–1:15 p.m.	Break
1:15–1:45 p.m.	Video recording
1:45–1:55 p.m.	Spill
1:55–2:10 p.m.	Strike

Let's examine more closely each of the time line's activities.

Crew call   This is the time when all production crewmembers (floor manager and assistants, TD, LD, camera operators, audio people, and other equipment operators) are expected to show up and start working.

Technical meeting   This meeting includes the major nontechnical and technical people: producer, director, interview host, PA, floor manager, TD, LD, and audio engineer. The director briefly explains the program objective and how she expects the show to look (simple interview set, bright lighting, fairly tight shots of the college president). This meeting is also to double-check all technical facilities and the scenery and props.

Setup and lighting   According to the floor plan, the setup is relatively easy for the floor manager and his crew. The lighting is routine and does not require any special effects. The two hours allotted should be sufficient for both activities.

Meal   It is important that everybody be back from lunch at exactly 12:00 p.m., which means that everyone has to be able to leave the studio at exactly 11:00 a.m., even if there are still minor setup and lighting details left. Minor adjustments can be made during the reset time.

Notes and reset   If there are no major setup and equipment problems, the period set aside for notes may be considerably shorter. The available time can then be spent on a more leisurely reset—fine-tuning the lighting, moving a plant that may interfere with the person in front of it, cleaning the coffee table, and so forth.

Briefing of guest   While the production crew is getting ready for the first run-through and camera rehearsal, the producer, the interview host, and the PA (and sometimes the director) meet with the college president in the Green Room to go over the program concept. The Green Room is a small, comfortable room specifically set up for such a briefing.

Run-through and camera rehearsal   This run-through is to familiarize the guest with the studio environment and procedures, to check on the various camera shots, and to rehearse the show's opening and closing. It is intentionally brief, to keep the guest as fresh as possible. Because of severe time constraints, news interviews are normally not rehearsed. The producer may brief the guest during camera setup and lighting.

Notes and reset   The run-through and camera rehearsals will inevitably reveal some minor problems with the lighting or audio. The floor manager may ask the makeup person to straighten the president's tie and put a little makeup on his forehead to hide the perspiration.

Break   Even when working on a tight schedule, it is important to give the talent and crew a brief break just before the production. This will help everybody relax and separate the rehearsal from the actual taping.

Video recording   The time allotted allows for a few false starts or closings. The fewer takes there are, however, the fresher the interview will be.

Spill   This is a grace period to fix things that went wrong unexpectedly. For example, the director might use this time to redo the introduction by the host because the president's name was inadvertently misspelled in the opening titles.

Strike   This activity does not refer to a protest by the crew but to the clearing of the studio of all scenery, properties, and equipment.

Such a detailed time line is especially important for an electronic field production. The EFP schedule normally includes additional items, such as loading and unloading equipment and transportation to and from the remote location.

Once you have a production schedule and a time line, you must stick to them. The best schedule is useless if you don't observe the deadlines or the blocks of time designated for a specific production activity. Experienced producers and directors move on to the next segment according to schedule, regardless of whether they have accomplished everything in the previous one. If you ignore the time limits too many times, your schedule becomes meaningless. **ZVL3 CUE 5** ▶ PROCESS→ Phases→ production

> ▶**KEY CONCEPT**
> Establish a realistic production schedule and time line and stick to them.

As you can see, knowing the functions of every member of the production team and coordinating them according to a precise schedule are essential to effective and efficient video productions.

M A I N   P O I N T S

▶ **Team Members**

The members perform nontechnical and technical functions. Nontechnical people do not normally operate equipment; technical people do. The nontechnical people are also called above-the-line personnel; the technical people, below-the-line personnel.

▶ **Preproduction Team**

These people plan the production. This team normally includes the producer, writer, director, art director, and, occasionally, technical director (TD). Small production companies or television stations often combine preproduction functions, such as producer-director. Larger productions employ additional preproduction personnel, such as a sound designer or a choreographer.

▶ **Production Team**

An electronic news gathering (ENG) "team" may consist of a single VJ (video journalist), who not only reports the story but also operates the camera and does the postproduction editing. The typical electronic field production (EFP) team comprises the talent, a camcorder operator, and a utility person. Larger field and studio productions employ a much larger team. It may include the producer and various assistants, such as associate producer and production assistant (PA); the director and the associate director (AD); and the talent. The production crew usually includes the floor manager and floor persons (grips or utility persons), technical director, camera operators, lighting director (LD), video engineer, audio engineer, video-recording operator, and C.G. (character generator) operator. In preproduction the producer is in charge of coordinating the various people and production details; in the production phase, the director is in charge.

▶ **Postproduction Team**

This team normally consists of the director, the editor, and, in more-complex productions, a sound designer, who remixes the sound track. The director and occasionally the producer guide the editor in the selection and the sequencing of shots.

▶ **Communication**

Always establish and maintain regular communication among all production personnel.

▶ **Production Schedule and Time Line**

A production schedule, prepared by the producer, is a calendar that shows the major preproduction, production, and postproduction activities. A time line, drawn up by the director, shows a breakdown of time blocks for a single production day.

Z E T T L ' S   V I D E O L A B   3 . 0

 For your reference, or to track your work, the Zettl's VideoLab 3.0 *program cues in this chapter are listed here with their corresponding page numbers.*

ZVL3 CUE 1 PROCESS→ People→ nontechnical | technical   **18**

ZVL3 CUE 2   PROCESS→ Phases→ preproduction   **24**

ZVL3 CUE 3 PROCESS→ Phases→ production   **24**

ZVL3 CUE 4 PROCESS→ Phases→ postproduction   **25**

ZVL3 CUE 5 PROCESS→ Phases→ production   **31**

II

Image Creation: Digital Video and Camera

Now that you have some idea of what video production is all about and who does what in producing a program, you are probably eager to produce a knock-your-socks-off documentary or movie. But you must exercise just a bit more patience and realize that mastering the art of video includes a healthy dose of technical know-how. Before you embark on an ambitious production, learning the technical basics of analog and digital video, the workings of a video camera, and how to use the camera to capture compelling images will save you time, money, and especially nerves. Even if a camera's automated features enable you to produce acceptable images in some cases, you won't know how to override them when the circumstances or your artistic intentions require you to go beyond the default settings. The basic knowledge of how an electronic image is formed and the difference between analog and digital processes is a necessary prerequisite to understanding how to use a camera to its fullest technical and artistic potential.

CHAPTER 3

KEY TERMS

480p A scanning system of digital television. The *p* stands for *progressive,* which means that each complete television frame consists of 480 visible lines that are scanned one after the other.

720p A scanning system of digital television. The *p* stands for *progressive,* which means that each complete television frame consists of 720 visible lines that are scanned one after the other. Generally considered high-definition television.

1080i A scanning system of high-definition television. The *i* stands for *interlaced,* which means that a complete frame is formed from two interlaced scanning fields. Generally considered the high-end HDTV system.

analog A signal that fluctuates exactly like the original stimulus.

binary digit (bit) The smallest amount of information a computer can hold and process. A charge is either present, represented by a 1, or absent, represented by a 0. One bit can describe two levels, such as on/off or black/white. Two bits can describe four levels (2^2 bits); three bits, eight levels (2^3 bits); four bits, sixteen (2^4 bits); and so on. A group of eight bits (2^8) is called a byte.

codec Stands for *compression-decompression.* Can be one of several compression systems of digital video, graphics, and audio files.

compression The temporary rearrangement or elimination of redundant picture information for easier storage and signal transport.

digital Pertaining to data in the form of digits (on/off pulses).

digital television (DTV) Digital systems that generally have a higher image resolution than standard television. Sometimes called *advanced television (ATV).*

field One-half of a complete scanning cycle, with two fields necessary for one television picture frame. In standard (NTSC) television, there are 60 fields, or 30 frames, per second.

frame A complete scanning cycle of the electron beam. In interlaced scanning, two partial scanning cycles (fields) are necessary for one frame. In progressive scanning, each scanning cycle produces one complete frame.

frame rate The time it takes to scan a complete frame; usually expressed in frames per second (fps). In standard (NTSC) television, there are 60 fields, or 30 frames, per second. In DTV the frame rate is flexible (ranging from 15 fps to 60 fps). HDTV cinema cameras have adopted the film standard of 24 fps, but you can change their frame rate.

high-definition television (HDTV) Includes the 720p, 1080i, and 1080p scanning systems. Because the 480p system produces high-quality video, it is sometimes included in the HDTV category.

high-definition video (HDV) A recording system that produces images of the same resolution as HDTV (720p and 1080i). The images are much more compressed than those of HDTV, resulting in a slightly lower image quality.

interlaced scanning The scanning of all the odd-numbered lines (first field) and the subsequent scanning of all the even-numbered lines (second field). The two fields make up a complete television frame.

progressive scanning The consecutive scanning of lines from top to bottom.

quantizing A step in the digitization of an analog signal. It changes the sampling points into discrete numerical values (0's and 1's). Also called *quantization.*

refresh rate The number of complete scanning cycles per second. Also expressed in frames per second.

sampling Taking a number of samples (voltages) of the analog video or audio signal at equally spaced intervals.

scanning The movement of the electron beam from left to right and from top to bottom on the television screen.

Image Formation and Digital Video

The past few years have seen a dramatic change from analog to digital video equipment. But why? After all, analog video produced amazingly good video and audio recordings. This chapter is a partial answer to why such a conversion took place. It will help you understand how video images are created, what digital processes are all about, and the major advantages of digital over analog video and audio processing.

▶ **BASIC IMAGE FORMATION**
Interlaced, progressive, and digital HDTV scanning systems; and flat-panel screens, including LCD and plasma panels

▶ **WHAT IS DIGITAL?**
Analog versus digital signals, sampling, and quantizing

▶ **WHY DIGITAL?**
Picture quality in dubs, signal compression, and picture and sound manipulation

BASIC IMAGE FORMATION

The basic principle of image formation is the same for black-and-white television, color television, standard analog television, and digital high-definition television (HDTV) that uses a standard television set, or more accurate, a cathode ray tube (CRT) display rather than a flat-panel display. To explain this principle, we'll start with a monochrome (black-and-white) television set.

The back end of the monochrome picture tube houses the *electron gun,* which emits a tiny but sharp *electron beam.* In a standard television set, this beam is guided through the long neck of the picture tube to scan the face of the tube, which is covered with thousands of tiny phosphorous dots. The stronger the beam, the brighter the dots light up. **SEE 3.1** When the beam is too weak to illuminate the dots, the screen appears to be black. When the beam hits the pixels at full strength, the screen looks white.

A color set, on the other hand, has three electron guns in the back of the tube that emit three separate electron beams. The face of the color picture tube has neatly

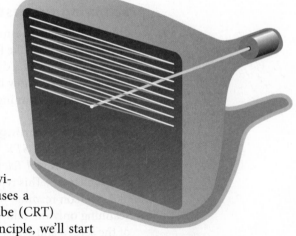

3.1 Video Image Formation

The electron gun in the back of the picture tube generates an electron beam. This beam is guided through the long neck of the tube to scan the thousands of dots covering the face of the tube.

3.2 Color Video Image Formation

The color receiver has three electron guns, each responding to either the red, green, or blue part of the video signal. Each beam is assigned to its specific color.

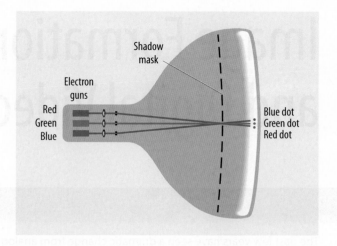

arranged groups of *RGB*—red, green, and blue—dots or tiny rectangles, which are activated by the three beams. One of the beams is designated to hit the red dots, the second to hit the green dots, and the third to hit the blue dots. These dots are now also called *pixels* (a contraction of *picture element*), a term borrowed from computer lingo. A pixel, similar to the tile of a mosaic, is the smallest element of a digital picture whose color can be controlled by the computer. **SEE 3.2** Various combinations of these three beams provide all the colors you see on the video screen. (See chapter 7 for a discussion of these three primary colors of light and how they mix into all the others.)

Scanning Process

The electron beam, emitted by the electron gun, uses **scanning** to "read" the television screen, much like how you read a printed page: from left to right and from top to bottom. There is a difference, however, between how the beam scans a standard television set and how it scans a computer monitor. A standard television set works with *interlaced* scanning; a computer screen works with *progressive* scanning.

Interlaced scanning   The television system that drives your home receiver is sometimes called *STV* (for *standard television*) or, more frequently, *NTSC,* which stands for *National Television System Committee.* (We discuss the NTSC system later in this chapter.) This type of system uses **interlaced scanning,** which means that, unlike a person reading, the electron beam skips every other line during its first scan, scanning only the odd-numbered lines. **SEE 3.3A** Then the beam returns to the top of the screen and scans all the even-numbered lines. **SEE 3.3B** Scanning all the odd-numbered lines, which takes exactly ⅟₆₀ second, yields one **field**. The subsequent scanning of all the even-numbered lines, which takes another ⅟₆₀ second, produces another field. The two fields, which take ⅟₃₀ second to produce, compose one complete picture, called a **frame**. **SEE 3.3C** Thus, for standard television there are 60 fields, or 30 frames, per second.

A complete television frame in the standard television NTSC system consists of 525 scanning lines.

3.3 **Interlaced Scanning**

A In interlaced scanning, the electron beam first scans all the odd-numbered lines, from left to right and from top to bottom. This first scanning cycle produces one field.

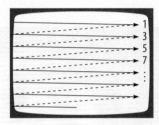

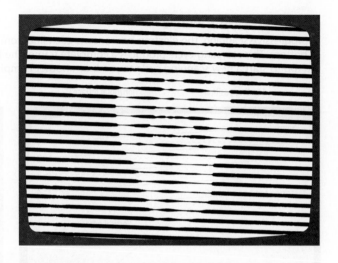

B The electron beam jumps back to the top and scans all the even-numbered lines. This second scanning cycle produces a second field.

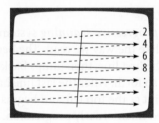

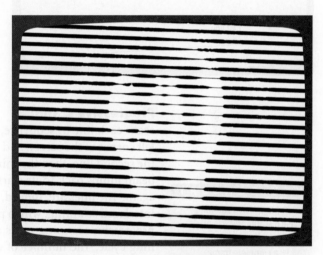

C The two fields make up a complete television picture, called a frame.

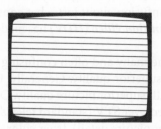

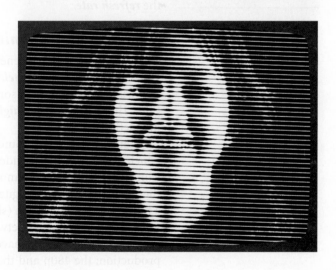

3.4 **Progressive Scanning**

In progressive scanning, the electron beam scans each line from left to right and from top to bottom. This scanning cycle produces a complete frame. The beam then jumps back to the top to start a new scanning cycle to produce another complete frame.

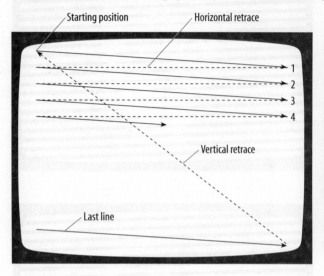

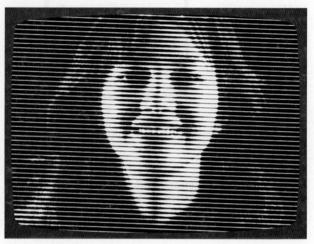

Progressive scanning   In the *progressive scanning* system, the electron beam scans each line in sequence, much like the way we read. The beam starts at the top-left corner of the screen and scans the first line, then jumps back to the left and scans the second line, then the third, and so forth. After the last line has been scanned, the beam jumps back to its starting point at the top left and begins the process all over again. The lines are, indeed, scanned in an orderly progression. **SEE 3.4** Contrary to interlaced scanning, which produces half a frame (one field) for each scanning cycle, progressive scanning reads all of the lines and produces a full frame for each scanning cycle. The number of complete scanning cycles per second (frames) is called the *refresh rate*.

Digital Video Scanning Systems

Although digital video is generally superior in quality to analog systems, not all digital video, also called *digital television* (*DTV*), is *high-definition television* (*HDTV*). You will find that there is some confusion about just what constitutes "high definition." The introduction of *high-definition video* (*HDV*) has made the high-definition distinction even fuzzier.

Let's try to sort out some of the many and often confusing abbreviations, all of which seem to describe video of superior quality. Generally, DTV—digital television—has become synonymous with superior picture quality. One of the reasons for the improved quality of digital video over STV (standard television) is that DTV has a higher picture resolution (sharper picture detail), truer color, and a wider contrast ratio (more-subtle grays between the brightest and darkest picture areas).

Three DTV systems have emerged as the most practical for all kinds of video production: the 480p and the 720p systems (*p* stands for *progressive scanning*) and the 1080i system (*i* stands for *interlaced scanning*).

480p system   The picture of the *480p* system is made up of 480 lines (just about what you actually see of the 525 lines of the NTSC system) that are progressively scanned. It normally produces 60 complete frames (not fields) per second. Because of the high picture quality, the 480p system is sometimes regarded as HDTV, although technical classifications do not include it in the high-definition category.

720p system   The *720p* system produces 720 lines that are progressively scanned. Its normal refresh rate is 60 frames per second. The high number of lines results in very sharp pictures that are definitely high-definition. The 720p system too belongs in the HDTV category.

1080i system   The *1080i* system uses interlaced scanning to save bandwidth. This means that its signals can be transported through a smaller pipeline than if its scanning were progressive. Although the 1080i system produces only 30 frames (60 fields) or less per second, its extremely high number of scanning lines contributes to higher-definition video than with either the 480p or the 720p system. It is currently the highest-quality HDTV system.

> **► KEY CONCEPT**
> The established DTV scanning standards are 480p, 720p, and 1080i.

Note, however, that video quality depends also on how little, or how much, the video signal is compressed. The more compression you impose on a signal, the less high-fidelity it becomes.

What about HDV—high-definition video? Although the HDV system was originally developed for small, prosumer camcorders, it uses the 720p or the 1080i scanning system, so its picture quality comes very close to that of the much more expensive professional HDTV camcorders. You would probably have a hard time distinguishing between HDV and HDTV by looking at the two videos on a standard television set. What, then, is the difference? One distinction is not electronic but physical: high-definition picture quality depends not only on the camcorder's scanning system but also on its lens. The lenses in professional HDTV camcorders can cost many times more than an entire HDV camcorder. The other factor is compression: HDV has a higher compression ratio than HDTV. Nevertheless, if you want high-quality video at a reasonable price, HDV is the way to go. **SEE 3.5**

3.5 DTV Systems

SYSTEM	SCANNING	COMPRESSION
Digital television (DTV)	480p, 720p, and 1080i	Superior picture and sound; various compressions
High-definition television (HDTV)	720p, 1080i, and 1080p	Usually MPEG-2
High-definition video (HDV)	720p and 1080i	Various; more compression than HDTV

Variable scanning systems   Some digital cameras, which are used primarily for electronic filmmaking, have a *variable* scanning system. Their normal refresh rate is 24 frames per second (fps), which is identical to film, but it can be lowered to 15 or boosted to 60. This variable *frame rate* allows for smooth accelerated or slow-motion effects.

Format conversion   To make digital scanning systems even more flexible, you can use a frame-rate converter to change the scanning systems, say, from 720p at 24 frames per second to 1080i at 30. This conversion takes place in the postproduction phase.

Flat-panel Screens

The need for larger display monitors has spurred the development of *flat-panel screens*. One of the great advantages of flat-panel displays is that the screen can get bigger—from the familiar small video display on a laptop computer to a large home theater–type screen—without getting thicker. Other advantages of flat-panel displays over the regular television CRT (cathode ray tube) are improved color rendition (more-subtle colors), greater contrast ratio (brighter whites and, therefore, darker blacks, and more-subtle shades in between), and generally a higher resolution (more pixels per square inch). The two most popular albeit incompatible flat-panel systems are the *liquid crystal display* (LCD) panels and the *plasma* panels.

LCD panels   The LCD panel comprises two transparent sheets that contain, sandwichlike, a liquid whose crystal molecules change when a video signal is applied. The many tiny transistors that compose the basic dots of the picture orient the liquid crystals in certain ways to allow back light to shine through.

Plasma panels   Instead of sandwiching a liquid, the two glass panels of the plasma system contain a thin layer of gas. When the gas receives the varying charges of the video signal, it activates the many tiny red, green, and blue dots that are arranged much like the ones on a standard television receiver.

Despite the technical differences between the two flat-panel systems, you would probably be hard-pressed to tell the difference when looking at their pictures. Before we continue praising the virtues of digital video, let's find out what *digital* actually means.

WHAT IS DIGITAL?

All digital video and the way computers process information are based on a binary code that uses on/off, either/or values for all their operations. The *on* state is represented by a 1, and the *off* state is represented by a 0. These **binary digits**, or **bits** for short, operate on the light-bulb principle: if you have a 1, the light bulb is on; if you have a 0, the light bulb is off. In the digital world—that pertaining to data in the form of digits, or on/off pulses—there is nothing between the 1 and the 0; the light bulb cannot burn at half-intensity.

The Difference Between Analog and Digital

An *analog* signal is an electrical copy of the original stimulus, such as somebody's singing into a microphone. The technical definition is that the analog signal fluctuates exactly like the original stimulus. The analog signal is also continuous, which means that it never skips any part of the signal, however small the skip may be. You may want to visualize the analog signal as a ramp, which is a continuous way to reach a certain height. Because it is continuous, you could divide the ramp into a virtually infinite number of points (values) that indicate their relative elevation. **SEE 3.6**

The *digital* signal, on the other hand, is discontinuous. It does not process the total original signal (the song) but skips from one point of the signal to the next, selecting a great number of successive points that represent the original signal—a process called *sampling*. In our analogy the digital signal looks more like a staircase. **SEE 3.7**

As you can see, we no longer have an infinite number of values, as in the analog signal, but a finite and measurable amount of steps. Very much in the on/off spirit of the digital world, you either stand on a certain step or you don't: you can't stand on the space between the steps. Technically, the signal has now been divided into a series of discrete on/off values.

Sampling   In *sampling*, the number of points along the ramp (analog signal) is determined for building the steps (digital values). With a low sampling rate, there

3.6 Analog Signal

The analog signal can be represented by a ramp that leads to a certain height.

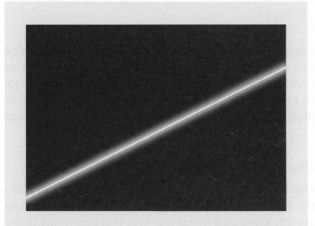

3.7 Digital Signal

The digital signal can be represented by a staircase that leads to a certain height in discrete steps.

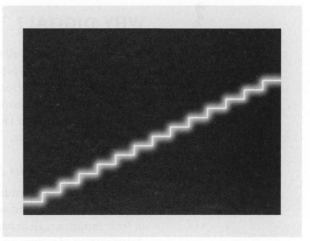

3.8 Low Sampling Rate

Sampling selects a portion of the original analog signal. A low sampling rate transforms this ramp into a few large steps. Much of the original signal is lost.

3.9 High Sampling Rate

A high sampling rate selects more parts of the original signal. The smaller steps more closely approximate the ramp. The higher the sampling rate, the higher the quality of the digital signal.

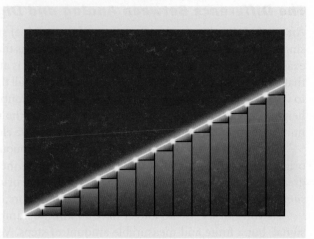

will be only a few points along the ramp, which translates into few, but large, steps. Obviously, those few large steps are not a good representation of the ramp (the original analog signal). **SEE 3.8**

A high sampling rate, on the other hand, will produce many little steps that much more closely approximate the original ramp. **SEE 3.9**

Quantizing   Once you have determined the number of steps (signal values) through sampling, you must identify each step (value) with a number. This numbering process is called **quantizing**, or *quantization*.

WHY DIGITAL?

Why do we go through all these technical maneuvers when we already have an analog signal that perfectly represents the original stimulus? The basic answer lies in this seemingly crude either/or, on/off principle. Among many other things, it lets you: (1) dub video and audio with little or no deterioration, (2) compress the signals to save storage space and facilitate signal transport, and (3) manipulate pictures and sound with relative ease.

Picture Quality in Dubs

Because a number identifies each step, the robust either/or digital system can identify and remove the bad steps. This means that the digital system can eliminate, or at least minimize, all *artifacts*—the unwanted signal elements that contribute to the deterioration of picture and sound. When you use digital video recorders, subsequent generations produce pictures and sound that are for all practical purposes identical to the original recording, an attribute called *transparency*. A *generation* is one of a number of dubs (copies) away from the original. For example, the first-generation dub is struck directly from the original; the second generation is two dubs away from the original. Digital recording systems produce images that show little or no deterioration even after thirty or more generations.

Not so with an analog signal. In the name of seamlessness, all values are equal: it does not distinguish between the desirable signal and the artifacts (the signal noise). This problem is compounded in subsequent analog dubs. With analog equipment each subsequent dub adds another layer of artifacts to the old ones, much like how printed text deteriorates when you progressively duplicate photocopies. Analog video equipment will yield marked picture deterioration after just a few generations.

Compression

What can you do when you have a lot of stuff to pack but only one suitcase? This type of dilemma faces digital systems all the time. Even a high-capacity digital system does not normally have enough room to store—or a pipe large enough to transport in real time—all the video and audio information necessary for high-quality, full-screen moving pictures and sound. The solution to this problem is compression. In the digital domain, **compression** means to repack data, including throwing away all data that are not absolutely necessary for preserving the original quality of the video and audio signals. The process of rearranging rather than throwing away is called *lossless* compression; the compression that actually deletes redundant data is the *lossy* kind.

Lossless compression   When you don't want to leave anything behind when packing your suitcase, you need to repack it and hope to make all the stuff fit. *Lossless compression* uses a similar tactic: it doesn't eliminate information, even if it is redundant, but simply rearranges it in various packets for easier storage and transport. The advantage of lossless compression is that it maintains the original makeup of the digital video and audio signals. The disadvantage is that the system still has to manage overly large files. Such files are usually too bulky for *streaming* your favorite music for uninterrupted listening or for watching a movie trailer on your computer without having to wait for a prolonged download.

Lossy compression   Now you have to make choices about what items to pack in the suitcase and what to leave behind. Do you really need three pairs of shoes or will one do? How about one instead of four sweaters, especially if you might not even need one? *Lossy compression* makes similar choices: to identify and "lose" any digital information that is not absolutely necessary for maintaining most of the original picture and sound quality.

One of the most widely used professional video compression systems is MPEG-2 ("em-peg two"). *MPEG* stands for *Moving Picture Experts Group,* which developed this compression standard. MPEG-2 systematically looks at an uncompressed video frame and memorizes all of its pixels. It then compares the next frame series with this key frame, usually called the *i frame,* to see which pixels are carried over from the previous frame. The duplications are ignored by the new frames, considerably reducing the pixel content of each frame. The only pixels used in the frame series are the ones necessary to show change.

For example, if the key frame and the subsequent frames show a hiker walking against the cloudless blue sky, the system tells the computer to simply ignore all the sky pixels in the subsequent frames and concentrate on the changing positions of the hiker. When an ensuing frame shows the hiker walking past a tree, the system uses the first tree image as a new key frame. MPEG-2 would ask that if you have two suitcases but need only one sweater, why put identical sweaters in both suitcases so long as you have access to suitcase 1? Confusing? Perhaps, but at least you now appreciate the highly complex process that goes into compression. In fact, the development of HDTV for home viewing is very dependent on such compression techniques.

> ►**KEY CONCEPT**
>
> Compression eliminates redundant picture information to increase storage capacity and speed up signal transport.

Codec   To complicate matters further, there are many different *codecs*—compression-*de*compression systems—used for a variety of compression purposes. Apple QuickTime, for example, has several codecs, such as a high-quality, less lossy one for screening your masterpiece and a fairly lossy one for sending it to your friend over the Internet. Such compression systems are, of course, not applicable with analog video.

Picture and Sound Manipulation

Because digital video and audio signals basically consist of 0's and 1's, they can be changed by simply rearranging the numbers. The fancy opening titles of your favorite television show or an animated weather map are both the result of calculated manipulation of digital information. In fact, you can create synthetic images by applying certain programs that let you "paint by numbers." Again, such extensive and predictable manipulation is not possible with analog signals. (See chapter 8 for more about digital video wizardry.)

M A I N   P O I N T S

▶ **Interlaced and Progressive Scanning**

A standard (NTSC) television frame is made up of two scanning fields, which are necessary for one complete frame. There are 30 frames (60 fields) per second. Interlaced scanning scans every other line, then goes back and scans the lines that were skipped. Progressive scanning scans every line. In progressive scanning, each scanning cycle produces not fields but a complete frame. The frame rate can vary.

▶ **Digital Scanning Systems**

The most prevalent digital television (DTV) scanning systems are 480p, 720p, and 1080i. All systems produce video with high resolution, improved color, and more-subtle shadings between the brightest and darkest picture areas. High-definition video (HDV) uses the 720p or 1080i scanning system, but with higher compression than HDTV.

▶ **Flat-panel Screens**

Flat-panel screens have many tiny transistors that are sandwiched between two transparent panels. There are liquid crystal display (LCD) and plasma flat panels. When a video signal is applied, these pixels orient liquid crystals or gas to let light shine through.

▶ **Binary Principle**

All digital systems are based on the on/off principle of binary code. An electric charge is either present or it is not. The on state is represented by a 1, the off state by a 0.

▶ **Sampling Rate**

A high sampling rate—smaller steps composing a ramp—is desirable in digitizing an analog signal.

▶ **Analog Versus Digital Signals**

Digital signals sample the analog signal and assign each sample a specific number, a process called quantizing. The higher the sampling rate, the higher the picture quality. Digital signals are very robust and can identify and eliminate interfering artifacts, so they do not deteriorate over multiple generations. Digital signals can be compressed; analog signals cannot.

▶ **Compression and Codecs**

Compression eliminates redundant picture information to increase storage capacity and speed up signal transport and video and audio processing. Lossless compression repackages the data into less space. Lossy compression throws away redundant or less important data. There are several codec (compression-decompression) systems that offer various degrees of compression.

CHAPTER 4

KEY TERMS

aperture Iris opening of a lens; usually measured in *f*-stops.

beam splitter Optical device within the camera that splits the white light into the three additive primary light colors: red, green, and blue.

camcorder A portable camera with the VTR or other recording device built into it.

camera chain The camera and associated electronic equipment, consisting of the power supply, the sync generator, and the camera control unit (CCU).

camera control unit (CCU) Equipment, separate from the actual camera, that allows the video operator to adjust the color and brightness balance before and during the production.

charge-coupled device (CCD) An imaging device that translates the optical image into a video signal. Also called *chip*.

chrominance channel Contains the RGB video signals or some combination thereof. Also called *color*, or *C, channel*.

ENG/EFP camera Highly portable, high-end self-contained camera for electronic field production.

fast lens A lens that permits a relatively great amount of light to pass through at its largest aperture (lowest *f*-stop number). Can be used in low-light conditions.

focal length With the lens set at infinity, the distance from the iris to the plane where the picture is in focus. Normally measured in millimeters or inches.

ƒ-stop The scale on the lens, indicating the aperture. The larger the *f*-stop number, the smaller the aperture; the smaller the *f*-stop number, the larger the aperture.

iris Adjustable lens-opening mechanism. Also called *lens diaphragm*.

luminance channel Contains the black-and-white part of a video signal. It is mainly responsible for the sharpness of the picture. Also called *luma*, or *Y, channel*.

slow lens A lens that permits a relatively small amount of light to pass through (relatively high *f*-stop number at its largest aperture). Requires higher light levels for optimal pictures.

viewfinder A small video monitor or flat-panel screen on a camera that displays the black-and-white or color picture the camera generates.

zoom lens Variable-focal-length lens. All video cameras are equipped with a zoom lens.

zoom range How much the focal length can be changed from a wide shot to a close-up during a zoom. The zoom range is stated as a ratio, such as 20:1. Also called *zoom ratio*.

The Video Camera

Your friend brags about the new digital camcorder he just purchased. It has a three-chip imaging device that allows video capture in both a 4 × 3 and a 16 × 9 aspect ratio, a fast 15:1 optical zoom lens, a black-and-white viewfinder, and a foldout color liquid crystal display. It uses mini-cassettes to record 720p or 1080i high-definition video, and it connects to the computer with a FireWire cable. He encourages you to get the same model because it produces superior video and audio and is especially well suited for nonlinear editing. But how do you know that these features really justify the relatively high price of the camcorder?

This chapter will help you answer this question. You will also learn how a video camera works, as well as the relative advantages of various camera types and systems.

▶ **BASIC CAMERA FUNCTION AND ELEMENTS**
Function, lens, imaging device, video signal processing, and viewfinder

▶ **TYPES OF CAMERAS**
Camcorders, studio cameras, field and ENG/EFP cameras, and HDTV cameras

BASIC CAMERA FUNCTION AND ELEMENTS

Whether digital or analog, and regardless of their size, cost, and quality, all video cameras operate on the same basic principle: they *transduce* (translate) the optical image that the lens sees into a corresponding video picture. More specific, the camera converts an optical image into electrical signals that are reconverted by a television receiver into visible screen images.

Function

To fulfill this function, each video camera needs three basic elements: (1) the lens, (2) the imaging device, and (3) the viewfinder. **SEE 4.1**

The *lens* selects a portion of the scene at which you point the camera and produces a sharp optical image of it. The camera contains a *beam splitter* and an *imaging device* that convert the optical image of the lens into weak electric currents, which are amplified and further processed by a variety of electronic components. The *viewfinder* reconverts these electrical signals into video pictures of the lens-generated scene. **SEE 4.2**

To explain this process, we start with how a lens operates and sees a particular portion of a scene, then we move on to how the beam splitter and the imaging device work, and, finally, to how the video signal is reconverted into a video picture by the

4.1 Basic Camera Elements

The video camera has three main elements: the lens, the imaging device, and the viewfinder.

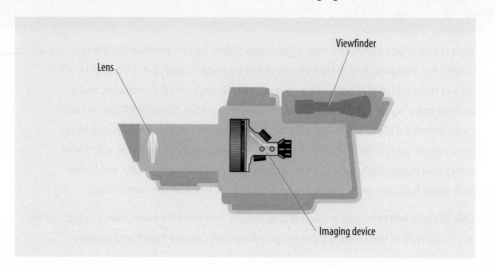

4.2 Functions of the Camera

The video camera translates the optical light image as seen by the lens into a corresponding picture on the screen. The light reflected off an object is gathered and transmitted by the lens to the beam splitter, which splits the white light into red, green, and blue (RGB) light beams. These beams are then transformed by CCDs into electric energy, which is amplified and processed into a video signal. It is then reconverted into video pictures by the viewfinder.

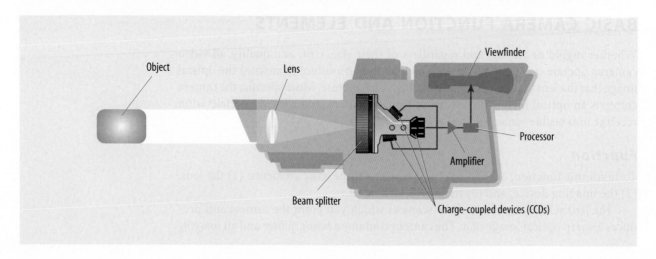

television receiver. Why bother with knowing all this, especially since most camcorders have automatic functions that can produce pretty good pictures and sound? The problem is that such automatic functions produce good pictures and sound only under ideal conditions. But what are ideal conditions? And what can you do when conditions are less than ideal? Knowing the basics of how a camera works will help you know when and how to override the automatic functions to produce optimal video. It will also aid you in understanding how other production elements such as lighting must be manipulated to meet the requirements of the camera. Most important, such knowledge will help you become a video professional. **ZVL3 CUE 1** ›CAMERA→
Camera introduction

Lens

Lenses determine what cameras can see. They are classified by *focal length*, which is a technical measure of the distance from the iris inside the lens to the plane where the projected image is in focus. This measurement assumes that the lens distance calibration is set at infinity (∞). This distance is normally given in millimeters (mm); thus, a still camera can have a 24mm or a 200mm lens. Lenses can also be classified by how wide a view you get from a specific camera position. A *wide-angle lens* (short focal length) gives a relatively wide vista. A *narrow-angle lens* (long focal length) gives a relatively narrow vista with the background greatly magnified. *Speed* refers to how much light a lens can let through.

The optical quality of the lens determines to a great extent how good the video picture will look. Regardless of the quality of the camcorder itself, a good lens is one of the principal prerequisites for good pictures. This is why the lenses for high-end cameras can cost many times more than your entire camcorder.

Focal length   The *zoom lens* on a camera can change from a short-focal-length, or wide-angle, position to a long-focal-length, or narrow-angle, position and back in one continuous move. A short-focal-length zoom position gives you a *wide-angle* view: you can see more than with a lens in the narrow-angle position. To bring a zoom lens into the extreme-wide-angle position, you need to zoom all the way *out*. You will see a relatively large portion of the scene in front of you, but the middle- and background objects look quite small and, therefore, far away. **SEE 4.3**

Zooming all the way *in* puts the zoom lens in a long-focal-length, or narrow-angle, position. The zoom lens will now give a much narrower, but enlarged, view

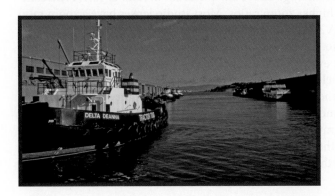

4.3 Wide-angle View

The wide-angle lens shows a wide vista, with the faraway objects looking quite small.

4.4 Narrow-angle View

The narrow-angle, or telephoto, lens shows only a narrow portion of the scene, with the background objects appearing much larger relative to the foreground objects than in a wide-angle view.

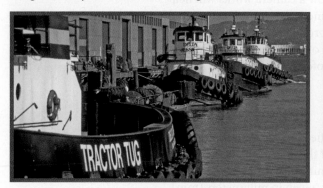

4.5 Normal View

The normal lens shows a vista and a perspective that are similar to what we actually see.

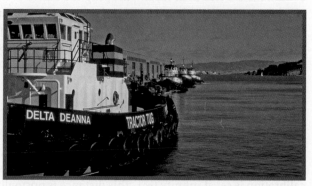

of the selected scene. Because the narrow-angle lens position functions similarly to binoculars, it is also called a *telephoto lens,* or telephoto zoom lens, position. **SEE 4.4**

When you stop a zoom in the middle of the zoom range (between the extreme-wide-angle and narrow-angle positions), you are more or less in the *normal lens* position. The angle of view of a normal lens approximates what you would see when looking directly at the scene. **SEE 4.5**

Because the zoom lens offers a great variety of focal lengths between its extreme-wide-angle and narrow-angle positions, it is also called a *variable-focal-length lens.* **ZVL3 CUE 2** CAMERA→ Zoom lens→ focal length

Zoom range   The *zoom range,* also called *zoom ratio,* refers to how close a view you can achieve when zooming in from the farthest wide-angle position to the closest narrow-angle position. The higher the first number of the ratio, the closer you can get to the object from the farthest wide-angle position. A 20:1 zoom lens lets you narrow the field of view (your vista) twenty times when zooming in from the farthest wide-angle position to the closest narrow-angle position. In practical terms you can move in to a pretty good close-up from a wide-angle shot. The 20:1 zoom ratio can also be indicated as 20×. **SEE 4.6**

Small camcorder lenses rarely go above an optical zoom ratio of 15:1. Field cameras, however, need much higher zoom ratios. Most studio lenses have a zoom ratio of between 15:1 and 30:1. A 30× zoom gets you a good close-up without moving the camera in even a large studio. Covering sports or other outdoor events demands lenses with zoom ratios of 40:1 or even 60:1. With such a lens, you can zoom in from a wide shot of the entire football field to a close-up of the quarterback's face. The large zoom range is necessary because these cameras are usually at the top of the stadium, far away from the event. Instead of moving the camera closer to the event, as is possible with a camcorder, the zoom lens must bring the event closer to the camera. Unfortunately, the higher the zoom ratio, the larger the lens gets. A 60:1 field lens is quite a bit larger and certainly heavier than the camera to which it is attached.

4.6 Maximum Wide-angle and Narrow-angle Positions of a 10:1 Zoom

A 10:1 zoom lens can narrow the angle of view by ten times.
It seems to bring a portion of the scene closer to the camera.

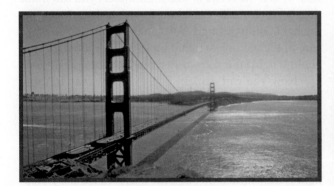 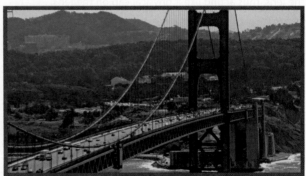

The focal length of a lens influences not only the *field of view* (how close or far away an object seems) but also how far apart objects appear to be. (You will read more about these and other aspects of framing and perception in chapters 5 and 6.)

Digital zoom   There is a great difference between an optical and a digital zoom. In an *optical zoom,* the elements inside the lens activate the change of angle of view. In a *digital zoom,* the center of the image is gradually magnified; we perceive this gradual magnification as the image coming closer. The problem with digital zooms is that the enlarged image becomes progressively less sharp and eventually displays oversized *pixels.* At best a digital zoom-in inevitably produces a slightly fuzzy image. An optical zoom does not influence the sharpness of the picture, which is why optical zooms are preferred.

Lens speed   As pointed out earlier, *speed* refers to how much light can pass through a lens to the imaging device. A **fast lens** can let a relatively great amount of light pass through; a **slow lens** is more limited in how much light it can transmit. In practice a fast lens allows you to produce acceptable pictures in a darker environment than does a slow lens. Fast lenses are therefore more useful than slow ones, but they are also larger and more expensive.

You can tell whether a lens is fast or slow by looking at its lowest f-stop number, such as $f/1.4$ or $f/2.0$ (see figure 4.7). The lower the number, the faster the lens. A lens that can open up to $f2.0$ is pretty fast; one that can't go below $f4.5$ is quite slow.

Lens iris and aperture   Like the pupil of your eye, all lenses have an **iris** that controls the amount of light transmitted. In a bright environment, your iris contracts to a smaller opening, restricting the amount of light passing through; in a dim environment, it expands to a larger opening, admitting more light.

The lens iris, or *lens diaphragm,* operates in the same way. Like your pupil, the center of the iris has an adjustable hole, called the **aperture,** that can be made large or

4.7 Iris Control Ring

The *f*-stop calibration is printed on a ring that controls the iris opening, or aperture, of the lens. The C on the control ring of this lens refers to cap, which means the iris is totally closed, letting no light pass through the lens, thus acting like a physical cap on the lens.

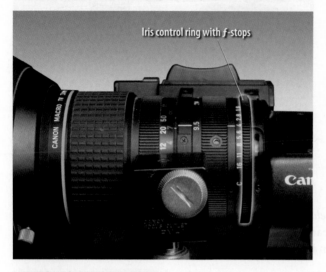

Iris control ring with *f*-stops

small. The size of the aperture controls how much light the lens transmits. When there is little light on a scene, you can make the aperture bigger and let more light through. This is called "opening the lens" or "opening the iris." When the scene is well illuminated, you can make the aperture smaller, or "close down" the lens, to restrict the light going through. You can thus control the exposure of the picture so that it looks neither too dark (not enough light) nor too washed out (too much light).

Now you can explain a fast or slow lens in more technical terms: a fast lens transmits more light at its maximum aperture (iris opening) than does a slow one. **ZVL3 CUE 3** Camera→ Exposure control→ aperture

f-stop   The means by which we measure how much light is transmitted through the lens is called the **f-stop**. All lenses have a ring at their base with a series of *f*-stop numbers printed on it (such as 1.4, 2.8, 4, 5.6, 8, 11, 16, and 22) that controls the iris opening. **SEE 4.7**

When you turn the ring so that *f*/1.4 lines up with the indicator, you have "opened" the lens to its maximum aperture; it now transmits as much light as it possibly can. When you turn the ring to *f*/22, the lens is "stopped down" to its minimum aperture, letting very little light pass through. A fast lens should have a maximum aperture of *f*/2.8 or better. Good lenses go as low as *f*/1.4 and occasionally even *f*/1.2. With these lenses you need considerably less light to produce good pictures than with slower lenses whose maximum aperture is *f*/4.5.

Notice that the *f*-stop numbers mean just the opposite of what you would expect: The lower the *f*-stop number, the larger the aperture and the more light is transmitted. The higher the *f*-stop number, the smaller the aperture and the less light is transmitted. **SEE 4.8** **ZVL3 CUE 4** CAMERA→ Exposure control→ *f*-stop

Auto-iris   Most camcorders enable you to choose between the manual iris control and an auto-iris feature. The auto-iris adjusts the aperture automatically to its optimal setting. The camera reads the light level of the scene and tells the auto-iris to open up or close down until the resulting picture is neither too dark nor too light. Such an automated feature is not without drawbacks, however. (We consider the advantages and disadvantages of the auto-iris in chapter 5.)

Imaging Device

A second main component within the camera is the *imaging device,* which transduces (changes) light into electric energy. Also called the *pickup device,* the imaging device in all electronic cameras is a *charge-coupled device,* often called a *chip.*

Beam splitter   The **beam splitter** separates ordinary white light into the three primary light colors: red, green, and blue (*RGB*). They are called *additive primaries,* or *primary light colors,* because you add, that is, shine on top of each other, the red,

4.8 *f*-stop Settings

The higher the *f*-stop number, the smaller the aperture and the less light is transmitted by the lens. The lower the *f*-stop number, the larger the aperture and the more light is transmitted by the lens.

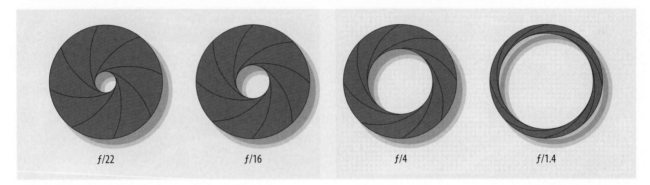

green, and blue light beams in various proportions. These three primary colors account for all the colors you see on the television screen. (See chapter 8 for more about color and its use in video.)

The actual beam splitter consists of a series of prisms and filters locked into a prism block. **SEE 4.9** The *prism block* splits the incoming light into the three colored beams and then directs the RGB light beams into the CCDs that transform the beams into electric energy—the RGB video signal. **SEE 4.10**

Charge-coupled device   A *charge-coupled device* (**CCD**) is small solid-state silicon chip that contains horizontal and vertical rows of thousands or even millions of light-sensing pixels. Each pixel can translate the light energy it receives into a

4.9 Beam-splitting Prism Block

The prism block contains prisms and filters that split the incoming white light into its three basic light colors—red, green, and blue (RGB)—and direct these beams to their corresponding CCDs.

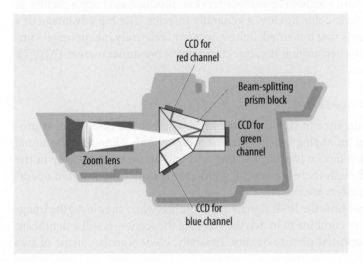

4.10 Video Camera Prism Block

In this photo of an actual video camera prism block, you can see the three CCDs firmly attached to the port (opening) for each RGB light beam.

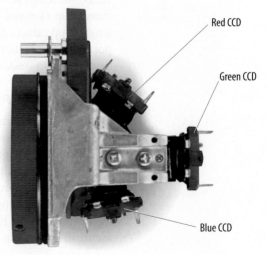

4.11 **Picture Resolution**

The picture on the right is composed of more pixels than the one on the left. It has a higher resolution and looks sharper. The more pixels a CCD contains, the higher the resolution of the video image.

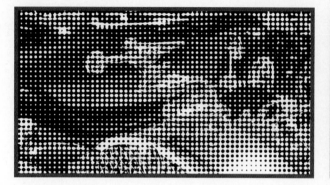 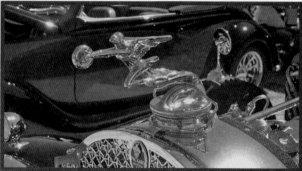

corresponding electric charge. The CCDs are the actual imaging device that delivers the RGB video signals that eventually compose the video image you see in the camera viewfinder.

Pixels function very much like the individual tiles in a mosaic or the dots in a magazine photo. The more pixels in a given picture area, the sharper the image will be. **SEE 4.11** Similarly, the more pixels a CCD contains, the sharper the resulting screen image. As you know, digital still cameras are usually rated by the number of pixels their chip contains. A 10-megapixel (10-million-pixel) still camera produces higher-definition pictures and truer colors than does a 5-megapixel one. As you can see, the resolution of the video image a camera can produce is determined not only by the number of scanning lines but also by the camera lens and the number of pixels on the CCDs.

> **▶ KEY CONCEPT**
>
> The CCD converts the light variations of an image into electric energy—the video signal.

High-quality cameras usually contain three CCDs—one for each of the RGB light beams as delivered by the beam splitter. Many of the smaller camcorders, however, have just a single chip. In this case, the incoming white light is divided by a filter into the three primary colors, which are then processed as individual signals by the single CCD. Although standard single-chip camcorders can produce as sharp a picture as three-chip cameras, their color fidelity is generally inferior. The big advantage of a single-chip camcorder is that it is small, lightweight, and relatively inexpensive—important considerations when aiming at a large consumer or prosumer market. **ZVL3 CUE 5**
CAMERA→ Camera introduction

Video Signal Processing

The most obvious difference in signal processing is whether the camcorder is producing and recording an analog video signal or a digital one. Note that the signal that leaves the imaging device is always analog and will become digital only in the processing stage. Although there are several good analog camcorders still in operation, most new camcorders are digital.

Signal processing—how the RGB signals are amplified when they leave the imaging device and how they combine to match the colors of the scene—is still a significant factor in producing optimal picture quality. Basically, color signals consist of two channels: a **luminance channel**, also called the *luma*, or *Y, channel* (*lumen* is Latin for "light"), which is mainly responsible for the picture's sharpness; and a **chrominance channel**, also called *color*, or *C, channel*. In high-quality video, these channels are kept separate throughout the signal processing and transport. In standard television both the Y and the C signals are then merged into a *composite* signal, called the *NTSC signal,* or *NTSC* for short.

Viewfinder

The **viewfinder** is a small video monitor attached to the camera that shows an image of what the camera sees. Most small analog camcorders have the familiar viewfinder tube through which you can view a monochrome video picture. You can adjust the tube vertically to facilitate eye contact during camera tilts. Most small digital camcorders have an additional flat-panel LCD viewfinder that can be folded out for more-convenient viewing when you handhold the camera rather than carry it on your shoulder. **SEE 4.12**

Because large camcorders do not have a foldout flat-panel monitor, some camera operators opt to connect the camera's video output to an independent larger, high-resolution monitor (see figure 4.22). This flat-panel monitor is mounted on a flexible arm, which lets you see the camera output even when taking the camcorder off your shoulder for certain shots. Note that all flat-panel monitors tend to drain the camera battery significantly faster than the built-in viewfinder.

4.12 Foldout Viewfinder

This relatively large LCD viewfinder gives the operator great flexibility in camera handling.

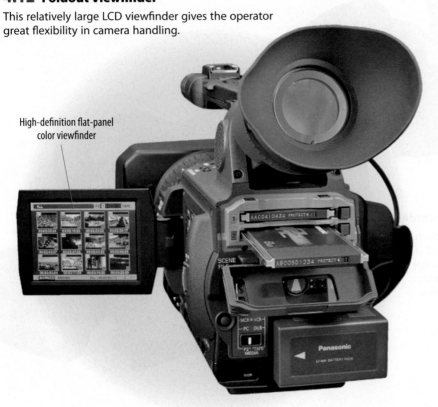

High-definition flat-panel
color viewfinder

TYPES OF CAMERAS

We normally classify video cameras by how they are used: camcorders, studio cameras, field cameras, and HDTV cameras.

Camcorders

As pointed out before, a **camcorder** (for *cam*era and re*corder*) is a portable video camera with its recording device attached to it or built into it. Many camcorders have a built-in videotape recorder, but the tendency is to use as a recording device the simpler hard drives and flash memory devices (memory cards), which have no moving parts at all. The advantage is that the recorded data can be transferred more quickly and easily to the computer for postproduction editing than can a digital video and audio signal recorded on videotape. **SEE 4.13 AND 4.14**

> **▶ KEY CONCEPT**
> A camcorder has its video recorder built-in.

All camcorders—large and small—have two audio inputs: one is normally used for the camera mic, and the other is for an additional, external microphone. In small camcorders the camera mic is built-in. Larger, more high-end models have two jacks (inputs) that let you plug in specific mics (see chapter 7). Most camcorders also have a camera light for illuminating small areas during ENG or to provide additional illumination. Note that if you run the camera light off the camcorder's battery, the battery will run down considerably faster; it's best to use a separate battery pack for the light.

4.13 High-end Small Camcorder

This high-end small camcorder has three CCDs, a 12× optical zoom lens, a built-in VTR that records high-quality video on a mini-cassette, and two professional (XLR) microphone inputs.

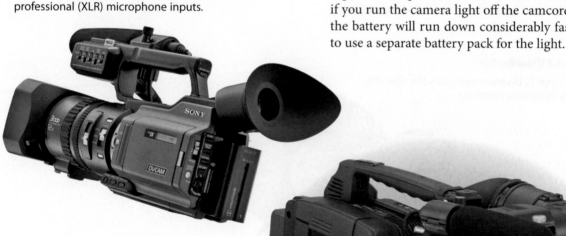

4.14 High-end Large Camcorder

This shoulder-mounted camcorder has three large, high-pixel CCDs; a fast (ƒ/1.4) 15× zoom lens; and two professional (XLR) microphone inputs. It records its video and audio on a flash drive.

HDV camcorders   To make high-definition video (HDV) more accessible to a wider community of videographers, small, high-end HDV camcorders have been developed by the major camera manufacturers. The HDV camcorder differs from the normal digital camcorder in several ways: (1) it has a high-quality lens, (2) it usually has three high-resolution chips that produce accurate colors and sharp video images, (3) its chips produce a native 16 × 9 aspect ratio (see chapter 6 for more about aspect ratio), (4) it has a superior signal processing system, and (5) it has a superior high-definition video recorder.

To prove that one-chip cameras can hold their own in the three-chip-camera domain, one manufacturer produced a high-quality single-chip HDV camcorder. It uses a CMOS imaging device—a modified CCD-like chip whose filter and pixel arrangement boosts the resolution of its Y (black-and-white) signal.[1]

HDV camcorders use either high-speed VTRs for mini-cassettes or relatively high-capacity flash drives that can be inserted into a camera slot. HDV camcorders can produce high-definition 720p or 1080i images. **SEE 4.15**

Quality difference   When you compare the pictures your friend took with his digital camcorder to a similar scene shot with an expensive and much larger and heavier camcorder, you will probably not see much difference in how the pictures look. Why, then, do you still see professional ENG shooters lugging heavy camcorders

---

1. *CMOS* stands for *complementary metal oxide semiconductor.*

4.15 HDV Camcorder

This HDV camcorder has a single CMOS image sensor and records video on a mini-cassette in the highest-quality HDTV format: 1080i. The high-resolution flat-panel color viewfinder facilitates critical focusing.

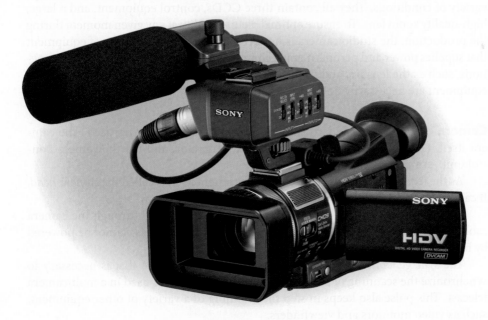

around on their shoulders? One of the main reasons is that television stations are reluctant to dump a perfectly fine camera that they purchased for a hefty price not too long ago. But there are also some technical advantages for using the larger camcorder for critical shoots.

When using a large camcorder, you can choose the lens that best fits your purpose. For example, you can use a very-wide-angle lens when shooting in confined quarters, such as the inside of an automobile, or a lens that lets you get a close-up view from far away. Additionally, the lens of a large ENG/EFP camcorder has better *optics* (high-quality lens elements) and a smoother zoom mechanism. Large camcorders also have more video and audio controls, more-robust recording devices, and usually a better processing system that ensures more-faithful colors even when shooting in low-light conditions.

But don't worry: even if you don't have a large ENG/EFP camcorder, you can still produce professional-looking video programs. You will find that shooting good video depends much more on what shots you select and how you frame them than on the technical specifications of the camcorder. (The discussion in chapter 6 about looking through the viewfinder will help you obtain maximally effective shots.)

Studio Cameras

The large, high-quality cameras you normally find in television studios are, appropriately enough, called *studio cameras*. Studio cameras are large and too heavy to be maneuvered without the aid of a pedestal or some other kind of camera mount. What makes the equipment so heavy is not necessarily the camera itself but the large zoom lens and, typically, the teleprompter attached to it. **SEE 4.16** Studio cameras are used in studio productions, such as interviews, news, and game shows, and also in big-remote telecasts, such as sporting events, where high-quality video is a must.

Studio cameras are built to produce exceptionally high-quality pictures under a variety of conditions. They all contain three CCDs, control equipment, and a large, high-quality zoom lens. To ensure optimal picture quality at any given moment during the production, the studio camera is hooked up via cable to a variety of equipment that supplies power and permits manual control of various electronic and optical functions, such as the lens iris and color fidelity. Because the camera and the associated equipment are necessarily linked together by cable, they are called a *camera chain*.

Camera chain   The standard *camera chain* consists of four parts: (1) the camera itself, (2) the power supply, (3) the sync generator, and (4) the camera control unit. **SEE 4.17**

As the front part of the camera chain, the camera itself is called the *camera head*. It cannot function by itself without the other parts of the chain.

The *power supply* feeds the electricity to the camera head through the camera cable. Unlike ENG/EFP cameras or camcorders, studio cameras cannot be powered by batteries.

The *sync generator* produces the uniform electrical pulse that is necessary to synchronize the scanning of the video pictures in all cameras used in a multicamera telecast. This pulse also keeps in step the scanning of a variety of other equipment, such as video monitors and viewfinders.

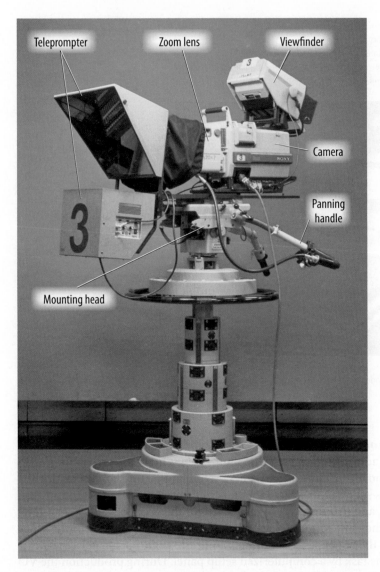

Teleprompter

Zoom lens

Viewfinder

Camera

Panning handle

Mounting head

4.16 Studio Camera

Studio cameras contain three high-end CCDs and a variety of picture-enhancing electronic circuits. They have a heavy lens and a large viewfinder. Most studio cameras also have a teleprompter attached, which makes the whole camera head much heavier than an ENG/EFP camera or camcorder.

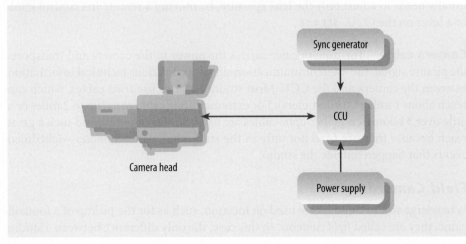

Sync generator

CCU

Camera head

Power supply

4.17 Standard Camera Chain

The standard camera chain consists of the camera head (the actual camera), the power supply, the sync generator, and the CCU.

4.18 Camera Control Unit

The CCU has a variety of controls with which the video operator can continuously monitor and adjust picture quality. The remote version of a CCU is called an RCU.

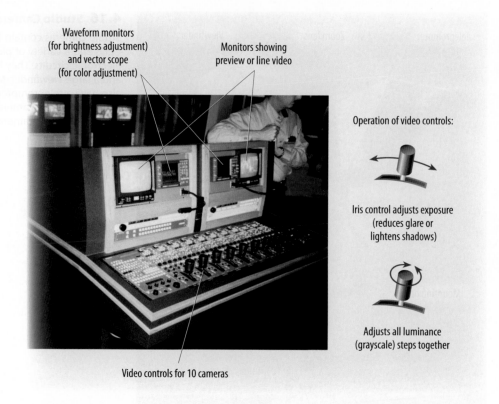

Waveform monitors (for brightness adjustment) and vector scope (for color adjustment)

Monitors showing preview or line video

Operation of video controls:

Iris control adjusts exposure (reduces glare or lightens shadows)

Adjusts all luminance (grayscale) steps together

Video controls for 10 cameras

The **camera control unit** (**CCU**) has two major functions: setup and control. *Setup* refers to the adjustments made when the camera is first powered up. The video operator (VO), who is in charge of the camera setup and picture control during the production, makes sure that the colors the camera delivers are true, that the iris is at the proper setting, and that the camera is adjusted for the brightest spot (white-level adjustment) and the darkest spot (black-level or pedestal adjustment) in the scene so that we can see the major steps within this contrast range. Fortunately, the VO is greatly aided in this task by a computerized setup panel. During production the VO usually needs to adjust only the lens aperture, by moving a remote iris control knob or a lever on the CCU. **SEE 4.18**

> **KEY CONCEPT**
>
> The camera chain consists of the camera head (the actual camera), the power supply, the sync generator, and the CCU.

Camera cable   The *camera cable* carries the power to the camera and transports the picture signal, the intercommunication signal, and various technical information between the camera and the CCU. Most studio cameras use *triax* cables, which can reach about 1 mile (1.6 kilometers). For extremely long cable runs (up to 2 miles or a little over 3 kilometers), *fiber-optic* cables are used. Studio cameras need such a great reach because they are used not only in the studio but also at *remotes*—scheduled events that happen outside the studio.

Field Cameras

When large studio cameras are used on location, such as for the pickup of a football game, they are called *field cameras*. In this case, the only difference between a studio camera and a field camera is not necessarily the camera itself but the lens. As you recall, field lenses have a higher zoom ratio and are generally larger than studio lenses. Despite their considerable size and weight, field cameras are usually mounted on heavy tripods or field dollies.

ENG/EFP Cameras

The basic difference between an ENG/EFP (electronic news gathering/electronic field production) camera and a camcorder is that the *ENG/EFP camera* does not have a built-in video recorder but must feed its output via cable into a stand-alone VTR or hard drive. Like a camcorder, the ENG/EFP camera is self-contained, but it can be connected with a camera cable to a *remote control unit* (*RCU*) and an external recording device. Why use an RCU when the camera is basically self-contained? First, although an ENG/EFP camera is capable of running on batteries, it is often better to power it with an external source. External power frees you from worrying about battery life during a long shoot or a live pickup. Second, the RCU allows the VO to tweak the camera for optimal performance under a variety of shooting conditions. **SEE 4.19**

Third, because the director can see on a monitor what the camera operators see in their viewfinders, he or she can give them the necessary instructions over the intercom headsets while the scene is in progress. All these production advantages considerably outweigh the slight disadvantage of having the cameras tethered to a remote truck or a temporary video control. As you probably noticed, the ENG/EFP camera operates now much like a highly portable studio camera.

Studio conversion of ENG/EFP camera   Because ENG/EFP cameras are considerably cheaper and easier to handle, they are often used in place of studio cameras, even if they can't quite match the quality. To adapt an ENG/EFP camera to studio conditions, you replace the small viewfinder with a larger one, attach a faster lens

4.19 ENG/EFP Camera Connected to RCU and External Video Recorder

This high-end ENG/EFP camera has no built-in video recorder but is connected to a remote control unit and from there to a high-capacity hard drive or studio VTR for high-quality recording.

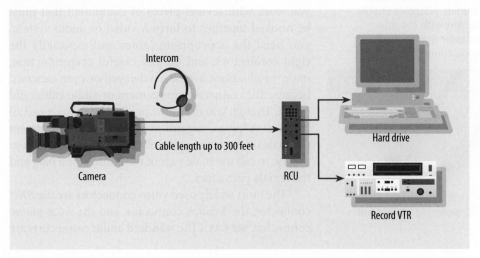

Intercom

Cable length up to 300 feet

Hard drive

Camera

RCU

Record VTR

4.20 Studio Conversion of ENG/EFP Camera

Converting a high-quality ENG/EFP camera for studio use usually requires adding a large viewfinder, a faster lens with a zoom range appropriate for the studio size, cables that allow zooming and focusing from the operator's position, and a frame and mounting devices for a tripod or studio pedestal.

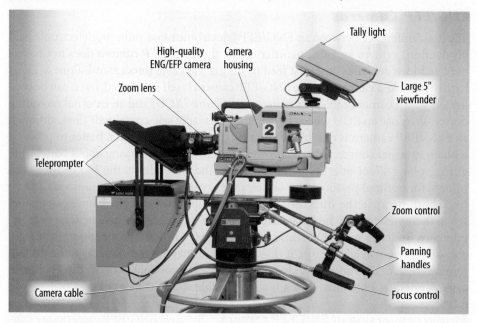

High-quality ENG/EFP camera
Camera housing
Tally light
Large 5" viewfinder
Zoom lens
Teleprompter
Zoom control
Panning handles
Camera cable
Focus control

(lower maximum f-stop number) that has a zoom range more appropriate for studio dimensions, affix cables for focus and zoom controls, and install a frame and mounting devices for a tripod or studio pedestal. An intercom box for the *P.L.* (*private line* or *phone line*) is usually attached to the mounting frame. **SEE 4.20**

4.21 Standard Video Connectors

The standard video connectors are the BNC, S-video, and RCA phono (also used for audio). Adapters enable you to join each of these connectors with the others. This illustration shows an adapter that changes a BNC connector to an RCA phono connector.

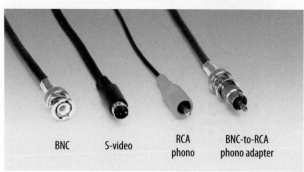

BNC   S-video   RCA phono   BNC-to-RCA phono adapter

Connectors   Is a discussion of connectors necessary in a book on video basics? Absolutely. Whenever you work with several pieces of equipment that must be hooked together to form a video or audio system, you need the appropriate cables and especially the right connectors; and despite careful preproduction, many productions have been delayed or even canceled because the connectors for camera or audio cables did not fit. Though you may hear production people call all connectors "plugs," regardless of whether they represent the male or the female part of the connector, it is more precise to call the male part of the connector a *plug* and the female part a *jack*.

The most widely used video connectors are the *BNC* connector, the *S-video* connector, and the *RCA phono* connector. **SEE 4.21** (The standard audio connectors are shown in figure 7.26.) A variety of adapters allow you to change from one plug to another, such as from a BNC to an RCA phono, but don't rely on them. An adapter is strictly a makeshift solution and always presents a potential trouble spot.

HDTV Cameras

Used in both the studio and the field, *HDTV cameras* generally produce much sharper pictures, better colors, and more-subtle light/dark contrast steps than do standard television cameras. To achieve an extremely high-resolution image, HDTV cannot rely only on the improved scanning system of 480p, 720p, or 1080i; it also requires high-quality CCDs, specific lenses, signal-processing equipment, viewfinders, and monitors that can accommodate the horizontally stretched 16 × 9 aspect ratio. The HDTV camera is usually connected to an HDTV recording device or has one built-in, similar to a large camcorder. **SEE 4.22**

Electronic cinema camera   The so-called *electronic cinema* cameras or camcorders are HDTV video cameras or camcorders that have cinematographic features built-in or attached. Some of these cameras have a tubelike viewfinder that displays extremely high-resolution monochrome images, and/or a large external high-resolution flat-panel screen. At the front of the lens is a *matte box,* which can hold a variety of filters. One of the most useful features for filmmaking with the HDTV electronic cinema camera is its variable *frame rate,* which permits a change from 24 fps scanning (modeled after the standard film frame rate) to a slower rate (as low as 15 fps) or a higher rate (to 60 fps). **SEE 4.23**

4.22 HDTV Camera

The HDTV camera has high-resolution CCDs, an HDTV lens, and a high-resolution 16 × 9 viewfinder.

4.23 Electronic Cinema Camera

The HDTV electronic cinema camera contains high-resolution CCDs, produces 16 × 9 images, and can adjust its frame rate to the film frame rate of 24 fps. Its VTR records the high-definition signals on a DVCPRO cassette. It has various cinematographic features, such as a matte box.

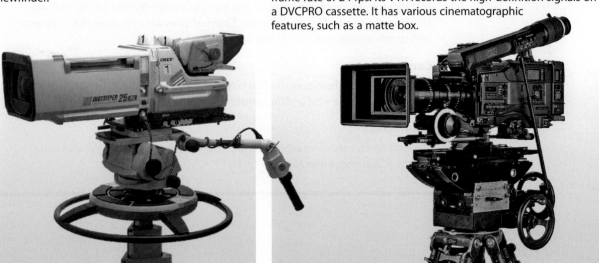

M A I N   P O I N T S

▶ **Basic Camera Elements**

These are the lens, the CCD imaging device, and the viewfinder.

▶ **Lenses**

Lenses are classified by the focal length (short and long), angle of view (wide and narrow), and speed (largest aperture expressed in the lowest f-stop). The zoom lens has a variable focal length. The zoom range is stated as a ratio, such as 20:1 or 20×. A 20:1 lens can show the angle of view twenty times narrower than the extreme-wide-angle position with the background magnified.

▶ **Lens Iris and Aperture**

The speed of the lens is determined by the maximum aperture, or iris opening. A fast lens lets a relatively large amount of light pass through; a slow lens, relatively little. The specific aperture is indicated by f-stops. The lower the f-stop number, the larger the aperture and the more light is transmitted. A fast lens has a low minimum f-stop number (such as f/1.4). The higher the f-stop number, the smaller the aperture and the less light is transmitted. A slow lens has a relatively high minimum f-stop number (such as f/4.5).

▶ **Beam Splitter and Imaging Device**

These devices change the optical image produced by the lens to a video signal. The beam splitter divides the light that comes through the lens into red, green, and blue (RGB) light beams. The imaging device—the charge-coupled device (CCD), or chip—transduces the colored light beams into electric energy, which is processed into the video signal.

▶ **Types of Cameras**

Camera types include small and large camcorders—portable cameras with the recording device attached or built-in; high-definition video (HDV) camcorders, which, despite their small size, produce high-resolution pictures with high color fidelity; studio cameras, which with a different lens are also used in the field; ENG/EFP cameras, which are high-end, shoulder-mounted field cameras; and high-definition television (HDTV) cameras, which produce the highest-quality video. Electronic cinema cameras are HDTV cameras with certain attachments carried over from film.

▶ **Camera Chain**

The studio camera chain consists of the camera head (the actual camera), the power supply, the sync generator, and the camera control unit (CCU).

▶ **Connectors**

The most widely used video connectors are the BNC connector, the S-video connector, and the RCA phono connector.

ZETTL'S VIDEOLAB 3.0

 For your reference, or to track your work, the Zettl's VideoLab 3.0 *program cues in this chapter are listed here with their corresponding page numbers.*

CHAPTER 5

KEY TERMS

arc To move the camera in a slightly curved dolly or truck.

calibrate the zoom lens To preset a zoom lens to keep in focus throughout the zoom.

cam head A camera mounting head that permits extremely smooth tilts and pans.

cant To tilt the camera sideways.

crane To move the boom of the camera crane up or down. Also called *boom*.

dolly To move the camera toward (dolly in) or away from (dolly out) the object.

jib arm A small camera crane that can be operated by the cameraperson.

mounting head A device that connects the camera to its support. Also called *pan-and-tilt head*.

pan To turn the camera horizontally.

pedestal To move the camera up or down using a studio pedestal.

shutter speed A camera control that reduces the blurring of bright, fast-moving objects. The higher the shutter speed, the less blurring occurs but the more light is needed.

Steadicam A camera mount that allows the operator to walk and run, with the camera remaining steady.

studio pedestal A heavy camera dolly that permits raising and lowering the camera while on the air.

tilt To point the camera up or down.

tongue To move the boom with the camera from left to right or from right to left.

tripod A three-legged camera mount. Also called *sticks*.

truck To move the camera laterally by means of mobile camera mount. Also called *track*.

white balance The adjustments of the color circuits in the camera to produce white color in lighting of various color temperatures (relative reddishness or bluishness of white light).

zoom To change the focal length of the lens through the use of a zoom control while the camera remains stationary.

Operating the Camera

Let's watch a tourist who is itching for something interesting to shoot with his brand-new camcorder. He quickly takes aim at one of the towers of the Golden Gate Bridge, tilts his camera up to the top, zooms in, zooms out again, tilts down to the bay just as a freighter passes below, zooms in on the containers, zooms out again, tilts up to the rail where some seagulls have perched, zooms in on one of the more aggressive birds that refuses to stay in the frame, and finally zooms out to catch a passing jogger, who waves at him.

Although such camera handling may be good exercise for the arm and the zoom mechanism, it rarely results in satisfactory footage. Such unmotivated camera motion produces images that seem restless and unsettling for anyone except, perhaps, the person who shot them. The tourist would have done much better had his camera been mounted on a small tripod.

When handling a small camcorder with a foldout viewfinder, you are virtually unrestrained in moving the camera. But when the camera is mounted on a tripod, its movements become much more restricted. Initially, you will probably feel that a tripod constrains your artistry and that it is much better to handhold the camera, so long as it is not too heavy. After some experience in camera operation, however, you will discover that it is actually easier to operate the camera and control picture composition when the camera is mounted on some kind of support. In fact, the art of operating a camera is not as dependent on its electronic design or basic operational controls as it is on its size and especially on how it is mounted.

This chapter explores basic camera movements and operation and how they can be accomplished.

▶ **BASIC CAMERA MOVEMENTS**
   Pan, tilt, cant, pedestal, dolly, truck, arc, crane, tongue, and zoom

▶ **CAMERA MOUNTS AND HOW TO USE THEM**
   Handheld and shoulder-mounted cameras, tripods, special camera mounts, and the studio pedestal

▶ **OPERATIONAL FEATURES**
   Focusing, adjusting shutter speed, zooming, and white balancing

▶ **GENERAL GUIDELINES**
   Checklists for camcorders and ENG/EFP cameras and for studio cameras

BASIC CAMERA MOVEMENTS

The various camera mounts are designed to steady the camera and help you move it as smoothly and easily as possible. To understand the features and the functions of camera mounting equipment, you should first learn about the major camera movements. The terms are the same regardless of whether the camera is carried on your shoulder or mounted on a tripod, a studio pedestal, or some other camera support.

There are nine basic camera movements: (1) *pan,* (2) *tilt,* (3) *cant,* (4) *pedestal,* (5) *dolly,* (6) *truck,* (7) *arc,* (8) *crane,* and (9) *tongue.* Sometimes *zoom* is included in the major camera movements, although the camera itself does not normally move during a zoom. **SEE 5.1**

Pan   To *pan* is to turn the camera horizontally, from left to right or from right to left. To *pan right* means to swivel or move the camera clockwise so that the lens points more to the right; to *pan left* means to swivel or move the camera counterclockwise so that the lens points more to the left.

Tilt   To *tilt* is to make the camera point up or down. A *tilt up* means to point the camera gradually up. A *tilt down* means to point the camera gradually down. A good rule to remember is that you need to pan and tilt in the direction of the shot you want to get.

Cant   To *cant* is to tilt the camera sideways. You can cant the camera either left or right. When you *cant left,* the horizon line will be slanted uphill; its low point will be screen-left, its high point screen-right. The *cant right* move will produce the opposite effect. Canting is easy with the handheld or shoulder-mounted camera, but you cannot cant a camera supported by a standard camera mount.

Pedestal   To *pedestal* is to elevate or lower the camera on the center column of a tripod or studio pedestal. To *pedestal up* you crank or pull up the center column, thereby raising the camera. To *pedestal down* you crank or pull down the center column, lowering the camera. This motion puts the camera into different vertical positions, which means that the camera sees the scene as though you were looking at it from the top of a ladder or while kneeling on the floor. You can "pedestal" a handheld camera by simply raising it slowly above your head or lowering it to the ground.

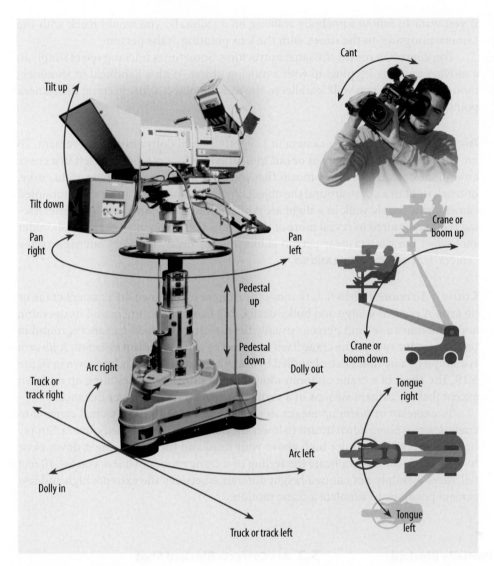

5.1 Major Camera Movements

The major camera movements are pan, tilt, cant, pedestal, dolly, truck or track, arc, crane or boom, and tongue.

Labels in figure: Tilt up, Tilt down, Pan right, Truck or track right, Arc right, Dolly in, Truck or track left, Cant, Pan left, Pedestal up, Pedestal down, Dolly out, Arc left, Crane or boom up, Crane or boom down, Tongue right, Tongue left

Dolly To *dolly* is to move the camera toward or away from an object in more or less a straight line by means of a mobile camera mount. When you *dolly in,* you move the camera closer to the object; when you *dolly out* or *dolly back,* you move the camera farther away.

With the handheld or shoulder-mounted camera, you simply walk the camera toward or away from the scene. Some directors call this "dollying" in or out, even though the camera is not mounted on a dolly; others simply ask you to get closer or back up.

Truck To *truck,* or *track,* is to move the camera laterally by means of a mobile camera mount. When you *truck right* or *truck left,* you move the camera mount to the right or left with the camera lens pointing at a right angle to the direction of travel.

If you want to follow somebody walking on a sidewalk, you would truck with the camera alongside on the street, with the lens pointing at the person.

Tracking often means the same as trucking. Sometimes tracking refers simply to a moving camera's keeping up with a moving object. With a handheld or shoulder-mounted camera, you walk parallel to the moving object while keeping the camera pointed at it.

Arc   To *arc* is to move the camera in a slightly curved dolly or truck movement. To *arc left* means that you dolly in or out in a camera-left curve, or truck left in a curve around the object; to *arc right* means that you dolly in or out in a camera-right curve, or truck right in a curve around the object. With the handheld or shoulder-mounted camera, you simply walk in a slight arc while pointing the camera at the scene. Arcing is often required to reveal more of the camera-far person in an over-the-shoulder shot when the camera-near person is blocking or nearly blocking our view of the camera-far person. **SEE 5.2 AND 5.3**

Crane   To *crane*, or *boom*, is to move the camera up or down on a camera crane or jib arm. A *crane* is a large and bulky device that can lift the camera and its operator, and sometimes a second person (usually the director), up to 30 feet aboveground in one impressive sweep. The crane itself is moved by a driver and an assistant. A *jib arm* is a simpler crane that can be handled by a single camera operator, as shown in figure 5.19. The effect of a crane or boom movement is similar to pedestaling up or down except that the camera swoops in a vertical arc over a much greater distance.

To *crane up* or *boom up* means to raise the boom with the attached camera; to *crane down* or *boom down* means to lower the boom and the attached camera. Simply holding a small camcorder high above your head and then swooping it down close to floor level will not duplicate the feeling of a crane motion. Unless you are 10 feet tall, there is simply not enough height difference between the extreme high and low camera positions to simulate a crane motion.

5.2 Camera-far Person Partially Blocked

In this over-the-shoulder shot, the camera-near person partially blocks the camera-far person.

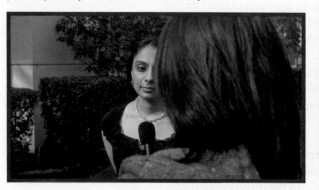

5.3 Arc Corrects Blocked Shot

By arcing left, the camera-far person is properly framed.

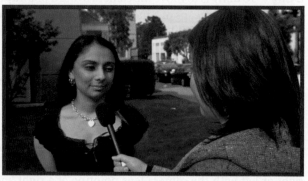

Tongue   To *tongue* is to move the whole camera from left to right or from right to left with the boom of a camera crane or jib arm. When you *tongue* left or right, the camera usually points in the same general direction, with only the boom swinging left or right. Tonguing creates an effect similar to a truck except that the horizontal arc of the boom with the camera is usually much wider and can be much faster. Tonguing is often combined with a boom-up or boom-down movement.

The crane and tongue movements are somewhat of a special effect. Even if you have access to a crane, use such extreme camera movements sparingly and only if they contribute to the shot's intensity.

Zoom   To *zoom* is to change the focal length of a lens through the use of a zoom control while the camera remains stationary. To *zoom in* means to change the lens gradually to a narrow-angle position, thereby making the scene appear to move closer to the viewer; to *zoom out* means to change the lens gradually to a wide-angle position, thereby making the scene appear to move farther away from the viewer. Although the effect of a zoom is the object's moving toward or away from the screen rather than the camera's moving into or out of the scene, the zoom is usually classified as one of the camera "movements." **ZVL3 CUE 1** ▸ CAMERA→ Camera moves→ dolly | zoom | truck | pan | pedestal | try it

CAMERA MOUNTS AND HOW TO USE THEM

You can support a camera in four ways: (1) by carrying it with your hands or on your shoulder, (2) with a tripod, (3) with special camera mounting devices, and (4) with a studio pedestal. They all influence greatly, if not dictate, how you operate the camera.

Handheld and Shoulder-mounted Camera

We have already mentioned that the small, handheld camcorder invites excessive camera motion. You can point it easily in any direction and move it effortlessly, especially if it has a foldout viewfinder. Although such high mobility can be an asset, it is also a liability. Too much camera movement draws attention to itself and away from the scene you want to show. Unless the camera has a built-in image stabilizer to absorb minor camera wiggles, you will find it difficult to keep the handheld camera steady. When zoomed all the way in (with the lens in the narrow-angle, or telephoto, position), it is almost impossible to avoid some shaking and unsteadiness in the handheld shot.

To keep the handheld camera as steady as possible, support the camera in the palm of one hand and use the other hand to support the camera arm or the camera itself. **SEE 5.4** With a foldout viewfinder, press your elbows against your body and use your arms as shock absorbers. Avoid operating the camera with your arms outstretched, which invites annoyingly quick pans and tilts. Inhale and hold your breath during the shot. The lack of oxygen will obviously limit the length of the shot, and that is probably a good thing. Shorter *takes* that show a variety of viewpoints are much more interesting than a long take with constant panning and zooming. Small handheld

5.4 Holding the Small Camcorder

Hold the small camcorder with both hands, with the elbows pressed against the body.

5.5 Steadying the Camera Operator

Leaning against a support will steady both camera operator and camera.

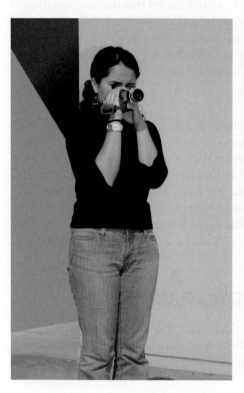

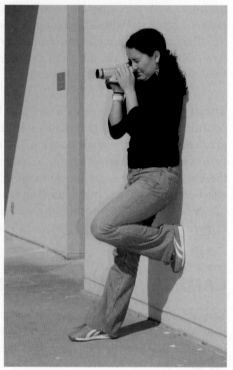

camera mounts can reduce the wobbles of small camcorders (see figure 5.15). When using your arms as a camera mount, bend your knees slightly when shooting or, better, lean against a sturdy support, such as a building, wall, parked car, or lamppost, to increase the camera's stability. **SEE 5.5**

If you or the event moves, keep the lens in the wide-angle position (zoomed out) to minimize camera wiggles. If you need to get closer to the scene, stop the videotape, walk closer to get the tighter shot, and start the tape again. If you need to zoom, work the zoom controls gently during the shot. For a relatively long take without a tripod, try to find something stable on which to place the camera, such as a table, park bench, or the roof or hood of a car.

When moving the camera, do it smoothly. To pan the camera, move it with your whole body rather than just your arms. Point your knees as much as possible to where you want to end the pan, while keeping your shoulders in the starting position. During the pan your upper body will uncoil naturally in the direction of your knees and will carry the camera smoothly with it. **SEE 5.6** If you do not preset your knees, you will have to coil your body rather than uncoil it when panning, which is much harder to do and usually results in jerky camera motion.

When tilting the camera (pointing it up or down), try to bend forward or backward at the waist as much as possible while keeping your elbows against your body.

As with a pan, your body motion makes the tilt look smoother than if you simply moved your wrists to point the camera up or down.

When walking with the camera, walk backward rather than forward whenever possible. **SEE 5.7** While walking backward you will lift your heels and walk on the balls of your feet. Your feet rather than your legs will act as shock absorbers. Your body, and with it the camera, will tend to glide along rather than bounce up and down.

For unconventional shots you can tilt the camera sideways, raise it above your head, and shoot over the people or other obstacles in front of you, or you can lower it close to the ground to get some low-angle views. Most regular viewfinders can be adjusted (at least tilted up and down) so that you can see what you are shooting during such maneuvers. The foldout viewfinder offers a great advantage in such situations, especially if you find that the only way to get a good shot is to hold the camera high above your head and aim it more or less in the direction of the event. The foldout display still enables you to see the shot the camera is getting. But even without a viewfinder display, you would probably get some usable shots.

Large camcorders are too heavy to be handheld for long and are best supported by the shoulder. Although the shoulder-mounted camera is slightly more restrictive than the small handheld camcorder, the basic moves are much the same. **SEE 5.8**

When carrying the camcorder on your shoulder, you need to adjust the viewfinder to fit your prominent (usually right) eye. Some camera operators keep the left eye open to see where they are going; others prefer to close it and concentrate on the viewfinder image. Most viewfinders of large camcorders can be flipped over for the left eye, and there are lenses with straps and zoom operating controls for the left hand.

5.6 Panning the Camcorder

Before panning, point your knees toward the end of the pan, then uncoil your upper body during the pan.

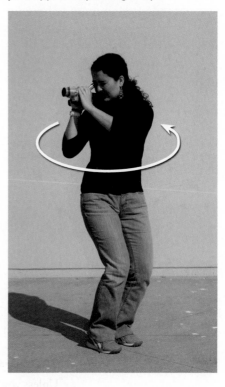

5.7 Walking Backward

Walking backward rather than forward makes it easier to keep the camera steady.

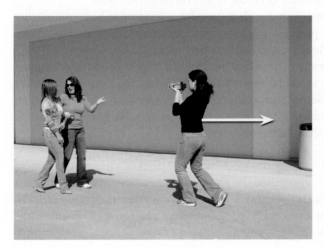

5.8 The Shoulder-mounted Large Camcorder

Carry the large camcorder on the shoulder. One hand slips through a strap attached to the lens, leaving the fingers free to operate the zoom control. The other hand steadies the camera and operates the focus ring.

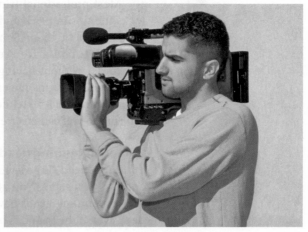

5.9 **Tripod with Spreader**

The tripod has three adjustable legs that are sometimes secured by a spreader.

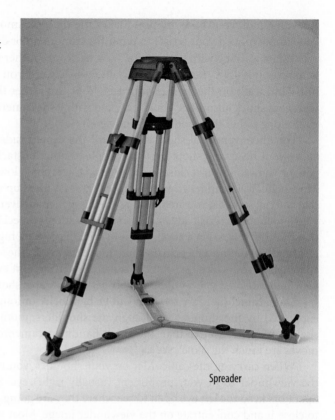

Spreader

Tripod-supported Camera

Unless you are running after a breaking news story, the best way to keep the camcorder or ENG/EFP camera steady and the movements as smooth as possible is to support it on a **tripod**, called *sticks* in production lingo, or some other kind of camera mount. A good tripod should be lightweight but sturdy enough to support the camera during pans and tilts. Its collapsible legs must lock securely in place at any extension point and should have rubber cups and spikes at the tips. The rubber cups prevent the tripod from slipping on smooth surfaces, as do the spikes on rough surfaces.

Most professional tripods come with a *spreader,* a triangular base mount that locks the tips in place and prevents the legs from spreading no matter how much weight is put on them. Some spreaders come as part of the tripod. **SEE 5.9**

Some tripods have a center column that enables you to elevate and lower a small camcorder without having to adjust the tripod legs. Unless the camcorder is very small, such columns may not be sturdy enough for smooth shots, especially when the column is fully extended. All good tripods have a leveling bubble at or near the top ring so you can ensure that the tripod is level.

Camera mounting head   One of the most important parts of a tripod is its camera **mounting head**. This device, also called the *pan-and-tilt head,* permits smooth pans and tilts. It also lets you attach the camera and remove it from the tripod quickly. Many mounting heads have a second leveling bubble so you can quickly adjust the head even if the tripod is on uneven ground.

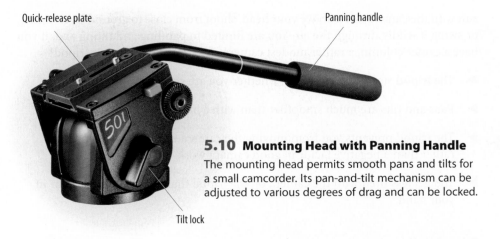

Quick-release plate

Panning handle

5.10 Mounting Head with Panning Handle
The mounting head permits smooth pans and tilts for a small camcorder. Its pan-and-tilt mechanism can be adjusted to various degrees of drag and can be locked.

Tilt lock

Most big tripod mounting heads have a load limit of 30 to 45 pounds—ample to hold even a large camcorder and a teleprompter. These days the problem is not whether the mounting head can support a heavy camera but whether it can operate smoothly with a small, lightweight camcorder. Even with a midsized camcorder, use a mounting head with a rating of 10 pounds or below. If the weight rating of the mounting head is much higher than the actual weight of the camera, even the lowest drag position will be too tight for smooth pans and tilts.

All mounting heads have similar basic controls. You move the mounting head (and with it the camera) with the attached panning handle. **SEE 5.10** Lifting the handle makes the camera tilt down; pushing it down makes the camera tilt up. Moving the panning handle to the left pans the camera to the right; moving the handle to the right pans the camera to the left. *Right* and *left* always refer to where the camera lens is supposed to point, not to movement of the panning handle.

To prevent jerky, uneven movements, a mounting head must provide a certain degree of *drag* (resistance) to panning and tilting. The pan and tilt drags can be adjusted to fit the weight of the camera and your personal preference. A small camcorder needs a lighter drag adjustment than does a large camcorder. Now you know why the weight rating for camera heads is important: the heads for large camcorders have a much higher minimum drag than is necessary or even desirable for small camcorders.

The mounting head also has pan and tilt lock mechanisms that prevent the camera from moving horizontally or flopping forward or backward when unattended. Lock the mounting head every time you leave the camera unattended, no matter how briefly. Don't use the drag mechanism to lock the camera.

Quick-release plate   This mechanism consists of a small rectangular plate that attaches to the bottom of the camera. The *quick-release plate* makes it easy to attach a camcorder in a balanced position. This feature is especially useful when you want to take the camera off the tripod to run after a new shot and then attach it again quickly when returning to the tripod position. You simply slide the camcorder into the plate receptacle on the mounting head, and it is locked in place and ready to go without having to rebalance its weight (see figure 5.10).

When switching from a handheld to a tripod-supported camera, you will find initially that the tripod severely restricts your use of the camera. You can no longer run with the camera, lift it above your head, shoot from close to ground level, cant it, or swing it wildly through the air. You are limited to panning and tilting and, if you have a center column, a rather modest camera elevation. So why use a tripod?

▶ The tripod steadies the camera, whether you are zoomed in or out.

▶ Pans and tilts are much smoother than with a handheld camera.

▶ The tripod prevents you from moving the camera excessively—a positive rather than a negative factor in good camera work.

▶ You get less tired with the camera on the tripod than on your shoulder or in your hand.

Tripod dolly   To dolly or truck with a tripod-mounted camera, you must put the tripod on a three-caster *tripod dolly,* which is simply a spreader with wheels. **SEE 5.11** When the casters are in a freewheeling position, you can dolly, truck, and arc. Most professional dollies let you lock the casters in position for straight-line dollying. Be sure to check that the floor is smooth enough for an "on-air" move while the camera is "hot" (operating). When moving the tripod dolly, you usually push, pull, and steer with your left hand while guiding the panning handle and the camera with your right hand.

5.11 Tripod Dolly

The tripod can be mounted on a three-wheel dolly, which permits quick repositioning of the camera.

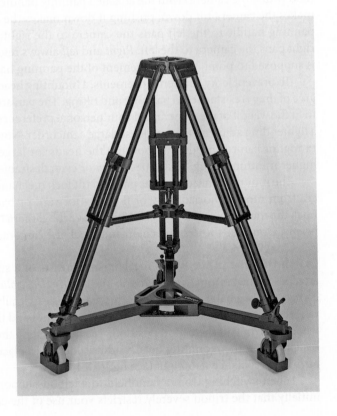

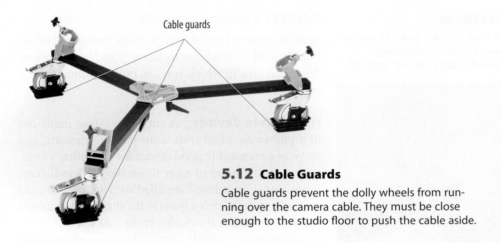

Cable guards

5.12 Cable Guards

Cable guards prevent the dolly wheels from running over the camera cable. They must be close enough to the studio floor to push the cable aside.

When a camera or camcorder is connected to a camera cable, you must adjust the *cable guards* so that the cable does not get wedged under the dolly casters. It is also a good idea to tie the cable to one of the tripod legs so that it is not pulled by its connector. **SEE 5.12**

Field dolly   When dollying on a rough surface, such as gravel or grass, you need to mount the tripod on a field dolly. A *field dolly* is a platform supported by four wheels with pneumatic tires. The steering mechanism works like the one you may remember from your red Radio Flyer wagon: a large handle turns the front wheels in the desired direction and lets you pull or push the entire platform. **SEE 5.13** When operating the camera, you can stand on the dolly or walk alongside while the dolly operator pushes or pulls it along the dolly path. When the surface is especially rough, you can underinflate the tires to make the trip smoother. Many dollies are homemade and constructed from parts readily available in most hardware stores.

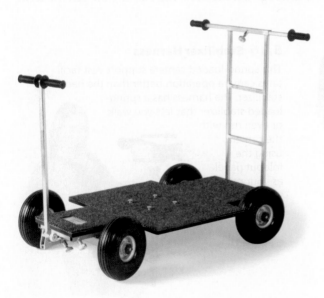

5.13 Field Dolly

The field dolly has a platform with four pneumatic tires that supports the tripod-mounted camera and the camera operator.

5.14 Beanbag as Camera Mount

A small pillowcase filled with foam packing peanuts cradles the camera and prevents minor wiggles. Professional beanbags are filled with a more flexible synthetic material.

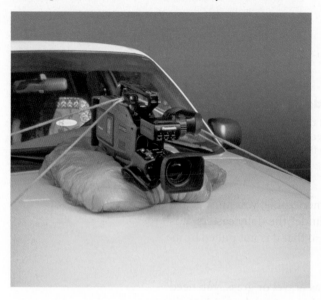

Special Camera Mounts

Special camera mounts range from beanbags, skateboards, and wheelchairs to heavy Steadicam mounts. This is an area in which you can put your imagination and creativity to work.

Homemade devices   A simple beanbag, made out of a pillowcase filled with foam packing peanuts, can serve as a reasonably good device for mounting a camcorder on the hood of a car or on bicycle handlebars. Professional "beanbags" are filled with a highly flexible synthetic material that adjusts to the shape of the camera yet remains highly shock absorbent. **SEE 5.14**

Mounting a small camcorder on a skateboard and pulling it along a smooth surface can give you an interesting low-angle dolly shot. And a wheelchair or shopping cart is a cheap but effective device for transporting camera operator and camcorder for a long tracking shot. If the floor is smooth, such tracking shots can rival the ones done with a much more expensive studio pedestal.

Handheld stabilizers   A variety of handheld stabilizers allow you to carry a small camcorder with one or both hands and keep the shot relatively steady so long as you don't jump up or down. You keep track of what the cameras sees by looking at the foldout viewfinder. **SEE 5.15**

Body-mounted stabilizers   A more elaborate but more comfortable way to operate a camera relatively wobble-free is by wearing a stabilizer harness, often called a "small Steadicam." *Steadicam,* although a trademark, has become the generic term for such devices. **SEE 5.16**

5.15 Handheld Stabilizer

This handheld stabilizer is built for small camcorders. If you're strong enough, you can carry it with one hand. The foldout viewfinder helps you get the right shots.

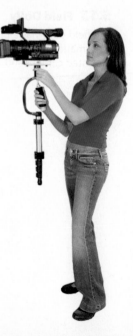

5.16 Stabilizer Harness

This spring-loaded camera support vest facilitates camera operation better than the handheld stabilizer. The harness has a spring-loaded stabilizer that lets you walk or even run with the camera, using the foldout panel as your primary viewfinder.

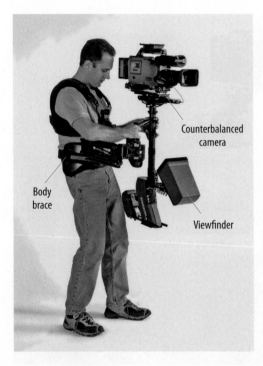

5.17 Body-mounted Steadicam®

This sturdy vest is designed to support a large camcorder or an ENG/EFP camera. It allows you to walk, run, or jump, with the camera remaining steady. Part of the counterweight is a large viewfinder.

Counterbalanced camera

Body brace

Viewfinder

For large camcorders, the bona fide **Steadicam** is similar to the support vest for small camcorders. Despite the wobble-inhibiting mechanism, wearing the Steadicam harness and operating the camcorder for a relatively short period of time can be a challenge for even a very strong person. **SEE 5.17**

Jib arms   The **jib arm** is a counterbalanced camera mount designed for shooting on location. You can clamp a *short-arm jib*, or *short jib*, to a doorframe, chair, or car window and then tongue the camera sideways and boom it up and down. **SEE 5.18**

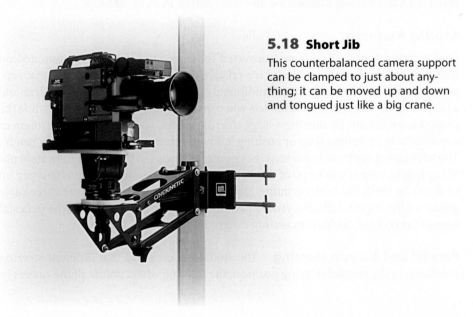

5.18 Short Jib

This counterbalanced camera support can be clamped to just about anything; it can be moved up and down and tongued just like a big crane.

5.19 Long Jib

This camera support, designed for on-location shooting, extends several feet and allows you to operate the ENG/EFP camera attached at the tip of the boom. It can do pretty much everything a big crane can do except carry you and the director aloft. It can be easily disassembled and transported in a car to a remote location.

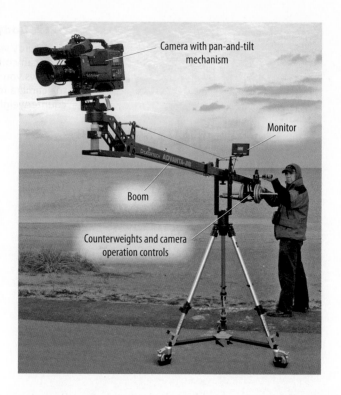

Camera with pan-and-tilt mechanism

Monitor

Boom

Counterweights and camera operation controls

For small camcorders there is a smaller jib arm attached to a body harness. This helps you get overhead shots without having to climb a ladder.

The *long jib is* designed for shooting on location and in large studios. It can do pretty much everything a studio crane can do except lift you up with the camera. In fact, you can run the jib arm and operate the camera or camcorder attached to it all by yourself. With the remote controls on the jib arm handles, you can tilt, pan, zoom, and focus the camera, using a small monitor. Some long jib arms have an 18-foot reach but can be easily dismantled and transported in a car. **SEE 5.19**

Studio Pedestal

Studio cameras, or EFP cameras converted for studio use, are usually mounted on studio pedestals. A **studio pedestal** is a relatively expensive camera mount that supports even the heaviest camera and additional equipment, such as a big zoom lens and a teleprompter. The studio pedestal lets you pan, tilt, truck, arc, and pedestal while the camera is on the air. By turning a large steering wheel, you can move the camera in any direction; by pulling it up or pushing it down, you can change the camera height. The telescoping center column must be counterbalanced so that the camera stays put at any height, even if you let go of the steering wheel. If the camera begins to creep up or down by itself, the center column must be rebalanced. Instead of the three cable guards of the tripod dolly, the studio pedestal has a skirt (housing) on the pedestal base to prevent the cable from getting caught in the casters. **SEE 5.20**

Parallel and tricycle steering   The studio pedestal has two different steering positions. In the *parallel* steering position, the steering wheel points all the casters in

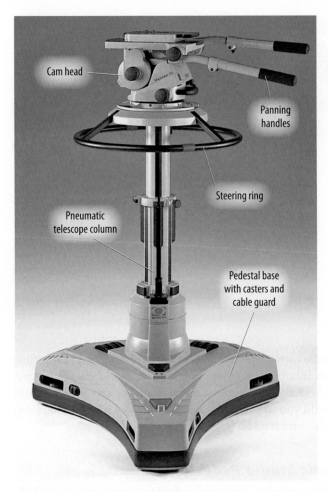

Cam head

Panning handles

Steering ring

Pneumatic telescope column

Pedestal base with casters and cable guard

5.20 Studio Pedestal

The studio pedestal permits you to pan, tilt, truck, arc, and pedestal while the camera is on the air. If the pedestal is equipped with a telescoping column, you can move the camera from about 2 feet to about 5 feet above the studio floor.

5.21 Parallel and Tricycle Steering

A In the parallel steering position, the three casters point in the same direction.

B In the tricycle steering position, only one wheel is steerable.

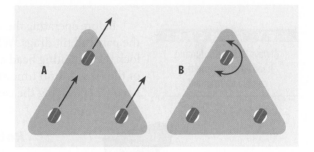

the same direction. **SEE 5.21A** Parallel steering is used for all normal camera moves. In the *tricycle* position, only one wheel is steerable. **SEE 5.21B** You use this steering position if you need to rotate the pedestal itself to move it closer to a piece of scenery or the studio wall.

Cam head   Like the tripod, the center column of the studio pedestal has a camera mounting head attached to it. To accommodate the combined weight of studio camera, heavy studio lens, and teleprompter, the customary tripod head has been replaced by a sturdier and more elaborate camera mount, called a ***cam head***. Its operational controls are similar to those of the mounting heads for lightweight cameras: pan and tilt drags, locking devices, and panning handles. Instead of the quick-release plate, the studio camera has an attached wedge mount, which fits a wedge mount receptacle on the top of the cam head. Once balanced, the wedge mount ensures proper camera balance every time the camera is put back on the pedestal. **SEE 5.22**

The cam head has two panning handles that allow you to pan and tilt smoothly while simultaneously operating the attached zoom and focus controls.

5.22 Cam Head with Wedge Mount Receptacle

The studio cam head is designed for heavy studio cameras and accessory equipment. It permits smooth pans and tilts despite the camera weight. Note that this mounting head has a wedge mount receptacle rather than one for a quick-release plate.

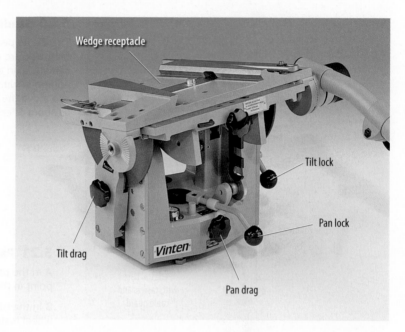

Wedge receptacle

Tilt lock

Pan lock

Tilt drag

Pan drag

Vinten

Before operating the studio camera, always unlock the mounting head and adjust the pan and tilt drags. When leaving the camera unattended, even for a short time, lock the mounting head and cap the lens (put the metal or plastic cap over the front of the lens). At no time should you use the drag controls for locking the mounting head when leaving the camera unattended.

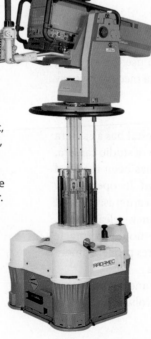

5.23 Robotic Studio Pedestal

The robotic studio pedestal can pan, tilt, dolly, truck, pedestal, and zoom according to computer instructions instead of those of a camera operator. It is used mainly for news presentations.

Robotic Studio Pedestal

You have probably seen small robotic camera mounts for little cameras in lecture halls. They are usually mounted on the wall and aimed at the podium. Robotic studio pedestals are much larger because they must support heavy studio cameras. You can see them in news studios, where two or three cameras are operated from the control room by a single robotic-pedestal technician/camera operator. Robotic pedestals can be preprogrammed to dolly, truck, pan, tilt, and zoom for specific camera shots, such as a two-shot of the anchors or a medium shot of the weather set. Much like in an outer-space movie, they move silently from place to place. **SEE 5.23**

OPERATIONAL FEATURES

Now that you know how to move the camera, you need to learn about focusing, adjusting shutter speed, zooming, and white-balancing before composing your unforgettable shots with a camcorder or studio camera.

Focusing

Normally, we want all pictures on the screen to appear in focus (sharp and clear). You can achieve focus by *manual* or *automatic* controls.

Manual focus   To ensure sharp, clear pictures, you should focus manually rather than rely on the automatic focus. The manual focus control of all nonstudio lenses is on a ring at the front of the lens that you can turn clockwise or counterclockwise. SEE 5.24 **ZVL3 CUE 2** CAMERA→ Focus ring→ try it

When operating a studio camera, you stay in focus by turning a twist grip mounted on the left panning handle and connected to the zoom lens by a cable. SEE 5.25

Calibration, or presetting the zoom lens   Assume that you are to videotape a local high-school fundraising event. The principal is auctioning off works of pottery made by students in the ceramic shop. She stands about 10 feet in front of the display tables along the back wall of the gym. During the video recording, you are asked to zoom from a medium shot of the principal to a fairly tight close-up of a ceramic pot, but during the zoom the shot gets progressively out of focus. When you reach the desired close-up, you can hardly make out the shape of the pot. What happened? You neglected to *calibrate*, or preset, the lens before zooming in for the close-up.

To **calibrate the zoom lens** means to adjust the zoom lens so that it will maintain focus during the entire zoom. To preset the lens, you must first zoom in to the desired close-up of the farthest target object—the pot—and bring it into focus by turning the focus ring at the front of the lens. When you then zoom back to the medium shot of the principal, she will be in focus (although you may have to adjust the focus a little).

5.24 **Manual Focus on Camcorder and ENG/EFP Cameras**

The manual focus control on small camcorders and ENG/EFP cameras is a ring at the front of the lens, which can be turned by hand.

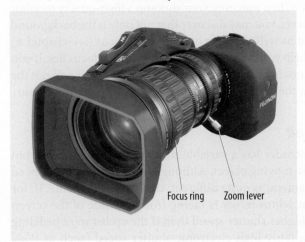

Focus ring   Zoom lever

5.25 **Manual Focus Control on Studio Camera**

The focus control on a studio camera is a twist grip attached to the left panning handle. To focus you turn it either clockwise or counterclockwise.

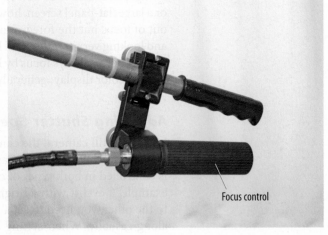

Focus control

When you zoom in again to another piece of pottery, you will stay in focus and the close-up of the new pot will be sharp and clear. As soon as you reposition the camera, however, or if the principal moves toward or away from the display tables, you will need to recalibrate the lens. This means zooming in on the pot again, focusing, zooming back to include the principal, and seeing whether you have to tweak the focus a little to keep her sharp and clear in subsequent zooms.

Now let's move into the studio, where your camera is assigned to cover a classical pianist from the side so that you can zoom in from a medium shot to a tight close-up of the keyboard and the pianist's hands. How do you preset the zoom lens for this? You zoom in for a tight close-up of the keyboard and bring the lens into focus by turning the twist grip on the left panning handle. But exactly where on the keyboard should you focus? Probably the far end because you can then zoom in and out and stay in reasonably sharp focus regardless of whether the pianist displays his virtuosity at the near or the far end of the keyboard.

> **▶KEY CONCEPT**
>
> To preset (calibrate) a zoom lens, zoom in as closely as possible on the farthest target object and bring it into focus. All subsequent zooms will be in focus so long as the camera-to-subject distance remains the same.

Auto-focus   Most small camcorders and some large cameras are equipped with an automatic focusing system, called the *auto-focus*. Through some electronic wizardry (reading the angle of a little radar beam or measuring the contrast), the camera focuses on the scene all by itself. Most of the time, these systems work well, but there are times when the camera cannot accommodate very bright or low-contrast scenes, leaving you with a blurred image. Or it may not detect exactly which object in the picture to bring into focus. You may not want to focus on the obvious foreground object but instead on the middleground. Unable to infer your artistic intent, the auto-focus will focus on the most prominent object closest to the camera. To achieve such a selective focus (see "Lenses and Depth of Field" in chapter 6), you need to switch from auto-focus to manual. The auto-focus can also have trouble keeping up with rapidly changing scenes in fast zooms. **ZVL3 CUE 3** CAMERA→ Focusing→ auto focus

When working with a high-definition video (HDV) camera, you may initially have trouble focusing. Because everything looks so much sharper than with standard television (STV), you may not see in the relatively small viewfinder when your shots are slightly out of focus. The increased sharpness of the HDV image also lures you into perceiving a much greater depth of field than you actually have—foreground and background seem to be in focus. When watching your shots on a high-quality monitor or a large flat-panel screen, however, you may discover that not only is the background out of focus but the foreground as well. *Racking* in and out of focus (see chapter 6) and looking very carefully will help you determine where the optimal focus lies. If you have a choice, always focus by looking at the black-and-white viewfinder and not the foldout color display; generally, the black-and-white image has a higher resolution.

Adjusting Shutter Speed

Like on a still camera, the camcorder has a variable **shutter speed** control to avoid image blur when shooting a fast-moving object. Although the way the shutter speed is controlled in both types of cameras is quite different, the effect is the same. If, for example, a cyclist with a bright yellow jersey is racing from one side of the screen to the other, you need to set a higher shutter speed than if the cyclist were pedaling along casually. When setting a fairly high electronic shutter speed (such as $\frac{1}{2,000}$

5.26 Camcorder Zoom Control

Camcorders have a rocker switch near the lens that controls the zoom-in and zoom-out motion.

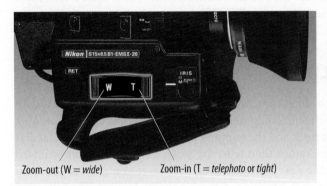

Zoom-out (W = *wide*)   Zoom-in (T = *telephoto* or *tight*)

5.27 Studio Zoom Control

The zoom control of the studio camera is a rocker switch on the right panning handle that is activated by the thumb of your right hand.

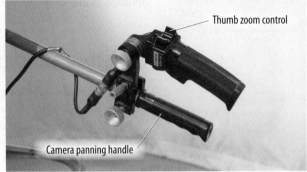

Thumb zoom control

Camera panning handle

second), you will notice that the yellow jersey looks considerably darker than with lower shutter speeds. All of this translates into a simple formula, which is similar to still photography: the higher the shutter speed, the more light you need.

> **KEY CONCEPT**
>
> The higher the shutter speed, the more light you need.

Zooming

All small and ENG/EFP camcorders have a rocker switch on the lens that activates the zoom mechanism. By pressing the front of the switch, usually labeled *T* for *telephoto* or *tight,* you trigger a motor that rearranges various elements in the zoom lens for the zoom-in effect. By pressing the back of the switch, labeled *W* for *wide,* you zoom out. This motorized *servo-zoom* mechanism, which is activated by the zoom rocker switch, keeps your zooming smooth and steady. **SEE 5.26** Some cameras offer a choice between a slow and a fast zoom speed. Some lenses for large camcorders have an additional manual zoom control that allows you to override the motorized mechanism by turning the zoom lever on the lens barrel for extremely fast zooms (see figure 5.24).

Studio cameras have a similar rocker switch mounted on the right panning handle. This thumb-operated switch is connected by cable to the servo-zoom mechanism of the studio lens. By pressing the *T* side of the switch, you zoom in; by pressing the *W* side, you zoom out. **SEE 5.27**

Because the servo-zoom mechanism makes zooming relatively easy, you may be tempted to zoom in and out even if your zooms are not necessary. Keep zooming to a minimum; frequent and unmotivated zooming reveals the inexperience of the camera operator as readily as excessive camera movement. **ZVL3 CUE 4** CAMERA→ Zoom lens→ focal length | zoom control

> **KEY CONCEPT**
>
> Keep zooming to a minimum.

White-balancing

To **white-balance** means to adjust the camera so that a sheet of white paper looks white on the television screen, regardless of whether the light that illuminates the sheet is reddish, such as candlelight, or bluish, such as outdoor daylight. Most small camcorders do this automatically, although some have you set the white-balance switch to the proper setting, such as outdoors or indoors.

Large camcorders and ENG/EFP cameras have a semiautomatic white-balance, which means that you have to activate a white-balance switch. (See chapter 8 for a more detailed explanation of white-balancing.) **ZVL3 CUE 5** ▶LIGHTS→ Color temperature→ white balance

GENERAL GUIDELINES

Whether you are operating a small camcorder or a large studio camera, treat it with extreme care as with all electronic equipment. Always be mindful of safety—yours and others'. Do not risk your neck and the equipment to get an especially spectacular shot that merely embellishes, rather than tells, the story. Do not abandon standard operational procedures for the sake of expediency. Whatever you do, use common sense. Like bicycling, you learn to operate a camera only by doing it. The following guidelines can make learning easier and also serve as useful checklists.

CHECKLIST: CAMCORDERS AND ENG/EFP CAMERAS

☑ *Don't expose the camera to the elements* Never leave the camera unprotected in the sun or in a hot car. Also watch that the viewfinder is not pointed into the sun; the magnifying glass in the viewfinder can collect the sun's rays and melt the viewfinder housing and electronics. Use plastic camera covers, called "raincoats," or a large umbrella when shooting in the rain or extreme cold. In case of emergency, a plastic grocery bag will do.

☑ *Leave the camera with care* Lock the mounting head on the tripod whenever you leave the camera unattended. When putting the camera down, place it upright. Laying it on its side may damage the viewfinder or attached microphone.

☑ *Use the lens cap* Even if a camera can be "capped" internally to prevent light from reaching the imaging device, always put the plastic cap over the front of the zoom lens. This lens cap protects the delicate front surface of the expensive lens.

☑ *Use fully charged batteries* Always see to it that the battery is fully charged. Some older batteries develop a "memory," which means that they signal a full charge even when only partially charged. To avoid this problem, discharge the batteries fully before recharging them. New batteries must first be "trained" to avoid memory. When first using a new battery, run it until it is totally discharged. Then charge it again. From now on it should fully charge without a memory effect. Do not drop batteries or expose them to extreme heat.

☑ *Verify the videotape format* Make sure that the videocassettes fit the camera model. Even though the cassettes look similar from the outside, they may not fit a particular camera.

☑ *Examine all connections*   Check all connectors, regardless of what they connect, to see whether they fit their designated jacks (see figure 4.21). Use adapters only in an emergency; an adapter is by design a stopgap and, as such, a potential trouble spot. Small camcorders normally use smaller (RCA phono) connectors; all larger camcorders have three-pin (XLR) audio connectors. (See chapter 7 for further information on audio connectors.)

☑ *Test the camera*   Even when in a hurry, always do a brief test recording to verify that the camcorder operates properly. Bring headphones along to check the audio. Use the same power supply and connectors that you intend to use during the actual video recording. Check the full range of the zoom lens and the focus. In extremely cold or damp weather conditions, zoom lenses sometimes stick or give up altogether.

☑ *Set the switches*   Have all the switches, such as auto- or manual focus, auto-iris, zoom speed, and shutter speed, in the desired positions. The faster the action in front of the camera, the higher the shutter speed must be to prevent the moving object from blurring. Remember that higher shutter speeds require higher light levels.

☑ *Perform a white balance*   White-balance the camera before beginning the video recording, unless the system is fully automatic. White-balance under the light that actually illuminates the event.

☑ *Always capture audio*   Always turn on the camera microphone and record ambient sound with the pictures. This sound will help you identify the location of the event and will aid shot continuity during postproduction editing.

☑ *Heed the warning signs*   Take note of caution signals in the viewfinder display and try to address the problem immediately. You may be able to dismiss the "low light level" warning on the camera if you are not concerned with picture quality, but you cannot ignore a "low battery" warning.

CHECKLIST: STUDIO CAMERAS

☑ *Get in touch and in control*   Put on your headset to establish contact with the control room and the video operator. Unlock the mounting head and adjust the pan and tilt drags. Pedestal up and down to get a feel for the pedestal range and motion. A properly balanced pedestal should prevent the camera from creeping up or down when left in a vertical position.

☑ *Tame the cables*   Position the cable guards close enough to the floor to prevent the pedestal from rolling over the camera cable. Uncoil the cable and check its reach. To avoid the inevitable tug of the cable during a dolly, tie it to the pedestal but leave enough slack so that you can freely pan, tilt, and pedestal.

☑ *Test-zoom and focus*   Ask the video engineer to uncap the camera so that you can rack through the zoom and focus ranges and, if necessary, adjust the viewfinder.

Practice calibrating the zoom lens so that the scene remains in focus during subsequent zooms.

✅ *Practice your moves*   Use masking tape on the studio floor to mark the critical camera positions. Write down all on-air camera moves so that you can set the zoom lens in the wide-angle position before the required move.

✅ *Move carefully*   Ask the floor person to help you steer the camera during an especially tricky move. If the cable gets tangled up during a dolly, don't drag the whole mess along. Signal the floor person to untangle it for you. When dollying or trucking, start slowly to overcome the inertia of the heavy dolly and slow down just before the end of the dolly. When raising or lowering the camera, brake the pedestal column before it reaches its maximum or minimum height; otherwise the camera and the picture might receive a hefty jolt.

✅ *Don't jump the red light*   Wait for the *tally light* (the red light inside the viewfinder and on top of the camera) to go out before moving the camera into a new position or presetting the zoom. The tally light tells the camera operator, the talent, and the studio production crew which camera is hot. During special effects the tally light may remain on even if you think your shot is finished. Normally, the ENG/EFP camera or camcorder has only a viewfinder tally light, which tells only you—the camera operator—when the camera is operating.

✅ *Avoid nervous camera movements*   Keep your eyes on the viewfinder and correct slowly for minor compositional defects. If a subject bounces back and forth on a close-up, don't try to keep it in the frame at all costs. It is better to let it move out of the frame from time to time than to play catch-up by rapid panning.

✅ *Let the director direct*   Always follow the director's instructions even if you think he or she is wrong. Do not try to outdirect the director from your position—but do alert the director if you are asked to do such impossible things as dollying or trucking on the air with your lens in the narrow-angle (zoomed-in) position.

✅ *Be observant and attentive*   Be aware of the activity around you. Pay particular attention to where the other cameras are and where they are asked to move. By listening to the director's instructions, you will be able to stay out of the way of the other cameras. When moving a camera, especially backward, watch for obstacles that may be in your path. Ask a floor person to guide you. Avoid unnecessary chatter on the intercom.

✅ *Anticipate your next shot*   Try to line up the next shot before the director calls for it, even if you work without a shot sheet that lists the nature and the sequence of your shots. For example, if you hear on the intercom that the other camera is on the air with a close-up, pull out to a medium shot or get a different angle to provide the director with another field of view. Do not duplicate the shot of another camera.

✅ *Put all tools away properly*   At the end of the show, wait for the "all clear" signal before preparing your camera for shutdown. Ask the video operator to cap the camera. As soon as the viewfinder goes dark, release the pan and tilt drags, lock the mounting head, and cap the lens. Park the camera in its usual place and coil the cable in the customary figure-eight loops.

MAIN POINTS

▶ **Camera Movements**

The movements include pan, tilt, cant, pedestal, dolly, truck or track, arc, crane or boom, and tongue. The zoom is also included, although the camera does not move.

▶ **Camera Mounts**

These include a variety of tripods, special mounts such as the jib arm and the Steadicam, and studio pedestals. Whenever possible, put the camcorder or the ENG/EFP camera on a tripod. Keep the handheld or shoulder-mounted camera as steady as possible and zoomed out when moving.

▶ **Camera Mounting Head**

This mechanism connects the camera to the tripod or the studio pedestal. It facilitates pans and tilts. Always lock the mounting head when leaving the camera unattended.

▶ **Focus and Shutter Speed**

Normally, we want all pictures on the screen sharp and clear. You can achieve focus by manual or automatic controls. Shutter speed reduces the blurring of bright, fast-moving objects. The higher the shutter speed, the less blurring occurs but the more light is needed.

▶ **Calibrating the Zoom Lens**

To preset a zoom, the lens must be zoomed in on the farthest target object and brought into focus. All subsequent wider-angle zoom positions will be in focus so long as the camera-to-subject distance remains the same.

▶ **White-balancing**

This procedure ensures that white and all other colors look the same under different lights. It needs to be done every time the camera operates under new lighting conditions, unless it has a fully automatic white-balance mechanism.

ZETTL'S VIDEOLAB 3.0

 For your reference, or to track your work, the Zettl's VideoLab 3.0 program cues in this chapter are listed here with their corresponding page numbers.

ZVL3 CUE 1 ▶ CAMERA→ Camera moves→ dolly | zoom |truck | pan | pedestal | try it   73

ZVL3 CUE 2 ▶ CAMERA→ Focus ring→ try it   85

ZVL3 CUE 3 ▶ CAMERA→ Focusing→ auto focus   86

ZVL3 CUE 4 ▶ CAMERA→ Zoom lens→ focal length | zoom control   87

ZVL3 CUE 5 ▶ LIGHTS→ Color temperature→ white balance   88

CHAPTER 6

KEY TERMS

aspect ratio The ratio of the width of the television screen to its height. In STV (standard television), it is 4 × 3 (4 units wide by 3 units high); for HDTV (high-definition television), it is 16 × 9 (16 units wide by 9 units high).

close-up (CU) Object or any part of it seen at close range and framed tightly. The close-up can be extreme (extreme or big close-up) or rather loose (medium close-up).

cross-shot (X/S) Similar to the over-the-shoulder shot except that the camera-near person is completely out of the shot.

depth of field The area in which all objects, located at different distances from the camera, appear in focus. Depends primarily on the focal length of the lens, its f-stop, and the distance from the camera to the object.

field of view The portion of a scene visible through a particular lens; its vista. Expressed in symbols, such as *CU* for close-up.

headroom The space between the top of the head and the upper screen edge.

leadroom The space in front of a laterally moving object or person.

long shot (LS) Object seen from far away or framed very loosely. The extreme long shot shows the object from a great distance. Also called *establishing shot*.

medium shot (MS) Object seen from a medium distance. Covers any framing between a long shot and a close-up.

noseroom The space in front of a person looking or pointing toward the edge of the screen.

over-the-shoulder shot (O/S) Camera looks over the camera-near person's shoulder (shoulder and back of head included in shot) at the other person.

psychological closure Mentally filling in missing visual information that will lead to a complete and stable configuration. Also called *closure*.

vector A directional screen force. There are graphic, index, and motion vectors.

z-axis Indicates screen depth. Extends from camera lens to horizon.

Looking Through the Viewfinder

As soon as you point a camera at some object or event, you need to make certain decisions about what to shoot and how to shoot it. Despite the trend for bigger video displays, television has remained a close-up medium. Because of the relatively small screen and the limited presentation time, you cannot usually introduce a scene by moving from an overall view to a close-up. Rather, you need to select only the most significant event details and show them as a series of close points of view. This way you not only reveal the features necessary to tell the story but also establish the energy of an event that might otherwise get lost on the small screen. Such a close-up technique is also effective when composing shots for the wider HDTV screen. Even large-screen motion pictures have finally learned from television the high-energy impact of telling a story primarily in a series of close-ups.

Effective camera operation depends on more than just knowing the technical requirements of the camera. It first and foremost requires a keen and sensitive eye and a basic knowledge of picture *aesthetics*—how to frame static or moving objects and events.

Familiarity with some basic compositional principles will help you not only produce pictures that have impact and meaning but also understand how and when to use the camera's operational controls and zoom lens positions. The technical and operational features of the camera cannot make aesthetic decisions for you: they merely enable you to carry out your artistic intentions as efficiently as possible.

We have all had, at least once, the rather trying experience of watching someone's vacation videos. Unless the person shooting the videotapes was an expert camera operator, you probably saw annoyingly fast zooms, shots with too much sky or too much ground, an incessantly moving view that shifted almost randomly from object to object, and people who seemed to be glued to either the sides or the top of the screen or who had background trees or telephone poles seeming to grow out of their heads.

To help you avoid such aesthetic pitfalls, this chapter takes a closer look at the aesthetics of picture composition. Note that in video, you are working mostly with moving images, so some of the traditional compositional principles for still photography must be modified to fit a shot series rather than a single picture. Such considerations are especially important when editing a shot series. (We discuss such principles in chapter 13.)

▶ **FRAMING A SHOT**
   Aspect ratio, field of view, vectors, composition, and psychological closure

▶ **MANIPULATING PICTURE DEPTH**
   Z-axis, lenses and perceived z-axis length, lenses and depth of field, and lenses and perceived z-axis speed

▶ **CONTROLLING CAMERA AND OBJECT MOTION**
   Camera movement and zooms, and shooting moving objects

FRAMING A SHOT

The most basic considerations in framing a shot are how much territory you include in the shot, how close an object appears to the viewer, where to place the object relative to the screen edges, and how to make viewers perceive a complete object when only parts of it are visible on the screen. In the terminology of photographic arts, including video, these factors are aspect ratio, field of view, vectors, composition, and psychological closure.

Aspect Ratio

Your framing of a shot depends to a great extent on the kind of frame you have available—the relationship of the width of the screen to its height, or **aspect ratio**. In video you will most often work with the standard television (STV) aspect ratio of 4 × 3—the screen is 4 units wide by 3 units high. When working in digital television (DTV), many cameras allow you to switch between the standard 4 × 3 ratio and the wide-screen 16 × 9 ratio of high-definition television (HDTV). The aspect ratio for HDTV is exclusively 16 × 9. You will find that on the small screen, your compositions will not differ significantly between the two aspect ratios. This is why even most high-definition video cameras still use the 4 × 3 aspect ratio for their viewfinders and foldout display panels. **SEE 6.1 AND 6.2**

On a large video screen or when video is projected onto a large movie screen, however, the difference between the two aspect ratios is prominent. A close-up of a face is much simpler to compose in the 4 × 3 aspect ratio than on the HDTV screen. On the other hand, the 16 × 9 aspect ratio allows you to frame wide vistas without losing too much event impact. Also, special effects are much more obvious, if not overbearing, on the wide HDTV screen. Most digital camcorders allow you to choose between the two aspect ratios. To help you frame for the wider screen, we display all the pictures in this book in the 16 × 9 aspect ratio. **ZVL3 CUE 1** ▶CAMERA→ Screen forces→ aspect ratio

6.1 4 × 3 Aspect Ratio

The aspect ratio of STV (standard television) is 4 units wide by 3 units high.

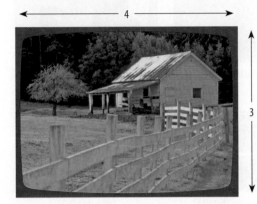

6.2 16 × 9 Aspect Ratio

The HDTV (high-definition television) aspect ratio is 16 units wide by 9 units high. Most DTV (digital television) cameras permit switching between the standard 4 × 3 ratio and the wide-screen 16 × 9 ratio.

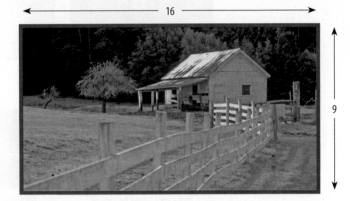

Field of View

Field of view refers to how close the object seems to the viewer, or how much of the "field," or scenery, in front of you is in the shot. When organized by how close we see the object, there are five field-of-view designations: *extreme long shot (ELS or XLS)*, *long shot (LS)*, *medium shot (MS)*, *close-up (CU)*, and *extreme close-up (ECU or XCU)*. **SEE 6.3**

When categorized by how much of a person we see, the shots are called: *bust shot*, which frames the upper part of a person; *knee shot*, which shows the person

6.3 Field-of-view Distance Steps

The field-of-view distance steps are relative and depend on how a long shot or a close-up is visualized.

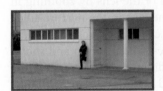

Extreme long shot (ELS), or establishing shot

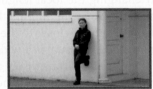

Long shot (LS), or full shot

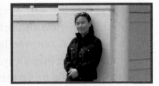

Medium shot (MS), or waist shot

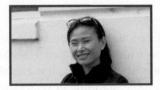

Close-up (CU)

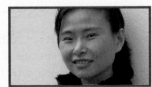

Extreme close-up (ECU)

6.4 Area Field of View

Other shot designations tell where the subject is cut off by the upper or lower part of the frame or by how many subjects are in the frame or how they are arranged.

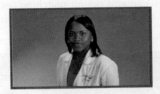

Bust shot

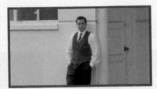

Knee shot

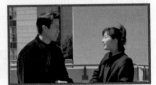

Two-shot (two persons or objects in frame)

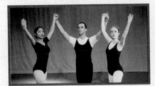

Three-shot (three persons or objects in frame)

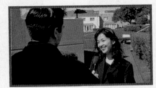

Over-the-shoulder shot (O/S)

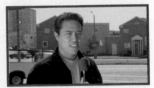

Cross-shot (X/S)

approximately from the knees up; *two-shot,* which shows two people or objects in the frame; *three-shot,* which shows three people or objects in the frame; **over-the-shoulder shot (O/S)**, which shows the camera looking at someone over the shoulder of another person nearer to the camera; and **cross-shot (X/S)**, which looks alternately at one or the other person, with the camera-near person completely out of the shot. **SEE 6.4**

The field of view is relative, which means that what you consider a close-up someone else may think of as a medium shot. As mentioned, the relatively small size of the standard video screen made the close-up the most frequently used field of view in video production. These field-of-view designations hold true regardless of whether you shoot for a small screen or a large screen, that is, a 4 × 3 or a 16 × 9 aspect ratio.

You can change the field of view either by moving the camera closer to the event or farther away from it or by changing the focal length of the lens by zooming in or out. As you learned in chapter 4, zooming in puts the lens in the narrow-angle (telephoto) position and brings the subject closer to the camera for a close-up view. When you zoom out, the lens gradually assumes a wide-angle position and shows more territory farther away. There are important visual differences between moving the camera closer or farther away from the subject and zooming in and out. (We discuss these differences in the context of controlling camera and object motion later in this chapter.) **ZVL3 CUE 2** CAMERA→ Composition→ field of view

> ▶ **KEY CONCEPT**
> Video is a close-up medium.

Vectors

A **vector** is a directional screen force with various strengths. This concept will help you understand and control the specific screen forces generated by someone looking, pointing, or moving in a particular direction or even by the horizontal and vertical lines of a room, desk, or door. A thorough understanding of vectors will aid you in *blocking*—designing effective positions and movements of talent and cameras.

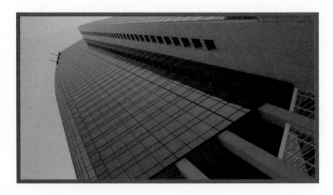

6.5 Graphic Vectors

Graphic vectors are created by lines or an arrangement of stationary objects that leads the eye in a certain direction.

6.6 Index Vectors

Index vectors are created by someone or something that points unquestionably in a particular direction.

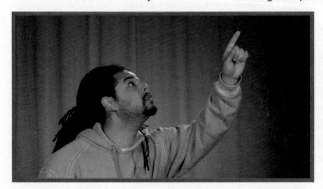 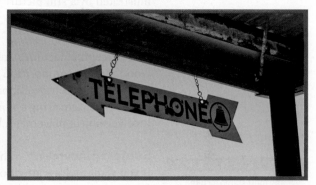

There are three basic vectors: graphic vectors, index vectors, and motion vectors.

Graphic vectors   These vectors are created by lines or an arrangement of stationary objects that lead the eye in a general direction. Look around you. You are surrounded by *graphic vectors,* such as the horizontal and vertical lines that are formed by this book, the window and door frames in the room, or the line where the walls meet the ceiling. Neatly lined-up houses create graphic vectors, as do the lines created by wires and a power pole. **SEE 6.5**

Index vectors   *Index vectors* are created by something that points unquestionably in a specific direction, such as an arrow, a one-way-street sign, or somebody looking or pointing in a certain direction. **SEE 6.6** The difference between graphic and index vectors is that index vectors are much more definite as to direction. Going against the index vector of a one-way sign may jolt your sense of good composition as well as your body.

Motion vectors   A *motion vector* is created by an object that is actually moving, or is perceived to be moving, on the screen. People walking, a car speeding along the highway, a bird in flight—all form motion vectors. For an illustration of motion

6.7 Screen-center Placement

The most stable screen position is screen-center. All screen forces are neutralized at this point.

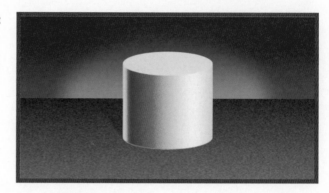

vectors, look around you where things are moving (they obviously cannot be illustrated by a still picture). **ZVL3 CUE 3** CAMERA→ Screen forces→ vectors

Composition

Our perceptual faculties are always striving to stabilize the chaotic world around us. Good picture composition helps us in this task. In fact, professional videographers apply effective compositional principles even when shooting under extreme pressure, such as while covering a storm or a war. Some of the most basic compositional factors involve subject placement, headroom and leadroom, and the horizon line.

Subject placement   The most stable and prominent picture area is screen-center. If you want to draw attention to a single subject, place it there. **SEE 6.7** The same goes for framing a person who is addressing viewers directly, such as a newscaster or a company president. **SEE 6.8**

> **▶KEY CONCEPT**
>
> The most stable picture area is screen-center.

If the newscaster has to share screen space with a visual, such as the secondary frame—the box—over his or her shoulder, you obviously need to move the newscaster to one side, not only to make room for the visual but also to balance the two picture elements within the frame. **SEE 6.9**

6.8 Screen-center Placement of Newscaster

A single newscaster should be placed screen-center. This position draws undivided attention to the newscaster and what she is saying.

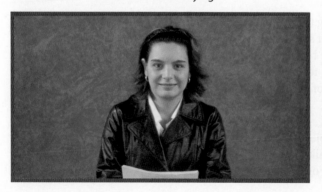

6.9 Picture Balance

When the newscaster has to share the screen space with other visuals, the elements must be placed in opposite screen halves so that they balance each other.

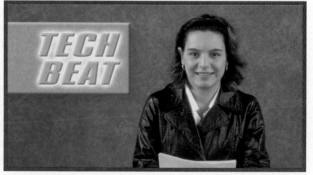

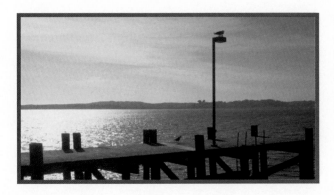

6.10 Nonsymmetrical Framing

A prominent horizontal line can best be divided by a vertical object located at about two-fifths (for the STV aspect ratio) or one-third (for the HDTV aspect ratio) the distance from either the left or the right screen edge. This way the screen is not divided visually into two equal halves, which makes for a more dynamic and interesting composition.

Sometimes when you frame large vistas that contain a distinct single vertical element, such as a telephone pole, a tree, or a fencepost, you can place the single vertical element off-center, at about the one-third or two-thirds mark of screen width. Such nonsymmetrical framing in which the two unequal parts of the screen contain different visual elements is often called the *rule of thirds* or *golden section framing*. It makes the picture look more dynamic and the horizon less divided than if you placed the vertical object at exactly midpoint. This rule of thirds is also used for placing horizontal graphic vectors, such as the horizon or printed titles. **SEE 6.10**

Headroom and leadroom   Somehow the edges of the video screen seem to act like magnets and attract objects close to them. This pull is especially strong at the top and bottom edges of the screen. For example, if you frame a man so that his head touches the upper screen edge, his head seems to be pulled up, or even attached, to the frame. **SEE 6.11** To counteract this pull, you must leave adequate space, called **headroom**. **SEE 6.12** As a rule of thumb, correct headroom places the eyes of the person in the upper third of the screen, unless the person wears a hat.

If you leave too much headroom, however, the bottom edge exerts its force and seems to pull the man downward. **SEE 6.13** Because you inevitably lose some picture

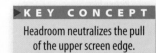

▶KEY CONCEPT
Headroom neutralizes the pull of the upper screen edge.

6.11 No Headroom

Without headroom the person seems glued to the top edge of the screen.

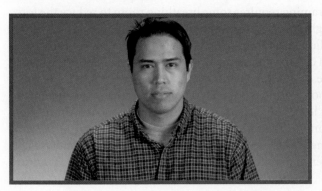

6.12 Proper Headroom

Correct headroom neutralizes the magnetic pull of the upper edge and makes the person look comfortable within the frame.

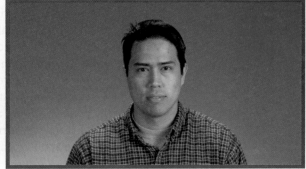

6.13 Too Much Headroom

Too much headroom tends to dwarf the person and push the image against the lower half of the screen.

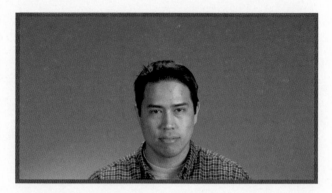

6.14 Headroom for Transmission

The framing on the left is correct for the viewfinder display, but the inevitable picture loss during transmission or video recording requires more initial headroom. The framing on the right is therefore more appropriate.

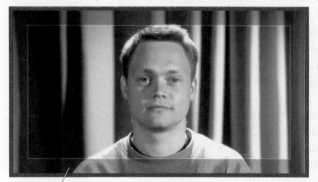

Picture loss

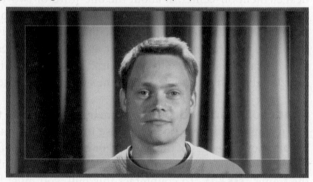

space when showing videotape on a television set, or when actually transmitting via cable or an on-the-air channel, you should leave just a little more headroom than what seems appropriate. This way the viewer will see framing with exactly the right headroom. **SEE 6.14** **ZVL3 CUE 4** CAMERA→ Composition→ headroom

The sides of the frame contain similar graphical "magnets" that seem to pull persons or objects toward them, especially when they are oriented toward one or the other side of the screen. Take a look at the next figure. **SEE 6.15** Do you feel that this is a good composition? Of course not. The person seems to push his nose into the right screen edge. Correct framing requires some breathing room to reduce the force of his glance—his screen-right index vector—and the pull of the frame, which is why this type of leadroom is called ***noseroom***. **SEE 6.16** Note that the rule of thirds also applies to noseroom: as you can see, the center of the person's head is approximately in the left third of the frame.

The same "breathing room" principle applies when you frame someone moving laterally. **SEE 6.17** You must leave some room in the direction of movement to show where the person is going and to absorb some of the directional energy of the motion vector. Because the camera must be somewhat ahead of the subject's motion and should lead the action rather than follow it, this is called ***leadroom***. It is not always

6.15 No Noseroom

Without any space between the nose and the screen edge, the person seems to be glued to the frame or crashing into it.

6.16 Proper Noseroom

This noseroom is sufficient to counter the pull of the screen and the force of the glance.

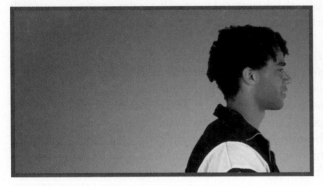

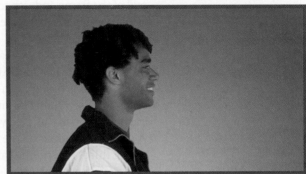

6.17 No Leadroom

Without proper leadroom the laterally moving subject or object seems oddly impeded by the screen edge.

6.18 Proper Leadroom

With proper leadroom the laterally moving subject or object seems able to move freely in the given direction.

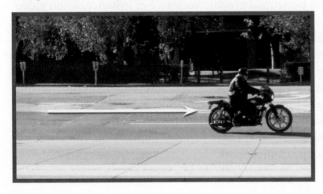

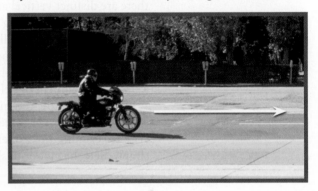

easy to keep proper leadroom for a moving person or object, especially if the subject moves rather quickly. **SEE 6.18** `ZVL3 CUE 5` CAMERA→ Composition→ leadroom

With an understanding of vectors, we can more accurately explain these basic compositional principles. When we frame a telephone pole or a fencepost somewhat off-center to divide a smooth horizon line, we basically divide a prominent horizontal graphic vector with a strong vertical one. To avoid dividing the screen symmetrically—into two equal halves—we place the vertical graphic vector at approximately one-third of the screen width. This way the horizontal vector is divided into balanced yet more dynamic proportions than with a symmetrical division.

If someone is looking or pointing directly screen-left or screen-right, you must give this index vector some room to play out by giving leadroom in the direction indicated, as shown in figure 6.16. As soon as the person looks straight into the camera, however, the index vector loses its force. Consequently, you must adjust the framing so that the person is screen-center. The same principle applies for motion vectors: if someone is running laterally in front of the camera, you must pan the camera ahead of the person to compensate for the strong motion vector, as illustrated in figure 6.18.

As you can see, leadroom must compensate for two screen forces: the magnetic pull of the frame and, especially, the directional force of the index or motion vector. It is this combination of forces that causes a composition to look so bad when leadroom is inadequate.

Now that you have learned all about the rule of thirds, a word of caution is in order: if you always apply this rule in a mathematical fashion, your pictures will look mechanical, as though you consistently edited them to the beat of the music without exception. In certain circumstances you need to break this rule and frame the subject unconventionally to give your pictures additional aesthetic energy. For example, if you want to emphasize the beautiful colors of the evening sky, you should ignore the rule of thirds and tilt the camera up to lower the horizon line as much as possible. Or you may want to place a person right next to the screen edge to intensify his claustrophobia. As you can see, you can—and should—bend the compositional rules if it intensifies the message. But before you can bend a rule, you must understand it.

Horizon line   Normally, we expect buildings and people to stand upright on level ground. This principle is especially important when you shoot outdoors and where there are distinct vertical and horizontal graphic vectors. For instance, when videotaping a reporter standing on a street corner, make sure that the background lines (graphic vectors) are parallel to the upper and lower screen edges. **SEE 6.19** A slight tilt of the handheld camcorder may not readily show up on the foreground person but is easily detectable by the tilted horizon line. For example, you may want to upset a stable environment by deliberately canting the camera and, with it, the horizon line. A tilted horizon line can make the picture more dynamic and give it more aesthetic energy. Of course, the subject matter must lend itself to such aesthetic manipulation. **SEE 6.20**   Canting the camera on a dull speaker will not improve his speech; it will simply alert the viewer to sloppy camera work.

6.19 Level Horizon Line

When framing a person standing in front of a prominent horizon line, make sure that it is level.

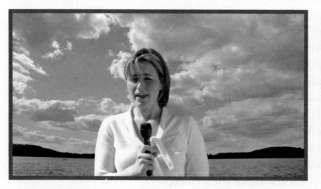

6.20 Tilting the Horizon Line

A tilted horizon line increases the dynamic tension of the event.

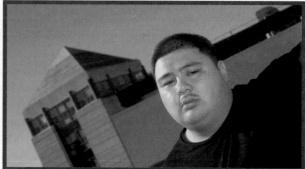

Psychological Closure

Our minds try to make sense out of the bombardment of impressions we receive every second and to stabilize the world around us as much as possible. Our perceptual mechanism does this by ignoring most sense impressions that are not immediately relevant and by combining visual cues or filling in missing visual information to arrive at complete and stable configurations. This process is called ***psychological closure***, or *closure* for short.

Take a look at the arrangement of angle brackets to the right. Although we actually see three separate brackets, we perceive a single triangle. Through psychological closure we have automatically filled in the missing lines. In fact, we have a hard time seeing them as three isolated angles. **SEE 6.21**

Now look at the close-up to the right. **SEE 6.22** Again, you mentally fill in the rest of the subject's body although you actually see only her head and shoulders on-screen.

The graphic vectors of the shoulders that led your eye outside the frame helped you to apply closure—to fill in the missing parts. One of the most important principles in framing a close-up in which only part of the subject is shown is to provide sufficient visual clues (graphic vectors) that enable the viewer to complete the figure mentally in off-screen space. Below are two different ECUs of the same person. Which one do you prefer? **SEE 6.23**

6.21 Psychological Closure

We perceive these three angle brackets as a triangle by mentally filling in the missing parts.

6.22 Framing a Close-up

A properly framed close-up leads our eyes into off-screen space to complete the figure.

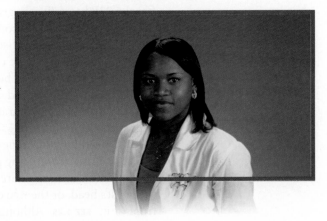

6.23 Choosing the Proper Framing

Here are two extreme close-ups. Which one looks better to you?

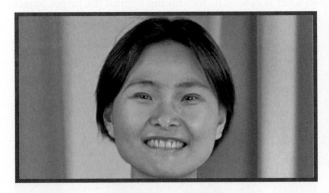
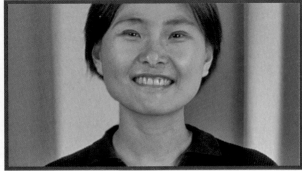

6.24 **Improper and Proper Framing**

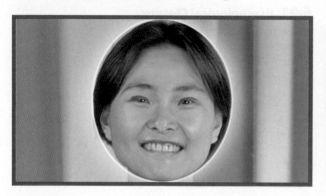 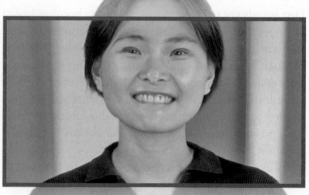

A This extreme close-up is improperly framed because it invites us to apply closure within the frame (a circle) without extending it into off-screen space.

B This framing properly extends into off-screen space and makes us apply closure to the whole figure.

Most likely, you chose the photo on the right as the better ECU. But why? Because figure 6.23B has sufficient graphic clues (vectors) to tell us that the subject is continuing in off-screen space. In contrast the framing of 6.23A gives practically no visual cues that would lead us into off-screen space. In fact, our perceptual mechanism is happy with having found a stable configuration within the frame: the head forms an oval. **SEE 6.24** The disagreement between our experience, which tells us that there must be a body attached to the head, and our automated perception, which is perfectly happy with the circlelike configuration, is the principal reason why we feel uncomfortable with such a composition. **ZVL3 CUE 6** CAMERA→ Composition→ close-ups | try it

The need for psychological closure can also produce visual paradoxes and bad compositions by combining parts of the foreground and the background into a single configuration. Examples are the rubber plant on the set that seems to grow out of the guest's head, or the tree or street sign that extends out of the person standing in front of it. **SEE 6.25** Although we know that such elements are in the background, our perceptual need for stable figures makes us perceive these visual paradoxes as a single unit.

When looking through the viewfinder, you must learn to see not only the foreground (target) object but also what is *behind* it. By looking behind the target object

6.25 **Undesirable Closure**

Because of our tendency to stabilize the environment, we perceive this background object as part of the main figure.

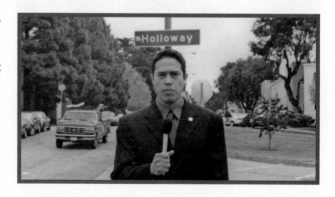

or scene, you will readily discover potential closure problems, such as the street sign that the reporter seems to balance on his head. Looking behind may also reveal other visual hazards, such as billboards that compete with your sponsor, or garbage cans, camera or mic cables, or light stands. **ZVL3 CUE 7** ▸ CAMERA→ Composition→ background

MANIPULATING PICTURE DEPTH

So far we have been concerned mainly with organizing the two-dimensional area of the video screen.[1] This section explores the depth dimension. Whereas the width and the height of the video screen have definite limits, the depth dimension extends from the camera lens to the horizon. Although illusory, the screen depth, or *z-axis* (a term borrowed from geometry), is the most flexible screen dimension. The ***z-axis*** is an imaginary line that stretches from camera lens to horizon, regardless of where the lens is pointing. You can place many more objects along this depth axis than across the width of the screen. You can also have objects move toward and away from the camera at any speed without having to worry about losing them in the viewfinder or providing adequate leadroom. **ZVL3 CUE 8** ▸ CAMERA→ Picture depth→ z-axis

Defining the Z-axis

If you point a camera at the cloudless sky, you have just about as long a z-axis as you can get—but it does not show its depth. To show screen depth, you need to define the z-axis by placing objects or people along it. The traditional way of creating the illusion of depth is to place objects in a distinct foreground, middleground, and background. **SEE 6.26** Even on a relatively small set, a prominent foreground piece or person will help define the z-axis and suggest screen depth. **SEE 6.27**

---

1. For more information on picture composition, see Herbert Zettl, *Sight Sound Motion: Applied Media Aesthetics,* 4th ed. (Belmont, Calif.: Thomson Wadsworth, 2005), pp. 73–113.

6.26 Foreground, Middleground, Background

A distinct division of the z-axis into foreground (the bench, bushes, and tree), middleground (the boat and the dock), and background (the skyline and the bridge) creates the illusion of depth.

6.27 Foreground Person to Create Depth

The person standing in the foreground increases the illusion of depth.

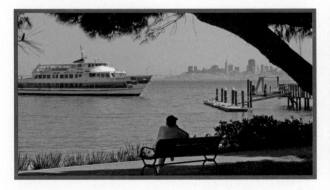

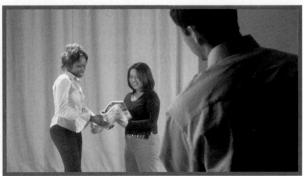

6.28 Wide-angle Z-axis

The wide-angle lens stretches the z-axis and increases the perceived distance between objects.

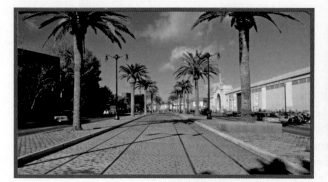

6.29 Narrow-angle Z-axis

The narrow-angle (telephoto) lens shrinks the z-axis and compresses the distance between objects.

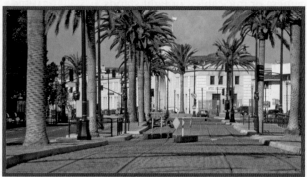

Lenses and Z-axis Length

The focal length of a lens has a great influence on our perception of z-axis length and the distance between objects placed along the z-axis.

Wide-angle position   When zoomed all the way out (wide-angle position), the z-axis appears to be *elongated,* and the objects seem to be *farther apart* than they really are. **SEE 6.28**

Narrow-angle position   When zoomed all the way in (narrow-angle, or telephoto, position), the z-axis seems to be *shorter* than it really is, and the distance between the objects placed along it seems reduced. The z-axis and its objects seem *compressed.* **SEE 6.29**

Lenses and Depth of Field

You have probably noticed when zoomed all the way in (with the lens in the telephoto position) that you have more trouble keeping an object traveling along the z-axis in focus than when zoomed all the way out to a wide-angle position. When zoomed in, the z-axis area that is in focus is considerably more shallow than when zoomed out. We call this area in which objects are in focus *depth of field*. **SEE 6.30**

6.30 Depth of Field

The area of the z-axis in which the objects appear in focus is called depth of field.

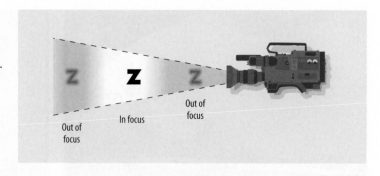

6.31 Shallow Depth of Field

Narrow-angle (telephoto) lenses have a shallow depth of field. When zoomed in, the depth of field is shallow.

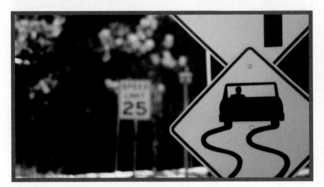

6.32 Great Depth of Field

Wide-angle lenses have a great depth of field. When zoomed out, the depth of field is great.

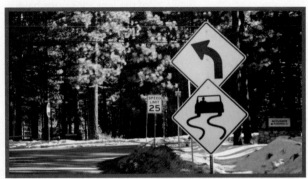

In the narrow-angle position, lenses have a shallow depth of field. This means that if you are focused on a foreground object, objects in the middleground and the background are out of focus. If you shift your focus to an object in the middleground, the foreground and background objects are out of focus. If you focus on the background, the middleground and foreground objects are out of focus. Note that with a shallow depth of field, an object can move only a short distance along the z-axis before it gets out of focus. **SEE 6.31** **ZVL3 CUE 9** ▶CAMERA→ Focusing→ depth of field | shallow

A wide-angle position creates a great depth of field: objects that are widely scattered along the z-axis are all in focus. For example, when you focus on the foreground object in a large depth of field, the middleground and background objects remain in focus as well, and an object can travel a great distance along the z-axis and still stay in focus. **SEE 6.32**

In practice this means that when zoomed out to a wide-angle position, you don't have to worry much about staying in focus. But when zoomed in to a narrow-angle position, you need to adjust the focus constantly whenever the camera or the object moves along the z-axis.

Depth of field is also influenced by object-to-camera distance and the size of the lens aperture. The closer the camera is to the object, the shallower the depth of field becomes; the farther away you are, the greater the depth of field. A large aperture reduces the depth of field; a small one increases it. (See chapter 4 for a discussion of lens apertures.) **ZVL3 CUE 10** ▶CAMERA→ Focusing→ depth of field | great

You will find that a great depth of field is desirable for most routine productions. Especially when running after a news story, you want to show as much of the event as clearly as possible without having to worry about keeping the picture in focus. This is why you should zoom out and keep the zoom lens in the wide-angle position. When you need a closer shot, you simply move the camera closer to the event. With the wide-angle lens position, the depth of field remains great enough to keep in focus, even when you or the object moves.

For a more deliberate production, there are many instances in which a shallow depth of field is preferred. By focusing on the target object while keeping everything else out of focus, you can emphasize the target without eliminating the environment.

> **KEY CONCEPT**
>
> Depth of field is dependent on the focal length of the lens, the distance from camera to object, and the aperture.

6.33 Shallow Depth of Field in Close-ups

Regardless of the focal length of the lens, close-ups have a shallower depth of field than long shots. The clue is the out-of-focus background.

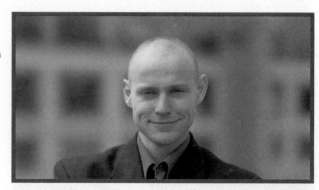

> **KEY CONCEPT**
>
> With the zoom lens in a narrow-angle position (zoomed all the way in), depth of field is shallow and keeping focus is difficult. With the zoom lens in a wide-angle position (zoomed all the way out), depth of field is great and keeping focus is relatively easy.

Another favorite technique is to shift emphasis from person to person by alternately focusing on one person, with the other person out of focus, and then switching. Realize, however, that this *racking focus* effect is so popular that it has become a cliché.

You will find that if you move the camera extremely close to the object, the depth of field will shrink even if the lens is zoomed out to the wide-angle position. Because the camera-to-object distance influences the depth of field as does the focal length of the lens, we can say that, in general, tight close-ups have a shallow depth of field. SEE 6.33 **ZVL3 CUE 11** ▶ CAMERA→ Focusing→ depth of field

> **KEY CONCEPT**
>
> A narrow-angle lens position compresses the z-axis and slows down z-axis motion. A wide-angle lens position stretches the z-axis and speeds up z-axis motion.

Lenses and Z-axis Speed

Because a narrow-angle lens position compresses the z-axis, the movement of objects along the z-axis is equally compressed. When the lens is zoomed all the way in, cars seem to be much more crowded and moving more slowly than they actually are. With the lens zoomed all the way out, they seem to be farther apart and moving much faster than they actually are. By simply putting the zoom lens in a narrow-angle or wide-angle position, you can manipulate the viewer's perception of the distance between objects and how fast they move along the z-axis. **ZVL3 CUE 12** ▶ CAMERA→ Picture depth→ lens choice | perspective and distortion **ZVL3 CUE 13** ▶ CAMERA→ Screen motion→ z-axis

CONTROLLING CAMERA AND OBJECT MOTION

Here we cover a few of the main aesthetic principles of camera and object motion. These include the most obvious do's and don'ts of moving the camera, zooming, and blocking object movement. (Additional information about controlling camera and object motion is presented in subsequent chapters.)

Controlling Camera Movement and Zooms

If there is a single indication of an inexperienced camera operator, it is excessive camera movement and zooms. The wildly roaming camera reminds us more of a firefighter's hose than photographic artistry, and the fast out-of-focus zooms produce more eyestrain than dramatic impact.

Moving camera   For some reason most beginners think that it is the camera that has to do the moving rather than the object in front of it, especially when there is not much object motion. If nothing moves, so be it. Aesthetic energy does not come from unmotivated camera movement but from the event itself, regardless of whether it is in motion. If there are any hard-and-fast aesthetic rules in camera operation, this is one of them: *always try to keep the camera as steady as possible and have the people and objects in front of the camera do the moving.* The problem with an incessantly moving camera is that it draws too much attention to itself. It is, after all, the *event* you want to show, not your virtuosity of zooming and camera handling.

For variety and to provide viewers with different points of view, you can shift camera angles or change the camera-to-object distance. Even if there is absolutely no movement in the event, different angles and fields of view will provide enough change to give viewers more information about the event and hold their interest. To keep camera movement to a minimum, use a tripod or other camera mount whenever possible, even if the camera is small.

▶ **KEY CONCEPT**
Whenever possible, keep the camera still and let the event do the moving.

Fast zooms   Fast, unmotivated zooms are as annoying as the needlessly roving camera. The major problem is that the zoom—even more than camera motion—is a highly visible technique that easily draws attention to itself. One of the worst things you can do is follow a fast zoom-in or zoom-out with an equally fast zoom in the opposite direction. Rest on the target object for a while before switching to another angle and point of view. Constant zooming in and out makes viewers feel cheated: you bring the event to them through zooming in only to take it away again by immediately zooming out. In the worst case, it may make viewers slightly nauseated. Unless you are planning a highly dramatic effect, a zoom should remain largely unnoticed by the viewer. If you must zoom, do it slowly.

In general, zooming in to a close-up increases tension; zooming out releases it. You will find that it is easier to start with a close-up view of an object and then zoom out than the other way around. When zooming out from a close-up, it is also easier to stay in focus than when zooming in, especially if you do not have time to calibrate (preset) the zoom lens (see chapter 5). Even with auto-focus, fast zooms cause focus problems because the auto-focus mechanism may not be able to keep up with constantly changing picture requirements. Consequently, the picture will pop in and out of focus during the zoom.

▶ **KEY CONCEPT**
Avoid fast and constant zooming in and out.

Zoom versus dolly   There is an important aesthetic difference between a zoom and a dolly. When you *zoom* in or out, the event seems to move toward or away from the viewer; when you *dolly* in or out, the viewer seems to move toward or away from the event.

If, for example, you want to show that the ringing telephone bears an important message, you zoom in on the phone rather than dolly in. The fast zoom virtually catapults the phone toward the screen and the viewer. But when you want to have the viewer identify with a student who is late for class, you dolly the camera toward the only empty chair rather than zoom in on it. The dolly will accompany the student—and the viewer—to the empty chair. A zoom would bring the chair to the student (and the viewer), and that rarely happens, even in a friendly classroom atmosphere. The reason for this aesthetic difference is that the camera remains stationary during the zoom, whereas during a dolly it actually moves into the scene, usually by means of a mobile camera mount. **ZVL3 CUE 14** CAMERA→ Camera moves→ dolly | zoom

▶ **KEY CONCEPT**
A zoom-in brings the object to the viewer; a dolly-in takes the viewer to the object.

6.34 Z-axis Blocking

Blocking along the z-axis suits the small video screen.

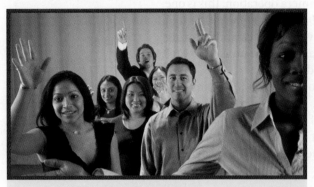

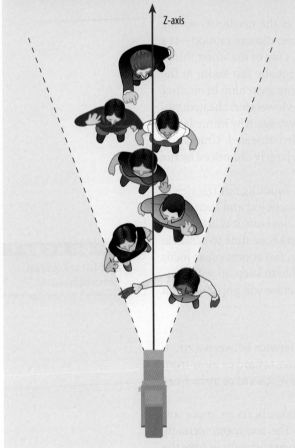

Controlling Object Motion

Despite all the theory on providing leadroom for an object moving laterally from one screen edge to the other, it is hard to keep it properly framed on the traditional 4 × 3 STV screen. Sometimes even experienced camera operators have trouble following an object that moves laterally in a tight shot. Just try following somebody moving sideways fairly close to the camera—you will be glad just to keep the person in the viewfinder! Framing lateral motion—that is, motion along the *x-axis*—is somewhat easier with a wide-angle lens position or when shooting for the 16 × 9 aspect ratio. In any case, when the subject moves in a straight line along the z-axis—toward or away from the camera—you will have much less trouble keeping the person in the shot and properly framed, even if he or she walks briskly. Blocking people along the z-axis rather than the x-axis not only is easier on the camera operator but also produces shots with greater impact.

Z-axis blocking refers to placing people behind rather than next to one another. **SEE 6.34** This arrangement makes it relatively easy to keep several people in a single shot and to capture their movements without excess camera motion. With the lens in the wide-angle position, z-axis movement can look dramatic and spectacular. Also, as you have just learned, the wide-angle lens provides a large enough depth of field so that you need do little, if any, focusing.

Even when you have no control over the event and cannot influence the blocking, as is the case in most electronic news gathering, you can still conform the object motion to the aesthetic requirements of the small screen and the stable camera: simply position the camera in such a way that most of the object movement occurs along the z-axis. For example, if you cover a parade, don't stand on the sidewalk and try to capture the various bands and floats as they move past you; instead, step onto the street and shoot against the oncoming parade traffic. With a zoom lens in the wide-angle position, you will have little trouble covering the event in long shots and close-ups while staying in focus. **ZVL3 CUE 15** CAMERA→ Picture depth→ z-axis

Framing effective shots is a basic requirement for competent camera work, regardless of whether you work with a small analog camcorder or an HDTV studio camera.

MAIN POINTS

▶ **Aspect Ratio**

The standard television (STV) aspect ratio is 4 × 3. The high-definition television (HDTV) aspect ratio is 16 × 9.

▶ **Field of View**

The field of view is usually expressed in five shots, ranging from extreme long shot (ELS) to extreme close-up (ECU). Other shot designations refer to how much of a person we see (such as bust shot or knee shot) or how many people we see (two-shot or three-shot). In an over-the-shoulder shot (O/S), we see the shoulder and the back of the head of the camera-near person while looking at the camera-far person. A cross-shot (X/S) is closer, with the camera-near person out of the shot.

▶ **Close-up Medium**

Video is a close-up medium. Select those event details that tell the real story with clarity and impact.

▶ **Vectors**

Vectors are directional screen forces of various strengths that influence composition and the blocking of talent and cameras. There are graphic vectors, which suggest a direction through lines or objects that form a line; index vectors, which point unquestionably in a specific direction; and motion vectors, which show the actual event or its screen image in motion.

▶ **Screen Forces**

The most stable picture area is screen-center. Headroom neutralizes the pull of the upper screen edge. Noseroom and leadroom neutralize the index and motion vector forces, respectively, and the pull of the frame.

▶ **Psychological Closure**

Through psychological closure we are able to perceive a complete figure even if it is shown only partially in a close-up. Close-ups that show only part of the object must provide sufficient visual cues for closure in off-screen space.

▶ **Picture Depth**

The depth dimension depends on defining the z-axis into foreground, middleground, and background. Wide-angle zoom positions (zoomed out) make the z-axis look longer; objects seem farther apart, and their z-axis movement appears faster than it actually is. Narrow-angle positions (zoomed in) make the z-axis look shorter; objects seem more compressed, and their z-axis movement appears slower. Wide-angle lens positions show a great depth of field; narrow-angle lens positions show a shallow one.

▶ **Motion**

Whenever possible, keep the camera still and let the event do the moving. A zoom-in brings the object to the viewer; a dolly-in takes the viewer to the object. Z-axis movement is well suited to the relatively small TV screen.

ZETTL'S   VIDEOLAB   3.0

For your reference, or to track your work, the Zettl's VideoLab 3.0 program cues in this chapter are listed here with their corresponding page numbers.

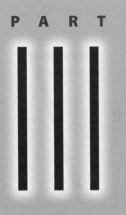

Image Creation: Sound, Light, Graphics, and Effects

When you review your latest video recordings a little more critically, you can see that your composition has improved considerably. You left proper headroom and leadroom, and your horizons are level. But now you are discovering other problems that went unnoticed before. What is most annoying are the hollow sounds you got when you interviewed people in their living room and the crackling of wind and traffic noise when the interview took place on a street corner. Apparently, you forgot to listen to the environment while composing your impressive shots. Despite the good composition, some of your video looks grossly overexposed; other shots hide all the detail in dense shadows. Some of the indoor shots have a strange green tint, and the white wedding gown of your friend's bride looks light blue in your outdoor shot. The following three chapters on image creation will introduce you to the basic audio and lighting techniques that will help you avoid such problems—and also give you some pointers on effective graphics and visual effects.

KEY TERMS

ATR Stands for audiotape recorder.

cardioid Heart-shaped pickup pattern of a unidirectional microphone.

condenser microphone High-quality, sensitive microphone for critical sound pickup.

DAT Stands for *digital audiotape.*

digital versatile disc (DVD) The standard DVD can store 4.7 gigabytes of video and/or audio information.

dynamic microphone A relatively rugged microphone. Good for outdoor use.

fader A volume control that works by sliding a button horizontally along a specific scale. Identical in function to a pot. Also called *slide fader.*

hypercardioid A very narrow pickup pattern with a long reach. The mic can also hear sounds coming directly from the back.

jack A socket or receptacle for a connector.

lavaliere A small microphone that is clipped to clothing. Also called *lav.*

mini disc (MD) A small optical disc that can store one hour of CD-quality audio.

mini plug Connector used for some consumer audio equipment.

omnidirectional Pickup pattern with which the microphone can hear equally well from all directions.

pickup pattern The territory around the microphone within which the mic can hear well.

polar pattern The two-dimensional representation of the microphone pickup pattern.

pop filer A wire-mesh screen attached to the front of a mic that reduces breath pops and sudden air blasts.

RCA phono plug Connector for video and audio equipment.

ribbon microphone High-quality, highly sensitive microphone for critical sound pickup in the studio, usually for recording string instruments.

sweetening The postproduction manipulation of recorded sound.

unidirectional Pickup pattern with which the microphone can hear best from the front.

volume-unit (VU) meter Measures volume units, the relative loudness of amplified sound.

windscreen Acoustic foam rubber that is put over the entire microphone to cut down wind noise.

XLR connector Professional three-wire connector for audio cables.

Audio and Sound Control

You have probably heard over and over again that television is primarily a visual medium. You have also no doubt heard that the worst sin you can commit in video production is showing "talking heads"—a criticism that is a total misconception. Video programs rely on the sound portion much more than films do. The audio portion not only conveys information but adds aesthetic energy and structure to the video sequences. You will find that there is nothing wrong with talking heads so long as they are well spoken and have something worthwhile to say.

In fact, much of the information in video programs is conveyed by somebody talking. You can do a simple experiment to prove this point: turn off the video portion of the program and try to follow what is going on; then turn on the video again but turn off the audio. You will probably have little trouble following the story by only hearing the sound track, but in most cases you will have difficulty knowing what is going on by only seeing the pictures. Even if you can follow the story by watching the pictures, the lack of sound leaves the message strangely incomplete.

Most amateur video is characterized not just by the madly moving camera and the fast zooms but also by the bad audio. Even professional video productions tend to suffer more from poor sound than bad pictures. Why? At first glance the production of sound seems much easier to achieve than the corresponding video. When working a camcorder, you are probably concentrating so hard on getting good pictures that you don't pay much attention to the sounds that surround you. You probably assume that the built-in microphone will do the job of picking up the necessary audio—and sometimes this may be sufficient. Most of the time, however, sticking a microphone into a scene at the last minute is not the way to go. Unless you do a routine show, you need to consider the audio requirements as an essential part of the production process. The better the original audio pickup, the more time you will save in postproduction. **ZVL3 CUE 1** ▶AUDIO→ Audio introduction

115

This chapter examines the various tools and techniques of producing good audio for video.

▶ **SOUND PICKUP PRINCIPLE**
   How microphones change sound waves into sound signals

▶ **MICROPHONES**
   How well they hear, how they are made, and how they are used

▶ **SOUND CONTROL**
   Working the audio mixer and the audio console

▶ **SOUND RECORDING**
   Analog and digital recording equipment and other audio-recording devices

▶ **SYNTHESIZED SOUND**
   Computer-generated sounds

▶ **SOUND AESTHETICS**
   Context, figure/ground, sound perspective, continuity, and energy

SOUND PICKUP PRINCIPLE

Like the translation process in video, in which the lens image of the object is converted into the video signal, in audio the sounds we actually hear are *transduced* (transformed) into electric energy—the audio signal. This signal is made audible again through the loudspeaker. The basic sound pickup tool is the microphone, or *mic* (pronounced "mike").

You can also create sounds synthetically, by electronically generating and recording certain frequencies, a process similar to creating computer-generated video images. We focus first on microphone-generated sounds, then turn briefly to synthesized sounds.

> ▶**KEY CONCEPT**
>
> Microphones transduce sound waves into electric energy—the audio signal.

MICROPHONES

Although all microphones fulfill the same basic function of transducing sounds into audio signals, they do so in different ways and for different purposes. Good audio requires that you know how to choose the right mic for a specific sound pickup—not an easy task when faced with the myriad mics available. Despite all the brand names and numbers, you can make sense out of the different microphones by classifying them by how well they hear, how they are made, and how they are generally used.

How Well Mics Hear: Sound Pickup

Not all microphones hear sounds in the same way. Some are built to hear sounds from all directions equally well; others favor sounds that come from a specific direction. The directional characteristic—the zone within which a microphone can hear well—is specified by its ***pickup pattern***. Its two-dimensional representation is called the ***polar pattern***.

In general, you will find that most microphones used in video production are omnidirectional or unidirectional. The ***omnidirectional*** mic hears equally well from all directions. Visualize the omnidirectional mic at the center of a sphere. The sphere itself represents the pickup pattern. **SEE 7.1** The ***unidirectional*** mic is designed to hear especially well from one direction—the front. Because the pickup pattern of a unidirectional mic is roughly heart-shaped, it is also called ***cardioid***. **SEE 7.2**

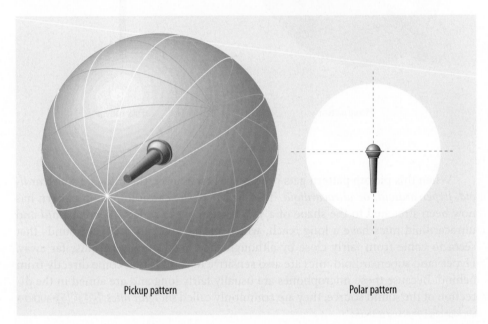

Pickup pattern   Polar pattern

7.1 Omnidirectional Microphone Patterns

The omnidirectional microphone hears equally well from all directions.

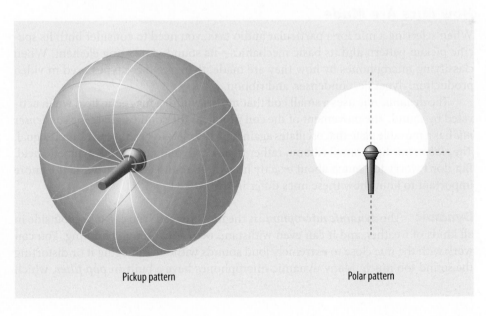

Pickup pattern   Polar pattern

7.2 Cardioid Microphone Patterns

The unidirectional microphone favors sounds that are in front of it. Its pickup pattern is heart-shaped, hence the term *cardioid*.

7.3 Hypercardioid Microphone Patterns

The hypercardioid pickup pattern is narrower than the cardioid and has a longer reach. Hypercardioid mics can also hear sounds coming from behind the mic.

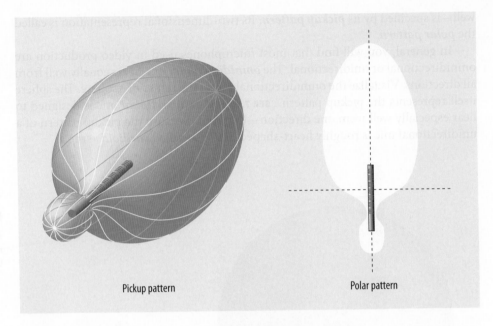

Pickup pattern   Polar pattern

When this pickup pattern gets progressively narrower, the mics are *supercardioid, hypercardioid,* or *ultracardioid.* The "heart" of the cardioid pickup pattern has now been stretched to the shape of a watermelon. **SEE 7.3** The **hypercardioid** and ultracardioid mics have a long reach, which means you can produce sounds that seem to come from fairly close by although they may actually be quite far away. Hyper- and supercardioid mics are also sensitive to sounds that come directly from behind. Because these microphones are usually fairly long and are aimed in the direction of the sound source, they are commonly called *shotgun mics.* **ZVL3 CUE 2** AUDIO→
Microphones→ pickup patterns

> **▶ KEY CONCEPT**
>
> The pickup pattern indicates the zone in which a microphone can hear well—its directionality.

How Mics Are Made

When selecting a mic for a particular audio task, you need to consider both its specific pickup pattern and its basic mechanics—its sound-generating element. When classifying microphones by how they are made, there are three types used in video production: dynamic, condenser, and ribbon.

The *dynamic mic* uses a small coil that moves within a magnetic field when activated by sound. The movement of the coil produces the sound signal. The *condenser mic* has a movable plate that oscillates against a fixed plate to produce the sound signal. The *ribbon mic* has a small ribbon, rather than a coil, that moves in a magnetic field. But don't worry too much about exactly how these sound elements work; it is more important to know how these mics differ in their use.

Dynamic   The **dynamic microphone** is the most rugged. You can take it outside in all kinds of weather, and it can even withstand occasional rough handling. You can work with the mic close to extremely loud sounds without damaging it or distorting the sound too much. Many dynamic microphones have a built-in **pop filter**, which eliminates the breath pops that occur when someone speaks into the mic at very close range. **SEE 7.4** `ZVL3 CUE 3`

AUDIO→ Microphones→ transducer→ dynamic mic

Condenser   These microphones are much more sensitive to physical shock and temperature than are dynamic mics, but they produce higher-quality sounds. *Condenser microphones* are generally used for critical sound pickup indoors, but they are also used in the field. They are especially prominent in music recording. Unlike dynamic mics, condenser microphones need a power supply to activate the sound-generating device inside the mic. Some have a battery in the microphone housing. **SEE 7.5** Others get their power supply through the cable from the audio console (usually called *phantom power*). If you use a battery, see to it that it is inserted properly (with the + and – poles as indicated in the housing) and that the battery is not run-down. Always have a spare battery handy when using a condenser mic. `ZVL3 CUE 4` AUDIO→ Microphones→ transducer→ condenser mic

When using a condenser shotgun mic (or any shotgun mic) outdoors, you need to protect the entire microphone from wind noise by covering it with a *windscreen*. **SEE 7.6** Windscreens are made of acoustic foam rubber or other synthetic material, which lets normal sound frequencies enter the mic but keeps most of the lower wind rumbles out. For ENG/EFP microphones that are used primarily outdoors, you may want to add a *windsock*, also called *wind jammer*—a fuzzy cloth resembling a mop that can be pulled over the windscreen. **SEE 7.7**

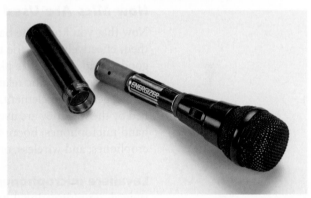

7.4 Dynamic Microphone with Pop Filter

Dynamic microphones are the most rugged. They can withstand rough handling and extreme temperatures. The built-in pop filter reduces breath pops.

7.5 Battery Power Supply for Condenser Mic

Most condenser mics use a battery to charge the condenser plates. When fed to the microphone from the audio console, the power is called phantom power.

7.6 Windscreen on Shotgun Microphone

The windscreen, made of porous material, protects the microphone from excessive wind noise.

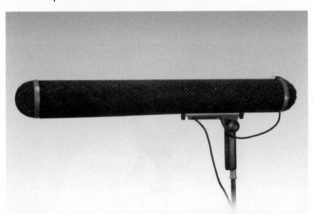

7.7 Windsock Pulled over Windscreen

The windsock is used on top of the windscreen to further reduce wind noise.

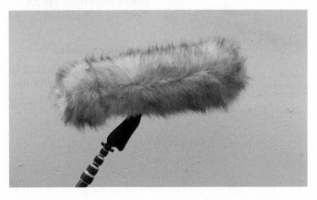

7.8 Ribbon Microphone for High-quality Sound Pickup

Ribbon microphones are very sensitive and are used mainly to capture the complex sound waves of string instruments in studio recordings.

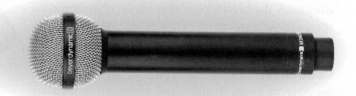

Ribbon   You may still find *ribbon microphones* in some audio-recording studios or for some critical music pickup for television. These highly sensitive microphones are normally used for the recording of string instruments. **SEE 7.8** For normal video work, however, ribbon mics are just too sensitive. A loud sound burst close to the mic can cause permanent damage. The star of a television western learned an impressive lesson about the ribbon mic's sensitivity quite accidentally during a live promo for his series. When he punctuated his quick-draw skills by firing a blank close to the mic, he blew the delicate ribbon right out the microphone. Only a lip reader could follow his subsequent pitch. **ZVL3 CUE 5** AUDIO→ Microphones→ transducer→ ribbon mic

How Mics Are Used

Now that you know the basic types of microphones, you need to learn how to use them effectively. Even the most sophisticated and expensive mic will not guarantee good sound unless it is placed in an optimal pickup position. In fact, the proper positioning of the mic relative to the sound source is often more important than its sound-generating element. In video production, microphones are therefore identified by the way they are used rather than how they are made: lavaliere microphones; hand microphones; boom microphones; desk and stand microphones; headset microphones; and wireless, or radio, microphones.

Lavaliere microphones   The *lavaliere* mic, or *lav* for short, is a very small, rugged, omnidirectional microphone (dynamic or condenser) that is used principally for voice pickup. The quality of even the smallest lav, which is about the size of a fingernail, is amazingly good. The combination of small size, ruggedness, and high quality has made the lavaliere indispensable in video production. It is usually clipped to clothing, such as the lapel of a jacket or the front of a shirt, 6 to 8 inches below the chin. **SEE 7.9**

7.9 Lavaliere Microphone

The small lavaliere microphone is usually clipped to the clothing of the performer. It is normally used for voice pickup.

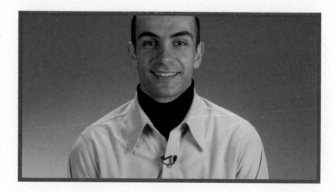

Although it is primarily intended for voice pickup, you can also use the lavaliere for music. Sound technicians have used the lav successfully on violins and string basses. Don't be overly influenced by the normal use of such mics: try them out in a variety of ways and listen to the sound they deliver. If it sounds good to you, you've got the right mic.

The obvious advantage of the lavaliere is that the talent has both hands free when he or she wears it, but there are numerous other advantages to using a lavaliere mic, as well:

▶ Because the distance from mic to sound source does not change once the mic is properly attached, you do not have to *ride gain* (adjust the volume) once you adjust the volume at the beginning of the shoot.

▶ Unlike lighting for the boom mic, which must be done in such a way that the boom shadows are hidden from camera view, the lavaliere needs no special lighting considerations.

▶ Although the talent's action radius is somewhat limited by the microphone cable, the lavaliere lets him or her move more quickly than with a boom mic or even a hand mic. For greater mobility you can plug the talent's lavaliere into a body-pack transmitter and use it as a wireless or radio mic.

Unfortunately, there are also some disadvantages to using a lavaliere mic:

▶ If the environment is very noisy, you cannot move the mic closer to the talent's mouth. Consequently, the surrounding (ambient) noise is easily picked up.

▶ You need a separate mic for each sound source. In a two-person interview, for example, you need separate lavalieres for the host and the guest. In a five-person panel show, you obviously need five mics.

▶ Because it is attached to clothing, the lavaliere may pick up rubbing noises, especially if the talent moves around a great deal. You may also get occasional popping noises from static electricity.

▶ If the mic must be concealed under clothing, the sound often takes on a muffled character and the danger of rubbing noises is greatly increased.

▶ One of the advantages we listed can also be a disadvantage: because the distance from the mic to the mouth does not change, the sounds do not seem to come from a closer distance on a close-up or from farther away on a long shot. Therefore you cannot achieve a desirable *sound perspective*. (You will read more about sound perspective later in this chapter.)

Here are some points to consider when using a lavaliere microphone:

▶ Once the microphone is attached to the mic cable but not yet to the talent, watch that you do not pull the mic off a table or chair and drop it on the floor. Although the lavaliere is fairly rugged, it does not tolerate mistreatment. If you accidentally drop the mic during the setup or strike (clearing of the production space), test it immediately to check that it still functions properly. Ask the talent to avoid hitting it with his or her hand or some object that might be demonstrated on-camera.

▶ Be sure to put the mic on. As obvious as this sounds, on the opening cue many a performer has been found sitting on the mic rather than wearing it.

▶ To put on the microphone, bring it up underneath the talent's shirt, blouse, or jacket and attach it securely on the outside. Do not put the mic next to jewelry or buttons. If you have to conceal the mic, don't bury it under layers of clothing; try to keep the top of the mic as exposed as possible. Tuck the cable into the talent's belt or clothing so that it cannot pull the mic sideways or, worse, completely off. To further avoid pops and rumbles, put a small loop in the cable just below the mic clip, or try putting a loose knot in the mic cable where it leaves the mic. Wedging a small piece of foam rubber between mic and clothing will further reduce rubbing noises.

▶ When outdoors, attach the little windscreen that slips over the top of the mic.

▶ When using a wireless lav, tell the talent to switch the body-pack transmitter to the *off* position during each break. This keeps the battery from running down prematurely and also prevents the transmission of sounds that might be embarrassing to the talent.

▶KEY CONCEPT

Treat all microphones gently, even when turned off.

▶ After the show watch that the talent does not get up and walk off the set without first removing the microphone. **ZVL3 CUE 6** ▶AUDIO→ Microphones→ mic types→ lav mic

Hand microphones   As the name implies, *hand microphones* are handled by the talent. You select a hand mic for situations in which the talent needs to exercise some control over the sound pickup.

A reporter can move a hand mic closer to his or her mouth when working in noisy surroundings, thereby eliminating much distracting ambience; the reporter can also point it toward the person he or she is interviewing. Because the talent can point the microphone toward whoever is doing the talking, you need only a single microphone for an interview with one or even several guests. Performers who do audience participation shows like the hand mic because it allows them to approach people and talk to them spontaneously without any elaborate multiple-microphone setup.

A singer can control the intimacy of the sound (its presence) by holding the unidirectional hand mic very close to his or her mouth during an especially tender passage and pulling it farther away when the song gets louder and more external. Experienced singers use the hand mic as an important visual element; they work the mic during a song by switching it from one hand to the other to signal—visually—a transition or change of pace or simply to supply additional visual interest. **SEE 7.10**

When the hand mic is used outdoors for numerous production tasks and under a great variety of weather conditions, you need a rugged mic that tolerates rough handling and extreme conditions. Dynamic hand mics with built-in pop filters are popular for such productions. Singers, on the other hand, demand much more sound quality than a field reporter and prefer high-quality condenser hand mics.

The control of the mic by the talent can also be a disadvantage. Inexperienced talent often block their own and their guests' faces; this no-no becomes especially apparent when the mic has a large, colored pop filter attached to it. Also, in the excitement of the interview, an inexperienced reporter may aim the microphone toward the guest when asking the question and toward himself or herself when listening to the answer. As humorous as this unintentional comedy routine may seem to the bystander or viewer, it is not funny to the production people who see their efforts undermined by this maneuver.

Other disadvantages of using a hand mic are that the talent's hands are not free to do other things, such as demonstrate a product. And, unless it is a wireless hand mic, pulling the cable while working a hand mic is not always easy to do.

These hints may help you work with a hand microphone:

▶ During rehearsal, check the action radius of the mic cable. Also see that the cable has free travel and will not catch on furniture or scenery. Checking the reach of the cable is especially important when the mic is connected to a camcorder.

▶ Test the microphone before the video recording or live transmission. Say a few of the opening lines so that the audio engineer or camcorder operator can adjust the volume of the audio signal. When there are several mics in the immediate vicinity and you need to find out which one is turned on, do not blow or whistle into it—or, worse, whack it; rather, lightly scratch the pop filter. This scratching noise will enable the audio technician to identify your microphone and separate it from the others.

▶ When using a hand mic in the field under normal conditions (the environment is not excessively loud, and there is little or no wind), hold the microphone at chest level and speak *across* rather than into it. **SEE 7.11** In noisy and windy conditions, hold the mic closer to your mouth. **SEE 7.12**

▶ When using a directional hand microphone, hold it close to your mouth and speak or sing directly into it, as shown in figure 7.10.

▶ When using a hand mic to interview a child, do not remain standing; squat down so that you are at the child's level. This way you establish more-personal contact with the child, and the camera can get a good two-shot. **SEE 7.13**

▶ If the mic cable gets tangled during a take, do not panic and yank on it. Stop where you are and

7.10 Use of Directional Microphone by Singer

To emphasize the richness of her voice, the singer holds the directional hand mic close to her mouth.

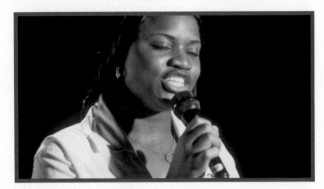

7.11 Normal Position of Hand Microphone

In a fairly quiet environment, the hand mic should be held at chest height. The performer speaks across the mic rather than into it.

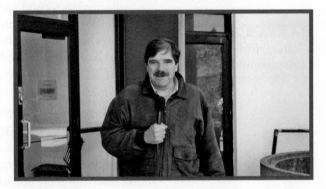

7.12 Position of Hand Microphone in Noisy Surroundings

In environments with a lot of ambient noise, the performer holds the mic closer to the mouth and speaks into the mic rather than across it.

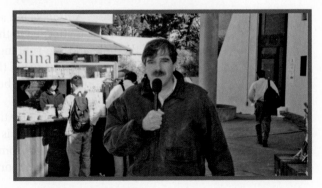

7.13 Interviewing a Child

When interviewing a child, squat down and hold the mic toward the child. The child is now more aware of you than the mic, and the camera operator can include both faces in the shot.

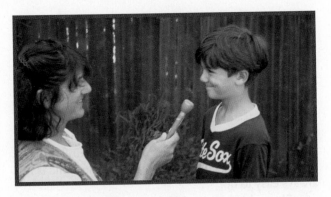

continue your performance while trying to get the attention of the floor manager or somebody else who can untangle it for you.

▶ If you need to use both hands while holding a hand mic, tuck it temporarily under your arm so that it can still pick up your voice.

▶ When the hand mic is connected directly to a camcorder, the camera operator should also turn on the camera mic (built-in or attached). The camera mic will supply a second audio track with the ambient sounds without interfering with the hand mic, which is supplying the primary audio. In fact, you should always turn on the camera mic, even if you don't intend to use the ambience. Most likely, these sounds will come in handy during postproduction editing. **ZVL3 CUE 7** AUDIO→ Microphones→ mic types→ camera mic

Boom microphones   Whenever the microphone is to be kept out of the picture, it is usually suspended by a *fishpole* or a *big boom*. Whatever microphone is suspended from such a device is called a *boom mic*, regardless of its pickup pattern or its sound-generating element. But because the boom mic is usually farther away from its sound source than a lavaliere or hand mic, hypercardioid or supercardioid shotgun mics are used. As you recall, such highly directional microphones can pick up sounds over a fairly great distance and make them seem to come from close by. You can aim the mic toward the principal sound source while eliminating or greatly reducing all other sounds that lie outside its narrow pickup pattern. Note, however, that it is equally efficient at picking up extraneous noise that lies in its pickup path.

Fishpole   A *fishpole* is a sturdy, lightweight metal pole that can be extended. The shotgun mic is attached to the pole with a *shock mount*, which absorbs the vibrations of the pole and the rubbing noises of the mic cable. Always test the microphone before each take to see if the shock mount is transferring the handling noise or pole vibrations. Even the best shotgun mic is rendered useless by a noisy pole or shock mount.

If a scene is shot fairly tightly (with tight medium shots and close-ups), you can use a short fishpole, which is much easier to handle than a long one. You can position it to pick up the sound from either above or below the source. If the sound pickup is from above, hold the boom in your outstretched arms and dip it into the scene as

7.14 Short Fishpole Used from Above

The short fishpole is normally held high and dipped into the scene as needed.

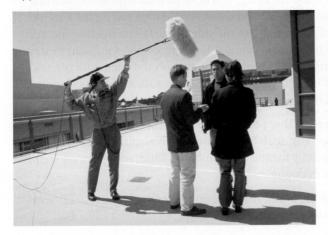

7.15 Short Fishpole Used from Below

The short fishpole can also be held low with the mic pointed up for good sound pickup.

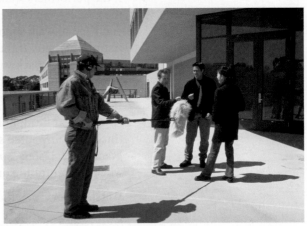

needed. **SEE 7.14** If the sound pickup is from below the source, turn the pole so that the mic is pointing up toward the person speaking. **SEE 7.15**

When the shots are wider and you need to be farther away from the scene, you must use a long fishpole. Because the long fishpole is heavier and more difficult to handle, you should anchor it in a belt and raise and lower it as you would an actual fishing pole. The long fishpole is usually held above the sound source. **SEE 7.16**

Here are some additional hints for operating a shotgun mic mounted on a fishpole:

▶ With a fishpole it is especially important that you check the reach of the mic cable. Because you must concentrate on the position of the mic during the pickup, you will not be able to monitor the cable.

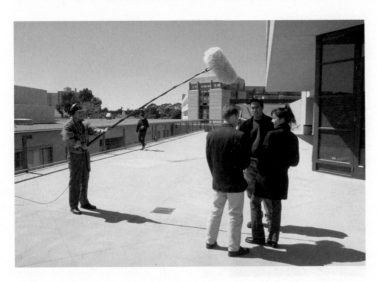

7.16 Long Fishpole

The long fishpole can be anchored in a belt and raised and lowered much like an actual fishing pole. It is usually held above the sound source.

▶ Check that the cable is properly fastened to the pole and that it does not tug on the microphone.

▶ If the performers walk while speaking, you need to walk with them, holding the mic in front of them. If the camera shoots straight on (along the z-axis), you need to walk slightly ahead and to the side of the talent, holding the mic in front of them. If the blocking is lateral (along the x-axis), you need to stay in front, walking backward. While keeping your eyes on the talent and the mic, be careful not to bump into obstacles. Rehearse the walk a few times before the actual take. If possible, have a floor person guide you during the take.

▶ Always wear headphones so that you can hear what the mic is picking up (including unwanted sounds, such as the drone of an airplane during a Civil War scene). Listen especially for the low rumble of wind, which is easy to miss when concentrating on dialogue.

▶ Watch for shadows that the boom may cast on persons or objects in camera range. **ZVL3 CUE 8** AUDIO→ Microphones→ mic types→ boom mic

Handholding a shotgun mic is as simple as it is effective. You become the boom—and a very flexible one at that. The advantage of holding the shotgun mic is that you can walk up to the scene as close as the camera allows, aiming the mic quickly and easily in various directions. **SEE 7.17**

Some audio people insist on covering the handheld shotgun with a windsock even when shooting indoors, but it is a must when shooting outdoors. As you have learned, the windsock reduces and often eliminates wind noise. Hold the microphone only by its shock mount—never directly. This minimizes handling noise and also prevents covering up the microphone *ports*—the openings in the mic barrel that make the mic directional.

Big boom   When used for an elaborate studio production, such as the video recording of a soap opera, shotgun mics are suspended from a large boom, called a *studio boom* or *perambulator boom.* A boom operator, who stands on the boom platform,

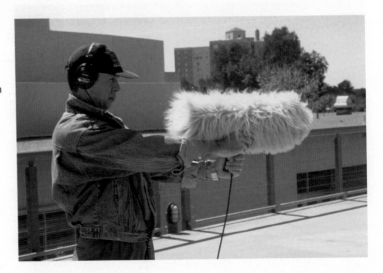

7.17 Handheld Shotgun Microphone

Hold the shotgun mic only by its shock mount. When it's used outdoors, the windscreen and windsock are a must.

can extend or retract the boom, tilt it up and down, pan it sideways, rotate the mic toward the sound source, and even have the whole boom assembly moved. This is all to have the microphone as close to the sound source as possible while keeping it out of the camera's view.

A studio boom is quite large and takes up a lot of operating space, and you will discover that operating a boom is at least as difficult as running a camera.

Desk and stand microphones   *Desk microphones* are hand mics mounted on a tabletop stand. You use them for panel shows, public hearings, speeches, and news conferences. Because the people using them are usually more concerned with what they are saying than with the quality of the audio, they frequently (albeit unintentionally) bang on the table or kick it while moving in their chairs, and sometimes even turn away from the microphone while speaking. Considering all these hazards, which microphones would you suggest for a desk mic? If you recommend an omnidirectional dynamic mic, you are right. This type of microphone is best suited to abuse. If you need more-precise sound separation, use a unidirectional dynamic mic.

When placing the microphones, you can use a single mic for each performer or to serve two people simultaneously. Because microphones can cancel each other's frequencies when positioned too close together—known as *multiple-microphone interference*—you should place the individual mics at least three times as far apart as any mic is from its user. **SEE 7.18**

Despite your careful placement of the multiple desk mics, inexperienced—and even experienced—users are sometimes compelled to grab the mic and pull it toward them as soon as they are seated. To save your nerves and optimize sound pickup, simply tape the mic stands to the table.

Stand mics are hand microphones that are clipped to a sturdy microphone floor stand. They are used for singers, speakers, musical instruments, and any other sound source that has a fixed position. The quality of mics used on stands ranges from rugged

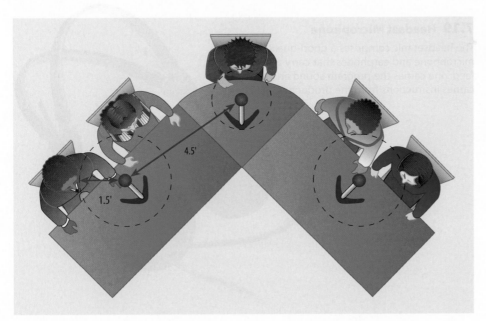

4.5'

1.5'

7.18 Setup for Multiple Desk Microphones

To avoid multiple-microphone interference when using several desk mics for a panel show, place them at least three times as far apart as any mic is from its user.

dynamic mics for news conferences and speeches to high-quality mics for singers and instrumental pickups.

For some performers, such as rock singers, the microphone stand is an important prop. They tilt it back and forth, hold themselves up by it, and even swing it through the air like a sword (not recommended, by the way, especially if the microphone is still attached).

Headset microphones   Sportscasters and other performers who are announcing an event often use a *headset microphone*. **SEE 7.19** This type of mic combines an earphone headset with a good-quality microphone. The earphones can carry a split audio feed, which means that the talent can hear the program sound (including his or her own voice) in one ear and instructions from various production people in the other.

Wireless, or radio, microphones   *Wireless microphones* are also called *radio mics* because they broadcast the audio signal from a microphone transmitter to a receiver, which in turn is connected to the mixer or audio console.

The most popular wireless microphones are hand mics used by singers. These high-quality mics have a transmitter and an antenna built into their housing. The performer is totally unrestricted and can move about unimpeded by a mic cable. The receiver is connected by cable to the audio console for sound control and mixing. Because each wireless mic has its own frequency, you can use several simultaneously without signal interference.

Another popular radio mic is the wireless lavaliere, which is often used in news and interviews, in electronic field production, and occasionally in sports. If, for example, you are asked to pick up the breathing of a bicyclist during a race or the clatter of the skis during a downhill run, a wireless lav is the obvious choice. Wireless lavs are sometimes used for dramatic studio productions instead of boom mics.

7.19 Headset Microphone

The headset mic comprises a good-quality microphone and earphones that carry a split audio feed: one carries the program sound and the other carries instructions from the production team.

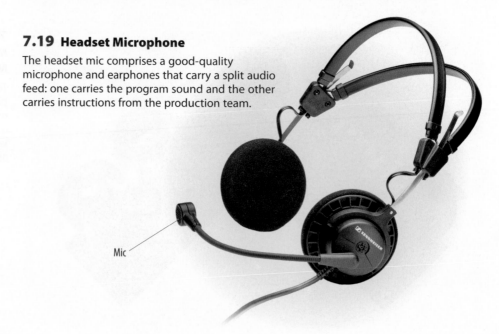

Mic

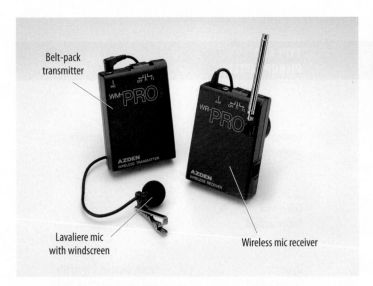

7.20 Wireless Lavaliere Microphone and Receiver

Wireless lavalieres are connected to a small transmitter worn by the talent. The receiver picks up the signal and sends it by cable to the audio console.

Belt-pack transmitter

Lavaliere mic with windscreen

Wireless mic receiver

The wireless lavaliere is plugged into a small transmitter that is worn by the talent. You simply put the transmitter into the performer's pocket or tape it to the body and string the short antenna wire along the pants, skirt, or shirt sleeve or around the waist. The receiver is similar to that used with wireless hand mics. **SEE 7.20**

Unfortunately, using wireless mics is not without drawbacks. The signal pickup depends on where the talent is relative to the receiver. If the talent walks beyond the transmitter's range, the signal will first become intermittent and then be lost altogether. For example, if the talent moves behind a tall building, or near high-voltage lines or strong radio transmitters, the audio may become distorted or totally overpowered by the extraneous signals. Concrete walls, X-ray machines, and even the talent's perspiration can affect the transmission and reduce or distort the signal strength. Although wireless equipment has an assigned frequency that is purposely different from police and fire transmissions, you may occasionally pick up a police or fire call instead of the talent's comments. **ZVL3 CUE 9** AUDIO→ Microphones→ mic types→ wireless mic

> **►KEY CONCEPT**
> Wireless, or radio, microphones are subject to interference.

The table on the following page gives an overview of some of the most popular microphones. Realize, however, that new mics are developed all the time and that model numbers change accordingly. **SEE 7.21**

SOUND CONTROL

When using a small camcorder to record a friend's birthday party, you are probably unconcerned about the various steps of audio control. All you need to do is put a tape or a *flash memory device* in the camcorder and check that the built-in mic is turned on and in the AGC mode. *AGC* stands for *automatic gain control*—it automatically adjusts the volume of the various sounds to optimal levels, eliminating the need for manual volume control. But because the AGC cannot distinguish between desirable sounds and noise, it amplifies both indiscriminately.

7.21 **Table of Microphones**

MICROPHONE	TYPE AND PICKUP PATTERN	USE
Sennheiser MKH 70	Condenser Supercardioid	Studio boom, fishpole. Good for EFP and sports.
Sony ECM 672	Condenser Supercardioid	Fishpole. Excellent for indoors.
Azden SGM-1	Dynamic Supercardioid	Small shotgun. Especially well suited for small digital camcorders.
Electro-Voice 635A or RE50	Dynamic Omnidirectional	Rugged hand mics. Good for all-weather ENG.
Shure SM63L	Dynamic Omnidirectional	Fairly rugged. Excellent for ENG.
Electro-Voice RE16	Dynamic Supercardioid	All-purpose hand mic. Good outdoors (ENG/EFP).
Shure SM58	Dynamic Cardioid	Hand mic for singer. Crisp, lively sound.
Beyerdynamic M160	Ribbon Hypercardioid	Classic hand mic for singer. Warm sound.
Sony ECM 55 or ECM 77	Condenser Omnidirectional	Lavalieres. Good voice pickup. Good studio mics that mix well with boom mics.
Sony ECM-88	Condenser Omnidirectional	Very small lavaliere. Excellent quality. Low handling and wind noise.
Sennheiser ME 2	Condenser Omnidirectional	Very small lavaliere mic.

If the audio requirement is more demanding, such as controlling the volume during an outdoor interview or when somebody is playing a musical instrument, you need to switch from AGC to manual control.

Manual Volume Control

As mentioned previously, the better (and more expensive) camcorders have two XLR (balanced) microphone inputs and allow you to switch from AGC to manual volume control for both inputs by using the menu on the foldout screen. Try to do this switchover before you are in the field; the commands are often hidden in submenus and are not always easy to activate when you are in a hurry. Also, you will quickly learn that even the best foldout screens wash out in bright sunlight, making the menus hard to see. Once you've switched to manual volume control, you can set a level for each of the two mic inputs before you start recording. You can then monitor the input volume in the viewfinder display.

Try to use one channel (normally channel 1) for the external mic and the other (channel 2) for recording ambient sound with the camera mic. If there are more than two sound sources, you need to control and mix them before they can be recorded on one of the two audio tracks. The necessary equipment to do so consists of the audio mixer; the audio console; and the audio cables and the patch panel.

Audio Mixer

The *audio mixer* amplifies the weak signals that come from the microphones and/or other sound sources and lets you control the sound volume and mix (combine) two or more sounds. Actually, what you control and mix are not the sounds themselves but the signals, which are then translated back into actual sounds by the loud-speaker. **ZVL3 CUE 10** AUDIO→ Systems→ try it

A normal monophonic audio mixer has three or four inputs and one output of the manipulated signal. A stereo mixer has two outputs, one for the left channel and another for the right. There is a rotary *pot* (for *potentiometer*) for each input, also called a **fader** or *slide fader;* one *master pot* or fader (two for stereo mixers); and a monitor **jack** (outlet) for your earphones so you can hear the outgoing signal. A **VU meter,** which measures in *volume units* the relative amplitude (loudness) of the incoming sound signals, helps you visually monitor the volume of each incoming source and the final *line-out* signal that leaves the mixer. **SEE 7.22** **ZVL3 CUE 11** AUDIO→ Consoles and mixers→ parts

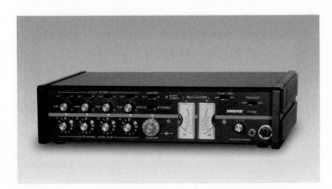

7.22 Audio Mixer

The audio mixer allows you to control the volume of a limited number of sound inputs and mix them into a single or stereo output signal.

Mic- and line-level inputs   All professional mixers give you a choice between mic and line inputs. The difference between the two is that the *mic-level input* is for weak audio signals, such as those coming from a microphone. The *line-level input* is for relatively strong audio signals, such as from a video recorder or CD player. If you plug the output of a CD player into the mic input, a preamplifier will unnecessarily boost the sound; most likely, it will become grossly distorted. If you plug a microphone into the line input, you need to turn the volume control way up to hear anything and in so doing will inevitably cause extensive noise in the audio signal. If you don't know whether an input source is suited for the mic-level input or the line-level input, do a brief test recording. `ZVL3 CUE 12` AUDIO→ Consoles and mixers→ signals

Controlling the volume   Controlling sound volume—or *riding gain*—is not only to make weak sounds louder and loud sounds softer but also to keep the sounds at a level where they do not get distorted. To increase the loudness of a sound, you turn the pot clockwise or push the horizontal fader up, away from you. To reduce the sound volume, you turn the pot counterclockwise or pull the fader down, toward you. The VU meter reflects the gain adjustment by oscillating along a calibrated scale. **SEE 7.23** Some larger audio mixers and consoles have VU meters with *LED* (light-emitting diode) displays instead of oscillating needles.

If the volume is very low and the needle of the standard VU meter barely moves from the extreme left, or if the LED meter remains at the bottom of the scale, you are riding the audio "in the mud." When loud sounds make the needle hit the right side of the meter, you are "bending or pinning the needle" and should turn the volume down to avoid distortion.

When recording analog sound, try to keep the needle between 60 and 100 percent on the lower scale (or between –5 and 0 on the upper scale). Don't worry if the needle spills occasionally into the red, but keep it from oscillating entirely in this overload zone. Most LED meters change color when the sound is overmodulated, that is, when the audio signals are boosted too much. All these systems indicate visually whether there is a sound signal in the system and how loud the electrical signal is relative to a given volume scale.

When working with digital audio, you need to keep the volume lower than with analog audio. Because digital audio does not tolerate "bending the needle," keep the master fader at about –6 dB (decibel) instead of the 0 dB level. Newer machines lower the VU scale so that you can set the master fader at the accustomed 0 dB as the standard volume level. If the incoming volume is too high, it simply clips the signal,

7.23 VU Meter

The volume-unit (VU) meter indicates the relative loudness of sound. The scale is given in volume units, ranging from –20 to +3 (upper scale), and percentages, ranging from 0 to 100 (lower scale).

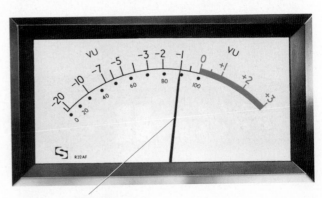

Adjust peak levels to fall near 0

which translates into sound distortion. Even if volume levels are rather low, they can be cranked up to normal levels in postproduction without adding too much noise, but you cannot eliminate the distortion that resulted from recording at too high a volume. Overloading digital audio not only results in distorted sound but adds considerable noise to the recording. **ZVL3 CUE 13** AUDIO→ Consoles and mixers→ control | try it

Sound calibration   When the sound signals go through a mixer or the console before reaching the camcorder or an audio-recording device, you must adjust the recorder's volume meter so that it reads the identical volume units as on the mixer or console VU meter. This adjustment is called *sound calibration.* Generally, the audio technician feeds a 0 VU tone to the video recorder or other recording system. The video-record operator adjusts the volume of the incoming sound signal until the VU meter shows 0 VU. To avoid overload distortion in digital audio, some audio technicians suggest calibrating the system at a designated VU setting that is below the standard analog operating level of 0 VU. **SEE 7.24** **ZVL3 CUE 14** AUDIO→ Consoles and mixers→ calibration

Live field mixing   *Mixing* means combining two or more sounds. You don't need a mixer if you simply interview somebody in the field: you plug the interviewer's hand mic into the appropriate input on the camcorder, turn on the camera mic for ambience, and start recording. But if you have a complicated audio assignment that requires more than two inputs or more-precise volume control than the AGC or the camcorder volume controls can give you, a small mixer will come in handy.

7.24 Calibrating Audio Console and Video Recorder Volume Levels

The VU meter on the video recorder input is adjusted to the 0 VU line-out signal of the console. Once calibrated, both VU meters must read 0 VU (or the designated standard operating level).

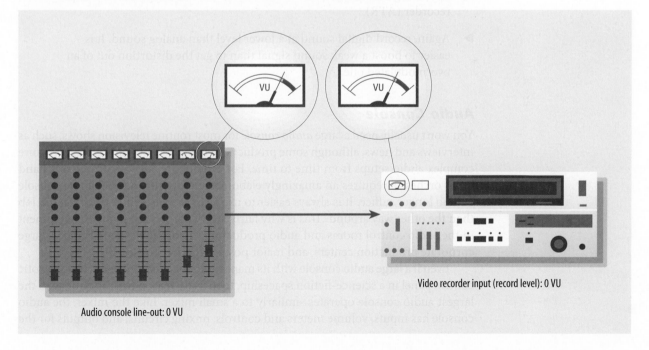

Audio console line-out: 0 VU

Video recorder input (record level): 0 VU

The following guidelines are intended to assist you with field-mixing tasks, but observe this caveat: if at all possible, try to avoid intricate sound mixing in the field. It is usually easier to achieve a satisfactory mix if you record the various sound sources separately and then do the mixing in postproduction. That said, here are some of the most basic field-mixing guidelines:

▶   Even if you have only a few inputs, label each one with what it controls: mic for the host and the guest, ambience mic, and so forth.

▶   Double-check all inputs from wireless microphone systems. They have a pesky habit of malfunctioning just before the start of an event.

▶   Always send a test tone at 0 VU (or whatever standard operating level you are working with) from the mixer to the video recorder before the actual record-ing. Adjust the VU meter on the recorder (either the camcorder or a separate unit) so that it also reads 0 VU (or other standard). You have now calibrated the output from the mixer with the input of the recorder.

▶   Be sure to switch each input to the correct input level (mic or line). Many field productions have been ruined by somebody's not paying attention to the correct input setting.

▶   When working a mixer, set the master pot to 0 VU (or other standard), then adjust the volume of the various inputs for the proper mix. Watch the VU meter of the master pot (line-out). If it spills into the red zone, readjust the volume of the inputs but leave the master pot at the designated standard operating level.

▶   If you have to do a complicated sound pickup in the field, protect yourself by feeding it not only to the camcorder but also to a separate audiotape recorder (ATR).

▶   Again, record digital sound at a lower level than analog sound. It is easier to boost a weak sound signal than to get the distortion out of an overmodulated one.

Audio Console

You won't usually need a large *audio console* for most routine television shows, such as interviews and news, although some productions in high schools and colleges require complex audio setups from time to time. For example, a video recording of a band or an orchestra requires an amazingly elaborate audio setup; a small audio console will no longer suffice. It is always easier to use a larger console for a small audio job than the other way around. This is why fairly large consoles are standard equipment in the audio control rooms and audio production rooms of television stations, large corporate production centers, and major postproduction houses.

Even if a large audio console with its many buttons and levers resembles an exotic control panel in a science-fiction spaceship, there is no reason to be intimidated: the largest audio console operates similarly to a small mixer. Like the mixer, the audio console has inputs, volume meters and controls, mixing circuits, and outputs for the

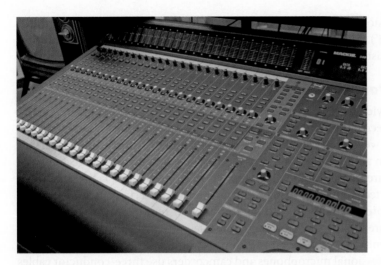

7.25 Audio Console

The audio console has many inputs (twenty-four or more for large video productions), each of which has its own slide fader volume control, a variety of quality controls, various on/off and assignment switches, and a VU meter.

manipulated signal. Unlike the mixer, however, the console has many more inputs and outputs, slide faders instead of rotary pots, and a variety of additional quality controls as well as assignment and on/off switches.

The audio console is relatively large because, instead of the four inputs of the small mixer, it may have twenty-four or even sixty-four. Each input has a separate slide fader and an array of quality controls and switches. Some of the larger consoles have a VU meter for each input channel. The console has additional subgroup faders that control the mix of various inputs before it gets to the master fader, and two master faders that control the two channels of the outgoing stereo signal. Each outgoing channel has its own VU meter. **SEE 7.25**

An audio console lets you control the volume of all inputs, mix some or all of the input signals in various ways, and manipulate the sound signals of each input channel for the final mix. For example, with the quality controls you can add *reverberation* (echo) to the incoming sounds; reduce unwanted frequencies such as a hum or squeal; boost or *attenuate* (reduce) the high, middle, or low frequencies of each sound; and *pan* (move) a sound to a specific horizontal position between the two stereo speakers. Some controls allow you to adjust the strength of the signal input before it is amplified or to turn off all other inputs except the one you want to hear. You can also group some inputs into subgroups that can then be further mixed with other inputs or subgroups.

Why so many inputs? Because even a simple six-person panel discussion may use up to ten inputs: six for the panel's microphones (assuming that each panel member has his or her own mic), one for the moderator's mic, one for the CD that contains the opening and closing theme music, and two more for the two servers that play back program segments during the discussion.

Considering the many microphones and other sound equipment used in a rock concert, even twenty-four inputs seem modest. Large professional recording consoles are called *in-line,* which means for each input they have a corresponding output. Many digital consoles are computer-controlled, which reduces their physical size despite increased mixing capabilities. **ZVL3 CUE 15** AUDIO→ Consoles and mixers

Much professional audio postproduction mixing is done with a *digital audio workstation* (*DAW*). Most of the signal processing, including the mixing, is accomplished with sophisticated computer software.

Cables and Patch Panel

Audio *cables* provide an essential link between the sound sources and the audio console or other recording equipment. Because cables have no moving parts or complicated circuitry, we tend to consider them indestructible. Nothing could be farther from the truth. An audio cable, especially at the connectors, is vulnerable and must be treated with care. Avoid kinking it, stepping on it, or rolling a camera pedestal over it. Even a perfectly good cable may pick up electrical interference from lighting instruments and produce a hum in the audio—another reason for checking out the audio system before the director calls for a rehearsal.

Another potential problem comes from the various connectors that terminate the cables. All professional microphones and camcorders use three-conductor cables (called *balanced* cables) with three-conductor **XLR connectors**. They are relatively immune to outside interference from unwanted frequencies. With an XLR jack in a camcorder, you can use any professional audio cable to connect a high-quality microphone to the camera. Most consumer microphones and small camcorders use the smaller **RCA phono plug** or the **mini plug** for their (unbalanced) cables. Some audio cables terminate with the larger *phone plug*, which is often used for short cable runs to connect musical instruments, such as electric guitars. **SEE 7.26** **ZVL3 CUE 16** AUDIO→ Connectors

Adapters make it possible to hook up cables with different connectors. Although you should always have such adapters on hand, avoid using them as much as possible. As with video adapters, an audio adapter is at best a makeshift solution and always a potential trouble spot. **ZVL3 CUE 17** AUDIO→ Connectors→ overview

> **► KEY CONCEPT**
>
> Always check that the connectors on the cable fit the microphone output and the inputs at the other end (such as camcorder, mixer, or recording device).

> **► KEY CONCEPT**
>
> Keep cable connections and adapters to a minimum; each one is a potential trouble spot.

7.26 Audio Connectors

All professional microphones use the three-wire cables with XLR connectors. Other audio connectors include the phone plug, the RCA phono plug, and the mini plug.

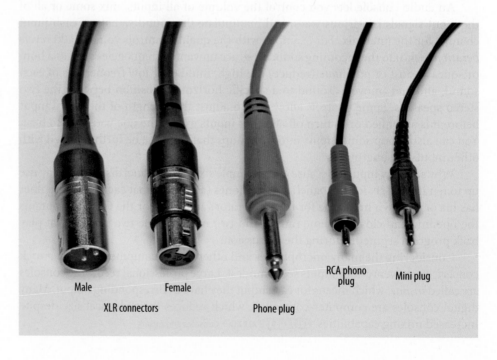

Male   Female

XLR connectors

Phone plug

RCA phono plug   Mini plug

Using the *patch panel* will make your life easier by bringing the various sound inputs (microphones, CD players, remote inputs, and the audio tracks of the video recorder) into a desired order on the audio console. For instance, if the various audio sources correspond to widely dispersed faders on the console (such as the lavaliere mic of the interviewer at fader 1, the CD player at fader 2, the videotape playback at fader 3, and the second lav at fader 4), you may want to move the two lavalieres to adjacent faders, with the video playback at fader 3 and the CD player at fader 4. Rather than change the cables to different inputs, you simply *patch* these sound sources so they appear in the desired order on the console.

Patching can be done in two ways. The old (highly reliable) way is to connect with small cables the incoming signals (called *outputs* because they are carrying the outgoing audio signals that are to be connected with the audio console) to the various faders on the audio console (called *inputs*). **SEE 7.27** The most efficient way is to have a computer take over the signal routing, which accomplishes the same task faster and without additional cables and connectors.

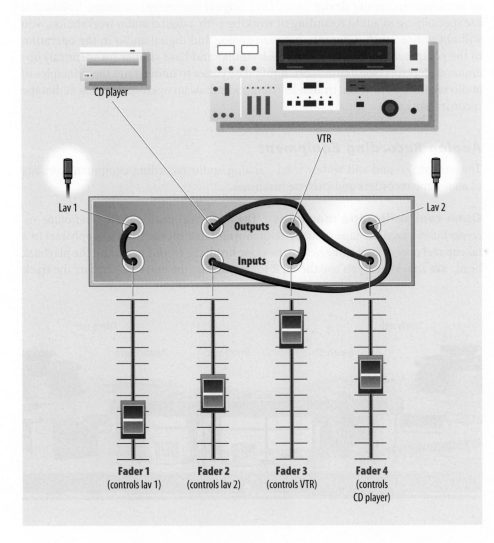

7.27 Patching

The four audio sources (lav 1, CD player, videotape playback, and lav 2) are rerouted through patching (lav 1, lav 2, videotape playback, and CD player).

SOUND RECORDING

Sound, like video, can be recorded as analog or digital signals. Despite the inherent differences between analog and digital equipment, there is relatively little difference in the operation of these two systems. The recording is only as good as the signal you feed into the recorder. Careful attention to sound pickup will often save you many frustrating hours of postproduction. But even the best sound pickup is useless if you don't record it properly.

In most video productions, sound is recorded on the audio tracks of the videotape or nonlinear recording device (computer hard drive or flash memory device) simultaneously with the video (see chapter 11). More-ambitious projects require audio postproduction, wherein you try to eliminate unwanted sounds or add something to the existing audio track on the videotape—a process called *sweetening*. In audio postproduction you can also create an entirely new audio track and add it to the video that has already been shot and edited.

In video production all audio is recorded on the audio tracks of the videotape or nonlinear recording device or on *DAT* (*digital audiotape*) cassettes. Unless you are specializing in audio recording or working with a digital audio workstation, you will not notice much difference between analog and digital audio in the operation of the equipment. Both types often look similar and have similar (or identical) operational controls (see figure 7.29). It might be easier to understand the principles of audio recording, however, by first learning about how an open-reel analog audiotape recorder works.

Analog Recording Equipment

The surviving—and still widely used—analog audio-recording equipment consists of audiotape recorders and cassette machines.

Open-reel audiotape machines   The open-reel analog *ATR* (*audiotape recorder*) uses magnetic tape (usually ¼-inch wide) that moves from a supply reel to a takeup reel over at least three heads: the erase head, the record head, and the playback head. **SEE 7.28** When you use the ATR for recording, the erase head clears the track

7.28 Analog Head Assembly

In a reel-to-reel audiotape recorder, the tape moves from a supply reel over the head assembly to the takeup reel.

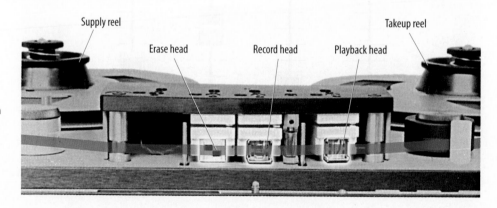

Supply reel   Erase head   Record head   Playback head   Takeup reel

of all previous recordings so that the record head can put the new audio on a clean tape. The playback head then plays the recorded material back so you can hear what you are recording. In the playback mode, the ATR plays back what has been previously recorded. The erase head and the record head are not activated during playback. Sometimes heads are combined or serve a dual function, depending on whether you are in the playback or recording mode.

Multitrack machines   Simple stereo ATRs use only two channels or tracks, one for the left channel and the other for the right channel, on a ¼-inch tape. More-complex recorders put twenty-four or even more tracks on a 2-inch tape.

Analog audiocassette machines   You certainly know what an analog cassette looks like and how the cassette recorder functions. The major advantages of the cassette system over the open-reel system are that the cassette is smaller, it can hold more continuous information (up to 180 minutes), and the recorders are much more portable than are open-reel machines.

Operational controls   Although their arrangement may differ from one model to the next, almost all audio recorders (including digital ones) have the same five operational controls: *record, play, stop, rewind,* and *fast-forward.* **SEE 7.29**

Digital Audio Production Equipment

The major digital audio production equipment includes: digital audiotape recorders; CDs, DVDs, and mini discs; digital cart systems; computer hard drives and flash memory devices; and digital audio workstations.

Digital audiotape recorders   Recorders for *digital audiotape,* or **DAT**, can be open-reel recorders or, more common, cassette recorders. They look similar to their analog cousins and have comparable or identical operational controls. The advantage of DAT is that the recording and the playback are relatively noise-free and more easily

7.29 Operational Controls on Audiotape Recorder
The standard operational controls on ATRs are *record, play, stop, rewind,* and *fast-forward.*

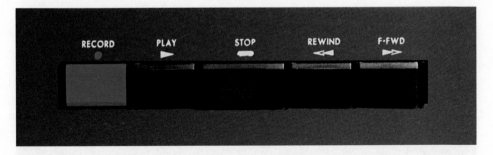

7.30 DAT Cassette

The digital audiotape (DAT) cassette is slightly smaller than the analog audiocassette yet it delivers much higher-quality sound.

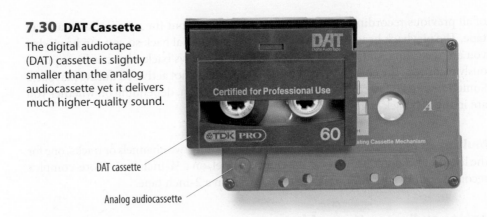

DAT cassette

Analog audiocassette

stored and synchronized with digital video recordings. DAT cassettes are even smaller than analog cassettes, yet they deliver much higher-quality audio. **SEE 7.30**

CDs, DVDs, and mini discs   As you know, the professional optical *compact disc* (*CD*) is a popular digital recording and playback device. The CD player uses a laser beam to optically read the digital information on the small (about 5-inch) disc. The advantage of the CD is that it reproduces almost noise-free sound (assuming the recording was relatively noise-free in the first place). A highly accurate LED read-out system, which functions much like a counter, allows you to select a precise starting point regardless of how deep the segment may be buried on the disc.

The standard CD display consists of seven basic controls: *play, pause, stop, down* button, *up* button, *fast-forward*, and *fast-rewind*. Pressing the *down* button takes you to the beginning of the current track; repeated pressing skips to previous tracks. The *up* button takes you to the end of the current track; repeated pressing selects subsequent tracks. *Fast-rewind* moves the laser back until you release the button. *Fast-forward* moves the laser forward until you release the button. You can hear the audio in the fast-forward and rewind modes. **SEE 7.31**

7.31 CD Operational Display

The standard CD display consists of seven basic controls: (1) *play,* (2) *pause,* (3) *stop,* (4) *down* button, (5) *up* button, (6) *fast-forward,* and (7) *fast-rewind.* The *down* button jumps to the beginning of the current track and to previous tracks. The *up* button jumps to the end of the current track and to subsequent tracks.

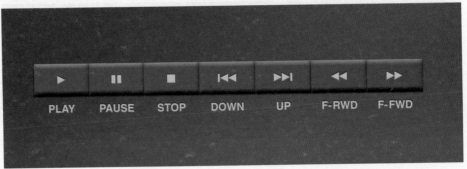

Writable CDs allow you to record new material as you would with audiotape or computer disks. All you need is a CD or DVD burner in your laptop or desktop computer. The **digital versatile disc (DVD)** can hold many times more video and audio information than can the standard CD. The **mini disc (MD)** is also an optical disc but is designed for smaller applications.

Digital cart systems   These systems are specialized computers that can record, store, and play back a great number of audio files. They operate much like a CD player or iPod: you can select a particular audio segment and start the audio track instantly. **SEE 7.32** Some systems have an additional slot for a second, smaller removable disk that allows you to store and exchange a limited amount of audio material (45 minutes or so).

Computer hard drives and flash memory devices   The ubiquitous iPod is one of the most popular hard-drive audio storage and playback devices. In fact, you may be using one right now to make reading this chapter a little more pleasant. Such wonder machines can record up to 60 gigabytes of music and make downloading a snap. Much of television audio is also stored on *flash memory devices,* also called *flash drives* or *memory cards,* of some camcorders.

Digital audio workstations   The typical DAW has a relatively large-capacity hard drive and software that combines a digital audio-recording system with an audio console and editing system. **SEE 7.33** You can call up and operate with the mouse a virtual audio console and editing controls. It also displays multiple audio tracks for

7.32 DigiCart II Plus®

This popular cart system uses a high-capacity hard drive for recording, storage, and instant playback of audio files. You can edit with this system, exchange audio data via a removable 100 MB Iomega Zip disk, and operate the system through a remote panel.

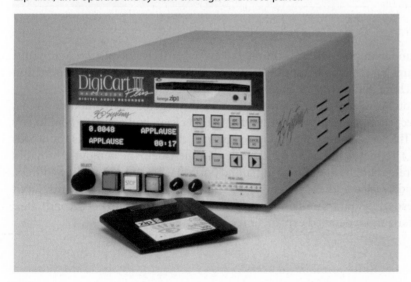

7.33 Digital Audio Workstation Display

Multiple computer interfaces display a variety of audio control and editing functions.
They also activate hardware, such as audio consoles and recorders.

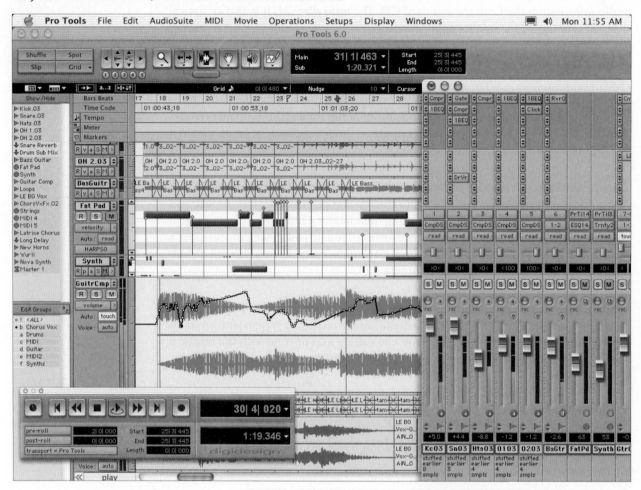

accurate sound manipulation and editing. But even relatively inexpensive audio software programs for desktop computers are powerful tools for audio postproduction
and for matching audio with video in postproduction editing.

Once you have learned to interpret the sound image on the computer screen,
you can select certain sound portions with great precision and arrange them in any
sequence. (The visual sound track on the cover of this book represents the words
video basics.) To match the new sound track with the video, the computer provides
each video frame and the accompanying sound portion with a corresponding address.
The most widely used address system is called the *SMPTE time code.* The displayed
time code reads out hours, minutes, seconds, and frames (30 frames per second). (See
chapter 12 for a more detailed explanation of the SMPTE time code.)

SYNTHESIZED SOUND

If we can translate sound into digital information and then manipulate it, could we not use the computer to create digital information that can be translated into actual sound? Yes. The *audio synthesizer,* commonly called a *keyboard,* can generate a great variety of complex frequencies that we perceive as sounds produced by musical instruments. A single key can approximate the sound of a piano, an electric or acoustic guitar, a drum, or a trumpet. A synthesizer, which you can easily carry under your arm, offers more sounds than a large rock band and a symphony orchestra combined.

The computer can also be used to grab brief portions of a regular sound, such as a telephone ring, translate it into digital form, store it, and make it available for all sorts of manipulations. Through a digital device called a *sampler,* or with the help of sampling software, you can repeat the telephone ring as often as you want, transform it into a shrill beat, speed it up or slow it down, play it backward, have it overlap, or distort it to the point that you can no longer recognize the original sound.

> **▶KEY CONCEPT**
> Sounds and sound mixes can be entirely computer-generated.

SOUND AESTHETICS

Even the most sophisticated digital sound equipment is of little use if you cannot use your ears—that is, exercise some aesthetic judgment. Sounds can make us feel about pictures in a certain way. You can make the same scene appear happy or sad by simply putting some happy or sad sounds behind it.

There are five basic aesthetic factors that can help you achieve an effective audio/video relationship: context, figure/ground, sound perspective, continuity, and energy.

Context

In most studio sound-recording sessions, we try to eliminate as much of the ambient sound as possible. In the field, however, the ambient sounds are often as important as the principal ones: they help establish the general context of the event. If you shoot a scene at a busy downtown intersection, the environmental sounds of cars, horns, streetcars, and buses; people talking, laughing, and moving about; the doorman's whistle for a taxi; and the occasional police siren—all are important clues to where you are, even if you don't show these sound sources in the video portion.

Think of recording a small orchestra. If you do a studio recording, the coughing of one of the crewmembers or musicians during an especially soft passage would certainly prompt a retake. Not so in the context of a live concert. We have learned to interpret the occasional coughing and other such environmental sounds as proof of the live quality of the event.

As pointed out previously, in normal field recording you should try to use one mic and audio track for the primary sound source, such as a reporter standing on a street corner, and another mic (usually the camera mic) and the second audio track for recording environmental sounds. Separating the sounds on different videotape tracks as much as possible makes it easier to mix the two in the proper proportions in postproduction editing.

Figure/Ground

One important perceptual factor is the *figure/ground* principle. This refers to our tendency to organize our environment into a relatively mobile figure (a person or car) and a relatively stable background (wall, houses, or mountains). If we expand this principle a little, we can say that we single out an event that is important to us and assign it the role of the figure while relegating all other events to the background or, as we just called it, the environment. For example, if you are waiting for your friend and finally see her in a crowd, she immediately becomes the focus of your attention—the foreground—while the rest of the people become the background. The same happens with sound. We have the ability to perceive, within limits, the sounds we want or need to hear as the figure while pushing all other sounds into the background. When re-creating such a figure/ground relationship with sound, we usually make the "figure" somewhat louder or give it a distinct quality in relation to the ambient sounds. In the same way, we can easily bring a background sound up in volume to become the figure and relegate the other sounds to the ground.

> ►**KEY CONCEPT**
>
> The figure/ground principle in audio means to make a selected sound or group of sounds (figure) louder and more distinct than the ambient sounds (ground).

Sound Perspective

Sound perspective means that close-up pictures are matched with relatively close sounds, and long shots are matched with sounds that seem to come from farther away. Close sounds have more *presence* than far sounds—a sound quality that makes us feel as though we are near the sound source. Faraway sounds seem to be more distant from us.

As mentioned earlier in this chapter, this desirable variation of sound presence is virtually eliminated when using lavaliere mics. Because the distance between mic and mouth remains the same regardless of whether the performer is seen in a close-up or a long shot, the sound has the same presence. This is why you should use boom mics when controlling sound presence. The boom mic can be moved close to a performer during a close-up and somewhat farther away during a long shot—a simple solution to a potential audio problem.

> ►**KEY CONCEPT**
>
> Close-ups need closer sound presence than do long shots.

Continuity

Sound *continuity* is especially important in postproduction. You may have noticed the sound quality of a reporter's voice change depending on whether he or she was speaking on- or off-camera. In this case, the reporter used one type of microphone when on-camera and another when off-camera; the reporter also changed environments from on-location to the studio. This change in microphones and locations gives speech a distinctly different quality. Although this difference may not be too noticeable during the actual recording, it becomes readily apparent when the two audio sources are edited together in the final show.

What should you do to avoid such continuity problems? Use identical microphones for the on- and off-camera narration or at least ones that sound alike and, if necessary, mix the off-camera narration with some of the separately recorded ambient sounds. You can feed the ambient sounds to the reporter through earphones while recording the voice-over narration, which will help the reporter re-create the on-site energy.

Sound is also a chief element for establishing *visual* continuity. A rhythmically precise piece of music can help achieve continuity in a series of pictures that otherwise do not cut together very well. Music and sound are often the critical link among abruptly changing shots and scenes.

> **►KEY CONCEPT**
> Sound is an important factor in providing shot continuity.

Energy

Unless you want to achieve a special effect through contradiction, you should match the general energy of the pictures with a similar energy of sound. *Energy* refers to all the factors in a scene that communicate a certain degree of aesthetic force and power. Obviously, high-energy scenes, such as a series of close-ups of a rock band in action, can stand higher-energy sounds than a more tranquil scene, such as lovers walking on a beach. Also, as you have just learned, close-ups should have more sound presence and energy than should long shots.

The easiest way to match audio/video energies is to control the sound volume and/or presence. High-energy scenes should be matched with louder sounds than low-energy scenes. A close-up of two people confessing their love by whispering into each other's ears needs more sound presence than if the scene were shown in a long shot.

Good audio depends a great deal on your ability to sense the general energy of video sequences and adjust the volume and the presence of the sound accordingly. But what are the correct levels? You simply need to sense them. No volume meter in the world can substitute for your aesthetic judgment.

> **►KEY CONCEPT**
> High-energy pictures should be matched with high-energy sounds; low-energy pictures, with low-energy sounds.

M A I N   P O I N T S

▶ **Sound Pickup Principle**

Microphones transduce (transform) the sounds we hear into electric energy— the audio signal.

▶ **Directional Characteristics of Mics**

Omnidirectional mics can hear equally well from all directions; unidirectional, or cardioid, mics can best hear sounds that come from the front. Hyper- and supercardioid mics make faraway sounds that lie in the pickup pattern appear close to the mic.

▶ **Mechanics of Mics**

Classified by how they are made, there are three types of mics: dynamic (the most rugged), condenser (high-quality but sensitive), and ribbon (high-quality and very sensitive).

▶ **Use of Mics**

Classified by how they are used, there are six types of microphones: small lavaliere mics, which are clipped to the clothing of the performer; hand mics, which are carried by the performer; boom mics, which are suspended from a fishpole or a studio boom assembly; desk and stand mics, which are mounted on a tabletop stand or an adjustable floor stand; headset mics, which are worn by the performer and include earphones with a split audio feed; and wireless, or radio, mics, which broadcast the audio signal from a transmitter to a receiver. Treat all mics gently and test them before going on the air.

▶ **Audio Connectors**

As with video equipment, check whether the audio connectors fit their respective jacks. Carry adapters but use them only in an emergency.

▶ **Audio Mixer and Audio Console**

The mixer amplifies the incoming sound signals, controls the volume of each sound, and mixes (combines and balances) them in specific ways. A field mixer is small and normally has a maximum of four inputs. The audio console is much larger; it has many more inputs, each of which has a volume control and various quality and sound selection controls.

▶ **Analog Recording and Playback**

High-quality reel-to-reel audiotape recorders (ATRs) use various tape widths, depending on the number of audio tracks recorded on them. Twenty-four-channel ATRs normally use 2-inch tape.

▶ **Digital Recording and Playback**

Digital recording and playback equipment includes digital audiotape (DAT) recorders; compact discs (including read/write CDs), digital versatile discs (DVDs), and mini discs; digital cart systems; computer hard drives and flash memory devices; and digital audio workstations (DAWs).

▶ **Synthesized Sound**

Once sounds are in digital form, the computer can manipulate them. Computerized sound equipment, such as the keyboard, can create—synthesize—its own sounds.

▶ **Sound Aesthetics**

The five basic aesthetic factors that can help you achieve an effective audio/video relationship are context, figure/ground, sound perspective, continuity, and energy.

ZETTL'S VIDEOLAB 3.0

For your reference, or to track your work, the Zettl's VideoLab 3.0 program cues in this chapter are listed here with their corresponding page numbers.

CHAPTER 8

KEY TERMS

additive primary colors Red, green, and blue. Ordinary white light (sunlight) can be separated into the three primary light colors. When these three colored lights are combined in various proportions, all other colors can be reproduced.

attached shadow Shadow that is on the object itself. It cannot be seen independent of (detached from) the object.

background light Illumination of the set pieces and the backdrop. Also called *set light*.

back light Illumination from behind the subject and opposite the camera; usually a spotlight.

baselight Even, nondirectional (diffused) light necessary for the camera to operate optimally. Refers to the overall light intensity.

cast shadow Shadow that is produced by an object and thrown (cast) onto another surface. It can be seen independent of the object.

color temperature Relative reddishness or bluishness of white light, as measured on the Kelvin (K) scale. The norm for indoor video lighting is 3,200K; for outdoors, 5,600K.

contrast The difference between the brightest and the darkest spots in a video picture.

diffused light Light that illuminates a relatively large area with an indistinct light beam. Diffused light, created by floodlights, produces soft shadows.

dimmer A device that controls the intensity of light by throttling the electric current flowing to the lamp.

directional light Light that illuminates a relatively small area with a distinct light beam. Directional light, produced by spotlights, creates harsh, clearly defined shadows.

falloff The speed (degree) with which a light picture portion turns into shadow areas. *Fast falloff* means that the light areas turn abruptly into shadow areas and there is a great difference in brightness between light and shadow areas. *Slow falloff* indicates a very gradual change from light to dark and a minimal brightness difference between light and shadow areas.

fill light Additional light on the opposite side of the camera from the key light to illuminate shadow areas and thereby reduce falloff; usually done with floodlights.

floodlight A lighting instrument that produces diffused light.

foot-candle (fc) The unit of measurement of illumination, or the amount of light that falls on an object. One foot-candle is 1 candlepower of light (1 lumen) that falls on a 1-square-foot area located 1 foot away from the light source.

high-key lighting Light background and ample light on the scene. Has nothing to do with the vertical positioning of the key light.

incident light Light that strikes the object directly from its source. To measure incident light, point the light meter at the camera lens or into the lighting instruments.

Kelvin (K) The standard scale for measuring color temperature, or the relative reddishness or bluishness of white light.

key light Principal source of illumination; usually a spotlight.

light intensity The amount of light falling on an object that is seen by the lens. Measured in lux or foot-candles. Also called *light level*.

light plot A plan, similar to a floor plan, that shows the type, size (wattage), and location of the lighting instruments relative to the scene to be illuminated and the general direction of the light beams.

low-key lighting Fast-falloff lighting with dark background and selectively illuminated areas. Has nothing to do with the vertical positioning of the key light.

lux European standard unit for measuring light intensity. One lux is 1 lumen (1 candlepower) of light that falls on a surface of 1 square meter located 1 meter away from the light source. 10.75 lux = 1 foot-candle. Most lighting people figure roughly 10 lux = 1 foot-candle.

photographic principle The triangular arrangement of key, back, and fill lights, with the back light opposite the camera and directly behind the object, and the key and fill lights on opposite sides of the camera and to the front and the side of the object. Also called triangle, or three-point, lighting.

reflected light Light that is bounced off the illuminated object. To measure reflected light, point the light meter close to the object from the direction of the camera.

RGB Stands for red, green, and blue—the basic colors of television.

spotlight A lighting instrument that produces directional, relatively undiffused light.

triangle lighting The triangular arrangement of key, back, and fill lights. Also called three-point lighting or photographic principle.

white balance The adjustments of the color circuits in the camera to produce white color in lighting of various color temperatures (relative reddishness or bluishness of white light).

Light, Color, and Lighting

Lighting has changed radically over the past ten years—mostly because digital cameras and their lenses are more sensitive and need less light than the older analog cameras. Concurrent with the development of cameras that are more light sensitive are lighting instruments that are highly efficient. For example, some of the newer fluorescent-type instruments produce more light with much lower wattage and much less heat than the traditional incandescent lights.

Nevertheless, good lighting still calls for deliberate illumination— where and from what angle the light falls, whether the light is soft or harsh, and what color the light has—and the control of shadows and their relative transparency. This chapter will introduce you to the basic principles of lighting and how they can be adopted to various studio and field techniques. **ZVL3 CUE 1** ▶LIGHTS→ Light introduction

> ▶ **K E Y C O N C E P T**
> Lighting is deliberate illumination and shadow control.

▶ **LIGHT**
Directional and diffused light, light intensity and how to measure it, measuring incident and reflected light, and contrast

▶ **SHADOWS**
Attached and cast shadows and controlling falloff

▶ **COLOR**
Additive and subtractive mixing, the color television receiver and generated colors, and color temperature and white-balancing

▶ **LIGHTING INSTRUMENTS**
Spotlights, floodlights, and instruments for specific tasks

▶ **LIGHTING TECHNIQUES**
Operation of lights, lighting safety, studio lighting and the photographic principle, and field lighting

LIGHT

Learning about light and shadows seems like a strange assignment, considering that you have been seeing light and shadows all your life. But it makes more sense when you realize that what you see on a video or film screen is nothing but blobs of light and shadows and that lighting is the calculated interplay of these two elements.

Types of Light

No matter how the light is technically generated, you will work with two basic types: directional and diffused.

Directional light has a precise beam that causes harsh shadows. The sun, a flashlight, and the headlights of a car all produce directional light. You can aim directional light at a specific area without much spill into other areas.

Diffused light causes a more general illumination. Its diffused beam spreads out quickly and illuminates a large area. Because diffused light seems to come from all directions (is omnidirectional), it has no clearly defined shadows; they seem soft and transparent. A good example of diffused light occurs on a foggy day, when the fog operates like a huge diffusion filter for the sun. Watch the shadows during bright sunlight and on an overcast or foggy day; they are quite distinct and dense in sunlight, but hardly visible in fog. The fluorescent lighting in elevators and supermarkets is exclusively diffused light. Diffused light is used to minimize the harsh shadows on a face or an object and to light large areas.

Light Intensity

An important aspect of lighting is controlling **light intensity**, or how much light falls onto an object. Also called *light level,* light intensity is measured in American *foot-candles* or in European *lux.* A foot-candle is simply a convenient measurement of illumination—the amount of light that falls on an object. One **foot-candle (*fc*)** is 1 candlepower of light (called a *lumen*) that falls on a 1-square-foot area located 1 foot away from the light source. The European measure for light intensity is **lux**—1 lumen of light that falls on a surface of 1 square meter that is 1 meter away from the light source. If you have foot-candles and want to find lux, multiply the foot-candle figure by 10. Twenty foot-candles are approximately 200 lux ($20 \times 10 = 200$). If you have lux and want to find foot-candles, divide the lux number by 10. Two thousand lux are approximately 200 fc ($2{,}000 \div 10 = 200$). A room that has an overall illumination of 200 fc, or 2,000 lux, is pretty well lighted. **ZVL3 CUE 2** LIGHTS→ Measurement→ meters

Sometimes you may hear the lighting director (LD) or the video operator (VO) complain that there is not enough baselight. **Baselight** refers to general illumination, or the overall light intensity, such as the 200 fc in the room we just talked about. You determine baselight levels by pointing a *light meter* (which reads foot-candles or lux) from the illuminated object or scene *toward the camera.* To check the baselight of your living room, you would walk to the different corners of the room and point the light meter toward a real or imaginary camera position (probably in the middle of the room). **ZVL3 CUE 3** LIGHTS→ Measurement→ baselight

Although some camera manufacturers claim that their cameras can see in the dark, you need a certain amount of light to make the cameras see the colors and the shadows that you see when looking at the scene. In technical parlance you need to activate the imaging device and the other electronics in the camera to produce an optimal video signal at a given *f*-stop (see chapter 4). Although newer cameras and lenses are much more sensitive than older ones and need less light, good, crisp video still demands a generous amount of illumination. A small camcorder may be able to produce recognizable pictures at light levels as low as 1 or 2 lux; but for high-quality pictures, you need more light. Top-of-the-line studio cameras may still require about 1,000 lux (100 fc) at an *f*-stop of about *f*/5.6 for optimal picture quality.[1]

If there is insufficient light even at the maximum aperture (lowest *f*-stop number), you need to activate the *gain* circuits of the camera. Most consumer camcorders do this automatically. On camcorders, studio cameras, and ENG/EFP cameras, the gain is activated either via the camera control unit (CCU) or by a switch on the camera. The gain will boost the weak video signal electronically. Digital cameras can tolerate a relatively high gain before they show picture "noise," that is, artifacts that show up as colored specks. When video quality is of primary concern, it is better to raise the baselight level than to activate the gain switch.

Measuring Illumination

In critical lighting setups, before turning on the cameras you may want to check whether there is enough baselight and whether the *contrast* between the light and dark areas falls within the acceptable limits (normally 50:1 to 100:1, depending on the camera; see Contrast on the next page). You can check this with a light meter, which simply measures the amount of foot-candles or lux emitted by the lighting instruments—the **incident light**—or reflected off an object—the **reflected light**.

Incident light   An incident-light reading gives you an idea of the baselight level in a given area, which translates into how much light the camera receives from a particular location on the set. To measure incident light, stand next to or in front of the illuminated person or object and point the light meter *toward the camera lens*. Such a quick reading of incident light is especially helpful when checking the prevailing light levels at a remote location.

If you want a more specific reading of the light intensity from certain instruments, point the light meter *into the lights*. To check the relative evenness of the incident light, point the light meter toward the major camera positions while walking around the set. If the needle or digital read-out stays approximately at the same intensity level, the lighting is fairly even. If the needle or read-out dips way down, the lighting setup has *holes* (unlighted or underlighted areas).

Reflected light   The reading of reflected light is done primarily to check the contrast between light and dark areas. To measure reflected light, stand close to the lighted object or person and point the light meter *at the light and shadow areas from the direction of the camera*. Be careful not to block the light whose reflection you are

---

1. An *f*-stop between *f*/5.6 and *f*/8.0 produces an optimal depth of field. This is why camera specifications use *f*/5.6 as the norm for optimal light levels. Of course, with larger apertures you can shoot with less light.

trying to measure. As mentioned before, the difference between the two readings will indicate the lighting *contrast*. Note that the contrast is determined not only by how much light falls on the object but also by how much light the object reflects back into the camera. The more reflective the object, the higher the reflected-light reading will be. A mirror reflects almost all of the light falling onto it; a black velour cloth reflects only a small portion.

Now that you've mastered the light meter, don't become a slave to it. After all, the best way to tell whether the lighting is right is to look at the video monitor.

Contrast

Contrast refers to the difference between the brightest and the darkest spots in a video picture. Contrary to your eye, which can distinguish subtle brightness steps over a contrast ratio of 1,000:1 or more, even high-end video cameras are usually limited to a lower contrast. Whereas some equipment salespeople might tell you that high-end video cameras can tolerate a contrast that is close to that of our vision, LDs and VOs say that too high a contrast is one of the most common obstacles to producing optimal video. Believe the people who use the cameras rather than sell them. Video professionals prefer a contrast ratio that does not exceed 100:1 for studio cameras. The high number of the 100:1 contrast ratio indicates that the brightest spot in the scene is 100 times more intense than the darkest spot. Small digital camcorders will have trouble producing high-quality video that shows bright highlights as well as transparent shadows if the contrast ratio is higher than 50:1.

Measuring contrast   To measure contrast, point a reflective-light meter close to the bright side of the object, then close to the shadow side. (You will read more about measuring contrast in the next section.) The light meter reads the reflected light, first of the bright side (a high reading), then of the shadow side (a low reading). If, for example, the light meter reads 800 fc in an especially bright area, such as one side of the reporter's face in direct sunlight, and only 10 fc in the dark background, the contrast ratio is 80:1 (800 ÷ 10 = 80). Even with a fairly good digital camcorder, this contrast may be too high for good pictures. **ZVL3 CUE 4** ›LIGHTS→ Measurement→ contrast

High-end small camcorders and all professional cameras will tell you just which picture areas are overexposed, by showing a vibrating zebra-striped pattern over them. By stopping down the lens (closing the aperture by selecting a higher *f*-stop), you may eliminate the white glare (and get rid of the zebra pattern); in the process, however, you will also compress the shadow areas into a dense, uniform black.

To lower the contrast, you can do several things:

1. In the case of the reporter, you can activate one of the *neutral density (ND) filters* that are built into the camcorder. They act like sunglasses, reducing the overall brightness without affecting the colors too much. If possible, lighten up the harsh shadows (how to do this is explained later in this chapter).

2. If you use lighting instruments, you can reduce the light intensity by moving the lighting instrument farther away from the object, putting a light-diffusing material in front of the lighting instrument, or using an electronic dimmer.

3. Remove overly bright objects from the scene, especially if you are operating with an automatic iris. A pure white object always presents a lighting hazard, no matter

how high a contrast the camera can tolerate. The real problem is that even if the camera can manage a high contrast ratio, the average television set can't. `ZVL3 CUE 5`

LIGHTS→ Measurement→ try it

SHADOWS

Although we are quite conscious of light and light changes, we are usually unaware of shadows, unless we seek comfort in them on a particularly hot day or if they interfere with what we want to see. Because shadow control is such an important aspect of lighting, we'll take a closer look at shadows and how they influence our perception.

Once you are aware of shadows, you will be surprised by the great variety of shadows that surround you. Some seem part of the object, such as the shadow on your coffee cup; others seem to fall onto other surfaces, such as the shadow of a telephone pole that is cast onto the street. Some shadows are dark and dense, as though they were brushed on with thick, black paint; others are so light and subtle that they are hard to see. Some change gradually from light to dark; others do so abruptly. Despite the great variety of shadows, there are only two basic types: *attached* and *cast*. `ZVL3 CUE 6`

LIGHTS→ Light & shadow→ light

Attached Shadows

Attached shadows seem affixed to the object and cannot be seen independent of it. Take your coffee cup and hold it next to a window or table lamp. The shadow opposite the light source (window or lamp) on the cup is the attached shadow. Even if you wiggle the cup or move it up and down, the attached shadow remains part of the cup. **SEE 8.1**

Attached shadows help us perceive the basic form of an object. Without attached shadows the actual shape of an object may remain ambiguous when seen as a picture. In the figure at the bottom right of this page, the object on the left looks like a triangle; but when you see it with the attached shadows, the triangle becomes a cone. **SEE 8.2**

8.1 Attached Shadow

The attached shadow is always bound to the illuminated object. It cannot be seen separate from the object.

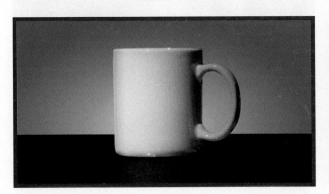

8.2 Attached Shadows Define Shape

Attached shadows help define the basic shape of the object. Without attached shadows, we perceive a triangle on the left; with attached shadows, we perceive a cone on the right.

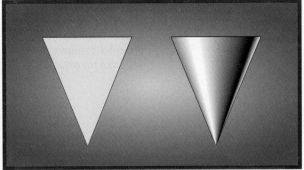

8.3 **Rough Texture**

Prominent attached shadows emphasize texture. The surface of this Styrofoam ball looks rough.

8.4 **Smooth Texture**

Here the attached shadows are almost eliminated, so the surface of the ball looks relatively smooth.

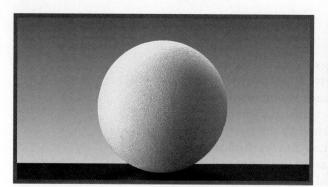

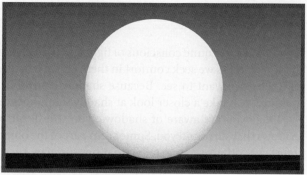

Attached shadows also contribute to perception of texture. A great amount of prominent attached shadows emphasizes texture; without them things look smoother. Attached shadows on a Styrofoam ball make it look like a moonscape; but when the attached shadows are removed through flat lighting, the ball looks smooth. **SEE 8.3 AND 8.4**

If you had to shoot a commercial for skin lotion, you would want to light the model's face in such a way that the attached shadows are so soft that they are hardly noticeable. **SEE 8.5** But if you wanted to emphasize the rich, deep texture of the famous stone carving of the Aztec Sun Stone (generally known as the Aztec calendar), you would need to light for prominent attached shadows. **SEE 8.6** Slow-falloff lighting would make the patterns in the stone hard to see. **SEE 8.7** (How to control attached shadows is discussed in the context of lighting techniques later in this chapter.) **ZVL3 CUE 7** LIGHTS→ Light & shadow→ attached

> **▶ K E Y   C O N C E P T**
>
> Attached shadows reveal form and texture.

Because we normally see the main light source as coming from above (the sun, for example), we are used to seeing attached shadows below protrusions and indentations. When you lower the principal light source so that it illuminates an object, such as a face, from below eye level, we experience this departure from the norm as

8.5 **Attached Shadows Minimized**

To emphasize the smoothness of this model's face, attached shadows are kept to a minimum.

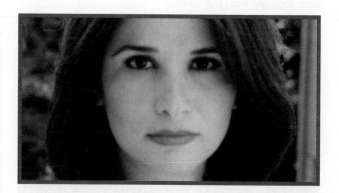

8.6 Attached Shadows Emphasized

With the light coming from the side, the attached shadows on this Aztec Sun Stone are more prominent, and the rich, deep texture is properly emphasized.

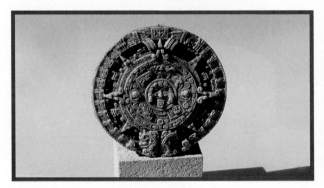

8.7 Attached Shadows Minimized

With the light shining directly on the Sun Stone, the lack of attached shadows makes the intricate carvings look relatively flat.

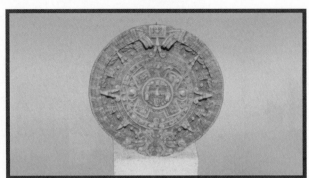

mysterious or spooky. There is probably not a single science fiction or horror movie that does not use such a shadow-reversal effect at least once. **SEE 8.8** **ZVL3 CUE 8** ▶LIGHTS→ Design→ horror

Cast Shadows

Unlike attached shadows, ***cast shadows*** can be seen independent of the object causing them. If you make some shadow pictures on a wall, for instance, you can focus on the shadows without showing your hand. The shadows of telephone poles, traffic signs, or trees cast on the street or a nearby wall are all examples of cast shadows. Even if the cast shadows touch the base of the objects causing them, they remain cast shadows and will not become attached ones. **SEE 8.9**

Cast shadows help us see where an object is located relative to its surroundings and help orient us in time, at least to some extent. Take another look at figure 8.9.

> **►KEY CONCEPT**
>
> Cast shadows help tell us where things are and when events take place.

8.8 Reversal of Attached Shadows

The below-eye-level light source causes the attached shadows to fall opposite their expected positions. We interpret such unusual shadow placement as spooky or mysterious.

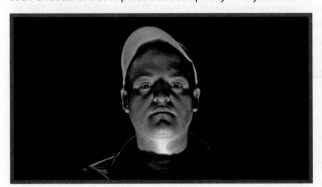

8.9 Cast Shadows

Cast shadows are usually cast by the object onto some other surface. In this case, the cast shadows of the parking meters fall on the sidewalk.

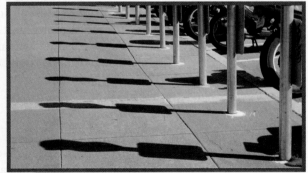

8.10 Fast Falloff

The change of light to shadow areas on these buildings is very sudden. The falloff is extremely fast, indicating an edge or a corner.

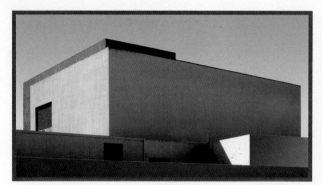

8.11 Slow Falloff

The attached shadow on this balcony gets gradually darker. The falloff is relatively slow, indicating a curved surface.

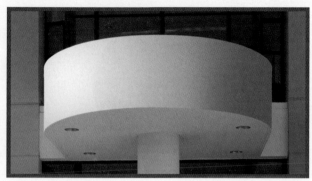

Stretching across the sidewalk, the relatively long cast shadows of the parking meters indicate early morning or late afternoon. **ZVL3 CUE 9** LIGHTS→ Light & shadow→ cast

Falloff

Falloff indicates the degree of change from light to shadow. Specifically, it refers to the relative abruptness—the speed—with which light areas turn into shadow areas, or the brightness contrast between the light and shadow sides of an object. An abrupt change from light to dense shadow illustrates *fast falloff*; it indicates a sharp edge or corner. **SEE 8.10** *Slow falloff* shows a more continuous change from light to shadow; the gradual shading indicates a curved object. **SEE 8.11**

Fast falloff can also refer to a high contrast between the light and shadow sides of a face. When the shadow side is only slightly darker than the light side and the shadows are highly transparent, the falloff is slow. If both sides of the face are equally bright, there is no falloff. The perception of texture also depends on falloff. Fast-falloff lighting emphasizes wrinkles in a face; slow-falloff or no-falloff lighting hides them (see figure 8.5). **ZVL3 CUE 10** LIGHTS→ Falloff→ fast | slow | none | try it

When generating lighting effects with a computer, the relationship between attached and cast shadows and the rate of falloff have to be carefully calculated. For example, if you simulate a light source striking the object from screen-right, the attached shadows must obviously be on its screen-left side (opposite the light source), and the cast shadows must extend in the screen-left direction. Such careful attention to shadow consistency is also important if you cut a live scene electronically into a photographic background (a process called *chroma keying*; see chapter 9).

> ►**KEY CONCEPT**
>
> Falloff defines the contrast between light and dark areas and how quickly light turns into shadow.

COLOR

Chapter 4 promised more-detailed information on color and its use in video. In this section we focus on the basic process of color mixing, the color television receiver and generated colors, and color temperature and white-balancing.

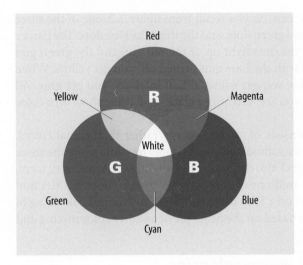

8.12 Additive Color Mixing

When mixing colored light, the additive primaries are red, green, and blue (RGB). All other colors can be achieved by mixing certain quantities of red, green, and blue light. For example, the additive mixture of red and green light produces yellow.

Additive and Subtractive Color Mixing

You will undoubtedly recollect the discussion about the beam splitter that divides the white light transmitted by the lens into the three primary light colors—red, green, and blue (**RGB**)—and how we can produce all video colors by adding the red, green, and blue light in certain proportions. These are called **additive primary colors** because we mix them by *adding* one colored light beam on top of others.

If you had three identical slide projectors, you could put a red slide into one, a green slide in the second, and a blue slide in the third and aim them at the screen so that their beams overlap slightly. **SEE 8.12** What you would perceive is similar to the three overlapping circles shown in the figure. The overlapped RGB light primaries show that mixing red and green light adds up to *yellow;* red and blue mix to a bluish red called *magenta;* and green and blue combine to make a greenish blue called *cyan.* Where all three primary light colors overlap, you get white. By dimming all three projectors equally, you get a variety of grays. By turning them all off, you get black. By dimming any one or all projectors independently, you can achieve a wide variety of colors. For example, if the red projector burns at full intensity and the green one at two-thirds intensity with the blue projector turned off, you get a shade of orange. The more you dim the green projector, the more reddish the orange becomes.

You may remember from your finger-painting days that the primary colors were red, blue, and yellow and that mixing red and green paint together does not produce a clean yellow but rather a muddy dark brown. Obviously, paint mixes differently from light. When paint is mixed, its built-in filters *subtract* certain colors (light frequencies) rather than add them. We call this mixing process *subtractive color mixing.* Because the video system processes colored light rather than paint, we concentrate here on additive mixing.

Color Television Receiver and Generated Colors

The color television set works on the additive color-mixing principle. Instead of three slide projectors, a color television receiver has three electron guns in the neck of the picture tube that shoot their beams at myriad red, green, and blue dots or rectangles

▶ **KEY CONCEPT**

The additive primary colors of light are red, green, and blue.

on the inside of the television screen. As you recall from figure 3.2, one of the three guns hits the red dots, the other the green dots, and the third the blue dots. The harder the guns hit the dots, the more the dots light up. If the red gun and the green gun hit their dots with full intensity with the blue gun turned off, you get yellow. When all three guns fire at full intensity, you get white; at half intensity, you get gray. All three guns work overtime when you are watching a black-and-white show on a color television set.

Because the video signal consists of electric energy rather than actual colors, couldn't we produce certain colors without a camera simply by stimulating the three electron guns with certain voltages? Yes, definitely! In a slightly more complex form, this is how computers generate millions of colors. The various colors in titles and other graphic displays, the colors on a Web page, and the controversial colorizing of black-and-white movies—all are based on the principle of additive color mixing and generating colors by computer.

Color Temperature and White-balancing

In chapter 5 you learned that white-balancing is an important operational camera feature. But what exactly is it, and why is it necessary? You need to white-balance a camera because not all light sources produce light of the same degree of whiteness. As mentioned in chapter 5, a candle produces a more reddish light than does the midday sun or a supermarket's fluorescent lights, which are more blue. Even the same light source does not always produce the same color of light: the beam of a flashlight with a weak battery looks quite reddish, for example, but when fully charged the flashlight throws a more intense, and also whiter, light beam. The same color temperature change happens when you dim lights: the more you dim the lights, the more reddish they get. The camera needs to adjust to these differences to keep colors the same under different lighting conditions.

> **▶ KEY CONCEPT**
>
> Color temperature, expressed in K, measures the relative reddishness or bluishness of white light. Reddish white light has a low color temperature; bluish white light has a high color temperature.

Color temperature   The standard by which we measure the relative reddishness or bluishness of white light is called **color temperature**. The color differences of white light are measured on the **Kelvin (K)** scale. The more *bluish* the white light looks, the higher the color temperature and the higher the K value; the more *reddish* it is, the lower its color temperature and, therefore, the lower the K value.

Keep in mind that color temperature has nothing to do with how hot the actual light source gets. You can touch a fluorescent tube even though it burns at a high color temperature; but you wouldn't do the same with the incandescent lamp in a reading light, which burns at a much lower color temperature.

Because outdoor light is much more bluish than normal indoor illumination, two color temperature standards have been developed for lamps in lighting instruments: 5,600K for outdoor illumination and 3,200K for indoor illumination. This means that the outdoor lights approximate the bluishness of outdoor light. The instruments for indoor lighting burn at the lower 3,200K; their white light is more reddish. **ZVL3 CUE 11 ▶**
LIGHTS→ Color temperature→ light sources

Because color temperature is measured by the relative bluishness or reddishness of white light, couldn't you raise the color temperature of an indoor light by putting a slightly blue filter in front of it, or lower the color temperature of an outdoor lamp by using a slightly orange filter? Yes, you can. Such color filters, called *gels* or *color media,* are a convenient way of converting outdoor instruments for indoor lighting and vice versa. Similar filters are used in some cameras for rough white-balancing.

White-balancing   As you recall, *white balance* means to adjust the camera so that it reproduces a white object as white on the screen regardless of whether it is illuminated by a high-color-temperature source (the sun at high noon, fluorescent lamps, and 5,600K instruments) or a low-color-temperature source (candlelight, incandescent lights, and 3,200K instruments). When white-balancing, the camera adjusts the RGB signals electronically so that they mix into white. Most small camcorders have an automatic white-balancing mechanism. The camera measures more or less accurately the color temperature of the prevailing light and adjusts the RGB circuits accordingly.

Large camcorders and ENG/EFP cameras have a semiautomatic white-balance control that is more accurate than a fully automatic one. The disadvantage is that you need to white-balance every time you move into a new lighting environment, such as from indoors to outdoors or from the fluorescent lights of a supermarket to the office that is illuminated by a desk lamp. The overriding advantage is that you white-balance a camera in the specific lighting in which you are shooting. When using a fully automatic white balance, you are never quite sure just what the camera considers to be white.

Some larger cameras allow you to use a bluish or orange filter to perform a rough white balance under extremely reddish (low K value) or bluish (high K value) light. The camera then fine-tunes the white balance by electronically adjusting the RGB mix. Studio cameras are white-balanced from the CCU or the RCU (remote control unit) by the video operator.

Proper white-balancing is very important for color continuity. For example, if you video-record a performer in a white dress first outdoors and then indoors, her dress should not look bluish in the outdoor scene and reddish in the indoor scene; it should look equally white in both. **SEE 8.13**

8.13 White Balance

To counteract tinting caused by variations in color temperature, it is necessary to white-balance the camera. This adjusts the RGB channels to compensate for the unwanted color cast and make white look white.

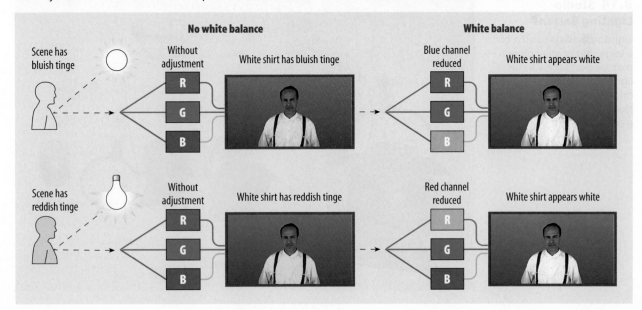

No white balance

Scene has bluish tinge
Without adjustment
R
G
B
White shirt has bluish tinge

White balance

Blue channel reduced
R
G
B
White shirt appears white

Scene has reddish tinge
Without adjustment
R
G
B
White shirt has reddish tinge

Red channel reduced
R
G
B
White shirt appears white

How to white-balance   To white-balance a camera with a semiautomatic system, take a screen-filling close-up of a white card, a white shirt, or even a clean tissue and press the white-balance button. Some camera utility bags have a white patch sewn into them, which gives you a handy white-balancing standard wherever you go. The viewfinder display (usually a flashing light) will tell you when the camera is seeing true white. Be sure that the white object fills the entire viewfinder and that it is located in the light that actually illuminates the scene you are shooting. For example, don't white-balance the camera in bright sunlight outside the hotel and then proceed to video-record the fashion show in the hotel lobby. (If you do, you may find that the video colors are quite different from the actual colors the models wore.) You need to white-balance every time you move into a new lighting environment; even if the light seems the same to the naked eye, the camera will detect the difference.

When operating a studio camera or an ENG/EFP camera that is connected to a camera cable, the video operator takes care of the white-balancing from the CCU or the RCU. **ZVL3 CUE 12** LIGHTS→ Color temperature→ white balance | controlling | try it

LIGHTING INSTRUMENTS

Despite the many lighting instruments available, there are basically only two types: spotlights and floodlights. *Spotlights* throw a directional, more or less defined beam that illuminates a specific area; they cause harsh, dense shadows. *Floodlights* produce a great amount of nondirectional, diffused light that yields transparent shadows. Some floodlights generate such slow falloff that they seem to be a shadowless light source. The heavier and more powerful lights are designed for studio use. They are usually suspended from a fixed lighting grid made of heavy steel pipes or from movable counterweighted battens. **SEE 8.14** Portable lights for ENG and EFP are more flexible and lightweight but are generally less sturdy and powerful.

8.14 Studio Lighting Battens

Lighting battens consist of a large grid of steel pipes that supports the various lighting instruments. In this case, the batten can be lowered or raised through a counterweight system.

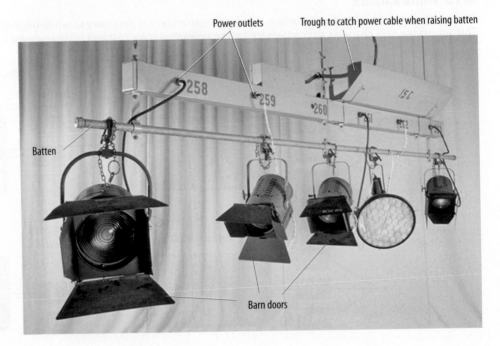

Power outlets

Trough to catch power cable when raising batten

Batten

Barn doors

Spotlights

Spotlights produce a relatively sharp, directional beam that illuminates a fairly distinct area. Most studio spotlights have glass lenses that help collect the light rays and focus them into a precise beam. There are also various special-purpose spotlights, which differ greatly in size and beam spread.

Fresnel spotlight   The workhorse of studio spotlights is the *Fresnel* (pronounced "fra-*nel*"). Its thin, steplike lens (developed by Augustin Jean Fresnel of France) directs the light into a distinct beam. It can be equipped with incandescent *TH* (*tungsten-halogen*), or *quartz,* lamps or with a specific type of fluorescent globe, not unlike the type you may use in your home. Most Fresnel spots have a reflector in the back of the instrument that directs almost all of its light toward the lens. **SEE 8.15**

The spread of the beam can be adjusted from a "spot" or "focus" position to a "spread" or "flood" position by turning a knob, ring, or spindle that moves the lamp-reflector unit. To flood, or spread, the beam in most common Fresnel spots, you move the lamp-reflector unit *toward* the lens. The light beam becomes slightly more diffused (less intense), and the shadows are softer than when focused. To focus the beam, you move the lamp-reflector unit *away from* the lens. This increases the sharpness and the intensity of the beam and makes its shadows fairly dense and distinct.

You can further control the light beam with *barn doors* (see figure 8.19), which are movable metal flaps that swing open and close like actual barn doors, blocking the beam on the sides or, when rotated, on the top and the bottom. Barn doors slide into a holder in front of the lens. To prevent them from sliding out and dropping, guillotinelike, on somebody, secure all of them to their instruments with a safety chain or cable.

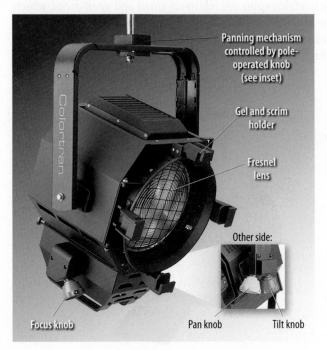

Panning mechanism controlled by pole-operated knob (see inset)

Gel and scrim holder

Fresnel lens

Other side:

Focus knob   Pan knob   Tilt knob

8.15 Fresnel Spotlight

The Fresnel spotlight is the workhorse of studio lighting. Its lens creates a relatively sharp light beam that can be partially blocked by barn doors. This spotlight can be focused, tilted up and down, and panned sideways by turning the knobs with a lighting pole (a wooden pole with a metal hook at the end).

The size of Fresnel spotlights is normally given in the wattage of their quartz-halogen lamps. In the studio the most common incandescent Fresnels are the 650-watt and 1K (1 kilowatt = 1,000 watts) instruments. For older, less sensitive cameras, the 2K (2,000-watt) Fresnel is still the workhorse. All incandescent studio Fresnel spots burn at the indoor color temperature of 3,200K.

These incandescent quartz Fresnels are being challenged more and more by highly efficient fluorescent spots that can produce an amazing amount of light with lamps in the 100- to 500-watt range. All lamps of the fluorescent-type spots have a built-in ballast, very much like the fluorescent spiral-type lamps that are replacing the ordinary pear-shaped household light bulb. Although they burn at slightly different color temperatures from the incandescent standard (3,000K instead of 3,200K, and 4,200K instead of 5,600K), they seem close enough for proper white-balancing. **SEE 8.16**

Before using fluorescent spotlights, test them out on-camera. Some of the older lamps emit a greenish or blue-green tint. This slight color shift may not be visible to the naked eye, but it is certain to show up on-camera, even if you have done some careful white-balancing. Newer lamps are generally free of such "green spikes," but it may still be a good idea to test them on-camera before using them in productions that rely heavily on accurate color reproduction.

During an elaborate EFP or a large remote telecast, you may come across another type of Fresnel spotlight, called an *HMI*. These expensive spotlights have highly efficient arc lamps that deliver three to five times the illumination of a normal Fresnel spot of the same size—and use less electricity to do so. All HMI spotlights burn at the outdoor standard of 5,600K. The disadvantage of HMI lights is that they are quite expensive and need an external ballast to operate properly.

Portable spotlights   Although you can, of course, take small Fresnel spotlights on location, there are portable spotlights that are hybrids of spots and floods. To keep their weight to a minimum, these portable spots are relatively small and *open-faced*, which means they do not have a lens. Without a lens, they cannot deliver as precise a beam as Fresnel spots, even when in the spot or focus position. They are all designed to be mounted on a light stand or with a clip-on device. Some of the more popular models

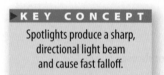

▶KEY CONCEPT

Spotlights produce a sharp, directional light beam and cause fast falloff.

8.16 Fluorescent Fresnel Spotlight

This fluorescent Fresnel spot has a built-in ballast. It has a high light output with relatively low-wattage fluorescent lamps.

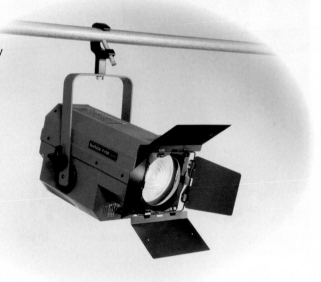

8.17 Lowel Omni-light

This popular lightweight instrument doubles as a spot and a floodlight and is used mainly in ENG/EFP. You can plug it into any normal household outlet and hold it or fasten it to a light stand or any other convenient mounting device.

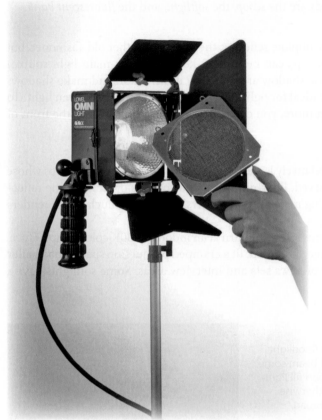

8.18 Lowel Pro-light

The Pro is a small, powerful (250-watt) ENG/EFP spotlight that can be handheld, clipped to the camera, or mounted on a light stand.

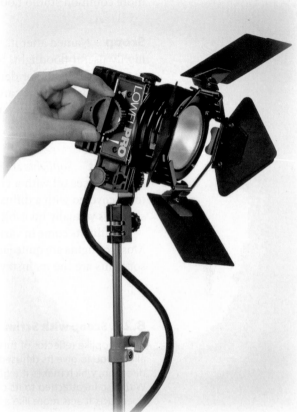

are the Lowel Omni- and Pro-lights. **SEE 8.17 AND 8.18** To reduce the harshness of the light emitted by the quartz lamp, attach a piece of spun-glass cloth to the barn doors with some wooden clothespins. The spun glass, which can withstand the considerable heat of the quartz lamps, acts as an efficient diffuser.

An old standby is the *clip light,* with its reflector built into its bulb. The PAR 38 lamp is especially popular for illuminating outdoor walkways and driveways. Clip lights are useful for supplemental illumination of small areas; you can easily clip them onto furniture, scenery, doors, or whatever the clip will fit. Metal housings with barn doors that fit over the clip light are also available. As with large ones, these barn doors control the spread of the beam. **SEE 8.19**

8.19 Clip Light with Barn Doors

Small spotlights, which use ordinary internal reflector lamps, are useful for illuminating small areas during field productions.

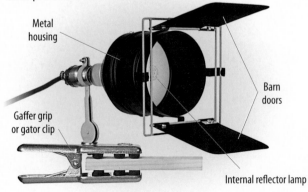

Metal housing

Barn doors

Gaffer grip or gator clip

Internal reflector lamp

Floodlights

Floodlights have no lens and use large, relatively low-powered lamps because their purpose is to create a highly diffused nondirectional light rather than a sharp beam. The diffused light creates soft and highly transparent shadows. When you illuminate an object with floodlights, the falloff is automatically slower than with a spotlight. The more common studio floods are the *scoop,* the *softlight,* and the *fluorescent bank.*

Scoop   Named after its scooplike reflector, the *scoop* is a rather old-fashioned but highly useful floodlight. Scoops can be used as key lights (the main light source) as well as fill lights for dense shadow areas to slow down falloff and make shadows more transparent. They are ideal for lighting large areas with relatively even light. To diffuse the light beam even more, you can attach a spun-glass scrim to the front of the scoop. **SEE 8.20**

Softlight   *Softlights* are relatively large instruments with long tubelike lamps whose light bounces off with a curved, light-diffusing reflector. The opening of the reflector is covered with a diffusing material that scatters the light so much that it renders shadows virtually invisible.

Softlights come in various sizes and burn at an indoor 3,200K color temperature. Most softlights are quite large and do not fit a cramped production space, but smaller softlights are the mainstay of news sets and interview areas. Some softlights have a

8.20 Scoop with Scrim

The scooplike reflector of this floodlight allows you to give its diffused beam some direction, which makes it a good fill light. With a scrim attached to its otherwise open face, it acts more like a broad.

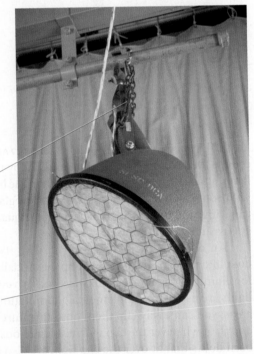

Safety chain

Scrim holder
with scrim

gridlike contraption, called an *egg crate,* attached instead of the customary diffusion cloth. The squares of the egg crate diffuser give you a little more control over the direction of the softlight beam than does the diffusion cloth. **SEE 8.21**

Fluorescent bank   The *fluorescent bank,* which consists of a row of fluorescent tubes, was one of the main lighting devices in the early days of television. After a hiatus the bank has made a comeback. It is highly efficient, produces extremely dif-fused light and slow falloff, and does not generate the heat of the other floodlights. You get fluorescent banks that burn at approximately 5,000K for outdoor light or at 3,000K for indoor light. The manufacturers of fluorescent lights try hard to make the light look similar to that of incandescent floodlights, without the telltale greenish look of the fluorescents. Before you settle on using a specific fluorescent bank, try it out: Light a white object with the fluorescent bank, white-balance the camera, and videotape it for a minute or two. Then do the same with an incandescent instrument (such as a softlight or a scoop with a scrim). The object should look similarly white in both segments. The disadvantage of all such lights is that the banks are relatively large and unwieldy, regardless of whether you use them in the studio or in the field. **SEE 8.22** **ZVL3 CUE 13** LIGHTS→ instruments→ studio

8.21 Softlight	**8.22 Fluorescent Bank**
This floodlight is covered with diffusing material and delivers extremely diffused light. It causes very slow falloff and renders shadows virtually invisible.	The fluorescent bank consists of a series of fluorescent tubes. It produces very soft light with slow falloff.

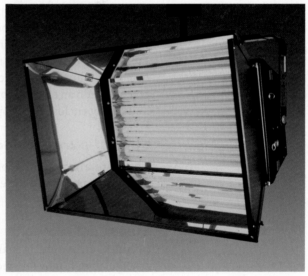

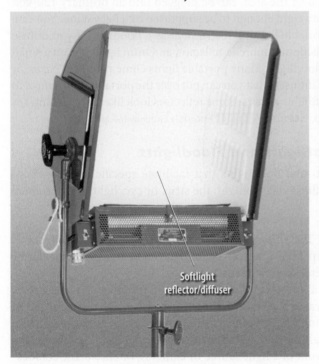

Softlight
reflector/diffuser

8.23 Diffusion Tent

Small portable lights, including small spot-lights, can be made into effective softlights by diffusing their beams with light tents.

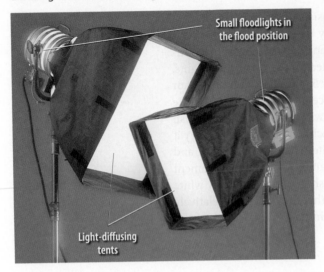

Small floodlights in the flood position

Light-diffusing tents

8.24 Chinese Lantern

These floodlights produce highly diffused light over a large area.

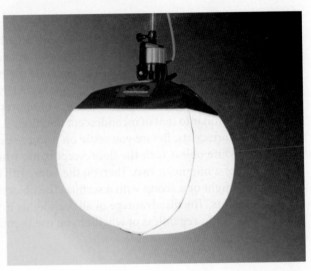

Portable floodlights   When choosing a portable floodlight, look for one that is small, produces a great amount of diffused light, has a reflector that keeps the diffused light from spilling all over the area, can be plugged into an ordinary 120-volt household outlet, and is lightweight enough to be supported by a light stand. You can, however, use any type of portable lighting instrument as a floodlight if you diffuse its beam. When mounted inside an umbrella reflector, an Omni light or even a small Fresnel spot can serve as a floodlight. Many portable lights come with *light boxes,* or *light tents,* which are tentlike diffusers that you can put over the portable light source to change it into an efficient softlight. **SEE 8.23** Some reflectors look like Chinese lanterns and totally enclose the lamp. **SEE 8.24** **ZVL3 CUE 14** LIGHTS→ instruments→ field

> ▶**KEY CONCEPT**
>
> Floodlights produce general, nondirectional illumination and cause slow falloff.

Special-purpose Spotlights and Floodlights

There are a variety of spot- and floodlights that facilitate specific lighting tasks. The most popular are the ellipsoidal spotlight; the strip, or cyc, light; and the small EFP floodlight.

Ellipsoidal spotlight   The *ellipsoidal spotlight* is used for special effects. It produces an extremely sharp, high-intensity beam that can be made rectangular or triangular with movable metal shutters. **SEE 8.25**

Some ellipsoidals have a slot next to the beam-shaping shutters that can hold a variety of metal sheets with variously patterned holes. Such metal sheets have acquired a variety of names, depending on the company that produces them or the LD who uses them. You may hear lighting people call them *gobos* (which can also mean the cutouts that are placed in front of a light source or camera), or *cucoloris* ("cookies" for short). Let's settle on *cookies*. When inserted in the slot of the ellipsoidal spot,

8.25 Ellipsoidal Spotlight

The ellipsoidal spotlight produces an extremely sharp, bright beam. It is used to illuminate precise areas.

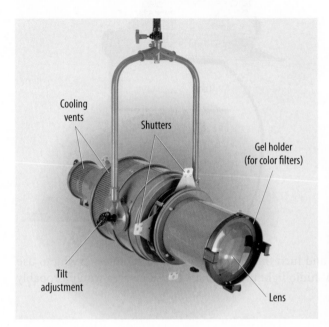

Cooling vents

Shutters

Gel holder (for color filters)

Tilt adjustment

Lens

8.26 Cookie Pattern

Some ellipsoidal spotlights double as pattern projectors. You can insert a variety of metal cutouts, called cookies, whose patterns are projected by the spotlight onto a wall or other surface.

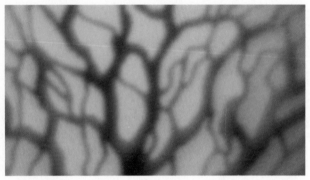

the cookie pattern can be projected onto a dull-looking surface to make it more interesting. **SEE 8.26**

Strip, or cyc, light   The *strip*, or *cyc, light* is used primarily to illuminate *cycloramas* (the seamless background curtain that stretches along studio or stage walls), drapes, or large areas of scenery. They are similar to theater border lights and consist of rows of four to twelve quartz lamps mounted in long, boxlike reflectors. These strips are usually positioned side-by-side on the studio floor and shined upward onto the background. **SEE 8.27**

Small EFP floodlight   There are a variety of very small floodlights on the market that run off regular household current. These are used to illuminate small areas that are difficult to reach with larger lights. **SEE 8.28** Much like the clip light, you can move

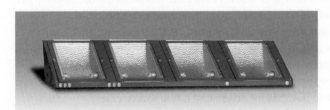

8.27 Strip, or Cyc, Light

These instruments are used primarily to illuminate cycloramas, drapes, or large scenic areas.

8.28 Small EFP Floodlight

This small EFP floodlight (Lowel V-light) runs off ordinary household current and can be used to illuminate small areas. When mounted inside an umbrella reflector, it serves as a softlight.

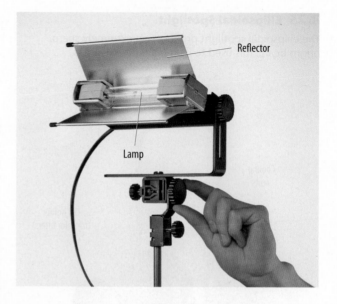

them into position quickly and turn them on in a matter of minutes. Trying to use a larger, more cumbersome studio light to illuminate the same area would probably take considerably longer.

LIGHTING TECHNIQUES

Now, let's find out what to do with all these instruments. Start your lighting task with an idea of how you would like a person, scene, or display to look on the video screen, then choose the simplest way of achieving that look. Although there is no universal recipe that guarantees good lighting for every situation, there are established techniques that you can easily adapt to the specific task at hand. But do not become a slave to such techniques. Although you may often wish you had more instruments, more space, and especially more time to do justice to the lighting, you should realize that the final criterion for video lighting is not how faithfully you imitate nature, or how closely you observe the standards as outlined in a book, but how it looks on the monitor and, especially, whether you got it done on time.

Let's take a look at some of the lighting basics: operation of lights, studio lighting, and field lighting.

Operation of Lights

Lighting presents some obvious hazards. Ordinary household current is powerful enough to kill. The lamps, barn doors, and sometimes the instruments themselves get so hot that they can cause serious burns. If placed too close to combustible material, lighting instruments can cause fires. The instruments with barn doors are suspended far above studio floor areas and, if not properly secured, can come crashing down. Staring into a bright, high-intensity light beam can cause temporary vision problems. Even so, you don't need to be intimidated and give up lighting before getting started. You can easily eliminate these hazards by observing a few safety rules.

CHECKLIST: LIGHTING SAFETY

☑ *Electricity*   Don't ever handle an instrument with wet hands, even if it is unplugged. Do not "hot-plug" an instrument: switch off the power before connecting or disconnecting the power cables or patch cords. Patch cords connect selected lighting instruments to specific *dimmers*. Wear gloves. Use fiberglass safety ladders rather than metal ones. Do not touch any metal while working with a power cable. If you need an adapter to connect a power cable or to plug it in, tape the connection with electrician's tape. Use only those instruments that are absolutely necessary. If you can, let the larger instruments warm up through reduced power before bringing the dimmer up full. Turn off the studio lights and use house lights for basic blocking rehearsals; this will keep the studio cooler and will also extend the life of the expensive bulbs. Do not waste electric energy.

☑ *Heat*   The quartz lamps (quartz housing and a tungsten-halogen filament) get extremely hot. They heat up the barn doors and even the housing of the lighting instrument itself. Never touch the barn doors or the instrument with your bare hands once it is turned on. Use gloves or a lighting pole (a long wooden pole with a metal hook at one end) to adjust the barn doors or the instrument.

Keep instruments away from combustible materials, such as curtains, cloth, books, or wood paneling. If you need to place a lighting instrument close to such materials, insulate the materials with a sheet of aluminum foil.

Let lamps cool down before replacing them. Don't ever touch quartz lamps with your fingers. Fingerprints or any other stuff clinging to the quartz housing will cause the lamp to overheat at those points and burn out. Use a tissue or, in case of emergency, your shirttail when exchanging lamps. Be sure the power is shut off before reaching into an instrument.

☑ *Placing and securing instruments*   Before lowering movable battens, see to it that the studio floor is clear of people, equipment, and scenery. Because the tie-off rails, where the counterweight battens are locked, are often hidden behind the cyclorama (so you can't see the studio floor), always give a warning before actually lowering the batten, such as "Batten 5C coming down!" Wait for an "all-clear" signal before lowering the batten, and have someone watch the studio floor while you do so. Tighten all necessary bolts on the *C-clamp*. **SEE 8.29** Secure the instrument to the batten, and the barn doors to the instrument with a safety chain or cable. Check the power connections for obviously worn or loose plugs and cables.

Whenever moving a ladder, watch for obstacles below and above. Don't leave a lighting wrench or other tool on top of the ladder. Never take unnecessary chances by leaning way out to reach an instrument. Whenever possible, have somebody steady the ladder for you.

☑ *Eyes*   When adjusting an instrument, try not to look directly into the light. Work from behind, rather than in front of, the instrument. This way you look *with* the beam, rather than into it. If you have to look into the light, do it very briefly and wear dark glasses.

8.29 C-clamp

Use the C-clamp to fasten heavy lighting instruments to the lighting battens. Even when tightly fastened to the batten, the C-clamp allows the lighting instrument to be turned.

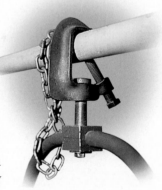

►**KEY CONCEPT**

Do not abandon safety for expediency.

Studio Lighting

Now you are ready to do some actual lighting assignments. Although you may struggle with lighting at remote locations more often than you do in fancy studio work, you will find that learning to light is easier in the studio than in the field. The art of lighting is neither mysterious nor complicated if you keep in mind its basic functions: to reveal the basic shape of the object or person, to lighten or darken the shadows, to show where the object is relative to the background, and to give the object or person some sparkle.

Photographic principle, or triangle lighting   Still photographers have taught us that all these functions can be accomplished with three lights: the *key light*, which reveals the basic shape; the *fill light*, which fills in the shadows if they are too dense; and the *back light*, which separates the object from the background and provides some sparkle. The various lighting techniques for video and motion pictures are firmly rooted in this basic principle of still photography, called the *photographic principle*, or *triangle lighting*. Some lighting people have yet another name for the photographic principle: *three-point lighting*. **SEE 8.30**

> **►KEY CONCEPT**
>
> The basic photographic principle, or triangle lighting, consists of a key light, a fill light, and a back light.

8.30 Basic Photographic Principle

The basic photographic principle uses a key light, a fill light, and a back light. They are arranged in a triangle, with the back light at its apex, opposite the camera.

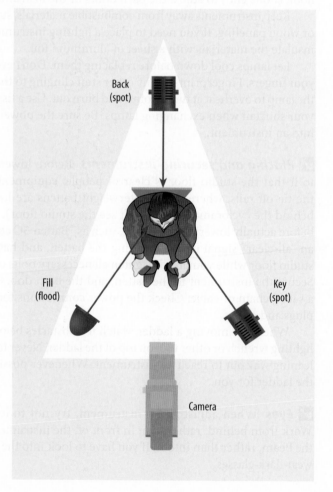

Back
(spot)

Fill
(flood)

Key
(spot)

Camera

8.31 Key Light

The key light is the principal light source. It reveals the basic shape of the object. A spotlight is generally used as a key.

8.32 Back Light Added

The back light outlines the subject against the background and provides sparkle. Focused spots are used as back lights.

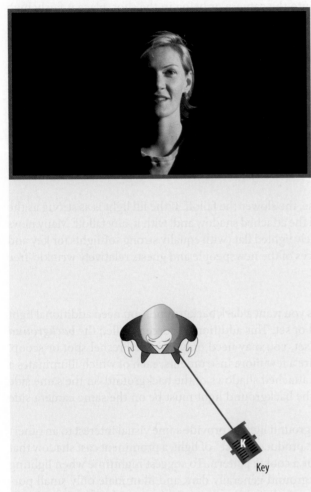

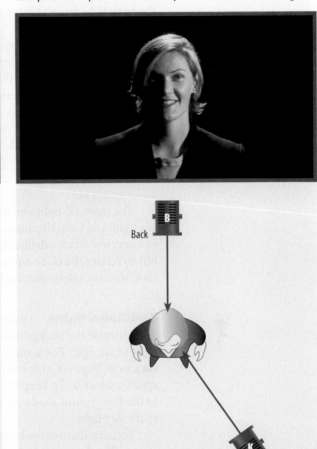

Applying the lighting triangle   In the studio slightly diffused Fresnel spots are normally used for key lights. Fresnels let you aim the beam at the object without too much spill into other set areas. But you can also use other instruments for a key light, such as an Omni light, a scoop, a softlight, or even a light that is reflected off a white card. As you can see, the *key light* is not defined by the instrument used but by its function: to reveal the basic shape of the object. The key light is usually placed above and to the right or left of the front of the object. **SEE 8.31** Note that when a spotlight is used as a key, it produces fast falloff (a dense attached shadow). **ZVL3 CUE 15**
LIGHTS→ Triangle lighting→ key

To outline the subject more clearly against the background, and especially to give the hair—and with it the whole picture—some sparkle and luster, you need a *back light.* Some lighting people believe that it is the back light in particular that gives the lighting its professional polish. **SEE 8.32**

As the name suggests, the back light falls on the back of the subject's head. You place it opposite the camera directly behind, and above, the subject. Because the area to be illuminated by the back light is rather limited, use Fresnel spots. To keep the back light from shining into the camera or being in the shot, place it fairly high behind the subject.

Some LDs insist on having the back light burn with the same intensity as the key. Such a rule makes little sense because the intensity of the back light depends on the relative reflectance of the object or subject. A blond woman who wears a white blouse certainly needs a less intense beam than a man in a dark suit who has curly black hair. **ZVL3 CUE 16** ►LIGHTS→ Triangle lighting→ back

To slow down falloff and thereby render dense shadows more transparent, you use a *fill light.* Floodlights are generally used, but you can of course also use Fresnels (or any other spotlights) for fill. Obviously, you place the fill light on the side opposite the key light and aim it toward the shadow area. **SEE 8.33** **ZVL3 CUE 17** ►LIGHTS→ Triangle lighting→ fill

The more fill light you use, the slower the falloff. If the fill light is as strong as the key light, you have eliminated the attached shadow and, with it, any falloff. Many news or interview sets are deliberately lighted flat (with equally strong softlights for key and fill) to render the close-up faces of the newspeople and guests relatively wrinkle-free (but, unfortunately, also flat).

Additional lights   Unless you want a dark background, you need additional light to illuminate the background or set. This additional source is called the **background light** or *set light.* For a small set, you may need only a single Fresnel spot or scoop. **SEE 8.34** A large set may require a few more instruments, each of which illuminates a specific set area. To keep the attached shadows of the background on the same side as the foreground shadows, the background light must be on the same camera side as the key light.

You can also use the background light to provide some visual interest to an otherwise dull background: you can produce a "slice" of light, a prominent cast shadow that cuts across the background, or a cookie pattern. To suggest nighttime when lighting an interior set, keep the background generally dark and illuminate only small portions of it. If you want to evoke daylight, illuminate the background evenly. You can colorize a neutral gray or white background simply by putting color gels in front of the background lights. Colored light can save you a lot of painting. **ZVL3 CUE 18** ►LIGHTS→ Triangle lighting→ background

Adapting the lighting triangle   Whenever possible, put up the set where the lights are rather than move the lights to the set location. If, for example, you have to light a simple two-person interview in the studio, look up at the lighting grid and find a key, fill, and backlight triangle and place the chair in the middle of it. Even if you can't find another lighting triangle for the other chair, you are still ahead—half of the lighting is already done. You will find that you cannot always apply the photographic principle so that the three instruments form the prescribed triangle. This is perfectly normal. Realize that the lighting triangle is a basic principle, not a mandate.

8.33 Fill Light Added

The fill light slows down falloff and renders shadows more transparent. Floodlights are generally used to fill in dense shadows.

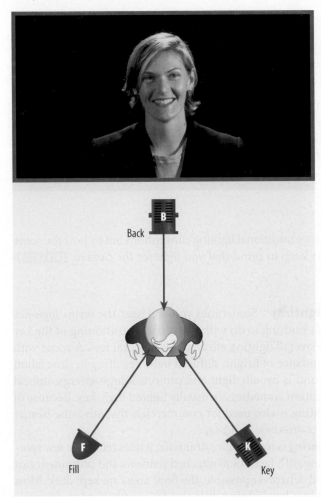

8.34 Background Light Added

The background, or set, light illuminates the background and various set areas. Spots or floodlights are used on the same side as the key.

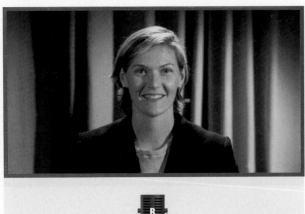
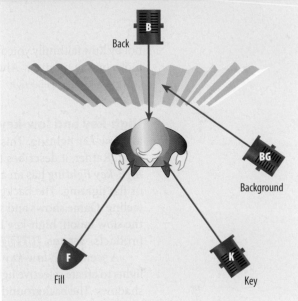

Always try to accomplish a lighting setup with as few instruments as possible. If the falloff from a diffused key light is slow enough (the shadow side is not too dense), you don't need a fill light. Even when doing studio lighting, you may find that a reflector is more effective for filling in shadows than setting up a fill light. (We discuss the use of reflectors in the context of field lighting later in this chapter.) Sometimes the key light will spill over onto the background and eliminate the need for a set light.

In any case, don't be a slave to the photographic principle. Sometimes a single Fresnel aimed at the windshield of a car is all you need to produce a convincing nighttime effect; at other times you may need four or five carefully placed instruments to re-create the effect of a single candle. The effectiveness of the lighting is determined

8.35 High-key Lighting

High-key lighting shows a bright scene with an abundance of diffused light. The background is usually light.

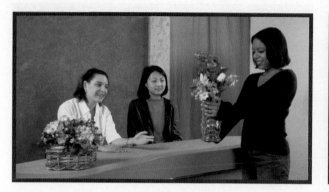

8.36 Low-key Lighting

Low-key lighting shows dramatic, selective lighting with fast-falloff attached and prominent cast shadows. The background is usually dark.

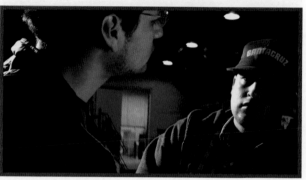

not by how faithfully you observe traditional lighting conventions but by how the scene looks on the monitor. Always keep in mind that you light *for the camera.* **ZVL3 CUE 19**
LIGHTS→ Triangle lighting→ try it

High-key and low-key lighting   Sometimes you will hear the terms *high-key* and *low-key* lighting. This has nothing to do with the vertical positioning of the key light. Rather, it describes the overall lighting effect and its general feel. A scene with **high-key lighting** has an abundance of bright, diffused light, resulting in slow falloff or flat lighting. The background is usually light and projects a high-energy, upbeat feeling. Game shows and situation comedies are usually lighted high-key. Because of the slow falloff, high-key lighting is also used for commercials that advertise beauty products. **SEE 8.35** **ZVL3 CUE 20** LIGHTS→ Design→ high key

A scene with **low-key lighting** is much more dramatic; it uses relatively few spotlights to create selective lighting with fast-falloff attached shadows and prominent cast shadows. The background and, wherever possible, the floor areas are kept dark. Most outdoor night scenes exhibit low-key lighting. It is also frequently used in dramatic scenes in soap operas, in mystery and crime shows, and sometimes in science-fiction movies. **SEE 8.36** **ZVL3 CUE 21** LIGHTS→ Design→ low key

Light plot   For more-complicated shows, you need to prepare a **light plot**. Some light plots are rough sketches to indicate the approximate position of lights. **SEE 8.37** Others are drawn on a floor plan grid, which shows the background scenery, the major action areas, and the principal camera positions. Some light plots show the position, type, and functions of the lighting instruments needed. Arrows indicate the approximate directions of the beams. **SEE 8.38**

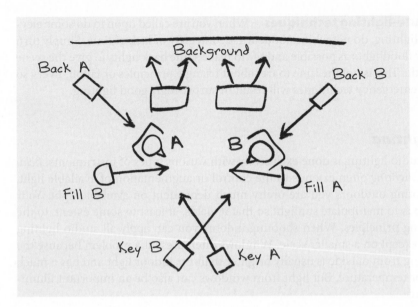

8.37 Simple Light Plot Sketch for Two-person Interview

Most light plots are rough sketches that indicate the types of lights used (spots or floods) and their approximate positions.

8.38 Detailed Light Plot for Two-person Interview

This light plot shows the type and the position of the lighting instruments used and the approximate direction of their beams. Sometimes light plots even indicate the size (wattage) of the instruments. Note that there are two overlapping lighting triangles—one for person A and the other for person B.

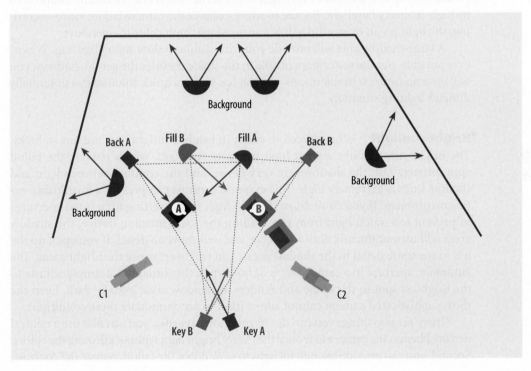

Last-minute-lighting techniques   When you are called upon to do some eleventh-hour lighting, do not whine about artistic integrity or lack of time. Simply turn on as many floodlights as possible and try to place some back lights to give the scene some sparkle. This is not the time to fret about triangle principles or falloff. Every so often such emergency techniques will result in surprisingly good lighting.

Field Lighting

Whereas studio lighting is done exclusively with various types of instruments, *field,* or *location, lighting* often extends to the control or augmentation of available light. When shooting outdoors you are pretty much dependent on available light. Your lighting job is to manipulate sunlight so that it yields, at least to some extent, to the basic lighting principles. When shooting indoors you can apply all studio lighting principles, except on a smaller scale. Windows often present a problem because the light entering from outside is usually brighter than the indoor light and has a much higher color temperature. But light from windows can also be an important illumination source.

Outdoors—overcast   An overcast or foggy day is ideal for outdoor shooting. The clouds and the fog act as giant diffusion filters: the giant and brutally bright spotlight of the sun becomes a huge but gentle softlight. The highly diffused light produces slow falloff and transparent shadows. The camera likes such low-contrast lighting and produces crisp and true colors throughout the scene. The scene is basically illuminated by high-intensity baselight. Be sure to white-balance the camera before video-recording; the light on an overcast day has a surprisingly high color temperature.

  A large shadow area will provide you with similarly slow-falloff lighting. Whenever possible, put the on-camera people in the shade. Besides the gentle shadows, you will have no contrast problems. As you can see, this is a quick solution to a potentially difficult lighting situation.

Bright sunlight   When forced to shoot in bright sunlight, you are not so lucky. The bright sun acts like a giant high-intensity spotlight, which renders the falloff appropriately fast; the shadows are very dense, and the contrast between light and shadow sides is extremely high. This extreme contrast can present a formidable exposure problem. If you close down the iris (high *f*-stop setting for a small aperture) to prevent too much light from overloading the CCD imaging device, the shadow areas will turn uniformly dark and dense and will show no detail. If you open up the iris to see some detail in the shadow areas, you will overexpose the bright areas. The automatic aperture in a camcorder is of no help in this situation: it simply adjusts to the brightest spot in the scene and renders all shadow areas equally dark. Even the most sophisticated camera cannot adjust itself to accommodate these conditions.

  There are two things you can do. As mentioned earlier, you can first use a neutral density filter on the camera to reduce the overly bright light without affecting the colors. Second, you can provide enough fill light to slow down the falloff, reduce the contrast,

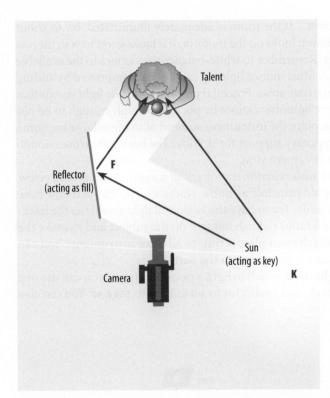

8.39 Use of a Reflector

The reflector acts like a fill light: it bounces some light back toward the dense shadow areas and slows down falloff.

and make the attached shadows more transparent without overexposing the bright areas. But where in the field can you get a fill light strong enough to offset the sun?

In expensive and elaborate productions, high-intensity spotlights (usually HMI lights), which burn at 5,600K, are used as outdoor fill lights. Fortunately, you can also use the sun to serve simultaneously as key and fill lights—all you need is a *reflector* to bounce some of the sunlight back toward the shadow area. **SEE 8.39** You can use a sheet of foam core or a white card as a reflector, or use crumpled aluminum foil taped to a stiff backing. You can also use a number of commercially available reflectors that fold up and prove effective over considerable distances. The closer you hold the reflector to the object, the more intense the fill light will be. Some LDs or *DPs* (*directors of photography*) use multiple reflectors to reflect light into areas that face away from the light source. In this case, the reflector becomes the principal light source. With good reflectors (mirrors), you can even guide sunlight indoors to light up a room or hallway without any lighting instruments.

Avoid shooting against any bright background, such as a sun-drenched white wall, the ocean, or a lake. Anyone standing in front of it will be rendered in silhouette, unless you use huge reflectors or other high-intensity fill lights. Whenever possible find some shade in which to position the subject. When shooting at a lakeshore or the ocean beach, use a large umbrella to create the necessary shadow area. The umbrella will not only make your lighting job considerably easier but also provide some visual interest. **ZVL3 CUE 22** ▶LIGHTS→ Field→ outdoor | use of reflectors

▶ **KEY CONCEPT**

Reflectors can replace lighting instruments.

Indoors without windows   If the room is adequately illuminated, try to shoot with available light and see how it looks on the monitor. If it looks good to you, there is no need for additional lights. Remember to white-balance the camera to the available light before starting to shoot. Most indoor lighting can be easily improved by adding some back lights in the appropriate areas. Potential problems include light stands that show up on-camera or a back light that cannot be positioned high enough to be out of camera range. In this case, place the instrument somewhat to the side, or use some 1 × 2 lumber to create a temporary support for it. Move the back light close enough to the subject to keep it out of camera view.

When lighting a person who remains stationary in a room, as in an interview, you use the same photographic principle as in the studio except that you now have to place portable lights on stands. Try to have the key or fill light double as the background light. To avoid the infamous reddish *hot spot* on the subject and to make the light look generally softer, attach spun-glass scrims to all three instruments. You can use wooden clothespins to attach the scrims to the barn doors.

If you have only two lights with which to light a person indoors, you can use one as the key, the other as the back, and a reflector to act as the fill. **SEE 8.40** You can also

8.40 Two-point Indoor Lighting

To achieve effective triangle lighting with only two lights, use one for the key light and the other for the back light. Fill light is achieved with a reflector.

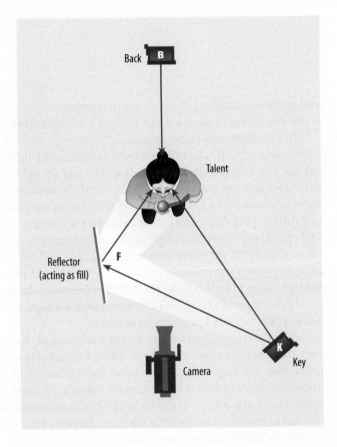

place a softlight for a key (light diffused by a light tent) almost directly opposite the person to avoid a dense shadow side, then use the second light as a back light.

If you have just one lighting instrument, such as an Omni light, you can use it as a key, with the reflector acting as the fill. In such a setup, you must necessarily sacrifice the back light. If you diffuse the key light and move it closer to the camera than it is in figure 8.40, however, you will light the face almost straight on. You can then use the reflector in the back (out of camera range) to provide the all-important back light.

To light an ordinary-sized room so that you can follow somebody walking through it, use the portable lights in the flood position and reflect them off the ceiling or walls, or diffuse their beams with scrims. If available, use light-diffusing umbrellas. Aim the instrument into the umbrella, with the opening of the umbrella toward the scene, or at reflectors rather than directly toward the action area. You can apply the same technique for lighting a large interior, except that you need more or higher-powered instruments. The idea is to get as much baselight (highly diffused overall light) as possible with a minimum of instruments.

Interiors with windows   As mentioned before, windows can present a formidable lighting problem. Even if you don't shoot against them, they admit a great amount of high-color-temperature light. If you try to augment the bluish 5,600K outdoor light with the normal indoor 3,200K lighting instruments, the camera will have trouble finding the correct white balance. The simplest way to match the lower 3,200K indoor color temperature with the prevailing 5,600K outdoor color temperature is to attach a light-blue gel to the indoor lighting instruments. The blue gel helps raise their color temperature to approximate the 5,600K outdoor light. Even if it is not a perfect match, the camera can be properly white-balanced for both types of light.

> ►**KEY CONCEPT**
>
> In the field, light for visibility rather than artistic impact.

The best way to cope with windows is to avoid them: draw the curtains and use a normal triangle lighting setup. Many times, however, you can use the window light as a back light or even as a key. For example, when using the window as a back light, you need to position the subject in such a way that the light strikes from the side and the back. Then position the key light and the camera. **SEE 8.41** Obviously, the window should be off-camera. By changing the window from a hazard to an asset and with only one lighting instrument in the room, you have achieved a professional lighting setup. What about the fill light? The spill from the window and the diffused key light should be enough to provide for relatively slow falloff. If not, you can always use a reflector to bounce some of the key light back as fill. **ZVL3 CUE 23** ►LIGHTS→ Field→ indoor | mixed

8.41 Window Acting as Back Light

In this interview setup, the lighting is done with a single instrument. A diffused Lowel Omni with a light-blue gel acts as the key light. The back light is provided by the window, which is kept out of camera range.

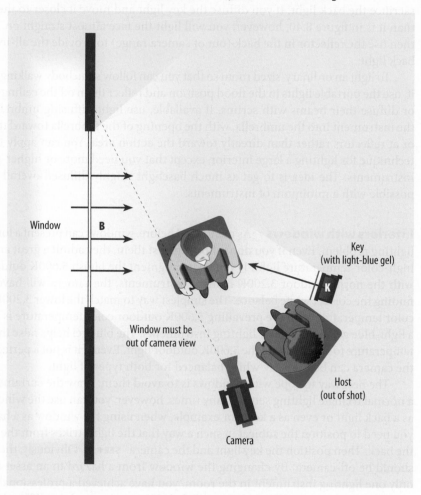

Window

B

Window must be
out of camera view

Key
(with light-blue gel)

K

Host
(out of shot)

Camera

GUIDELINES: FIELD LIGHTING

✔ **Scout ahead** Scout the location and determine the lighting requirements before the actual shooting date. Establish a contact person and get his or her name, address, and all phone numbers. Check the breaker box and determine the available power, the nature of the outlets, and the extension cords needed. Have adapters available that fit the various outlets.

✔ **Be prepared** Always take with you a few rolls of gaffer's tape, a roll of aluminum foil, gloves, a small wrench, some wooden clothespins (plastic ones melt), and a small fire extinguisher.

☑ *Don't overload circuits* Once on location don't overload the circuit. Although a normal 15-amp household outlet will accommodate 1,500 watts of lighting instruments, do not plug more than 1,000 watts into a single circuit. Realize that several outlets may be on the same circuit, even if they are in different corners of the room. To test which outlets are on the same circuit, plug a light into various outlets and turn off the breaker. If the light goes out, you are on the designated circuit. If the light stays on, the outlet is connected to another circuit. Keep in mind that even long extension cables can add to the circuit load.

☑ *Don't waste lamp life* Turn on the lights only as needed. The lamps for portable lighting instruments have a limited life span. Turning off the lights as much as possible will preserve energy, extend the life of the lamps, and reduce the heat in the performance area.

☑ *Secure the light stands* Be especially careful when placing lighting instruments on portable stands. Secure all light stands with sandbags so they won't tip over when somebody brushes against them. Route extension cords out of the main traffic pattern. If you have to lay them across a hallway or a threshold, tape them securely in place (here is where the gaffer's tape comes in handy) and/or put a rug or rubber doormat over them.

☑ *Move cords carefully* Don't pull on an extension cord that is connected to a lighting instrument; light stands tip over easily, especially when fully extended.

☑ *Be time conscious* Don't underestimate the time it takes to set up even simple location lighting.

M A I N   P O I N T S

▶ **Light and Shadow Control**

Lighting is the deliberate illumination of a performance area and the control of attached and cast shadows.

▶ **Types of Light and Light Intensity**

The two basic types of light are directional and diffused. Directional light is focused and causes harsh shadows. Diffused light is spread out and creates soft shadows. Light intensity is measured in foot-candles (fc) or European lux. There are approximately 10 lux per foot-candle.

▶ **Contrast and Measuring Light**

Contrast is the difference between the darkest and the brightest areas in the camera picture. This contrast is often expressed as a ratio, such as 60:1, which means that the brightest spot is 60 times the intensity of the darkest spot. Cameras tolerate a relatively limited contrast ratio, ranging from 50:1 to 100:1. When measuring contrast, the light meter must read reflected light. When measuring baselight levels, the meter reads incident light.

▶ **Shadows and Falloff**

There are two types of shadows: attached and cast. Attached shadows are affixed to the object; they cannot be seen independent of it. Cast shadows can be seen independent of the object that causes them. Falloff indicates the change from light to shadow and the contrast between light and shadow areas. Fast falloff means that the light area changes abruptly into dense shadow area; the contrast is high. Slow falloff means that the light turns gradually into the shadow side; the contrast is low.

▶ **Colors and Color Temperature**

Colors are generated through additive color mixing. All colors are mixed by adding the primary light colors—red, green, and blue (RGB)—in various proportions. Color temperature refers to the relative reddishness or bluishness of white light. White-balancing adjusts the camera to the color temperature of the prevailing illumination so that the camera will reproduce a white object as white on the video screen.

▶ **Lighting Instruments**

Lights are usually classified into spotlights and floodlights, and studio and portable lights. Spotlights produce a sharp, focused beam; floodlights produce highly diffused, nondirectional illumination. Studio lights are normally suspended from the ceiling. Portable lights are smaller and supported by collapsible light stands.

▶ **The Photographic Principle, or Triangle Lighting**

Lighting functions can usually be achieved with the basic photographic principle: a key light (principal light source), a fill light (fills in dense shadows), and a back light (separates the subject from the background and gives it sparkle). This is also known as three-point lighting. Reflectors frequently substitute for fill lights. The background light is an additional light used for lighting the background and set area. In field, or location, lighting, it is often more important to provide sufficient illumination than careful triangle lighting. In the field floodlights are used more often than spotlights.

▶ **High-key and Low-key Lighting**

High-key lighting uses an abundance of bright, diffused light, resulting in slow-falloff or flat lighting; the high-key scene generally shows a light background. Low-key lighting uses few spotlights to create fast-falloff lighting and prominent cast shadows; it illuminates only selected areas and projects a dramatic feel.

▶ **Windows**

In EFP lighting, a window can serve as a key or a side-back light, so long as it is off-camera. All incandescent instruments must have light-blue color media attached to match the color temperature of the light coming through the window.

Z E T T L ' S   V I D E O L A B   3 . 0

For your reference, or to track your work, the Zettl's VideoLab 3.0 program cues in this chapter are listed here with their corresponding page numbers.

CHAPTER 9

KEY TERMS

aspect ratio The ratio of the width of the television screen to its height. In STV (standard television), it is 4 × 3 (4 units wide by 3 units high); for HDTV (high-definition television), it is 16 × 9 (16 units wide by 9 units high).

character generator (C.G.) A computer dedicated to the creation of letters and numbers in various fonts. Its output can be directly integrated into video images.

chroma key Special key effect that uses a color (usually blue or green) for the key source backdrop. All blue or green areas are replaced by the base picture during the key.

digital video effects (DVE) Video effects generated by a computer with high-capacity hard drives and graphics software. The computer system dedicated to DVE is called a *graphics generator*.

electronic still store (ESS) system Stores many still video frames in digital form for easy access.

essential area The section of the television picture that is seen by the home viewer, regardless of minor misalignments of the receiver. Also called *safe title area*.

key An electronic effect in which the keyed image (figure—usually letters) blocks out portions of the base picture (background) and therefore appears to be layered on top of it.

matte key The key (usually letters) is filled with gray or a color.

super Short for *superimposition*. A double exposure of two images, with the top one letting the bottom one show through.

wipe A transition in which one image seems to "wipe off" (replace) the other from the screen.

Graphics and Effects

Now that you know what a video camera does and how to give lens-generated images effective composition, you can expand your creative efforts to synthetic video—images that are electronically manipulated or totally computer-generated. These synthetic images can be as simple as electronically generated titles that appear over a background image, or a computer-generated landscape that changes with your point of view. Although the camera still supplies the majority of video images, synthetic images are becoming increasingly more a part of video production.

This chapter explains analog and digital image manipulation and the major aspects of synthetic image creation.

▶ **PRINCIPLES OF GRAPHICS**
   Aspect ratio, essential area, readability, color, animated graphics, and style

▶ **STANDARD ELECTRONIC VIDEO EFFECTS**
   Superimposition, key, and wipe

▶ **DIGITAL EFFECTS**
   Digital image manipulation equipment, common digital video effects, and synthetic image creation

The relative ease with which you can change fonts and their appearance with a word-processing program has spilled over into television graphics. You are certainly familiar with the many variations of letters in titles: Some fly onto or dance across the screen. Weather maps not only display the temperatures but have clouds or fog drift over them or rain and snow fall on them. Traffic maps show where accidents occurred or how to get around a traffic jam. We have become so used to these graphics that we don't consider them special effects, although such effects demand highly sophisticated graphics software and especially skilled computer artists.

Unfortunately, many such dazzling displays do not always contribute to more-effective communication. Even if you don't intend to become a graphic artist or an art director, you need to understand the basic principles of video graphics and the common analog and digital video effects. This knowledge will help you integrate appropriate and effective graphics in your productions.

PRINCIPLES OF GRAPHICS

The basic elements and principles of video graphics include aspect ratio, essential area, readability, color, animated graphics, and style.

Aspect Ratio

As you recall from chapter 6, **aspect ratio** describes the basic shape of the television screen—the relationship between screen width and height. The STV aspect ratio is 4 × 3, which means its screen is 4 units wide by 3 units high. A *unit* can be any length—inches, feet, even meters. The ratio is also expressed as 1.33:1. This means that for every unit of screen height, there are 1.33 units of screen width. The HDTV aspect ratio is 16 × 9, or 1.78:1, which means the screen is horizontally stretched, not unlike the screen in a movie theater. Within the overall aspect ratio of the screen, you can generate digital picture frames with a variety of horizontal and even vertical aspect ratios (see figures 6.1 and 6.2).

The advantage of the HDTV aspect ratio is that you can include horizontally stretched scenes and titles that you would have to *crop* (cut at the sides) or rearrange in the standard aspect ratio. **SEE 9.1 AND 9.2** It can display wide-screen motion pictures without the need for *dead zones* (black bars) at the top and the bottom of the screen. Close-ups of faces, however, are more effectively framed in the STV aspect ratio.

Essential Area

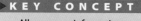

KEY CONCEPT

All necessary information must be contained within the essential (safe title) area.

Regardless of the aspect ratio, you need to keep all the important information within the **essential area**. Also known as the *safe title area,* this is the picture area displayed by the average home receiver, regardless of the minor loss of picture area during transmission or a slightly misaligned TV set. **SEE 9.3 AND 9.4** The viewfinders of most studio cameras allow you to switch to a secondary frame that outlines the safe title area.

9.1 Standard Television Aspect Ratio

The STV aspect ratio is 4 units wide by 3 units high, or 1.33:1.

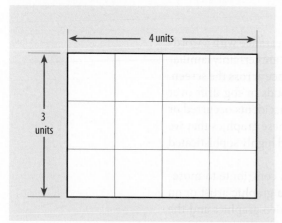

9.2 High-definition Television Aspect Ratio

The HDTV aspect ratio is 16 units wide by 9 units high, or 1.78:1.

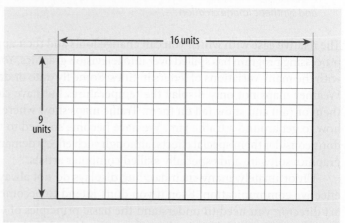

9.3 **Essential Area**

The essential, or safe title, area is centered within the television screen. All necessary information must be contained in the essential area.

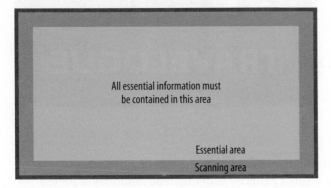

All essential information must
be contained in this area

Essential area

Scanning area

9.4 **Title Outside the Essential Area**

A Although we can read the complete title on a well-adjusted monitor . . .

B . . . the information that lies outside the essential area gets lost on the home receiver.

We now return to our regular programming.

Ne now return to ou egular programmin

Readability

Although the camera part of your camcorder may reproduce exceptionally fine picture detail, its video-recording system and your TV set may not. In practice this means that you need to choose lettering that can be easily read on-screen. Sometimes the titles dance so much or appear for such a short time that only a speed-reader can make sense of them. The following points will assist you in designing effective video graphics:

▶ Keep all the important information within the essential area. If you use the essential area of the 4 × 3 aspect ratio, your graphics will also show up clearly on a 16 × 9 screen.

▶ Use fonts that are big and bold enough to show up even when the picture resolution is less than ideal and when the background is especially cluttered. **SEE 9.5**

9.5 Bold Letters over a Busy Background

This title reads well despite the busy background. Its letters are bold and have enough contrast from the background to ensure readability.

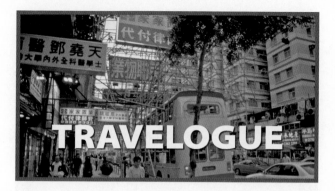

▶ Limit the amount of information and arrange the lettering in blocks. The information should form distinct patterns rather than be randomly scattered on the screen. This block design is especially important for Web pages, where display space is severely limited. **SEE 9.6 AND 9.7**

▶ Use a block design especially when dividing up the screen area for unrelated information. **SEE 9.8**

9.6 Block Organization of Titles

Information is easier to read when the titles are organized in graphic blocks.

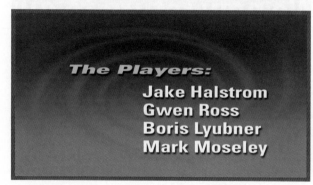

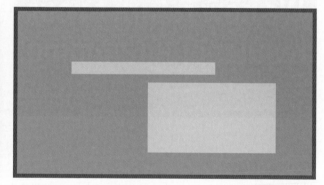

9.7 Disorganization of Titles

Visual clutter occurs when the information is not graphically organized. The scattered bits of information are hard to perceive, especially on a video screen.

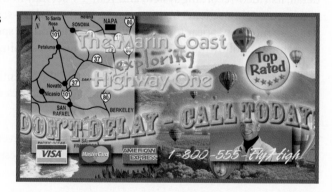

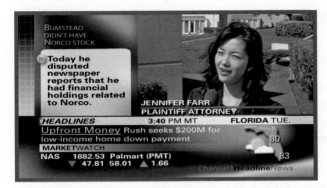

9.8 Multiscreen Blocks

When dissimilar pieces of information are graphically organized into blocks, or multiple screens, the information is easier to read.

Color

You already learned that the video camera and the television receiver produce all colors from the three additive (light) primaries of red, green, and blue (RGB). Now you need to arrange these colors so that they help clarify and intensify the intended message. Without going into complicated color theory, we'll jump directly to a practical way of using colors effectively in graphics and scenic displays: divide them not into their *hues*—their actual colors—but into high-energy and low-energy categories.

High-energy colors are what we ordinarily call "loud" or "bright," such as bold reds, yellows, and blues. *Low-energy* colors are the more washed-out, pastel colors, such as beige, pink, light blue, and various grays. To draw attention to a title or graphic area, use a high-energy color set off against a low-energy background. **SEE 9.9 AND 9.10** Applying high-energy colors to both the foreground (title) and the background is less effective—both shout with equal intensity and vie for attention. Many Web pages suffer from such an indiscriminate use of high-energy colors. As a result, the user is likely to ignore all of these areas and surf to a less demanding page. If both foreground and background colors are low-energy, the overall graphic is subdued. Many commercials that are deliberately low-energy are shot in black-and-white. The idea is to give you

> ►**KEY CONCEPT**
>
> Use high-energy colors for the foreground (titles) and low-energy colors for the background.

9.9 Low-energy Color

Low-energy colors are desaturated, which means they have little color strength. Most pastel colors are low-energy.

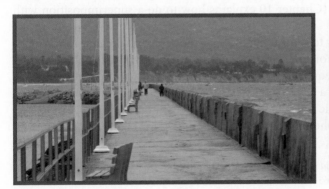

9.10 High-energy Color

High-energy colors have high saturation, which makes them bold. They are especially effective when set against a low-energy background.

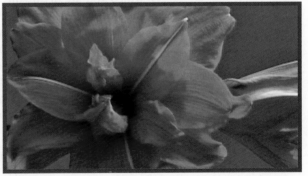

relief from loud, high-energy messages and stimulate you to mentally supply your own color palette.[1]

Animated Graphics

To capture your attention, titles are often *animated,* that is, made to move in some fashion. Written information *crawls* sideways across the screen, from one edge to the other. Some titles fly onto the screen or appear gradually from the sides or the top or bottom. Other titles zoom in or out, dancing or flashing on-screen. Although such titles draw immediate attention, they are apt to lose the viewer's attention just as quickly. When using animated titles, ask yourself whether they are appropriate for the content and the overall style of the show.

Style

Style in graphic design means that the visual display shows common elements that are appropriate for the message. The style of the opening titles should signal the nature of the show that follows. Bouncing cartoon letters are obviously the wrong choice for introducing a program that bares human suffering. So are titles that use somber, formal letters to announce a goofy cartoon. To learn more about style, watch the graphics of established news presentations or look through some chic fashion magazines.

> ►**KEY CONCEPT**
> Titles must match the style of the program.

STANDARD ELECTRONIC VIDEO EFFECTS

The standard electronic effects are achieved with an electronic switcher (see chapter 10) and a *special-effects generator (SEG)* that normally is built-in or connected to the switcher. Most postproduction editing software contains more special effects than you will ever need. Many special effects have become so commonplace that they are no longer "special" but are part of the normal video vocabulary, such as the superimposition and various types of keys.

Superimposition

The *superimposition* (or **super** for short) shows a double exposure; it is a simultaneous overlay of two pictures. In a super you can see both complete images at the same time. **SEE 9.11** A super is simply a *dissolve* at the halfway point. Stopping the dissolve a little before the midpoint gives you a superimposition that favors the image from which you were dissolving; stopping a little after the midpoint favors the image to which you are dissolving. (Chapter 10 explains how to do a superimposition with the switcher.)

> ►**KEY CONCEPT**
> The superimposition is a simultaneous overlay of two pictures.

Supers are used mainly to show inner events—thoughts and dreams—or to make an image more complex. You are certainly familiar with the overused close-up of a face over which a dream sequence is superimposed. To reveal the complexity of the movement and the grace of a ballet, you could superimpose a long shot and a close-up of the dancer. This synthetic image now generates its own meaning. As you can see, you are no longer simply photographing a dance but helping create it.

---

1. See Herbert Zettl, *Sight Sound Motion: Applied Media Aesthetics,* 4th ed. (Belmont, Calif.: Thomson Wadsworth, 2005), pp. 65–66.

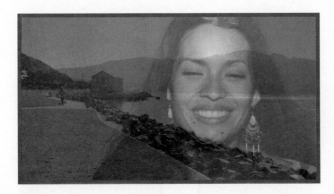

9.11 **Superimposition**

The superimposition, or super for short, shows two images simultaneously, as in a double exposure.

Key

The *key* is another method of electronically combining two video images. But unlike a super, where you can see the base picture through the superimposed image, the keyed image (figure) blocks out portions of the base picture (ground) and appears to be layered on top of it. Paradoxically, there are also keys that are partially transparent, revealing the background image.

To understand how a key works, consider the white lettering of a name that appears over a scene. The *character generator* (*C.G.*) supplies the white title against a black background; the studio camera supplies the picture of a scene. The C.G. title is called the *key source,* and the camera picture of the scene constitutes the *base picture,* or *background.* During the key, the key source cuts itself electronically into the base picture. The base picture replaces all the dark areas around the title but does not overlap the lettering itself. The effect is that the letters appear layered over the scene. **SEE 9.12** Instead of using the C.G., you can also paint the white title on a black card and take a picture of it with a second camera. The camera focused on the title card, rather than the C.G., is now the key source.

Of course, you can key any electronic image into a base picture, such as lines that divide the screen into different areas, or boxlike screen areas that highlight specific images. The box over the news anchor's shoulder is a well-known example of such a key (see figure 9.26).

Because the keying process has numerous technical variations, there are different—and often confusing—names for them. You may hear the terms *key, matte, matte*

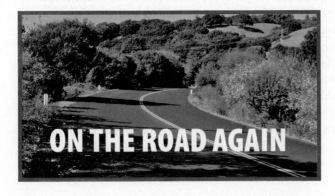

9.12 **Keyed Title**

The keyed letters seem pasted on top of the background image.

9.13 Basic Matte Key

In a basic matte key, the letters are filled with gray or a specific color.

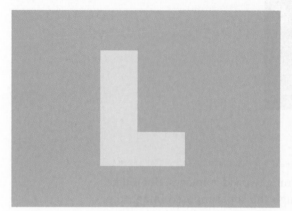

9.14 Edge Mode

In the edge mode, the matte key puts a black border around the letters. This separation from the background makes them more readable.

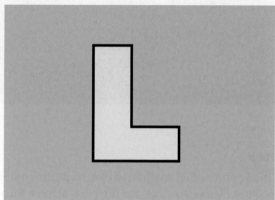

key, or *chroma key* used interchangeably. We group them here by the way they are commonly used: the normal, or luminance, key; the matte key; and the chroma key.

Normal, or luminance, key In a *normal key,* there are only two video sources: the base picture and the key source. The normal key simply replaces the dark areas around the title, making the lighter title appear to be layered on top of the base picture. Because the key process is technically triggered by the light/dark contrast between the title letters and the background, the normal key is also called a *luminance* (light) key. **ZVL3 CUE 1** SWITCHING→ Effects→ keys

Matte key In this key you add a third video source, which is generated by either the switcher or an external video source. Most often a **matte key** refers to the letters of a title that are filled with various colors or grays or that have different borders. **SEE 9.13** The matte keys that create borders around the letters are subdivided into the *edge mode,* the *drop-shadow mode,* and the *outline mode.* **SEE 9.14–9.16** **ZVL3 CUE 2** SWITCHING→ Effects→ key types

Chroma key When using a **chroma key,** the subject or object to be keyed is placed in front of a plain colored backdrop, which is usually blue or green, mainly because these colors are notably absent in skin tones. A typical example of chroma keying is the weathercaster who seems to stand in front of a large weather map. She's actually standing in front of a plain chroma blue (an even, saturated medium-dark blue) backdrop; the weather map is computer-generated. During the key the weather map replaces the blue areas, making the weathercaster appear to be standing in front of it. When she turns to point to the map, she actually sees only the blue backdrop. To coordinate her gestures with the actual weather map, she must watch a monitor that shows the entire key effect. **SEE 9.17** **ZVL3 CUE 3** SWITCHING→ Effects→ special effects

▶**KEY CONCEPT**

The key source cuts into the base picture, making the key seem layered on top of the base.

9.15 Drop-shadow Mode

The attached (drop) shadow gives the letters an added dimension and further separates them from the background.

9.16 Outline Mode

In the outline mode, you see only the contour of the letters. The outline mode requires a relatively simple background.

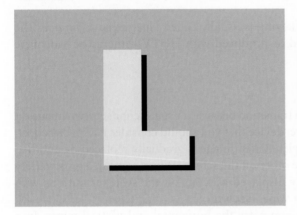

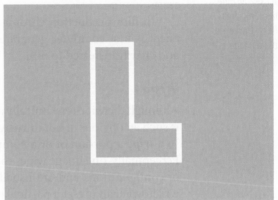

Assuming that you use blue as the chroma-key color, everything that is blue will be replaced by the weather map; therefore the weathercaster cannot wear anything that approximates the color of the backdrop. For example, if the weathercaster wore a blue jacket, you would see only her head and hands during the chroma key. Her jacket would act like the chroma-key backdrop and be replaced by the weather map. If the talent prefers to wear blue, however, you can switch to a green backdrop and a green chroma-key color on the switcher.

Chroma keying can also be used to achieve special effects. If, for example, you cover a dancer's upper body and head with a chroma-key blue material and have her move in front of the blue backdrop, the key will show only her legs dancing.

Chroma keys are often used to simulate backgrounds. You could replace the view of a parking lot from an office window with a spectacular view of the skyline by simply putting the desk and the chair in front of a chroma-key backdrop and using

9.17 Chroma-key Effect: Weathercaster

A In this chroma key, the weathercaster stands in front of a blue backdrop.

B During the key the backdrop is replaced by the computer-enhanced satellite photo.

C The weathercaster seems to stand in front of the photo.

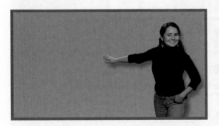

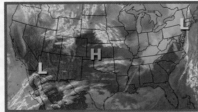

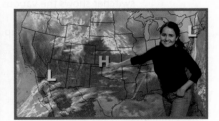

a photo of the skyline as the background source. During the chroma key, the person behind the desk would appear to be sitting in front of a high-rise picture window. The advantage of such a key effect is that you would avoid the formidable lighting problem of having the person silhouetted against the bright window (see chapter 8). **ZVL3 CUE 4**
SWITCHING→ Effects→ key types

In film production chroma keying is usually called *blue-screen technique*. The effect is first computer-generated or produced with HDTV cameras on videotape and later transferred to film.

Wipe

Although the wipe is technically a transition because it usually connects two images, it is such an obvious, if not intrusive, device that you should consider it a special effect. In a **wipe** a portion of or a complete video image is gradually replaced by another. Perceptually, one image wipes the other off the screen. Wipes come in a great variety of configurations and are usually displayed as icons on the switcher buttons with which you can preset a particular wipe. **SEE 9.18**

Some of the most common wipes are the horizontal and vertical wipes. In a *horizontal wipe,* the second image gradually replaces the base picture from the side. **SEE 9.19** A *split screen* done with an analog switcher is simply a horizontal wipe that is stopped midway. More often split screens are generated by digital effects, which give more control over the size of the split image than does the analog wipe. In a *vertical wipe,* the base picture is gradually replaced by the second image from the top down or from the bottom up. **SEE 9.20**

Other popular wipes are *corner wipes,* whereby the second image originates from one corner of the base image, and *diamond wipes,* in which the second image originates in the center of the base image and expands as a diamond-shaped cut-out. **SEE 9.21 AND 9.22** In a *soft wipe,* the demarcation line between the two images is purposely blurred. **SEE 9.23** **ZVL3 CUE 5** SWITCHING→ Transitions→ wipe

Don't go overboard with wipes simply because they are so easy to do. All wipes are highly visible and obvious transitions that need to fit the character and the mood of the video material. Using a diamond wipe during a news program to reveal a more detailed shot of a murder scene is hardly appropriate; but it is quite acceptable when changing from a medium shot of a new computer model to a close-up of its high-capacity hard drive.

9.18 Wipe Patterns

A group of buttons on the switcher shows the various wipe patterns available. Elaborate systems offer up to 100 different patterns.

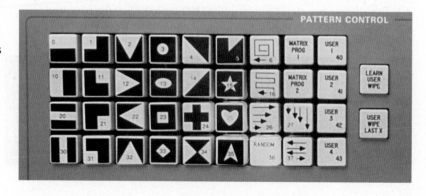

16 × 9 HDTV aspect ratio   On a large or even medium-sized HDTV screen, the wipe seems to travel a long distance and becomes especially noticeable and even intrusive.

9.19 Horizontal Wipe

In a horizontal wipe, the base picture is gradually replaced by another from the side.

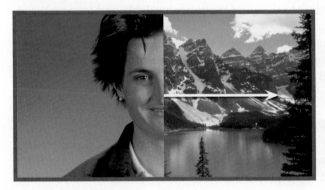

9.20 Vertical Wipe

In a vertical wipe, the base picture is gradually replaced by another from the top down or from the bottom up.

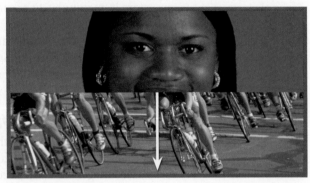

9.21 Corner Wipe

In a corner wipe, the base picture is gradually replaced by another that starts from a corner of the screen.

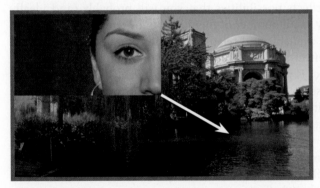

9.22 Diamond Wipe

In a diamond wipe, the base picture is gradually replaced by the second image in an expanding diamond-shaped cutout.

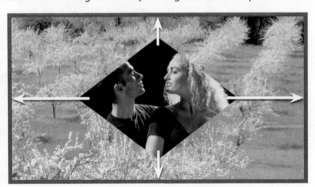

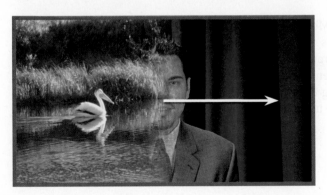

9.23 Soft Wipe

The soft wipe renders the demarcation line between the two images purposely less prominent.

DIGITAL EFFECTS

The computer has greatly expanded the range of possibilities for manipulation of the lens-generated image; it can even create still or animated images that rival high-quality lens-generated images in every respect. ***Digital video effects (DVE)*** change the normal analog video signal into digital data—or use the digital video from the camera—to create a variety of special effects. Basically, the DVE equipment can grab a frame from any video source (live camera or videotape), convert into digital data, store it, manipulate it according to the effects software available, and retrieve the effect on command.

To keep this topic manageable, we give a brief, basic overview of three major aspects of digital image manipulation and image creation: digital image manipulation equipment, common digital video effects, and synthetic image creation.

Digital Image Manipulation Equipment

All desktop computers with a generous amount of RAM (random-access memory), a high processing speed, and a large storage capacity are capable of manipulating video images—all you need is the proper software. Four types of systems facilitate image manipulation: an editing system with graphics software, a graphics generator, an electronic still store system, and a frame store synchronizer.

Editing system with graphics software   Most high-end desktop editing systems include so many effects possibilities that you will probably (and ideally should) use only a relatively small number of them. It may be tempting to try them all simply because they are available and relatively easy to use, but keep effects to a minimum. It is not the effect that makes a program interesting but its content. Realize that any digital effect is purposely visible, which means it is made to draw attention to itself. Ask yourself whether an effect is appropriate in the context of the show content and whether it is used to intensify, rather than falsify, the message. To add or remove a person digitally from a news story, for example, is certainly possible but definitely unethical.

In case you need even more effects than are included in your editing software, graphics software is available that is specifically designed for manipulating video images and creating special digital effects.

Graphics generator   Most television stations and independent production and postproduction companies use a digital *graphics generator* for manipulating and creating graphic images. Graphics generators are large-capacity, high-speed computers that can perform different jobs, depending on the software. Some have hardware attached, such as a drawing tablet, which allows you to draw with a light pen. Daily weather or traffic maps are usually created with a graphics generator.

Electronic still store system   With an *electronic still store* (***ESS***) ***system***, you can grab any video frame, digitize it, and store it on a disk. These systems—which can store tens of thousands of frames—perform like a superfast slide projector. You can call up and display any stored image in a fraction of a second. Once in digital form, the still image can be shrunk, expanded, and used in combination with other images. The familiar box above the newscaster's shoulder is usually a digitized frame that is keyed into the base picture of the news set.

Frame store synchronizer   The primary function of the digital *frame store synchronizer* is to stabilize a picture and synchronize two different video sources so that they don't roll when switching from one to the other, but some can also be used for simple DVE. With the frame store synchronizer, you can freeze a moving image, change it into a mosaic, advance it frame-by-frame at different rates (a process called *jogging*), or *solarize* it—mix the positive image with its negative. **SEE 9.24 AND 9.25**

Common Digital Video Effects

To understand the analog-to-digital translation process, try to visualize how a photo is transformed into a mosaic, as shown in figure 9.24. The analog video frame (complete picture) shows a continuous change of shape, color, and brightness. In digital form the same image is seen as a series of mosaic tiles, each representing a discrete picture element—a *pixel*. Because the computer can identify each pixel separately, you can take some out, move them, or replace them with a different color. Once satisfied with the manipulation, you can store the image on disk for later use.

9.24 Mosaic Effect

With the mosaic effect, the image is distilled into equal-sized squares, resembling mosaic tiles. In such an electronic mosaic, the size of the tiles can be manipulated.

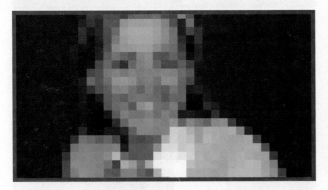

9.25 Solarization

Solarization is a special effect that is produced by a partial polarity reversal of an image. In a color image, the reversal results in a combination of complementary hues.

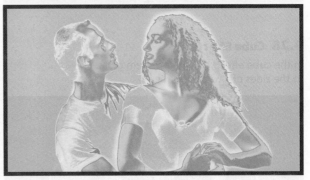

The box over the news anchor's shoulder is one of the most common digital effects. It can contain still or moving images. **SEE 9.26** More-elaborate DVE can change the size of the image (lettering or an actual scene), squeeze or stretch it, paste it on a cube, and have it tumble, flip, spin, bounce, and fly through the screen space. **SEE 9.27–9.29** `ZVL3 CUE 6` SWITCHING→ Effects→ special effects

Synthetic Image Creation

Synthetic images range from simple lettering of titles to complex 3-D motion sequences that rival well-shot and edited videotaped footage.

Character generator   The most common synthetic image creation is the production of various titles. The ***C.G. (character generator)*** is designed to produce letters and numbers of different fonts and colors. You can usually use a laptop computer as an efficient C.G., assuming you have the appropriate software. More-elaborate character generators are designated computers that offer a rich menu from which to

9.26 Box over the News Anchor's Shoulder

The box over the newscaster's shoulder can take on many shapes and sizes. The digital image inside the box can be stationary or moving.

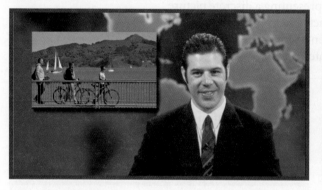

9.27 Stretching

Stretching changes the format of the frame and the image within it.

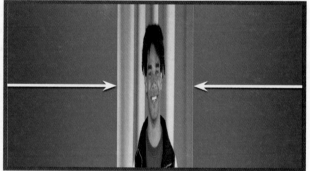

9.28 Cube Effect

In the cube effect, the images seem glued to the sides of a rotating cube.

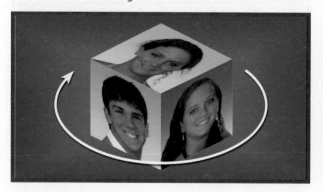

9.29 Fly Effect

In the fly effect, the image zooms from a certain spot to a full image or recedes to another screen position.

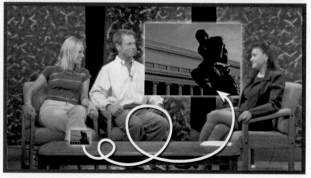

select the background and the size, style, and color of the letters and numbers. You then type the copy on the keyboard, colorize the characters, position them on the display screen, insert or delete words, scroll the copy up or down the screen, or have it crawl sideways—all with a few simple commands. **SEE 9.30** Using the switcher you can key the copy directly into the video of the program in progress or save it to a disk for later retrieval.

Graphics generator   With the appropriate software, a *graphics generator* lets you create a great variety of images independent of the video camera. This device needs a computer with a large RAM (random-access memory), a high-capacity hard drive, and a fast CPU (central processing unit). Drawing software enables you to create maps, floor plans, light plots, a variety of designs, and even simple storyboards. **SEE 9.31** With paint software you can simulate various painting styles, such as watercolor washes or the brushstrokes of oil paintings. **SEE 9.32**

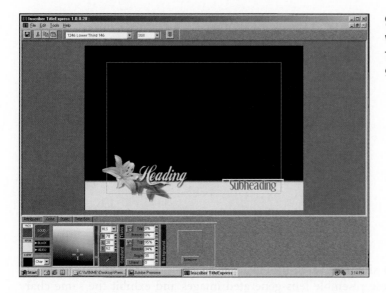

9.30 Video Created with Character Generator

The C.G. is designed to generate specific titles.

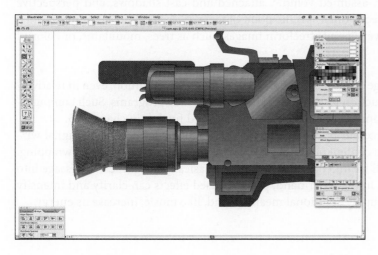

9.31 Image Created with Drawing Program

The drawing program facilitates technical drawings and two-dimensional images.

9.32 Computer-modified Photo

This photograph of a flower was given a watercolor quality using the computer.

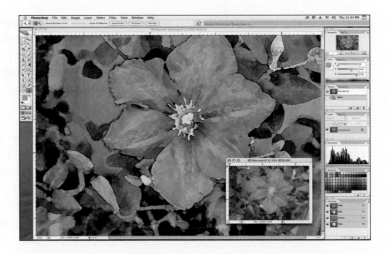

9.33 Fractal Landscape

Some computer programs allow you to "paint" irregular images using mathematical formulas.

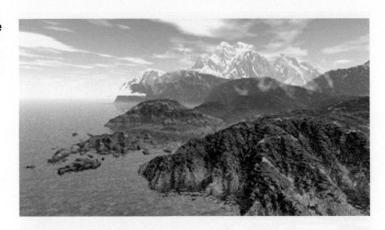

You can also simulate three-dimensional images that seem to occupy 3-D screen space. These resemble lens-generated images and exhibit the same characteristics: texture, assumed volume, attached and cast shadows, and perspective that shows the object from a specific point of view. With computer programs called *fractals,* you can even "paint" freeform images, such as trees, mountains, or colorful patterns. **SEE 9.33**

▶KEY CONCEPT

Synthetic images are entirely computer-generated.

Synthetic image creation is becoming more and more common, even in relatively simple video production processes and interactive video programs. Such computer-generated images and their applications are explored further in chapter 15.

Just to reinforce our basic caveat: don't get carried away by all the digital wizardry. After all, the content of the package is still more important than its wrapping. Even the best DVE treatment will not change a basically insignificant message into a significant one. On the other hand, properly used effects can clarify and intensify the screen event, supply additional meaning, and, like music, increase its energy.

M A I N   P O I N T S

▶ **Aspect Ratio**

Aspect ratio is the relationship of the width of the television screen to its height. In STV (standard television), it is 4 × 3 (4 units wide by 3 units high); for some DTV (digital television) and all HDTV (high-definition television), it is 16 × 9 (16 units wide by 9 units high).

▶ **Essential Area**

All the important information must be contained in the essential area—the screen area that is reproduced by the home television set even under adverse conditions. It is also called the safe title area.

▶ **Titles**

When using letters against a busy background, make them big and bold enough that they can be read easily on the home screen. In designing color graphics, try to set off high-energy colors (bright and rich hues) against a low-energy background (washed-out, pastel colors).

▶ **Special Effects**

Standard electronic video effects are achieved with an electronic switcher and a special-effects generator (SEG). They include superimpositions, normal (luminance) keys, matte keys, chroma keys, and wipes. Most chroma keys use either blue or green as the backdrop color. Although wipes function technically as transitions rather than effects, they are so obvious that they are usually considered an electronic effect. Digital video effects (DVE) can be generated by the switcher as well as by computers.

▶ **Character Generator**

The character generator (C.G.) is a computer with software designed to create titles; graphics generators are high-end computer systems that can create or manipulate 3-D still and animated images.

ZETTL'S VIDEOLAB 3.0

 For your reference, or to track your work, the Zettl's VideoLab 3.0 program cues in this chapter are listed here with their corresponding page numbers.

PART

IV

Image Control: Switching, Recording, and Editing

When you watch a live telecast of an interview, a newscast, or a football game, the changes from long shots to close-ups, the various transitions between shots, and some of the special visual effects are all done with a switcher. In a live telecast, the director selects the most effective shot and calls for the technical director (TD) to press the appropriate button on the switcher so that the shot is delivered to the line-out and put on the air. Many TDs think that there is nothing more exciting than switching a live or live-on-tape show. After all, it gives the audience a chance to witness, if not participate at least emotionally, in an event whose every moment has an open future. As you can see, sports are the ideal content for such live telecasts.

Although switching, or instantaneous editing, is essential for the live pickup of a football game, it is rarely appropriate for the production of a fully scripted play. Why do it live when every move has been scripted? There is no open future in such a production, unless somebody makes an obvious mistake. What you may gain in spontaneity you lose in production control. This is why many of the shows you see are assembled through postproduction editing. Postproduction editing allows you to be more deliberate in selecting and sequencing the most effective shots and enables you to correct minor mistakes. Unfortunately, some directors think that this type of postproduction activity gives them license to be sloppy in the production phase. This is why, when something goes wrong during videotaping, you may hear production people resort to the standard joke, "Don't worry—we'll fix it in post." But then they immediately do another take to fix whatever went wrong.

"Fixing it in post" is not only costly but a misconception of what postproduction is all about. Postproduction editing should not be seen as a convenient rescue operation for a sloppy production but as an organic extension of the production process in which the various segments are given form and order.

CHAPTER 10

KEY TERMS

downstream keyer (DSK) A control that allows a title to be keyed (cut in) over the picture (line-out signal) as it leaves the switcher.

effects bus Row of buttons on the switcher that can select the video sources for a specific effect. Usually the same as a mix bus that has been switched to an effects function.

fader bar A lever on the switcher that activates buses and can produce superimpositions, dissolves, fades, keys, and wipes of different speeds.

key bus Row of buttons on the switcher used to select the video source to be inserted into the background image.

line-out The line that carries the final video or audio output.

M/E bus Row of buttons on the switcher that can serve mix or effects functions.

mix bus Rows of buttons on the switcher that permit the mixing of video sources, as in a dissolve or a super. Mix buses are fundamental for on-the-air switching.

preview bus Row of buttons on the switcher that can direct an input to the preview monitor at the same time another video source is on the air. Also called *preset bus*.

program bus Row of buttons on the switcher, with inputs that are directly switched to the line-out.

switcher (1) A panel with rows of buttons that allows the selection and the assembly of various video sources through a variety of transition devices as well as the creation of electronic effects. (2) Production person who is doing the switching.

switching A change from one video source to another and the creation of various transitions and effects during production with the aid of a switcher. Also called *instantaneous editing*.

Switcher
and Switching

When you first look at a switcher, you may feel as puzzled as when you first saw an audio console: rows of buttons that light up in different colors—none of which makes any sense to you. But the TD assures you that you will be able to operate the switcher within a reasonable period of time once you understand the functions of the controls. To help you in this task, this chapter acquaints you with the basic switcher functions and switching operations.

▶ **PRODUCTION SWITCHER**
What a switcher does

▶ **BASIC SWITCHER FUNCTIONS**
Selecting, previewing, and mixing video sources and creating effects

▶ **SWITCHER LAYOUT**
Program bus, preview bus, key bus, fader bar and auto-transition, and delegation controls

▶ **SWITCHER OPERATION**
Cuts, dissolves, wipes, and keys, working the downstream keyer, chroma keying, and special effects

PRODUCTION SWITCHER

Switching refers to instantaneous editing using simultaneously available video sources. The term *switcher* can also refer to the person who does the switching, although usually the TD fills this production role. You accomplish this type of "editing-on-the-fly" with a switcher, which operates much like a pushbutton radio. The pushbutton radio lets you select and instantly switch from one radio station to another. Similarly, a production *switcher* allows you to punch up certain video sources, such as the pictures supplied by two or more cameras, a VTR, or a server file, while the production is in

10.1 Production Switcher

Large production switchers have many rows with buttons and several levers. The buttons permit the selection of various video sources, switching functions, and a variety of transitions and special effects. The levers control the speed of transitions and fades.

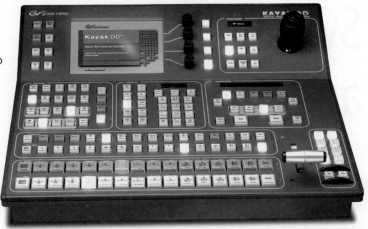

progress. Unlike a pushbutton radio, however, the switcher offers various transitions, such as cuts, dissolves, and wipes, with which you can join the selected pictures. It also has a number of standard electronic effects built into it (see chapter 9). The large production switcher is used primarily in multicamera studio productions or in *big remotes* for instantaneous editing. **SEE 10.1** **ZVL3 CUE 1** SWITCHING→ Switching introduction

There are also portable switchers that you could use for a local two-camera basketball game, and computer software whose interface looks and operates like a regular production switcher. **SEE 10.2 AND 10.3** Some switchers are used primarily in postproduction, where they function more as transition makers between two shots

10.2 Small Portable Production Switcher

Small, portable production switchers contain an astonishing variety of switching and effects functions. This PixBox has eight audio and four video inputs and a rich effects menu.

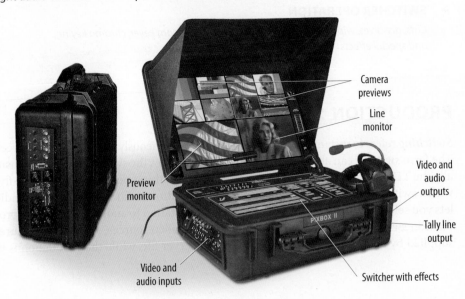

Camera previews

Line monitor

Video and audio outputs

Tally line output

Switcher with effects

Preview monitor

Video and audio inputs

10.3 **Interface for Production and Postproduction Switcher**

NewTek's VT[4] Live is a software program that serves as a production and postproduction switcher. The interface displays not only the switching equipment but also a variety of technical video controls.

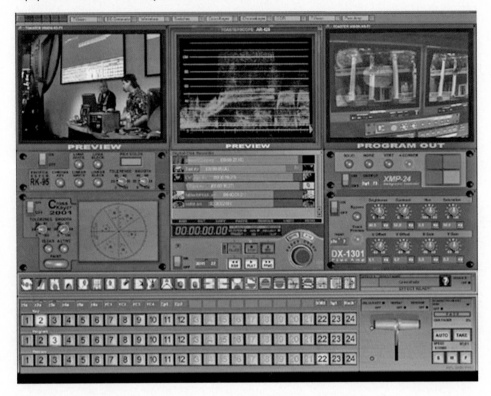

than as shot selectors, although these postproduction switchers can also be used for instantaneous editing.

All switchers allow you to make basic transitions between two shots, such as a *cut,* whereby one shot is instantly replaced by another; a *dissolve,* in which two images temporarily overlap; and a *wipe,* in which a portion of an image is gradually replaced—wiped off the screen—by another. They also offer a variety of effects, as you learned in chapter 9.

▶ **KEY CONCEPT**

Switchers allow the selection of multiple video inputs and the immediate creation of transitions and effects.

BASIC SWITCHER FUNCTIONS

The four basic switcher functions are: (1) selecting various video sources, (2) previewing upcoming video sources or special effects, (3) mixing video sources, and (4) creating effects.

A row of buttons on a switcher is called a *bus.* The selection of sources is done with the *program bus,* and the previewing is done with the *preview,* or *preset, bus.* These two buses can also be used as *mix buses,* which means you can mix two video sources for dissolves and supers. When you want to put titles over a scene, you need still another bus—the *key bus.*

10.4 **Production Switcher**

This production switcher has only three buses: a preview/preset bus, a program bus, and a key bus.
You can delegate the preview and program buses an M/E (mix/effects) function.

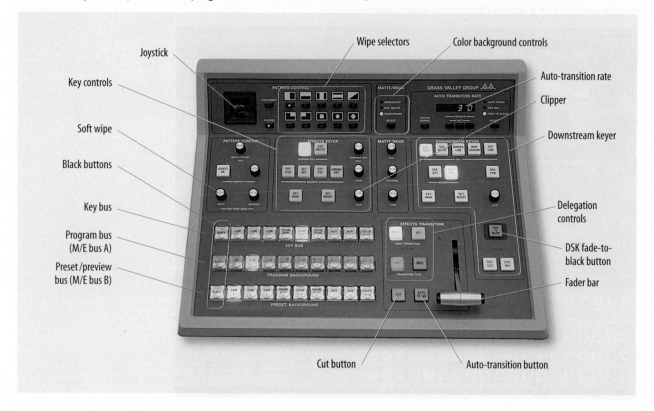

Let's take a look at how a relatively simple switcher is laid out.[1] **SEE 10.4** ZVL3 CUE 2

SWITCHING→ Switching functions→ select | connect | transitions | create effects

SWITCHER LAYOUT

Regardless of whether switchers are analog or digital, they all operate on a similar principle, called *switcher architecture.* This standardization helps you greatly when you're called upon to operate a variety of switchers.

Program Bus

To select and connect certain shots, you need several *video inputs.* If all you had were two cameras and you simply wanted to cut from one camera to the other, you could get by with only two switcher buttons: one that activates camera 1 and another for camera 2. By pressing the *C-1* (camera 1) button, camera 1 would be put "on the air";

---

1. The Grass Valley 100 switcher is used here because its architecture has become the standard for most multifunction production switchers. Even the more up-to-date digital switchers operate in similar ways.

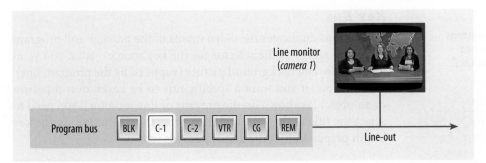

10.5 Program Bus
Whatever source is punched up on the program bus goes directly to the line-out.

that is, it would go to the ***line-out***—the line that carries the final video output—and from there to the video recorder (VTR) and/or the transmitter.

Because you would probably want to select from additional video sources, such as a VTR, a character generator (C.G.), and a remote source that is fed from a remote location, you need three additional buttons in the switcher row: *VTR, CG,* and *REM,* respectively. To quickly dump the video and "cut to black," you need still another button, called the *black (BLK)* button.

The switcher now has six separate buttons on a single bus. By pressing any one except the *BLK* button, the designated video source will be put on the air; the *BLK* button takes it off the air (actually, *BLK* selects a black video signal). This bus, which sends the chosen video source directly to the line-out, is called the ***program bus***. **SEE 10.5**

> **KEY CONCEPT**
> Whatever is punched up on the program bus goes directly to the line-out.

Preview Bus

Before putting the selected shots on the air, you will undoubtedly want to see whether the shots cut together properly—whether the sequence fulfills your aesthetic continuity or complexity editing requirements (see chapter 13). You may also want to see whether a superimposition has the right mix of the two images or whether you have the correct name for a title key over a guest. To preview the sources, the program bus buttons are simply repeated in an additional bus, appropriately called the ***preview bus***. **SEE 10.6** Because the preview bus is also used to preset more-complex effects, you may also hear it called the *preset bus.*

> **KEY CONCEPT**
> The preview bus sends its video to the preview monitor but not to the line-out.

10.6 Preview Bus
The preview bus lets you preview an upcoming source or effect before it is punched up on the air. The preview bus is identical to the program bus except that its output goes to the preview monitor rather than the line-out.

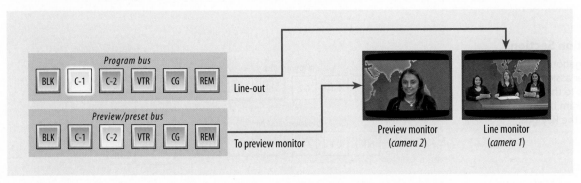

10.7 **Key Bus**

The key bus has the identical buttons as the preview and program buses. Each button functions as key source.

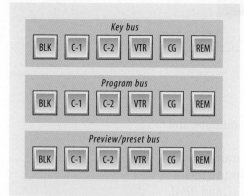

Key Bus

The **key bus** duplicates the video inputs of the preview and program buses but serves as the selector for the key source—what you want to appear over a background picture (supplied by the program bus). For example, if you want a specific title to be keyed over a person or an object (as shown on the preview or line monitor), you need to select the title at the C.G. and then press the *CG* button on the key bus in preparation of the actual key. **SEE 10.7**

Fader Bar and Auto-transition

To fade from black or fade to black, to superimpose two images, or to use various transitions other than cuts, you need to use a fader bar or an auto-transition (see figure 10.4). How to do this is described later in this chapter. The **fader bar** activates and regulates the speed of fades and dissolves. The faster you move the fader bar from one limit of travel to the other, the faster the dissolve or wipe will be. When stopped midway, the dissolve becomes a superimposition, and the wipe yields a split-screen effect.

The full travel of the fader bar can be substituted by the auto-transition button, although you must select the speed of the desired mix or effect before activating the auto-transition.

Delegation Controls

The *delegation controls* assign various functions to the program and preview buses. This prevents switchers from getting too large and keeps them manageable. Because the buses of digital switchers can be assigned to perform a great many functions, the switchers often look deceivingly small.

The preview and program buses of all switchers can also be assigned to function as mix buses, which allows them to work together to produce dissolves, supers, and wipes. They can also be assigned to function as effects buses, in which they usually serve as background images for keys.

These assignments are made possible by the delegation controls on the switcher (see figure 10.4). The various *mix/effects* (*M/E*) functions of the program and preview (preset) buses are assigned by pressing one or more of the delegation buttons in the effects/transition section of the switcher. **SEE 10.8** For example, by pressing the *background* (*BKGD*) and *MIX* buttons next to the fader bar, you delegate a mix function

10.8
Delegation Section

The delegation section of a switcher assigns various functions to the preview and program buses and activates the key bus.

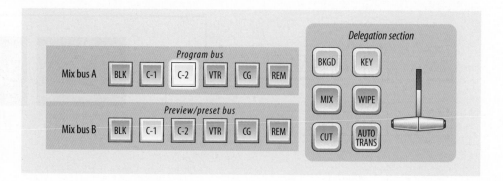

to the two **M/E buses** (program and preset). You can now dissolve from the picture punched up on the program bus (M/E bus A) to the one punched up on the preset bus (M/E bus B). By pressing the *WIPE* button located next to the *MIX* button, you can now wipe from the program source to the one punched up on the preset bus. The two buses have now become **mix buses**. By pressing the *KEY* button, the program and preview buses become **effects buses**. `ZVL3 CUE 3` SWITCHING→ Architecture→ program bus | preview bus | delegation controls | mix buses | key bus

► KEY CONCEPT

The delegation controls can assign the program and preview buses the function of mix and effects buses.

SWITCHER OPERATION

It's time now to press a few buttons and learn how to *switch*—select video inputs and sequence them through various transitions and effects. Yes, you certainly need a switcher, or at least a computer simulation of a switcher, to become proficient in the art of switching. By first studying the basic principles of switching, however, you will make your actual practice much more efficient and rewarding.

When you simply read the instructions on how to achieve a cut or a dissolve, you may be as puzzled as when reading about how to use new computer software. You should therefore pretend that the illustrations are part of a switcher and that you are actually pressing the buttons. If you have *Zettl's VideoLab 3.0* DVD-ROM available, engage in the switching exercises right away to reinforce the text.

Working the Program Bus: Cuts-only

As you recall, the program bus is basically a selector switch of video sources for the line-out. It has this function assigned to it by simply powering up the switcher. If you now want to cut from one video source, let's say C1 (camera 1), to another, C2 (camera 2), you can simply press the *C-2* button, assuming that C1 is already on the air (the *C-1* button has been pressed previously). Camera 1's picture will be instantly replaced by C2's picture; you have performed a *cut* from C1 to C2. **SEE 10.9** Because

10.9 Switching on the Program Bus

When switching on the program bus, the transitions will be cuts-only. With camera 1 on the air, you can cut to camera 2 by pressing the C-2 button.

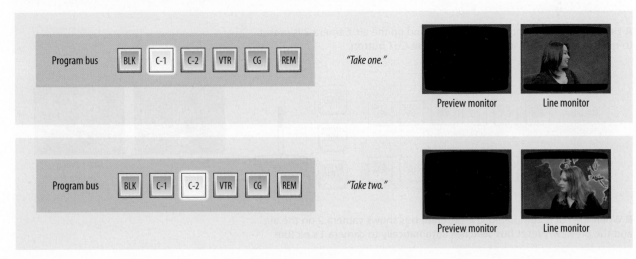

the program bus sends its signals directly to the line-out, you cannot preview the up-coming image (C2). The preview monitor remains black when you switch exclusively on the program bus. **ZVL3 CUE 4** ›SWITCHING→ Transitions→ cut

Working the Mix Buses: Cuts

If you want to preview the upcoming video source, or if you want to dissolve to camera 2 (mix) instead of cut to it, you first need to delegate a mix function to both buses. You do this on the Grass Valley 100 switcher (and the ZVL3 switcher) by pressing the *BKGD* and *MIX* buttons. To cut from camera 1 to camera 2, you need to punch up C2 on the preset bus (which is now M/E bus B) when the director calls "Ready 2," assuming that C1 is already punched up on the program bus. This action will place camera 2's picture on the preview monitor but will not yet replace camera 1's picture on the line monitor. Camera 1 is still on the line monitor (telling you that C1 is on the air). On the director's "Take 2" command, you press either the *CUT* button or the *AUTO-TRANS* button next to the preset bus. Camera 2 will instantly appear on the line monitor, and camera 1 will automatically jump to the preview monitor. The *C-2* button will light up full, called *high tally,* on the program bus, and *C-1* will have *low tally* (lighted halfway) on the preset bus. If you pressed the *CUT* button again, C1 would switch the line monitor, and C2 would appear on the preview monitor. **SEE 10.10** **ZVL3 CUE 5** ›SWITCHING→ Transitions→ try it

10.10 Switching in the Mix Mode

When delegated a background and mix function, the program bus becomes M/E bus A and the preview/preset bus becomes M/E bus B.

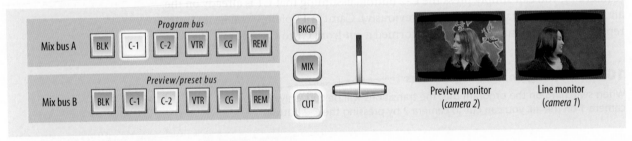

A Here camera 1 is punched up on bus A and on the air. Camera 2 is preset to replace camera 1 as soon as you press the CUT button.

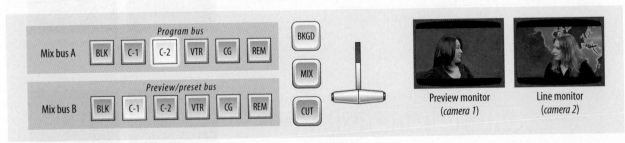

B When the cut is completed, the program bus shows camera 2 on the air, and the preview/preset bus switches automatically to camera 1's picture.

Working the Mix Buses: Dissolves

Because you have delegated both buses to the mix mode, you can also perform a dissolve. To *dissolve* from camera 1 (punched up on the program bus and, therefore, on the air) to camera 2, you need to press the *C-2* button on the preview bus and move the fader bar either up or down to the full extent of travel (or press the *AUTO-TRANS* button). On the switcher in figure 10.10, the fader bar is in the down position. You will have to move it all the way up to achieve the dissolve. **SEE 10.11**

Note that when you punch up C2 on the preview bus before the dissolve, the *C-2* button is low tally, indicating that the video source is preset but not yet activated. With the fader bar halfway through its travel, both cameras are activated (they show a temporary super on the line monitor). Both buttons show high tally. When the fader

10.11 Dissolve

Once assigned the mix function through the mix delegation control,
you can dissolve from camera 1 to camera 2.

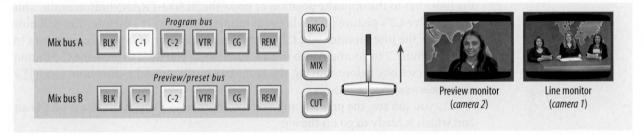

A Assuming that camera 1 is on the air on bus A, you need to preset camera 2 on bus B.

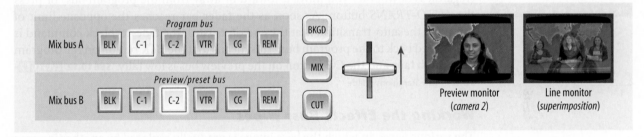

B When the fader bar is stopped midway, you have a super.

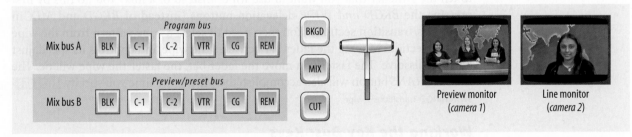

C By moving the fader bar to the full limit of travel, you activate the dissolve from camera 1 to camera 2. Once the dissolve is completed, camera 2 will replace camera 1 on the program bus.

10.12 Fade

When fading to black from camera 2, you need to punch up the BLK button on bus B (preset/preview) and dissolve to it by moving the fader bar down to its full limit of travel.

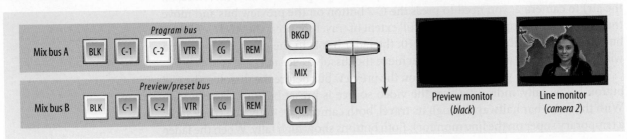

bar reaches the opposite limit of travel (in this case, up), finishing the dissolve from C1 to C2, camera 1 (which was punched up on the program bus) will be replaced by camera 2 on the program bus, with camera 1 appearing on the preview monitor and in low tally on the preset bus. If you now want to dissolve back to C1, you simply move the fader bar to the opposite position or press the *AUTO-TRANS* button again. This will dissolve C2's picture on the line-out monitor back to C1's picture. You will now see C1 on the line monitor and C2 on the preset monitor. If, however, you want to dissolve from C2 to another video source, such as C3, you need to press the *C-3* button on the preset bus before moving the fader bar in the opposite direction. **ZVL3 CUE 6**

SWITCHING→ Transitions→ mix/dissolve

As you can see, the preview and line monitors reflect which camera is on the air and which is ready to go on the air.

With camera 3 on the air, how can you fade to black? You simply press the *BLK* (black) button on the preset bus and move the fader bar in the opposite direction (regardless of whether you move it toward or away from the program bus) or press the *AUTO-TRANS* button. As soon as the fader bar reaches the opposite limit of travel (or the auto-transition is at the end of its run), the fade-to-black command is transferred back to the program bus. This means that the *BLK* button on the program bus is high tally and the *C-3* button on the preview bus is low tally. **SEE 10.12** **ZVL3 CUE 7**

SWITCHING→ Transitions→ fade

> **KEY CONCEPT**
>
> Mix buses (or buses in the mix mode) let you do cuts, dissolves, superimpositions, and fades.

Working the Effects Bus: Wipes

The various *wipes,* in which the base image is gradually replaced by another in some geometric pattern, are accomplished similarly to a dissolve except that you need to tell the switcher that you want to use wipes instead of a mix. You do this by first pressing the *BKGD and WIPE* delegation buttons (instead of *BKGD* and *MIX* in the effects/transition section). You then need to select a wipe pattern from the wipe selector section. Moving the fader bar activates the wipe and controls its speed, just like in a dissolve. The faster you move the fader bar, the faster the wipe will be. The *AUTO-TRANS* button will also accomplish the wipe in the time you specify. **ZVL3 CUE 8**

SWITCHING→ Transitions→ wipe

Working the Key Bus: Keys

Keying is not a transition but a special effect. It allows you to insert (cut electronically) an image (usually a title) into a background picture. Most often you will work with a *luminance key,* which is used to insert a title in the on-air background picture. Before you key a title over an on-the-air picture (the picture displayed by the line monitor), you should set up the key in preview and then transfer the completed key from the preview bus to the program bus.

Setting up a key is a little more involved than making a transition, and the exact sequence of keying differs from switcher to switcher. The picture you have on the air already (the dancer's image from camera 2) can serve as the background for the title you want to key over the dancer ("Palmatier Ballet Company"). If you want to preset this key on the preview monitor while C2's picture is already on the air, you must duplicate C2's picture on the preview monitor (by punching up C2 on the preview even though C2 is already punched up on the program monitor) before selecting the key source on the key bus and doing the keying. **SEE 10.13**

Regardless of the specific switcher architecture, you select the key source (usually the C.G. with the desired title) on the key bus. You then need to work some buttons and/or rotary controls (called the *clip control,* or *clipper*) to make sure the key has clean edges and does not tear. (Such an operation may differ from one switcher to another.) Then you press the *KEY* button in the delegation controls. This changes the

10.13 Key Effect

This key sequence is constructed for the preview monitor before it is transferred to the line-out. Assume that the key bus has been delegated.

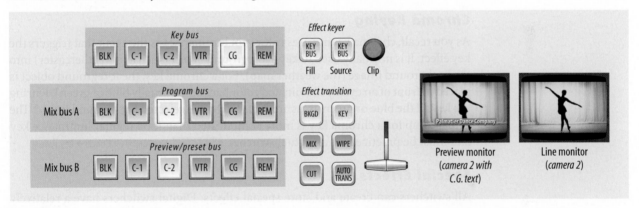

A The camera 2 close-up appears on both the line monitor (outgoing signal) and the preview monitor. By pressing the CG button on the key bus, the title is selected and appears on the preview monitor.

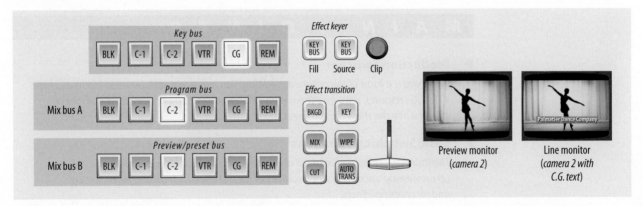

B Pressing the CUT button (or moving the fader bar) will transfer the complete key to the line-out monitor.

mix function of the buses to an effects function—in this case the key function. Once you have set up the complete key in the preview, you can transfer the background picture plus the keyed title to the line-out by pressing the *CUT* button. To dissolve into the complete key, you can use the fader bar or the *AUTO-TRANS* button.

Although it may seem confusing, remember that keying titles or other images simply takes practice. You can use *Zettl's VideoLab 3.0* for initial keying practice, but the keying procedures on this switching simulation are greatly simplified. The best way to learn keying is to sit down with an actual switcher and perform a variety of switching exercises. **ZVL3 CUE 9** SWITCHING→ Effects→ keys | key types

Working the Downstream Keyer

To complicate matters, there is still another—very important—key control. The **downstream keyer (DSK)** lets you key yet another title over the complete line-out video image as it leaves the switcher. In our example the DSK would enable you to add the name of the choreographer ("Robaire") to the original key ("Palmatier Ballet Company") without changing the original key. Note that the downstream keyer is independent of the program bus and puts its title on the air even if the program bus is in black. If you have used the downstream keyer, going to black on the program bus will not eliminate the DSK title: you need to use the DSK *BLK* button to eliminate this type of key. **ZVL3 CUE 10** SWITCHING→ Effects→ downstream keyer

Chroma Keying

As you recall, chroma keying uses color (not luminance) as the agent that triggers the key effect. It is normally used to key a foreground object (such as a weathercaster) into the background image (the weather map). For a chroma key, the foreground object is placed in front of an evenly illuminated color backdrop (usually blue or green). During the key all the blue or green areas are replaced by the selected background image. The actual setup for a chroma key is more complicated than for a regular luminance key and must be practiced on an actual switcher. **ZVL3 CUE 11** SWITCHING→ Effects→ key types

Special Effects

All switchers can create and store special effects. Digital switchers have a relatively large memory that can hold a great number of complex effects, which are recalled by their file name or number.

M A I N   P O I N T S

▶ **Production Switcher**

Switching is a form of instantaneous editing. You can select various video inputs (camera, VTR, C.G., remote), sequence them with different transitions, and create a number of effects while the show is in progress.

▶ **Basic Switching Functions**

The four basic switcher functions are (1) selecting various video sources, (2) previewing upcoming video sources or special effects, (3) mixing video sources, and (4) creating effects.

▶ **Switcher Layout**

Whatever is punched up on the program bus goes directly to the line-out. The preview bus sends its video to the preview/preset monitor. The key bus lets you select various key sources. The fader bar and the auto-transition facilitate transitions other than cuts.

▶ **Delegation Controls**

The delegation controls can assign the program and preview buses various mix and effects functions. The key bus has its own row of buttons and maintains its function.

▶ **Switcher Operation**

The program bus allows cut-only switching. The preview bus routs the upcoming picture to the preview monitor. When the preview and program buses are delegated as mix buses, you can create dissolves, superimpositions, and fades. The fader bar activates and regulates the speed of fades and dissolves and governs the extent of a wipe. The function of the fader bar can be duplicated by the auto-transition feature. Like the mix function, the effects function of the switcher must be assigned in the delegation section. This allows you to select the key source on the key bus and activate a key through a variety of additional controls. The downstream keyer (DSK) enables the addition of another title to the key just before the line-out signal leaves the switcher.

Z E T T L ' S   V I D E O L A B   3 . 0

For your reference, or to track your work, the Zettl's VideoLab 3.0 program cues in this chapter are listed here with their corresponding page numbers.

CHAPTER **11**

K E Y   T E R M S

audio track The area of the video-tape used for recording the audio information.

composite video A system that combines the Y (luminance, or black-and-white) and C (color—red, green, and blue) video information into a single signal. Also called *NTSC*.

control track The area of the videotape used for recording synchronizing information.

field log A record of each take during the videotaping.

flash memory device A read/write portable storage device that can download, store, and upload a limited amount of digital audio and video information. Also called *flash drive* or *memory card*.

interactive video A computer-driven program that gives the viewer some control over what to see and how to see it. It is often used as a training device.

luminance The brightness (black-and-white) information of a video signal. Also called *luma* to include the grayscale information.

multimedia Computer display of text, sound, and still and moving images. Usually recorded on CD-ROM or DVD.

nonlinear storage system Storage of video and audio material in digital form on a hard drive or read/write optical disc. Each single frame can be instantly accessed by the computer.

NTSC Stands for *National Television System Committee*. Normally refers to the composite video signal, consisting of the Y signal (luminance, or black-and-white information) and the C signal (red, green, and blue color information).

tapeless systems Refers to the recording, storage, and playback of audio and video information via computer storage devices rather than videotape.

time base corrector (TBC) An electronic accessory to videotape recorders that helps make videotape playbacks electronically stable. It keeps slightly different scanning cycles in step.

video server A large-capacity computer hard drive that can store and play back audio and video information.

video track The area of the video-tape used for recording the video information.

Y/C component video A system that keeps the Y (luminance, or black-and-white) and C (color—red, green, and blue) signals separate. Y and C are combined again when recorded on tape. Also called *Y/C system* or *S-video*.

Y/color difference component video Video-recording system wherein the three signals—the luminance, or luma (Y) signal, the red signal minus its luminance (R–Y), and the blue signal minus its luminance (B–Y)—are kept separate during the recording and storage process. All three signals are recorded separately on videotape.

Video Recording

You have undoubtedly used both tape-based and tapeless video- and audio-recording devices. Your VHS recorder or small camcorder uses tape to record video and audio information; your digital still camera records its pictures on a flash memory device; and your iPod has a large-capacity computer hard drive to store and play back your favorite music. Because the television industry has almost completely switched from analog to digital equipment and operation, it strives to do away with videotape altogether, yet videotape is still very much alive and widely used as a recording medium. Why? Because it can store a great amount of analog or digital information while taking up little space (think of the mini-cassette in your camcorder).

Videotape remains the primary recording medium in almost all camcorders. This means that you need VTRs for playing back the camera footage for viewing and for transferring it to the hard drive of a *nonlinear editing system* (*NLE*). Although tape is widely used, it has several disadvantages: it is a linear storage device, which means that you cannot randomly access specific information that might be buried in the middle of the cassette; it necessitates a complicated tape drive and record heads for video capture and playback; and the tape itself is subject to *dropouts* (which show up as specks in the picture) and wear and tear after repeated use.

As you can see, for the time being you need to learn about both types of recording media: videotape and nonlinear storage devices. This chapter will help you understand major video-recording systems, recording processes, and how to use and store video recordings.

▶ **VIDEOTAPE-RECORDING SYSTEMS**
Tape- and tapeless recording systems, basic videotape tracks, composite and component recording systems, types of videotape recorders, time base corrector, and tape formats and quality

▶ **VIDEOTAPE-RECORDING PROCESS**
The necessary checklists: before, during, and after

► **NONLINEAR STORAGE SYSTEMS**
*Computer disks and video servers, flash memory devices, read/write
optical discs, and ESS systems*

► **USE OF VIDEO RECORDING**
Multimedia and interactive video

VIDEOTAPE-RECORDING SYSTEMS

All videotape-recording systems operate on the same basic principle: the video and
audio signals are recorded and stored in analog or digital form on magnetic tape and
reconverted into pictures and sound during playback. These systems vary greatly,
however, in how the signals are put on the videotape. Some *videotape recorders,* or
VTRs, are designed for operational ease, such as the ones built into consumer camcorders or the popular *videocassette recorder (VCR).* Others are designed for high-
quality recordings whose pictures and sound maintain their quality even after many
generations during postproduction.

To make some sense out of the various systems, this section looks at tape- and tapeless recording systems, basic videotape tracks, composite and component recording systems, types of videotape recorders, the time base corrector, and tape formats and quality.

Tape- and Tapeless Recording Systems

Tape-based systems can record and play back analog or digital video and audio information. **Tapeless systems** use large-capacity computer disks, read/write (rerecordable)
optical discs, or flash memory devices. In television stations the storage and especially the playback of program material is done largely by *video servers*—high-speed,
large-capacity computers. Tape-based editing systems are called *linear systems,* and
disk-based systems are *nonlinear.* (You will read more about the important difference
between linear and nonlinear systems in chapter 13.)

Basic Videotape Tracks

All analog videotape recorders use separate tracks to record the video and audio as
well as various control data. Most videotape recorders put at least four tracks onto
a videotape: the **video track** containing the picture information, two **audio tracks**
containing all sound information, and a **control track** that controls the synchronization of the frames. **SEE 11.1**

11.1 Basic Analog Videotape Track System

The basic analog track system of
a videotape consists of a slanted
video track, two or more audio
tracks, and a control track.

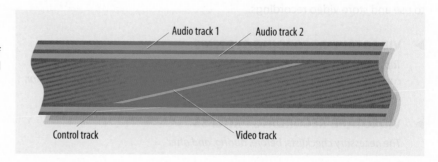

Audio track 1   Audio track 2

Control track   Video track

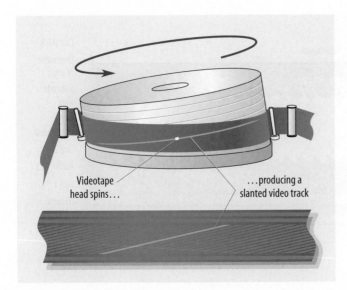

11.2 Video-recording Head

The videotape moves past the spinning head drum (or spinning heads inside the drum) at an angle, creating a slanted video track.

Videotape head spins...

...producing a slanted video track

To avoid superfast tape travel when recording the high-frequency video signal and to squeeze the maximum amount of information on the videotape, all recorders move the tape as well as the video-recording heads. In this way the tape moves in a loop around a head drum, which contains the spinning record heads. The video heads in digital systems spin at very high speeds. **SEE 11.2**

Simple VCRs and camcorders use a stationary head for erasure and only one set of rotating heads for video recording and playback. More-sophisticated models may use separate spinning heads for erasure, recording, and playback operations. The advantage of a separate erase head, often called a "flying erase head" for camcorders, is that it can precisely erase a recorded field without affecting the adjacent ones (remember, there are 60 fields for every second of video recording). Such precise erasure is an important prerequisite for stable edits.

The audio tracks—up to four high-fidelity digital tracks in the high-end digital VTRs—usually run lengthwise near the edges of the videotape. The control track, which also runs lengthwise, contains evenly spaced blips or spikes, called *sync pulses*, which keep the scanning in step, control the speed of the head drum, and mark each complete video frame—an important feature in videotape editing. **SEE 11.3** **ZVL3 CUE 1**

EDITING→ Postproduction guidelines→ tape basics

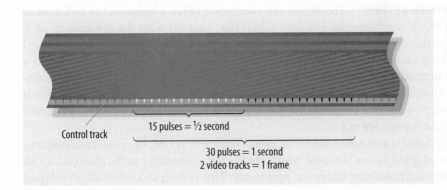

11.3 Control Track with Sync Pulses

The control track consists of equally spaced sync pulses. Thirty such pulses indicate one second of video.

Control track

15 pulses = ½ second

30 pulses = 1 second
2 video tracks = 1 frame

11.4
DVCPRO50 Tracks

This digital system uses twenty tracks for a single frame. Each track has specific video, audio, and code information.

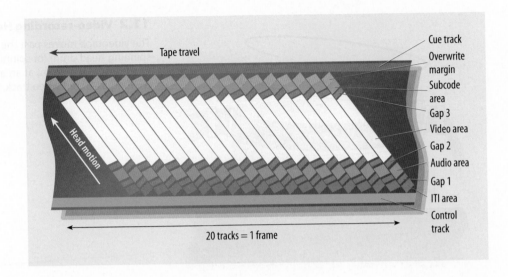

Tape travel

Head motion

Cue track
Overwrite margin
Subcode area
Gap 3
Video area
Gap 2
Audio area
Gap 1
ITI area
Control track

20 tracks = 1 frame

The *address code* information is recorded on yet another track—the *address code* or *time code track*—or mixed in with the video signal. Some digital systems, such as DVCPRO, split each track into video, audio, and code information. Contrary to analog tape, which records a complete field on each track and takes only two tracks for a complete frame, most digital systems use more tracks for a complete frame. The DVCPRO50 system, for instance, needs twenty tracks to complete a single frame. High-quality recording systems may use even more tracks for each frame. **SEE 11.4** The analog Hi8 recorders similarly incorporate video, audio, and code information on each track.

Composite, Y/C Component, and Y/Color Difference Component Recording Systems

Composite, Y/C component, and Y/color difference component systems refer to how the video signals are transported inside, and recorded by, the video recorder. The *composite system* is the one used in standard video and broadcast television equipment. The *Y/C component* and the *Y/color difference component* systems are designed to produce higher picture quality than the composite system and to resist deterioration in multiple videotape recordings.

Composite system   The signal for **composite video** combines the color, or *C* signal (which combines the red, green, and blue signals) with the **luminance**, or *Y* signal (which consists of the black-and-white, or *luma*, information). The combined C and Y signals are transported inside the VTR by a single signal and recorded as a single composite track on the videotape. In the composite system, each track contains a complete scanning field. Contrary to some high-end digital systems, which use twenty tracks for a single frame, the composite system needs only two tracks for a complete frame. **SEE 11.5**

This signal is also called the *NTSC signal*, or simply **NTSC**, because the configuration was adopted by the National Television System Committee as the standard for all U.S. video and broadcast television equipment. This system was originally developed

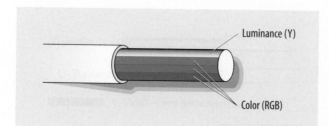

Luminance (Y)

Color (RGB)

11.5 **Composite System**

The composite system uses a video signal that combines the luminance Y (brightness) and color C information. It needs a single wire to be transported and recorded on videotape as a single signal. It is the standard NTSC system.

so that color broadcasts could be received in black-and-white on a monochrome receiver, and black-and-white broadcasts could be seen on a color receiver. Why NTSC is still the broadcast standard is not because of its superior picture quality but rather its narrow bandwidth. This means that the compact video signals take up relatively little space in the available electronic highway and that they can be transmitted with relative ease.

The disadvantage of NTSC composite video is that the Y and C signals occasionally get in each other's way, causing video "noise." A composite NTSC recording also tends to deteriorate relatively quickly in multiple generations, so the initial *artifacts* (video noise), which at first are hardly visible, are multiplied during each subsequent recording.

Not all countries in the world use the NTSC system. Many nations have standardized on other systems (such as PAL or SECAM), which are not compatible with NTSC. For instance, to play a videotape from Italy, which uses the PAL system, or a tape from French TV, which uses SECAM, you need a *standards converter*—an electronic device that changes other systems' signals to NTSC. Satellites that transmit global television have such converters built-in, but you would still need a VCR that translates the various recording standards.

Y/C component system   To reduce the interference between the Y and C signals in the NTSC composite system, the Y/C component, or *S-video*, system, was developed. The ***Y/C component video*** system keeps the Y signal (luminance, or black-and-white information) and the C signal (RGB color information) separate during its transport, but they are recorded together on the videotape. During the playback the two video channels (Y and C) are separated again. **SEE 11.6**

The advantage of this separation is that it ensures higher picture quality for both the original recording and any subsequent generations. To preserve this advantage, you need recorders, video monitors, and editing equipment specifically designed

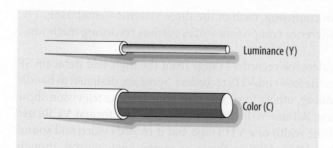

Luminance (Y)

Color (C)

11.6 **Y/C Component System**

The Y/C component system separates the Y (luminance) and C (color) information but combines the two signals on the videotape. It needs two wires to transport the two separate signals.

11.7 Y/Color Difference Component System

Like the RGB component system, the Y/color difference component system needs three wires to transport the three component signals: the Y (luminance) signal, the R–Y (red minus luminance) signal, and the B–Y (blue minus luminance) signal. The green signal is then generated from these signals.

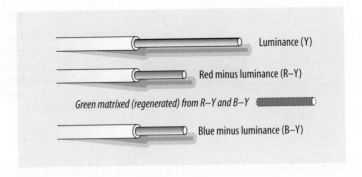

to handle the separate Y/C signals. You can play a regular VHS tape on an S-VHS recorder, but you cannot play an S-VHS tape on a VHS recorder. The S-VHS system is, therefore, only downward compatible.

Y/color difference component systems   For technical convenience and to save bandwidth (smaller cars can travel on narrower roads), the *Y/color difference component video* system takes the original RGB video signals and mixes them in different proportions to produce a Y (luminance, or luma) signal and two separate color difference signals: the R–Y (red minus luminance) signal and the B–Y (blue minus luminance) signal. The Y and two color signals are kept separate throughout the transport and recording process. As you might have guessed, this Y/color difference component video system also needs three wires to transport the three signals in the VTR and in all associated equipment. For all practical purposes, it is probably easier for you to envision the three component signals as RGB mixed in different proportions throughout the transport and recording process.   **SEE 11.7**

Confused? Well, it is somewhat confusing because the terminology is inconsistent. You may simply want to remember that the NTSC system is *composite* (all signals are mixed into one). The other two systems, which separate luminance from color, are *component*.

As with Y/C component video, the Y/color difference component systems require specific video monitors, switching, and editing equipment to accommodate the three separate video signals. But for transmission all signals must be converted to the NTSC composite standard, regardless of the recording system originally used. Most high-end component equipment therefore has NTSC composite inputs and outputs.

Types of Videotape Recorders

To make matters even more confusing, each of the three systems—composite, Y/C component, and Y/color difference component—uses various recording methods.

Analog VTRs   Analog videotape recorders range from the high-end Betacam SP (for *superior performance*) to the low-end VHS recorders. Some are designed to handle complex postproduction editing, others to simply tape your favorite television show or newscast for later viewing. All use ½-inch videotape. The Hi8 format VCRs use videotape that is about half the width of a VHS tape, but it records video and sound at a much higher quality than VHS. All have the same operational controls, though

11.8 Types of Analog Videotape Recorders

TYPE	CHARACTERISTICS
Betacam SP	Uses ½-inch videocassette. Y/C component and recorded on separate tracks. High quality.
S-VHS	Uses ½-inch videocassette. Y/C component signal transport but composite when actually recorded on tape. Good-quality first generation. Can play back VHS cassettes.
VHS	Uses ½-inch videocassette. NTSC composite. Quality not good enough for professional productions but is used extensively in off-line postproduction (product not intended for final release). S-VHS cassettes cannot be played back on VHS recorders.
Hi8	Uses 8mm (a little more than ¼-inch) videocassette. Y/C component or composite output. High-quality first generation.

the order may differ from one brand to another: *stop, rewind, play, fast-forward, pause,* and *record.* Refer to the table of the most commonly used analog VTRs. **SEE 11.8**

Time Base Corrector

The ***time base corrector*** (***TBC***) is an important piece of equipment for analog switching and videotape recording. Its main purpose is to make videotape playbacks, dubs, and edits electronically stable. It does so by keeping slightly different scanning cycles in step during recording and playback and adjusts the sync from various video sources so that they all scan exactly alike. Switching from one source to another will not cause a temporary *sync roll* (picture breakup). Most high-end VTRs have a built-in time base corrector. Lower-end equipment, however, needs to be hooked up to a TBC, especially during editing.

If this reminds you of the digital frame store synchronizer discussed in chapter 9, you are quite right. In digital operations, the frame store synchronizer has replaced the analog TBC. In fact, much of the higher-end equipment, such as VTRs and even switchers, has a frame store synchronizer built-in so that signals from different video sources can be switched, edited, and mixed without the danger of a temporary sync roll. Even switchers have built-in frame store synchronizers so that the signals have no chance to break up when switching among various video inputs.

Digital VTRs have replaced all but the best analog VTRs as stand-alone models and in camcorders.

Digital VTRs   When you look at studio digital VTRs, you can't tell the difference between analog and digital; they are about the same size and have similar, if not identical, operational controls. **SEE 11.9** They do differ, however, in several ways:

▶ Even the small *digital video* (*DV*) system VTRs that are built into consumer camcorders produce high-quality video and audio. Studio models that use

11.9 Analog and Digital Studio VTRs

The operational features of digital and analog VTRs are often quite similar.

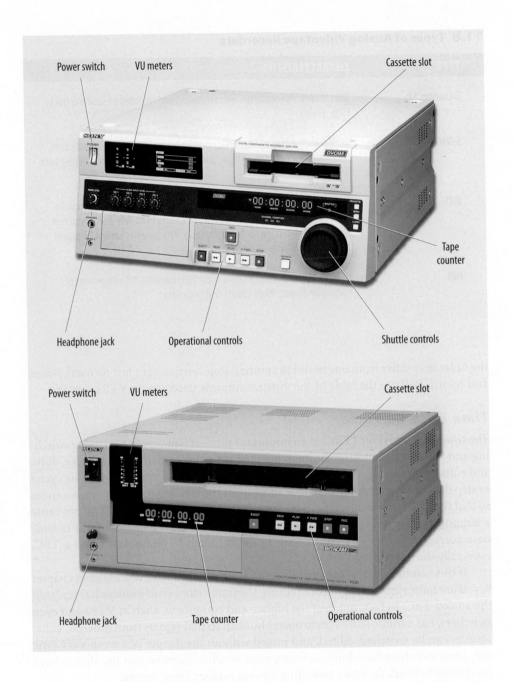

Power switch   VU meters   Cassette slot

Tape counter

Headphone jack   Operational controls   Shuttle controls

Power switch   VU meters   Cassette slot

Headphone jack   Tape counter   Operational controls

DVCAM (Sony) or DVCPRO (Panasonic) systems produce extremely high-quality video and audio that show no deterioration even after many generations. *High-definition video* (*HDV*) and *high-definition television* (*HDTV*) use exclusively digital VTRs for recording and editing.

▶ Digital VTRs use ¼-inch tape cassettes and MiniDV cassettes.

▶ The record heads in digital recorders are much smaller than in the average VHS or S-VHS machine and spin much faster.

▶ Digital recorders write several tracks for a single frame. For example, the DVCPRO50 system uses twenty tracks per frame.

▶ Most digital VTRs have a FireWire or i-link (IEEE 1394) port, which allows a two-way exchange of video and audio between the VTR and the computer editing station.

Refer to the table on the characteristics of the most common digital VTRs. **SEE 11.10**

11.10 Types of Digital Videotape Recorders

TYPE	RECORDING MEDIA	FEATURES
STV (STANDARD TELEVISION)		
Digital Betacam	½-inch tape cassette	Superior quality. Large tape. No loss in dubbing.
Digital-S	½-inch tape cassette	Good quality. Some loss in dubbing.
DVCPRO	¼-inch (6.35mm) tape cassette	Very good quality. Panasonic format. No loss in dubbing.
DVCPRO50	¼-inch tape cassette	Excellent quality. No loss in dubbing.
DVCAM	¼-inch tape cassette	Excellent quality. Sony format. No loss in dubbing.
MiniDV	¼-inch tape mini-cassette	Very good quality.
HDV (HIGH-DEFINITION VIDEO)		
Various models	¼-inch tape cassette	Excellent quality. Relatively slow (real-time) transfer to the nonlinear editing system (NLE).
	Small camcorder hard drives	Excellent quality. Rapid transfer to NLE. Random access.
	Small detached hard drives	Connected via FireWire to camera. High recording capacity.
Sony	Optical laser disc	Excellent quality. Easy transfer to NLE. Random access. High recording capacity. Still has moving parts.
Panasonic	Solid-state memory card	Excellent quality. No moving parts. Relatively low recording capacity.
HDTV (HIGH-DEFINITION TELEVISION)		
Various models, including Electronic Cinema	¼-inch DVCAM or DVCPRO	Superior quality: 1080i or 720p scanning formats.
Various models	¼-inch mini-cassette	Superior quality: 1080i or 720p formats.
Sony XDCAM HD	Optical disc	Superior quality: 1080i or 720p formats.
Grass Valley Infinity Digital Media Recorder	Removable Iomega 35 gigabyte hard disks or solid-state memory cards	Superior quality: 1080i or 720p formats. Supports DVCAM and DVCPRO.

Tape Format and Quality

Historically, *tape format* referred to the width of the videotape. In the early days of videotape recording, format was an important indicator of recording quality: the narrower the tape, the poorer the quality. Today the recording method or VTR type, rather than the tape width, determines recording quality. For example, the DVCAM and DVCPRO systems, which use a ¼-inch (6.35mm) tape width, are superior to the ½-inch (12.7mm) S-VHS system or even Betacam SP recordings, especially in subsequent generations.

You still need to know, however, which tapes are required for the various VTRs. Obviously, a ½-inch tape won't fit a VTR that uses ¼-inch tapes. But even if a VTR uses ½-inch tape rather than ¼-inch, it may still require a tape manufactured specifically for its model. For example, S-VHS recorders or Betacam SP VTRs require a much higher-quality tape than consumer VTRs, although all three use the ½-inch format. In an emergency you may use a high-quality VHS tape in an S-VHS recorder, assuming that the S-VHS recorder has a control that allows you to do an S-VHS recording with VHS tape. But the ¼-inch DVCPRO Panasonic tape cannot be used for the ¼-inch DVCAM Sony VTR and vice versa. The tapes may look alike, but they have different magnetic coatings. MiniDV cassettes, on the other hand, fit all DV camcorders and VTRs regardless of manufacturer.

Knowing the basic tape formats will help you choose the right tape for your VTR or camcorder, though it still pays to double-check each time you use a tape, even when you have become proficient as an ENG camcorder or VTR operator.

VIDEOTAPE-RECORDING PROCESS

The relative ease with which you can operate a VTR may cause you to put videotape recording at the bottom of your production priority list. Such an attitude often leads to huge problems and headaches. Taking the wrong videocassettes on an EFP shoot is as serious a problem as forgetting the camcorders, as is assuming that the studio VTRs will be available when you need them. As with any other major production activity, videotape recording requires careful preparation and meticulous attention to detail in the preproduction, production, and postproduction phases.

Similar to a pilot who must go through a checklist before every flight, you should establish your own "before, during, and after" VTR checklists. Such checklists are especially helpful when doing field productions. The following lists include major production items only; you may need to adapt or add to these lists to meet your specific equipment and recording requirements.

THE "BEFORE" CHECKLIST

☑ *Schedule* Is the videotaping equipment actually available for the studio or field production? Most likely, your operation will have more than one type of VTR available. Which VTR do you need? Be reasonable in your request. You will find that VTRs are usually available for the actual production or the remote shoot but not always for your playback demands. If you need a VTR simply for reviewing the scenes shot on location, don't request a high-end digital recorder: have the material dubbed down to a regular ½-inch VHS format and watch it on your home VCR. Be sure you have a recorder available that will actually play back the videotape.

✅ **VTR status**   Does the VTR actually work? A simple head clog can put even the most expensive VTR out of service. You can detect dirty heads if the picture starts to become progressively noisy or breaks up during playback. Sometimes one of the tiny switches on the VTR may be in the wrong position, preventing you from recording either video or audio. Sometimes you need an adapter to play MiniDV tapes in a regular digital VTR. Is the record-protect tab of the videotape in the *off* position? (See figure 11.11.) Always do a brief test recording and play it back before the actual videotaping.

✅ **Power supply**   When you use a VTR in the field, or when you use a camcorder, do you have enough batteries for the entire shoot? Are they fully charged? If you power the VTR, the camera, and perhaps even the camera light with the same battery, your recording time will be considerably less than if each piece of equipment had a separate power supply. Electronic image stabilization, which corrects minor camera wobbles, and using the foldout viewfinder screen also drain the battery quite rapidly. If you use household current for power, you will need the appropriate adapter. Check whether the connectors of the power cable fit the jacks of the power supply and the camera. Don't try to make a connector fit a jack it isn't designed for; even if you can force it in, you may blow more than a fuse.

✅ **Tape**   Do you have the correct tape? Does the cassette match the type and the format of the VTR? Check whether the boxes actually contain the correct tapes. Do not rely solely on the box label. Because cassettes can be loaded with various lengths of tape, look at the supply reel to verify that it contains the amount of tape indicated on the box.

Do you have enough tape for the proposed production? Videotape is relatively inexpensive and does not take up much room. Always bring more cassettes than you think you'll need. Running out of videotape during a field production does not win you any friends.

Are the cassettes in the record mode? All cassettes have a device to protect the videotape from accidental erasure, which means that you cannot record a new program over the old one. All tape cassettes have a tab that can be moved into or out of a record-protect position. VHS and S-VHS ½-inch cassettes have a tab on the lower left of the back edge. **SEE 11.11** When this tab is in the open position, or broken off, you cannot record on the cassette. To restore the cassette to the record mode, move the tab into the record position; for breakaway tabs, cover the hole with a piece of adhesive tape. Routinely check the status of the tab before using a cassette for videotape recording. The cassette will play back with or without record-protect devices in place.

> **▶ KEY CONCEPT**
> Always check that the cassette format matches the VTR and that the cassette tab is in place for recording.

✅ **Cables**   Do the cables work? The problem with defective cables is that ordinarily you can't see the damage. If you don't have time to test the cables beforehand, take some spares along. Do the cables fit the VTR jacks? As you recall, most professional recorders or camcorders use XLR jacks for audio inputs, but some have RCA phono

11.11 Cassette Record Protection

Digital ¼-inch and MiniDV cassettes have a movable tab that prevents accidental erasure, much like a small computer disk. When in the open position, the cassette will play back but not record. The tab on ½-inch VHS and S-VHS cassettes can be broken off.

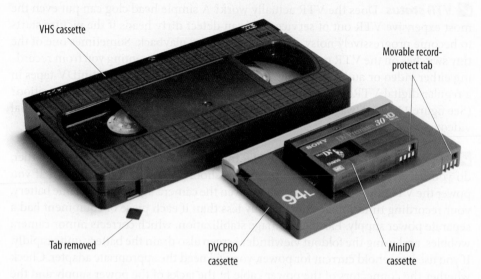

VHS cassette

Movable record-protect tab

Tab removed

DVCPRO cassette

MiniDV cassette

jacks. Video cables have either BNC, S-video, or RCA phono connectors (see figures 4.21 and 7.26). Keep a supply of adapters on hand, but try to have cables with the correct plugs. You will soon find out that each adapter is a potential trouble spot.

☑ *Monitor* Most portable monitors can be powered by battery or household current. When using such a monitor in a field production, bring a long extension cord as well as two fully charged batteries. You can feed the camera output directly into this monitor via a coaxial cable with a BNC connector at both ends.

THE "DURING" CHECKLIST

☑ *Video leader* Whenever possible, start each videotape with a *video leader*, which consists of a 30- to 60-second recording of color bars and a 0 VU test tone, an identification slate, black or leader numbers (from 10 to 2) that flash on-screen every second for eight seconds, and two seconds of black before the first frame of the program video. **SEE 11.12**

The *color bars* can be generated by the ENG/EFP camera you actually use or, in a studio production, from the camera control unit (CCU). Unfortunately, most consumer camcorders cannot generate color bars. The 0 VU test tone can come from a portable mixer or the studio console.

During playback you can use the color bars and the test tone as important references to match the colors of the playback monitor and the audio volume of the playback VTR with that of the videotape recording. Do not copy the video leader from another recording—you would be adjusting your playback equipment to the wrong standard.

11.12 **Video Leader**

The video leader helps adjust the playback machine to the video and audio values of the record machine.

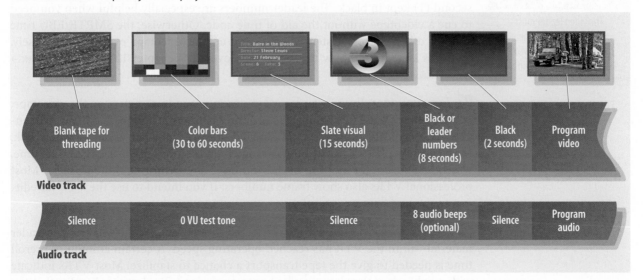

11.13 Character-generated Slate

The slate gives vital production information and is recorded at the beginning of each major take.

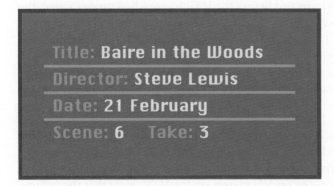

The *video slate* shows vital production information, such as the show title; the scene and take numbers; the date, time, and location of the recording; and frequently the name of the director and the producer. At a minimum the slate should indicate the name of the show and the take number. The slate is usually done with a character generator (C.G.) or the camcorder's built-in lettering function. **SEE 11.13** In field productions this information is sometimes hand-lettered on a board, also called a slate, or simply read into a microphone by the floor manager, the VTR operator, or even the talent. Each time you do another take, you need to update the take number on the slate.

The *leader numbers* that show the seconds remaining before the first frame of the program material are also produced by the C.G. These numbers, which were originally developed for film cueing, are used for cueing the videotape during playback. For instance, you can cue the tape at leader number 4, which gives you a 4-second preroll before the first frame of program video appears. These numbers are normally accompanied by corresponding audio beeps. Note that the last two seconds are usually in black and silent. Some leader numbers flash down to 2, with only the last second (1) kept in black. The leader numbers are especially helpful when you need to cue a videotape without the aid of time code. Otherwise, the SMPTE/EBU time code or other address system lets you cue up the videotape even more precisely. (Address systems and how they work are covered in chapter 12.) **ZVL3 CUE 2** EDITING→ Postproduction guidelines→ leader

✅ *Tape counter*   Even if you record some kind of address system on the videotape, you should reset the mechanical tape counter before starting the tape. This will enable you to quickly locate the approximate starting point when asked for a playback. Most consumer VTRs display hours, minutes, and seconds of elapsed recording time, which is sufficient for locating the beginning of a recording or show segment. Most professional VTRs also show frame numbers. If you intend to use the VTR for editing, frame numbers are essential.

✅ *Preroll*   When starting a VTR, do not record anything—not even the video leader material—until the VTR has reached operating speed. A certain amount of preroll time is needed to give the tape transport a chance to stabilize. Most VTRs indicate with a light when they have reached operating speed. To alert the director that the VTR has reached operating speed and is ready to record, give a "speed," "locked," or "in-record" cue. If you start to record before the VTR has reached proper speed, the recording will most likely suffer from picture and sound breakup.

During editing most VTRs in camcorders back up the tape automatically for the required preroll (see chapter 12). This procedure is called *backspacing*. In the playback mode, most high-end VTRs reach operating speed within a fraction of a second; they deliver a stable picture even when you shift directly to *play* from the pause mode that displays a freeze-frame.

✅ *Recording levels*   Watch carefully the video and especially the audio recording levels. You may get so carried away with the exciting visuals of a scene that minor—or even major—audio problems escape your attention. Many camcorders indicate these levels in the viewfinder display or on VU meters on the VTR. Note that the volume standard for digital audio is considerably lower than that of analog. In any case, the digital audio signal should never peak above 0 dB, or you will end up with an irreparable sound distortion.

✅ *Recording for postproduction*   When recording for postproduction editing, record enough of each segment so that the action overlaps the preceding and following scenes. Such cushions (called *pads* or *trim handles*) greatly facilitate editing. If you have enough tape, record the camera rehearsals. Sometimes you will get a better performance during rehearsal than during the actual take. Record a few seconds of black after each take before stopping the tape. This *run-out* signal acts as a pad during editing or, if you do a live-on-tape recording, as a safety cushion during playback.

✅ *Retakes*   As the VTR operator, tell the director right away if you feel that another take is necessary for some reason. It is far less expensive to repeat a take than to try to "fix it in post." Be ready to rewind the tape to the beginning of the flawed take without delay. You can do this quite easily if you keep an accurate *field log*.

☑ *Recordkeeping* Keep accurate records of each take during the recording. You will be surprised at how quickly you forget just where on the videotape your unforgettable shot or scene is located. A carefully kept field log can save you considerable time in finding takes during the field production and especially when preparing a more accurate *VTR log* in the postproduction phase. The **field log** should include the production title, the names of the producer and the director, the taping date and location, the tape number, the scene and take numbers and their sequence, whether the takes are good, and the tape counter or time code number. You may also list some important production details, such as mistakes made by the talent or especially serious audio problems. **SEE 11.14** If there is only a single column for the take number, circle the good takes.

> **KEY CONCEPT**
>
> Keep an accurate field log during the recording session and carefully label all videotapes.

11.14 Field Log

The field log is kept by the VTR operator during the production. It normally indicates the production title, names of producer and director, taping date and location, tape number, scene and take numbers and their sequence, whether the takes are good, tape counter or time code number, and what the take was all about. It facilitates locating the various cassettes and shots during postproduction previewing.

PRODUCTION TITLE: "impressions"   PRODUCER/DIRECTOR: Hamid Khani

TAPING DATE: 4/15   LOCATION: BECA Newsroom

CASSETTE NUMBER	SCENE	TAKE	OK or NO GOOD	TIME CODE IN	TIME CODE OUT	EVENT / REMARKS
C-005	2	1	NG	01:57:25	02:07:24	student looks into camera CU - Z axis
		②	OK	02:09:04	02:14:27	monitor + L news anchor MS getting ready
		③	OK	02:14:28	02:34:22	Pan R to reveal anchor in news set
		4	NG	02:34:22	02:45:18	Rack focus from Floor Mgr to L anchor - OUT OF FOCUS
		5	NG	02:48:05	02:55:12	Rack focus both out of focus
		6	NG	02:58:13	03:05:11	Rack OK LOST Audio
		⑦	OK	03:12:02	03:46:24	Hurrah! Rack OK
	3	①	OK	04:16:03	04:28:11	MS Floor Mgr + camera op from behind
		2	NG	04:35:13	04:49:05	CU of R anchor lost audio
		③	OK	05:50:00	06:01:24	CU of R anchor
		4	NG	06:03:10	06:30:17	CU of L anchor audio problem
		5	NG	06:40:07	07:04:08	LS of both anchors Floor Mgr walks through shot
		⑥	OK	07:07:15	07:28:05	Good! Floor Mgr silhouette against set
		⑦	OK	07:30:29	07:45:12	slow pullout
C-006	4	①	OK	49:48:28	51:12:08	MCU Marty talks to anchors
		2	NG	51:35:17	51:42:01	Lav comes off R anchor

THE "AFTER" CHECKLIST

☑ *Recording check* Before moving on to the next scene or striking the studio set or remote location, verify that you have actually recorded the scene as planned. Rewind the tape to the beginning shot, then fast-forward the tape two or three times to spot-check the entire recording. If the tape looks and sounds good, proceed to the next item on the production schedule. Pay attention to the sound. Sometimes you may think that the audio distortion is in the playback equipment, but more likely than not the problem was caused by connecting the incoming sound signal to the wrong mixer input (line instead of mic and vice versa).

☑ *Labeling* Label each tape with the title of the production, the recording date, the tape number, and the tape content. Label the box with the identical information. As obvious as such labeling seems, countless precious hours of postproduction time have been lost because someone labeled the tape boxes but not the tapes themselves. Watch that the tape labels match the information on the corresponding field log. Make a photocopy of the field log and label both the log and the corresponding tape with the same code so that you can match the two when preparing the VTR log.

☑ *Protection copies* As soon as possible, dub all source tapes in their entirety so you have a protection (backup) copy of all the material shot. During this dubbing session, you can also make *window dubs*—lower-quality (VCR) recordings that have the time code inserted over each frame. You can then proceed to prepare a VTR log, which we explain in chapter 12.

> **▶ KEY CONCEPT**
>
> Always make protection copies of all the source tapes.

NONLINEAR STORAGE SYSTEMS

Regardless of whether the video information stored on videotape is analog or digital, you can access it only serially: you need to roll through the first twenty-six shots, for example, before reaching shot 27. Unlike the linear videotape system, *nonlinear storage systems* allow random access. When this digital information is stored on a hard drive, an optical disc, or a flash memory device, you can access shot 27 directly. Instead of having to wait for the tape to roll to the desired frame, you can call up the frame in a fraction of a second. Shot 27 and shot 327 are as quickly and easily accessible as shot 1. This random access to each digitized frame has revolutionized postproduction editing (explored further in chapter 12).

> **▶ KEY CONCEPT**
>
> Nonlinear digital storage devices allow random and almost instantaneous access to each video frame.

The problem with using nonlinear digital video is that high-resolution, full-screen video requires a great amount of storage space, especially when dealing with moving images. Advances in data compression, however, let you squeeze more information on smaller storage devices. As you can see, a tapeless operation depends on improved storage devices as well as better compression techniques. The most popular nonlinear digital storage devices are computer disks and video servers, flash memory devices, read/write optical discs, and electronic still store (ESS) systems.

Computer Disks and Video Servers

Because video and audio information can be digitized, you can store it on any type of computer disk. The computer won't know whether the magnetic pulses it stores represent a reproduction of the *Mona Lisa* or your checkbook balance. So long as the pictures you want to store are still images rather than moving ones, you can store a great number of video images on a relatively small hard drive or flash memory device. Moving images need considerably more storage space. Realizing that just one second of video takes 30 individual frames, you can see why, despite high-capacity hard drives, some kind of image compression is necessary for the efficient storage and transport of full-motion video.

Fortunately, various compression methods let you cram more and more information onto ever-smaller disks. Recall from chapter 3 the discussion about lossless and lossy compression and the suitcase example. *Lossless compression* simply finds unused space on the disk and puts the information in the best possible order. *Lossy compression* reduces all nonessential and redundant information, usually borrowing the dropped information from one or two frames that originally carried it and restoring it when necessary.

Some small hard drives can be plugged into the camera part of a camcorder, but the recording time is still somewhat limited. There are, however, small external hard drives (such as Laird's CapDiv) that let you store 60 gigabytes of video and audio information. This translates into four-plus hours of high-quality video and audio. More camcorders are using nonlinear storage devices rather than videotape, especially for news and EFP.

Because of the ease with which computers can manage digital information, television stations are switching from videotape to video servers for on-the-air playback and as the central storage device for postproduction editing. A **video server** is a large-capacity computer hard drive that can store and play back a great amount of video and audio information. The advantage of such a server is that the computer can instantly call up a single frame for editing or an entire show for on-the-air playback. Because servers work with disk arrays, they can also accommodate multiple users; several editors can work on different projects simultaneously so long as the source material is stored on the server.

Flash Memory Devices

Solid-state **flash memory devices**, known as *flash drives, flash media, memory sticks,* or *memory cards,* come in various shapes and sizes, but they all have the same goal in mind: to replace videotape as the recording medium in camcorders. They operate very much like the small memory stick you may be using as a fast backup device for a limited amount of information. But the flash memory devices in camcorders hold more information—4 gigabytes per card, which is enough for capturing an average news story or several takes during EFP. Their great advantage is their ease of use and their extremely fast data transfer speed. Some, such as the Panasonic P-2 card, can be plugged directly into a compatible slot on a laptop computer for editing.

Because flash drives have no moving parts, they are quite rugged and can be carried in your shirt pocket. But there are also disadvantages. One is the relatively limited recording capacity. For example, you need several cards for a half hour of video and audio capture. Another problem is cost. Because the cards are quite expensive, you cannot afford to use them for editing or archiving the news footage but must transfer their content to a hard drive or server to free up the card for further use in the camera.

Read/Write Optical Discs

These laser-operated optical discs let you "read" (play back) previously recorded material and "write" (record) new material, just like with a hard drive. You are certainly familiar with the CDs that are used primarily for music, the CD-ROMs that are used for interactive programs and games, and the DVDs that have all but replaced VHS tapes as the favorite movie playback device. You also can use *CD-Rs* (recordable compact discs) or *DVD-RWs* (digital versatile discs–read/write) for storage and playback of short or long audio/video sequences.

The recording and playback equipment comes in various sizes and with varying degrees of sophistication. Even a small read/write optical disc the size of a regular CD-ROM (normally 650 megabytes) lets you record and play back about seventy minutes of high-fidelity digital audio and a relatively great amount of motion video. Depending on the format, a DVD can hold from 4.7 to 17.9 gigabytes of data—enough storage space for your favorite high-definition movie and then some. Again, the advantage of such an optical disc over videotape is that the disc allows random access, is easier to store, and produces better video and audio than VHS or S-VHS tape; it also does not wear out with repeated use.

There are ENG/EFP camcorders that use optical disc cartridges as their recording media. For example, one of the large Sony camcorders (XDCAM) uses an optical disc cartridge, whose 23-gigabyte capacity allows you to record eight-five minutes of high-quality audio and video. Such a disc provides all the advantages of a nonlinear recording but, contrary to flash memory devices, still needs moving parts to operate.

Electronic Still Store Systems

As mentioned in chapter 9, an *electronic still store (ESS) system* can store a vast array of still images and display any one of the stored frames in a fraction of a second. As you know, you can store hundreds of high-resolution photos on a single CD. Larger systems can store several thousand still frames. In fact, nonlinear editing systems are basically large ESS systems. They don't store actual moving images but rather myriad single-frame files.

USE OF VIDEO RECORDING

The original purpose of video recording was to temporarily preserve a live uninterrupted television program for repeated playback or for reference and study. Today, however, we use video recording in a great variety of ways: for personal communication, for constructing video events through postproduction editing, for producing electronic movies through HDTV electronic cinema cameras, and for archiving TV programming and various educational materials. All television stations maintain a large videotape library for their daily programming. Many of these recordings are transferred to video servers for automated retrieval.

Video as a field extends far beyond simply producing broadcast or cable television programs. The affordable high-quality camcorder made video recording an important personal communication medium. Your vacation and family videotapes and your demo reel when applying for a job are good examples. *Desktop video,* which originally meant using regular desktop computers and simple editing software for editing home video, has become an important professional video production tool. This marriage of computer and video has brought about other significant developments: multimedia and interactive video.

Multimedia

Multimedia refers to the simultaneous display of text, sound, and still and moving images. Although a great percentage of multimedia programs are entirely computer-generated, many still rely heavily on video production for content. Multimedia programs come on CD-ROM and DVD and must be played with the appropriate drives on personal computers or with stand-alone CD or DVD players. Such programs are used extensively for informational, instructional, and training programs; various types of presentations; and, of course, entertainment. As you know, interactive game shows have become a huge industry.

Though much more modest in scope, *Zettl's VideoLab 3.0* DVD-ROM is an example of an instructional interactive multimedia program. If you have been using the DVD-ROM with this book, you know that it presents the material with text, diagrams, narration, music, still and moving images, and various sound effects. It also invites you to make choices and gives you immediate feedback on their relative merit. The interactive program also provides a production laboratory in which you can work different equipment in a variety of production situations without tying up an actual studio. It is an effective transition between learning production from a book and doing it in the studio and the field.

Interactive Video

Interactive video is the type over which the viewer has some control of what he or she wants to see and how to see it. The viewer is no longer passive but has become an active partner in the communication process.

In its simplest form, such interactivity allows you to choose programs from a menu of options. You can also determine, at least to some extent, how a particular story will end, provided the show was produced with two or three different endings. Home shopping and video games are other well-known forms of interactive video.

As a training device, interactive video might show a critical traffic situation. You could then be asked (by the person appearing on-screen or an off-screen announcer) what you, as the driver, would do to avoid an accident. An elaborate interactive program would then show you the consequences of your answer. A simpler program will at least let you know immediately whether your answer was right or wrong. Or, after watching various scenes showing different shoppers in a department store, you may be asked to identify the shoplifter. The computer will then show you the culprit and demonstrate what behavior raised a red flag before the actual crime was committed.

The most important development in interactive video is the marriage of television and the Internet. Rather than use separate equipment—a television system for

Interactive video allows the
viewer to exercise choice
with immediate feedback.
It combines the functions of
television with the interactivity
of the desktop computer.

watching television and a desktop computer with a modem for accessing information—your television set can now take on many computer functions, and computers can act as little television systems. With a *digital subscriber line (DSL)*, you can receive digital audio and video streams for recording high-quality audio and full-motion video, although coaxial and fiber-optic cable systems are much better suited for transporting the huge amounts of digital data necessary for full-screen, real-time video and audio. The advantage of this high-capacity, high-speed transport system is that the Internet can expand its database to full-motion HDTV video.

M A I N   P O I N T S

► **Tape- and Disk-based Recording Systems**

Tape-based systems can record and play back analog or digital video and audio signals and other information necessary for the proper operation of the tape. Disk-based systems can record and play back only digital information.

► **Basic Videotape Tracks**

All analog videotape recorders (VTRs) use separate tracks for recording the video and audio as well as various control data. Most analog VTRs put at least four tracks onto a videotape: the video track containing the picture information, two audio tracks containing all sound information, and a control track for the synchronization of the frames.

► **Composite and Component Recording Systems**

The NTSC (National Television System Committee) standard is a composite video system that combines the color (C) and the luminance (Y, or black-and-white) part of the video signal into a single composite signal. The Y/C component video system separates the color (C) and luminance (Y) information; it is sometimes referred to as the S-video system. They are combined into the one NTSC signal only for transmission. The Y/color difference component system takes the original RGB video signals and mixes them in different proportions for technical convenience and to save bandwidth.

► **Composite and Component Video Playback**

Videotapes recorded as Y/C component or Y/color difference component signals cannot be played back on composite (NTSC) equipment.

► **Types of Videotape Recorders**

The two major types of videotape recorders are analog and digital. Although both types use videotape as the recording medium, they are not compatible: you cannot play back an analog tape on a digital VTR or a digital tape on an analog VTR.

► **Time Base Corrector**

The time base corrector (TBC) is needed to make analog and digital videotape playbacks, dubs, and edits electronically stable. The TBC keeps slightly different scanning cycles in step during videotape playback. The digital frame store synchronizer, which can also be used for analog VTRs, has largely replaced the TBC.

▶ **Tape Format**

Not all VTRs use the same videocassettes. Cassettes having the same tape width are not necessarily interchangeable. Always check that the cassette format matches the recording VTR and that the cassette tab is in place for recording.

▶ **Video Leader**

The video leader must be generated by the equipment actually used in the videotape recording.

▶ **Field Log and Protection Copies**

Keep an accurate field log during a recording and carefully label all videotapes. Whenever possible, make copies of the original source tapes right away.

▶ **Linear and Nonlinear Recording Systems**

All videotape recordings are linear, regardless of whether they are analog or digital. Linear systems allow no random access. Nonlinear systems are tapeless and permit random access of recorded material—any frame can be accessed instantaneously. The most common nonlinear storage device is the computer hard drive. A video server is a large-capacity hard drive for storage and on-the-air playback of program material. A single server can accommodate multiple users simultaneously. Flash memory devices are solid-state storage devices; they have no moving parts but have a low storage capacity. Read/write optical discs are used in some camcorders; they have a greater storage capacity than flash drives but still have moving parts. Electronic still store (ESS) systems can store thousands of still frames that can be quickly accessed for use in a live program or video recording.

▶ **Multimedia and Interactive Video**

Multimedia refers to the simultaneous display by the computer of text, sound, and still and moving images. Distributed on CD-ROM or DVD, these interactive programs are used extensively for information, instruction, and entertainment. Interactive video allows the viewer to exercise choice with immediate feedback. It combines the functions of television with the interactivity of the desktop computer.

Z E T T L ' S   V I D E O L A B   3 . 0

For your reference, or to track your work, the Zettl's VideoLab 3.0 *program cues in this chapter are listed here with their corresponding page numbers.*

ZVL3 CUE 1   EDITING→ Postproduction guidelines→ tape basics   **221**

ZVL3 CUE 2   EDITING→ Postproduction guidelines→ leader   **232**

KEY TERMS

assemble editing Adding shots on videotape in a consecutive order without first recording a control track on the edit master tape.

capture Moving video and audio from an analog or digital videotape to the hard drive of a computer with a nonlinear editing program. Analog signals must be converted to digital before they can be imported by the computer.

digitizing Similar to capturing analog audio and video. The analog signals of a videotape are converted to digital signals for storage on the computer hard drive.

edit controller A machine that assists in various editing functions, such as marking edit-in and edit-out points, rolling source and record VTRs, and integrating effects. It can be a desktop computer with a specific software program. Also called *editing control unit*.

edit decision list (EDL) Consists of edit-in and edit-out points, expressed in time code numbers, and the nature of transitions between shots.

edit master The videotape or disc that contains the final version of an edited program. Subsequent copies are struck from the edit master.

insert editing Produces highly stable edits. Requires the prior laying of a continuous control track by recording black on the edit master tape.

linear editing system Uses videotape as the editing medium. It does not allow random access of shots.

nonlinear editing system (NLE) Allows random access of shots. The video and audio information is stored in digital form on computer disks. Usually has two external monitors, small loudspeakers, and an audio mixer.

off-line editing In linear editing it produces an edit decision list or an edit master not intended for broadcast. In nonlinear editing the selected shots are captured in low resolution to save computer storage space.

on-line editing In linear editing it produces the final high-quality edit master for broadcast or program duplication. In nonlinear editing it requires recapturing the selected shots at a higher resolution.

pulse-count system An address code that counts the control track pulses and translates that count into time and frame numbers. Also called *control track system*.

rough-cut A preliminary off-line edit.

SMPTE time code A specially generated address code that marks each video frame with a specific number (hour, minute, second, and frame). Named for the Society of Motion Picture and Television Engineers, this time code is officially called *SMPTE/EBU* (for European Broadcasting Union).

VTR log A record of each take on the source tapes. Also called *editing log*.

window dub A dub of the source tapes to a lower-quality tape format with the address code keyed into each frame.

Postproduction:
Linear and Nonlinear Editing

Postproduction editing is the third and final stage of the production process, in which the various video and audio segments are given structure and meaning. Editing offers you the final chance to clarify and intensify the intended message. Assuming that the preproduction and production phases went according to plan, you can now use your grasp of the program objective and your creativity to build a program that has clarity and impact.

Most editors feel that postproduction editing is among the most creative aspects of video production. Very much like writing, editing is an exacting and painstaking activity. To tell the story effectively, you must not only understand the program objective, the angle the director has in mind, and the general feel of the program but also master a complex technical procedure. **ZVL3 CUE 1** EDITING→ Editing introduction

Although you may have done some simple editing already with a nonlinear editing program, you should acquaint yourself first with the basic principles of linear videotape editing. Nonlinear editing has taken over many terms from linear editing, and, although operationally different, many of the principles and procedures of linear editing also apply to nonlinear editing. Besides, if you are a good editor, it's likely you may be called upon to do some linear editing. **ZVL3 CUE 2** EDITING→ Functions

This chapter focuses on the various systems and processes of postproduction editing.

▶ **LINEAR EDITING**
Single-source linear system, multiple-source linear system, pulse-count and address code, assemble editing, and insert editing

▶ **NONLINEAR EDITING**
Nonlinear editing system and basic editing procedures

▶ **POSTPRODUCTION PREPARATIONS**
Shooting for continuity, making protection copies, adding time code, making a window dub, reviewing and logging the source footage, transcribing the audio text, and laying a control track

▶   **OFF-LINE AND ON-LINE EDITING**
     Linear and nonlinear off- and on-line editing procedures

LINEAR EDITING

The basic principle of linear editing is copying selected shots from the source tapes to an edit master tape in a desired sequence. The ***edit master tape*** is the first videotape that contains the final version of an edited program and from which subsequent copies are struck. Whenever you use a videotape recorder (VTR) for playing the source tapes and for copying the selected shots onto the edit master tape, you have a ***linear editing system***, regardless of whether the signal on the videotape is analog or digital. It is called "linear" because you cannot access the source material randomly. For example, if you want to edit shot 14 to shot 3, you must roll through the intervening eleven shots: the first two to reach shot 3, then another eleven to reach shot 14. You cannot simply call up shots 3 and 14. **ZVL3 CUE 3** ▶EDITING→ Linear editing→ system

Single-source Linear System

The most basic linear editing system consists of a source VTR and a record VTR. You use the source VTR to select the various shots and the record VTR to copy them and join them through cuts. The record VTR performs the actual video and audio edits. Both the source and record VTRs have their own monitor. In a single-source system, the source VTR monitor displays the source material to be edited, and the record VTR monitor displays the edited video portion of the edit master tape. **SEE 12.1**

Because there is only one source VTR, the single-source editing system is usually limited to cuts-only transitions. But speed is paramount in news editing, so such cuts-only editors are still very much in demand. There are highly portable ones that contain two digital VTRs, two flat-screen monitor displays, and basic editing controls—all packed tightly into a small suitcase. You can take them along in your news vehicle and edit news stories on location. **SEE 12.2**

12.1 Basic Single-source System

The source VTR supplies the chosen shots of the original video and feeds them to the record VTR. The record VTR copies the selections and joins them in the desired sequence through cuts. The source monitor displays the video of the source VTR, and the record monitor shows the video of the record VTR. In this case, the close-up will follow the two-shot.

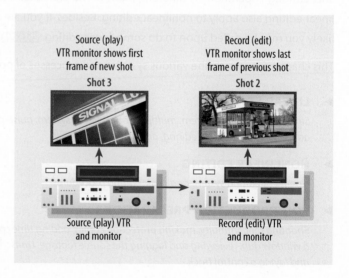

Source (play)
VTR monitor shows first
frame of new shot
Shot 3

Record (edit)
VTR monitor shows last
frame of previous shot
Shot 2

Source (play) VTR
and monitor

Record (edit) VTR
and monitor

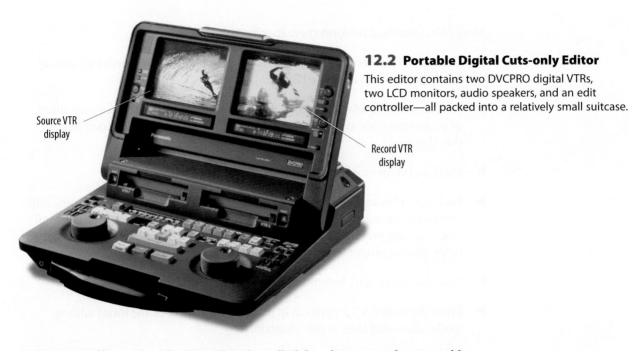

12.2 **Portable Digital Cuts-only Editor**

This editor contains two DVCPRO digital VTRs, two LCD monitors, audio speakers, and an edit controller—all packed into a relatively small suitcase.

Source VTR display

Record VTR display

Edit controller   The ***edit controller,*** also called the *editing control unit,* acts like an able and superefficient editing assistant. This computerized machine will mark and remember frame locations on the source and record tapes, preroll and synchronize the VTRs, allow you to treat the audio with the video or separately, and tell the record VTR when to switch to record mode (thereby performing the edit). Smart edit controllers also activate switchers and audio consoles for video and audio effects. Usually, the edit controller has separate operational controls for the source and record VTRs (*play, fast-forward, rewind,* and variable search speeds) and for common editing functions. Best of all, this editing assistant never complains about long hours in the editing bay. **SEE 12.3**

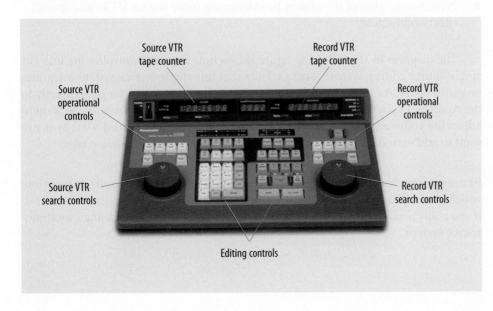

Source VTR tape counter

Record VTR tape counter

Source VTR operational controls

Record VTR operational controls

Source VTR search controls

Record VTR search controls

Editing controls

12.3 **Edit Controller**

The edit controller has separate operational controls for the source VTR and the record VTR, such as search and shuttle controls. The controls in the center activate the preroll and editing functions.

Most edit controllers perform these specific tasks:

▶ Control VTR search modes (variable forward and reverse speeds) separately for the source and record VTRs to locate shots.

▶ Read and display elapsed time and frame numbers from either a pulse-count or an address code system for each VTR. (Address code is discussed later in this chapter.)

▶ Mark and remember precise edit-in and edit-out points.

▶ Back up, or backspace, both VTRs to exactly the same preroll point. Some edit controllers have a switch that gives several preroll choices, such as a 2-second or a 5-second preroll. You may recall that prerolling the VTRs ensures that the tapes achieve proper speed and synchronization.

▶ Simultaneously start both machines and keep them running in sync.

▶ Make the record VTR perform in either the assemble or the insert editing mode (discussed later in this chapter).

▶ Tell the record VTR to edit either the video track or the audio track or both. The actual edits are performed by the record VTR.

▶ Run a trial edit so that you can preview it. This preview edit will appear on the monitor for the record VTR, although the record VTR has not yet performed the actual edit.

▶ Rewind the record VTR so that it can execute the actual edit. The edited shots will appear again on the second (edit) monitor, but this time the edit has actually been completed. You can now review, instead of preview, the edit.

▶ Permit expansion of the system by interfacing more source VTRs and special-effects equipment.

The diagram in the following figure shows how the edit controller fits into the single-source editing system. **SEE 12.4** Note that this single-source system integrates an audio mixer. As you can see, however, the output from the mixer goes directly to the record VTR, bypassing the edit controller. You will need the mixer if you want to adjust the volume of the source VTR before sending it to the record VTR or if you want to add various sounds, such as music, that were not on the source tape.

▶ KEY CONCEPT

Single-source VTR editing systems are typically limited to cuts-only transitions.

Preread function   Some single-source editors have a built-in preread function, which allows you to produce dissolves, supers, and wipes with a single-source VTR. If you really need such transitions, however, you would be better off using a multiple-source system.

12.4 Edit Controller in Single-source System

The edit controller in a single-source system starts and synchronizes the source and record VTRs and locates the in- and out-points for both.

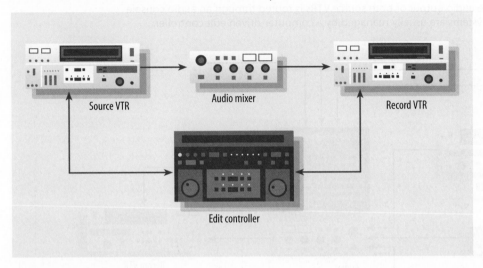

Source VTR

Audio mixer

Record VTR

Edit controller

Multiple-source Linear System

This system uses two or more VTRs as source machines, normally labeled with letters (A VTR, B VTR, C VTR, etc.), and a single record VTR.

With a multiple-source VTR system, you can edit the shots from the A and B (and/or C) VTRs without having to change tapes. The big advantage is that you are no longer restricted to cuts-only transitions. You can now perform fades, dissolves, and wipes between the *A-roll* (the material on the source A VTR) and the *B-roll* (the material on the source B VTR). To accomplish such transitions between the A and B rolls, you need to feed their video material into a postproduction switcher that will perform the actual switching function. Its line-out is then recorded by the record VTR. You can also use special effects provided by the switcher for a great variety of transitions.

The edit controllers for such multiple-source systems are usually computer-based. The computer will not only remember your commands—such as shot selection from the A and B rolls, type and length of transition, or special effects—but also make the source VTRs, the switcher, and/or the SEG (special-effects generator) perform various feats. Multiple-source systems normally interface an audio console rather than a mixer for more-ambitious audio manipulation during editing. **SEE 12.5**

Note that even if the source and record VTRs are digital, the editing is still linear. So long as you use videotape instead of a nonlinear storage device, such as a large-capacity hard drive, you do not have random access to shots. If you have the feeling that things are getting a bit more complicated than what you expected from a discussion of video "basics," you are right. Not only is postproduction editing a formidable aesthetic challenge, it is also technically complex. Even so, postproduction editing

> ▶ **KEY CONCEPT**
>
> Dissolves, wipes, and other special-effects transitions are possible with a multiple-source linear editing system.

12.5 Multiple-source Editing System

In a multiple-source system, two VTRs (A and B) supply the source material to the single record VTR. The video output of both source machines is routed through the switcher for transitions such as dissolves and wipe effects. The audio output of both source VTRs is routed through an audio console (or a mixer). Multiple-source systems are usually managed by a computer-driven edit controller.

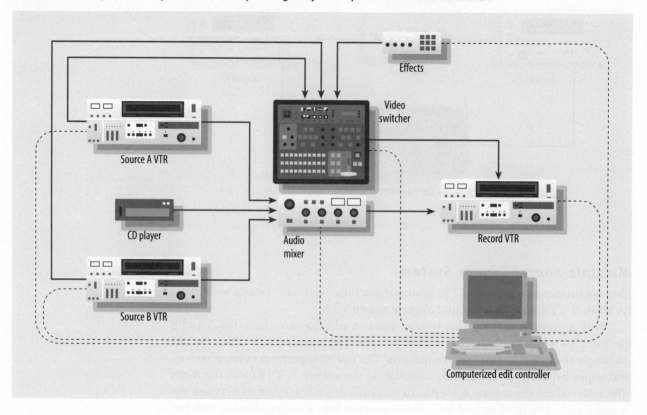

is not unlike learning a new software application: once you know how to use it, its complexity helps rather than hinders you in accomplishing your goals.

Pulse-count and Address Code

When you look at the edit controller, you see number displays for the source tape and the record tape. **SEE 12.6** These displays, which show elapsed hours, minutes, seconds, and frames, help you locate a shot or frame on the source and edit master tapes. These numbers are generated by either the pulse-count system or the time code system.

Pulse-count system   The *pulse-count system*, also called the *control track system*, uses the control track pulses to count the frames. **SEE 12.7** Recall that each pulse on the control track designates a video frame, so you can locate a specific spot on the videotape by counting the pulses on the control track. Thirty frames make up one second on the display, so each new second rolls over after the twenty-ninth frame. Each additional minute is generated by the sixtieth second, as is the hour after the sixtieth minute.

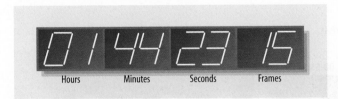

12.6 Pulse-count and Address Code Display

The pulse-count and address code displays show elapsed hours, minutes, seconds, and frames. The frames roll over (to seconds) after 29, the seconds to minutes and the minutes to hours after 59, and the hours to 0 after 24.

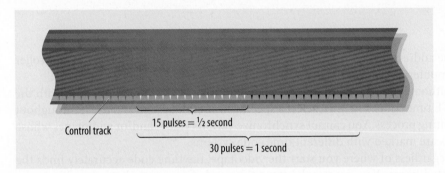

Control track

15 pulses = ½ second

30 pulses = 1 second

12.7 Pulse-count System

The pulse-count, or control track, system counts the control track pulses to find a specific spot on the videotape. Thirty pulses make up one second of elapsed tape time.

The pulse-count system is not frame-accurate: you will not get the same frame each time you move the tape to a specific pulse-count number because some of the pulses are skipped in the high-speed tape shuttle. For example, if you had to find the tenth house on a street, you would have no trouble. But if you were asked to go to the thirty-six-hundredth house, you would probably have more difficulty finding it. Considering that 3,600 pulses constitute only two minutes of videotape recording, you can understand why the counter may be off a few frames when you're trying to find a specific spot some twenty or more minutes into the tape.

This system switches to zero when you insert a tape, regardless of whether the tape starts from the very beginning or from somewhere in the middle. If you want to find a spot on the tape by the time and frame numbers displayed on the tape counter, you must rewind the tape completely and set the counter to zero before logging or editing.

The advantage of the pulse-count system is its speed. It does not require a prerecorded address code on a separate videotape track. For that reason the pulse-count system is still used in some analog news-editing rooms even though it isn't perfectly frame-accurate. **ZVL3 CUE 4** EDITING→ Postproduction guidelines→ tape basics

Time code system   For more-accurate editing, you have to use a *time code,* or *address code, system,* which marks each frame with a different number and a specific address. With time code the edit controller will guide you precisely to the tenth or thirty-six-hundredth house. To get to the tenth house, the edit controller does not have to start counting from 1 to 10 but simply looks for house number 10. It finds the thirty-six-hundredth house just as easily by looking at its house number: 3600.

The most widely accepted address system is the ***SMPTE time code*** (pronounced "sempty"); its full name is *SMPTE/EBU time code* (for Society of Motion Picture and Television Engineers/European Broadcasting Union). It gives each frame a specific and

12.8 **Time Code Address System**

The time code system marks each frame with a unique address.

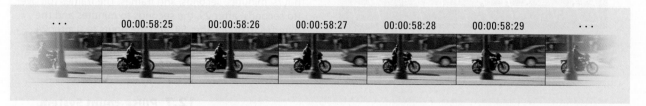

| · · · | 00:00:58:25 | 00:00:58:26 | 00:00:58:27 | 00:00:58:28 | 00:00:58:29 | · · · |

▶**KEY CONCEPT**

The time code provides a unique address for each frame of recorded video.

unique address, which you can use by looking at the read-out on the edit controller or computer display. **SEE 12.8** **ZVL3 CUE 5** EDITING→ Postproduction guidelines→ time code

Although there are similar time code systems, they are not compatible with the SMPTE time code. You must select a specific time code system and use it throughout the editing process. You cannot synchronize various video- and/or audiotapes whose frames are marked with different time code systems.

Regardless of where you start the videotape, the time code accurately finds the requested frame. You can use the same time code for your audiotape and have the computer synchronize the audio and the video frame-by-frame. The disadvantage of the address code system is that you need a time code generator to record the code on a cue track on the videotape or on one of the audiotape tracks. You then need a time code reader to display it. But for accurate editing, you can't do without it. All ENG/EFP camcorders can generate their own time code or import it from a time code generator.

You can record the time code while videotaping or, as is common in smaller productions and EFP, add it later to one of the cue tracks or audio tracks of the videotape. Because videotape segments rarely exceed one hour, the hour digit is sometimes reserved to indicate the tape number. For example, a time code of 04:17:22:18 would mean that the shot you are seeking is 17 minutes, 22 seconds, and 18 frames into tape number 4. This labeling is an added protection so that you can find the right tape even if the physical labels have come off the tape or—more commonly—were never put on it.

Assemble Editing

All linear editing systems give you the choice between *assemble* and *insert* mode. Generally, assemble editing is faster than insert editing but less electronically stable at the edit points. The major drawback is that assemble editing will not allow you to edit video and audio independently.

In ***assemble editing*** the record VTR erases everything (video, audio, control, and time code tracks) on the edit master tape to have a clean slate before copying the video and audio material supplied by the source tape. During the transfer everything that is recorded on the selected portion of the source tape is copied to the edit master. The record VTR supplies a new control track for the edit master tape that is modeled exactly on the control track of the source segment. To achieve a stable edit, the record VTR must align and space the sync pulse segments so that they form a continuous control track. **SEE 12.9**

12.9 Assemble Editing

In the assemble mode, the record VTR lays down a new control track section based on the sync information for each edited shot. In this illustration the first sync pulse of shot 2 is accurately spaced from the last sync pulse of shot 1 on the edit master tape. The sync pulses from both sections form a continuous control track. Any other spacing at the edit point would cause the picture to tear.

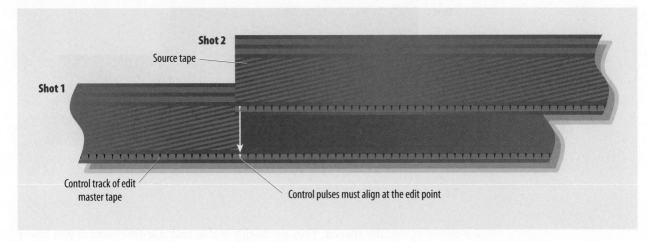

Unfortunately, even fairly high-quality VTRs do not always succeed in this task. For example, when the record VTR adds the control track of the first frame of shot 2 to the last frame of shot 1, the sync pulses may be a little farther apart or closer together at the edit point. This slight discrepancy will result in a "tear," which means the picture will break up or roll momentarily at the edit point during playback.

Because all tracks of the edit master tape are erased prior to copying the new shot from the source tape, you cannot copy the audio track first and then go back to add the corresponding video, nor can you first record the video segments and then match them with the appropriate audio. All you can do is add sections of video and audio together from the source tape to the edit master tape.

As already mentioned, the advantage of assemble editing is that you do not have to record a continuous control track (by recording black) for the edit master tape before the actual editing.

Insert Editing

Although it requires the previous recording of a continuous control track on the edit master tape, ***insert editing*** is the preferred editing mode because it produces highly stable edits and you can edit the video and audio tracks separately. Recording black on the edit master—the tape you use in the record VTR—will provide the continuous control track without putting any pictures on it. Note that the recording of black happens in real time, which means you must run the blank edit master tape for 30 minutes to lay a 30-minute control track. Only then do you have a truly continuous guide for the edit points. **SEE 12.10**

During insert editing, the record VTR does not add a new control track but rather places the new shot to fit the existing control track on the edit master tape. All edits

12.10 **Insert Editing**

In the insert edit mode, the source material is transferred to the edit master tape without its control track and is placed according to the prerecorded control track of the edit master tape.

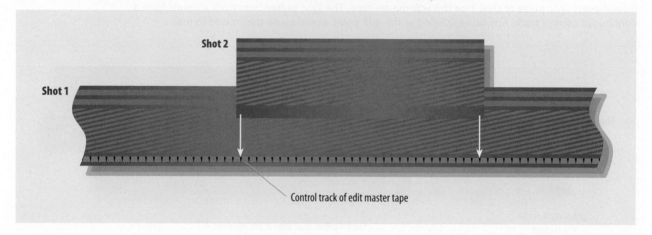

Shot 2

Shot 1

Control track of edit master tape

are therefore equally spaced. They are highly stable and tear-free, even if you insert a new shot in the middle of the edit master tape.

You will find that in all but the simplest editing jobs, you need to separate audio from video. For example, many news and documentary editors prefer to edit the audio track first and then "drop in" (match) the video so that it is synchronized with the sound. To speed up the editing process, they often have several "blackened" tapes on hand (with the control track already recorded). These tapes serve as edit masters for insert editing. Normally, however, the blackening of edit master tapes is part of the editing preparations.

> **KEY CONCEPT**
>
> The edit master tape must be prepared for insert editing by first recording black on it.

NONLINEAR EDITING

Instead of using VTRs to transfer shots from source tapes to an edit master in a specific order, with a *nonlinear editing system* you use a computer to organize and keep track of a huge electronic slide library that contains every frame of your source footage.

The basic nonlinear editing principle is digital file management rather than copying from one tape to another. Each of the files contains a single frame. You probably now see why this system is called "nonlinear": you can call up any one of the files (frames) instantly in any order, regardless of where the information was located on the source tapes. The selected frames or frame sequences, called *clips*, are then flagged by the computer so that they play back in the sequence you specify. Note that the video files themselves are not moved from where they are stored on the hard drive; they are simply played back in a particular order when triggered by the computer. **ZVL3 CUE 6**

EDITING→ Nonlinear editing→ system

> **KEY CONCEPT**
>
> The basic nonlinear editing principle is file management.

Nonlinear Editing System

A *nonlinear editing system* (**NLE**) consists of a high-end desktop computer that stores the digital video and audio information on a high-capacity hard drive. The typical

12.11 Nonlinear Editing System

The camcorder or an external video recorder feeds the video and audio source material into the nonlinear editing system (NLE)—the capture phase. The computer's editing software acts as the edit controller for the whole editing process—the editing phase. Once the final edit is done, the program is transferred to videotape or DVD—the exporting phase. The VTR produces the edit master tape. The DVD burner produces a DVD, the edit master disc.

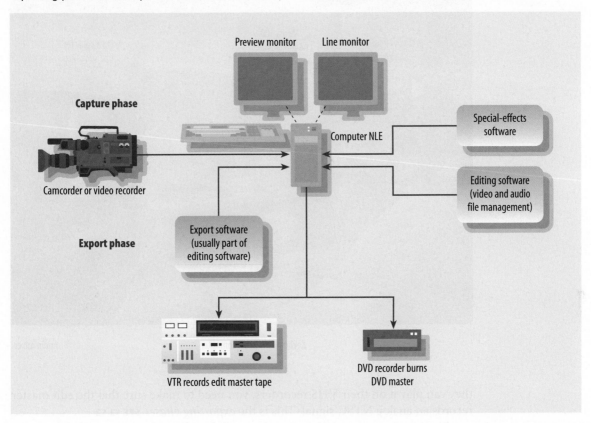

NLE includes two fairly large external monitors—one for the computer output and the other to show your edited sequences. It also has two small loudspeakers and a mixer to assist with importing additional audio tracks.

A computer used for editing must have the necessary software to accomplish the three phases of nonlinear editing—capture, the actual editing, and exporting—as well as additional special-effects software for creating transitions, graphics, and titles.

Most editing software allows you to import the video and audio information directly from the video recorder inside the camcorder (whether on videotape, hard disk, optical disc, or flash memory device) to the hard drive of the computer. This represents the *capturing phase.*

Once the information is on the hard drive, you can select clips and specify their order of play. You can also add new information, such as clips from another shoot or various audio segments, to heighten the impact of your creation. **SEE 12.11** The special-effects software enables myriad title possibilities. This is the actual *editing phase.*

Unless you play your masterpiece only on the NLE, you need to dub it onto an edit master (tape or disc). If you intend to broadcast it or send it to friends so that

12.12 **Nonlinear Editing Setup**

This nonlinear editing station consists of a computer, a keyboard, a large computer display monitor, a second monitor for playback of edited sequences, an audio mixer, and a digital VTR for feeding the source tapes into the computer.

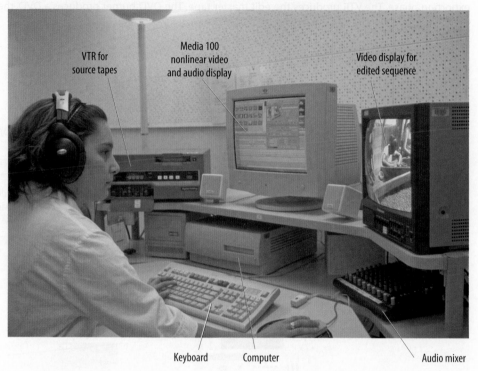

VTR for source tapes

Media 100 nonlinear video and audio display

Video display for edited sequence

Keyboard   Computer   Audio mixer

they can play it on their VHS recorders, you need to make sure that the edit master records an analog NTSC signal. This is the *exporting phase.* **SEE 12.12**

The *interface*—the window that shows all the editing features—differs from one editing program to another, but they all have some elements in common. The following figure shows a typical interface of the Apple iMovie HD. **SEE 12.13**

With this relatively simple editing program, you can accomplish astonishing digital editing tasks that far exceed the capabilities of the cuts-only, or even the multiple-source analog, editing setups. In fact, this "simple" program has so many features that you probably don't need anything more complicated for even your most ambitious projects.

With more-sophisticated software and the appropriate video and audio hardware, a desktop computer will drive a powerful professional nonlinear editing system. **SEE 12.14**

All systems are capable of displaying a variety of frames and of running shots and brief sequences, also called *clips,* so that you can preview the edit and see how well the shots cut together. The computer will also display the time code in- and out-numbers and the length of the shot. You can hear the sound track when running the sequence and can see its waveform displayed on the computer screen.

We'll next examine the three editing phases—capture, editing, and export—in more detail.

12.13 Simple Nonlinear Editing Interface

In this iMovie interface, the clips (files) are arranged on a "shelf" as slides. You can order and view the clips in the viewer space or sequence them on the time line. Below the large edit monitor are the controls for the source VTR, for the actual editing of clips, and for the playback of edited sections. Note that each clip has a unique filename.

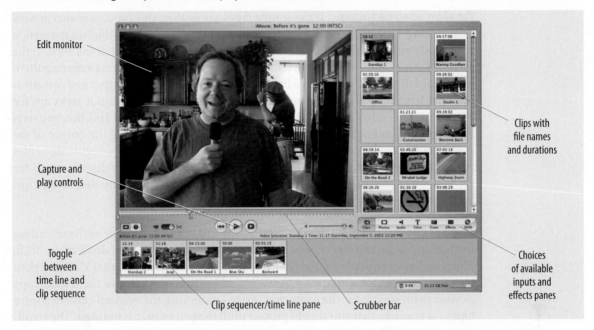

Edit monitor

Capture and play controls

Toggle between time line and clip sequence

Clip sequencer/time line pane

Scrubber bar

Clips with file names and durations

Choices of available inputs and effects panes

12.14 Advanced Nonlinear Editing Interface

This interface of an advanced nonlinear editing program has a window that displays editing functions, a source monitor (left), and an edit monitor (right) that shows the edited segments. Below are the time lines for the video and audio tracks. The edit, or line, monitor display is usually fed into a separate video monitor.

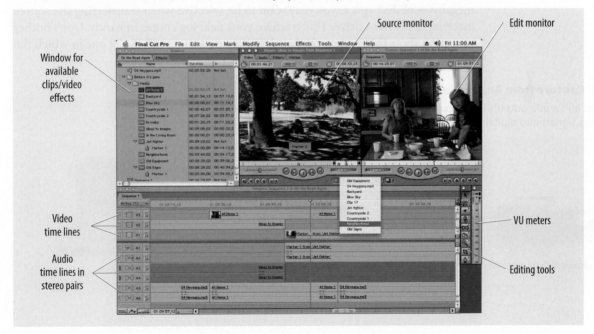

Source monitor

Edit monitor

Window for available clips/video effects

Video time lines

Audio time lines in stereo pairs

VU meters

Editing tools

Nonlinear Editing Phase 1: Capture

Before you can do any nonlinear editing, you need to transfer the videotaped source material to the computer and store it on the hard drive—the process called *capture*.

Analog source tapes   If the source tapes are analog, this process is also known as *digitizing*. One of the most important steps during capture is to digitize the analog video and audio signals so that they can be stored on the computer. If the VTR in the camcorder is analog, you must first digitize the source tapes before transferring them to the hard drive. You can do this by connecting the camcorder output to a converter box that has video and audio inputs and outputs. The various in/out jacks are for RCA phono, S-video, and IEEE 1394 (FireWire or i-link) cables. This box converts the video and audio signals from analog to digital. By connecting the output of the converter box to the computer, you can import the video and audio segments as files to the hard drive. **SEE 12.15** Note that some NLEs accept analog *or* digital signals for capture. The analog signals are digitized by a card inside the computer, so no converter box is necessary.

Digital source media   If your digital camcorder uses videotape as the recording medium, you can transfer the source material directly to the hard drive of the NLE. You may, however, prefer to first record the source material on a digital VTR and then transfer it to the computer via a FireWire cable. This way you use the digital copy as your main source for the capturing phase, preserving the original camera source tapes—a resource that you should protect until the edit master is finished. The stand-alone digital VTR, which is usually much more rugged than a camcorder VTR, now serves as the playback device for all the videotape segments you select for capture. The two-way FireWire connection between the digital VTR and the computer will also allow you to operate the VTR with computer commands. **SEE 12.16**

Because with normal compression each minute of video swallows up 228 megabytes of disk space, you may want to be selective when transferring the source material to the hard drive. This is where your field log comes in handy. Don't bother capturing shots that you marked as definitely no good, such as the one in which the

12.15 **Capture from Analog Camcorder VTR**

The video and audio outputs of the camcorder are connected to a converter box that changes the analog signals into digital ones. The digital signals are then exported to the computer.

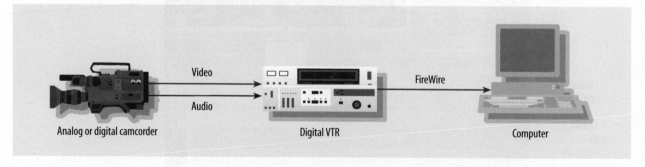

Analog or digital camcorder   Digital VTR   Computer

12.16 Capture from Digital VTR

When dubbed onto a digital VTR, the digital video and audio source material can be fed directly into the computer via a two-way FireWire cable.

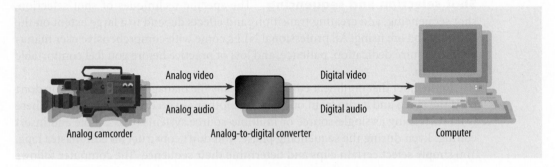

Analog video   Digital video

Analog audio   Digital audio

Analog camcorder Analog-to-digital converter Computer

talent showed the wrong book during an interview with the author. (We discuss the review and logging of source tapes later in this chapter.)

Nonlinear Editing Phase 2: Editing

This phase includes the major steps of editing the imported video: file identification, shot selection, sequencing, transitions, and effects. It also involves the building of the audio track: selecting the acceptable sound portions, importing new sound, mixing sound, and matching it with the video. But before we go into the editing process, a word of advice: Although a laptop computer can certainly function as a first-class NLE and will do just fine for the import phase, you will need additional equipment for serious editing. Instead of squinting at the small computer screen, try to get a large, high-quality flat-panel display for your editing interface. The larger image prevents eye fatigue and also gives you a better idea of how the pictures will cut together. Also get a second monitor for full-screen video playback. This will cause less confusion about whether you are watching the source clips or a partially edited sequence, and it will prove especially valuable when scrutinizing complex effects.

Unless your audio requirements are relatively simple, you will also need an audio mixer and high-quality speakers for monitoring audio. Don't rely on the little speakers that come with the computer unless you intend to wear headphones. Good speakers or headphones will reveal audio problems right away and tell you whether some audio *sweetening* is required.

Labeling the imported source material The computer of your NLE now functions as a huge slide library from which you can select specific clips, which, in effect, are brief slide series. The computer screen can display a selection of shots. But which ones? Choosing the appropriate clips is what editing is all about.

It should come as no surprise that finding the right slides presupposes that they are labeled properly. You need to give all imported files a specific filename and/or number—the best library in the world is useless if the books are not indexed accurately for quick retrieval. The same is true for files. All editing programs have a space for the filename of the imported clips as well as for some additional information, similar to a field log. In fact, you should use the names listed on the field log files for your captured clips. (We address labeling and creating an editing log later in this chapter.)

Shot selection and sequencing   The specific techniques of shot selection, shot sequencing, and creating transitions and effects depend to a large extent on the software you are using. All professional NLEs come with comprehensive user manuals and require dedication, patience, and lots of practice before you feel comfortable using them.

Remember that nonlinear editing is basically file management. Because you don't copy the video and audio from one tape to another as you do in linear editing, there is no such thing as single-source or multiple-source systems or assemble and insert editing. Even during the sequencing phase, you don't construct an edit master tape. You simply select certain clips and determine their sequence. The computer follows your instructions and tells every frame how to line up for playback. The random access of clips gives you extraordinary flexibility not only in selecting shots but also in rearranging them. Because each clip is simply assigned a playback number, the sequence can be changed more easily than physically rearranging slides.

You will discover that once you have mastered the actual editing techniques, the biggest challenge will be selecting the most effective shots and sequencing them to convey your message with clarity and impact. (The checklist on postproduction preparation on page 258 gives some tips on making the selection process more efficient and less stressful, and chapter 13 is devoted entirely to the basic aesthetic principles of postproduction editing.)

Nonlinear Editing Phase 3: Export to Videotape or Disc

Once you finish selecting the desired shots and joining them in a sequence through various transitions, it's time to get your masterpiece out of the computer and onto videotape or disc. Essentially, you need to export your file sequence to a recording medium, usually videotape or DVD. Once recorded on tape or disc, your program is finally and actually edited.

Because various software programs have different ways of exporting the edited piece, you need to determine how your specific software exports files. If you plan to distribute your edited program for playback on an STV (standard television) system, the final version must be recorded in the analog NTSC standard. Note that you can also connect the NTSC output of a digital VTR or DVD player to a television set without any conversion to an analog signal. **ZVL3 CUE 7** ▶EDITING→ Nonlinear editing→ exporting

POSTPRODUCTION PREPARATIONS

As with all other production activities, editing requires diligent preparation. The only editing for which preparations are kept to a minimum is in news. There is no way to predict the amount and the nature of news footage you may have to edit on a given day, and you always have precious little time to make deliberate editing decisions. All you can do is try to select the most telling shots and sequence them into a credible, responsible news story.

To make the best use of the usually insufficient postproduction time available, you should lay the groundwork with some necessary preparations: shooting with continuity in mind, making protection copies, adding time code to the source tapes, making a window dub, reviewing and logging the source footage, transcribing the audio text, and laying a control track.

Shoot for continuity   It may sound strange, but the postproduction process starts in the shooting phase. Good directors and camera operators not only have the ability to visualize each shot and give it composition and meaning but they also think ahead about how those shots will cut together and look in sequence. In complicated productions, such as dramas, commercials, or carefully constructed field productions, sequencing is determined by a storyboard. The *storyboard* shows key visualizations and the major sequencing of shots. **SEE 12.17**

If you don't have the time or luxury to prepare a storyboard, you can still facilitate postproduction editing by observing the following tips during production. You may have noticed that some of these points were made in earlier discussions; but because they can greatly facilitate postproduction editing, we reiterate them here.

12.17 Storyboard

The storyboard shows key visualizations and the major sequencing of shots, with action and audio information given below. It can be hand-drawn on preprinted storyboard paper or computer-generated.

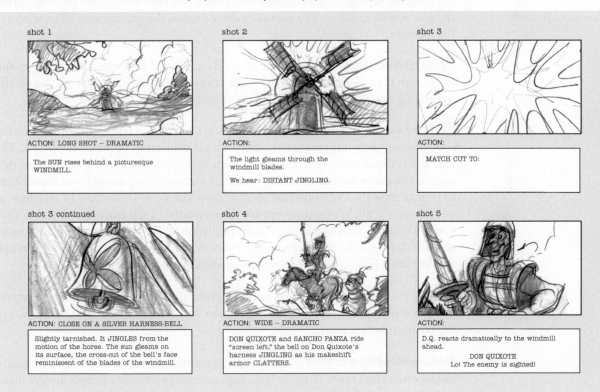

shot 1

ACTION: LONG SHOT -- DRAMATIC

The SUN rises behind a picturesque WINDMILL.

shot 2

ACTION:

The light gleams through the windmill blades.

We hear: DISTANT JINGLING.

shot 3

ACTION:

MATCH CUT TO:

shot 3 continued

ACTION: CLOSE ON A SILVER HARNESS-BELL

Slightly tarnished. It JINGLES from the motion of the horse. The sun gleams on its surface, the cross-cut of the bell's face reminiscent of the blades of the windmill.

shot 4

ACTION: WIDE -- DRAMATIC

DON QUIXOTE and SANCHO PANZA ride "screen left," the bell on Don Quixote's harness JINGLING as his makeshift armor CLATTERS.

shot 5

ACTION:

D.Q. reacts dramatically to the windmill ahead.

DON QUIXOTE
Lo! The enemy is sighted!

PRODUCTION TIPS TO MAKE POSTPRODUCTION EASIER

✓ *Slate each take* Identify each take with a visual or at least a verbal slate. In the studio this is usually done with the character generator (C.G.). In the field you should have a handheld slate or a small clapboard that shows the date of the shoot, the tape number, the scene number, and the take (shot) number. If you don't have a visual slate available, slate the various takes verbally. After calling out the take number, count backward from five to zero. This counting helps in locating the approximate beginning of a shot after the slate.

✓ *Leave margins for editing* When videotaping do not stop the tape exactly at the end of a shot; record a few more seconds before stopping. For instance, if the software company president has finished describing the latest nonlinear editing system, have her remain silent and in place for a few seconds before cutting the action and stopping the tape. When starting the next segment, roll the camera briefly before calling for action; when finished, have everybody remain in place for a few seconds before stopping the tape. Such *pads,* or *trim handles,* give you more flexibility in deciding on the exact edit in- and out-points.

✓ *Record background sounds* Even if you plan to reconstruct the audio track in postproduction, always record a few minutes of ambient sound (room tone, traffic noise, or the sounds of silence in the mountains) before changing locations or finishing the taping. This environmental sound will help mask silent periods during the edit or within a shot. You may even decide to use the sounds after all to reinforce the location.

✓ *Keep a field log* Keep an accurate field log of what you tape. Label all tapes and boxes with the tape number and the production title. The field log will aid you greatly in locating the videotaped material for the first screening.

✓ *Tape cutaway shots* Get some cutaways for each scene. A *cutaway* is a brief shot that will help improve or establish visual continuity between two shots. The cutaway is usually related to the event, such as a bystander looking at a parade or a reporter's camera during a hearing. Make the cutaways long enough—at least fifteen to twenty seconds. Cutaways that are too short can be as frustrating to an editor as no cutaways at all. When cutaways are too short, they look more like mistakes than continuity links. When shooting cutaways, always let the camera run for a few more seconds than you think necessary; the cutaway will then be just about long enough for the editor. **ZVL3 CUE 8** EDITING→ Production guidelines→ cutaways

The preceding tips show how certain production techniques can make postproduction more efficient. The following section lists activities that are already part of the postproduction phase.

Make protection copies Your production efforts are wasted if you lose the source media or damage them in some way. Experienced production people always make protection copies of all source material as soon as possible after the recording. If you shoot in a videotape format that suffers from generation loss during extensive post-production editing, such as Hi8 or S-VHS, you should "bump up" the source footage (dub it onto a higher-quality videotape format). For nonlinear editing you can make digital copies during the capturing phase. There is no quality loss in copying digital tape, even after many generations. **ZVL3 CUE 9** EDITING→ Production guidelines→ housekeeping

Add time code   Unless you recorded the time code during the videotaping, you may need to add it to all source tapes. You do this by "laying in" the time code signals from a time code generator on the address track of the videotape or on one of the audio tracks.

Make a window dub   When laying in the time code, you can simultaneously make another dub, called the **window dub**. This lower-quality, bumped-down (usu-ally VHS) copy has the time code "burned in"—keyed over each frame. Each frame displays a box, called a window, which shows its time code address. **SEE 12.18** Even if you have labeled some takes *NG* (no good), it is usually easier to window-dub all video, regardless of whether the takes are OK or no good. Every once in a while, the video from an initially NG take proves invaluable as a cutaway or a substitute shot in the actual editing. You can still eliminate the really bad ones during the capturing phase.

This window dub will serve you in the accurate logging of all recorded shots; in preparing an **edit decision list** (**EDL**), which lists the in- and out-points of each edit; and even in performing a **rough-cut**—a preliminary low-quality version of the edit master tape—in linear editing.

Review and log the source footage   It is now time to make a list of every-thing recorded on the source tapes, regardless of whether the take was properly field slated as usable. Note that we still use the term *VTR* for the logging operation, even if your camcorder recorded the shots on a hard drive, optical disc, or flash memory device. This list—called a **VTR log** or an *editing log*—is a written document based on the window dub. (Although *VTR log* is the traditional name for such a list, the new term *editing log* seems more appropriate given the rapid advance toward a tapeless

12.18 SMPTE Time Code Window Dub

The time code can be keyed directly into the copy of the source tape for off-line editing. Each frame displays its own unique time code address.

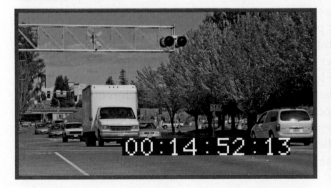
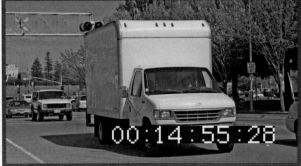

environment.) This log helps you locate specific shots and their principal screen directions without having to preview the source material over and over again.

Although logging may initially seem like a waste of time, an accurate and carefully prepared editing log will save you time, money, and ultimately nerves during the actual editing. Besides the usual data, such as the production title, the name of the director, and the production number and date, the editing log should contain the following information:

▶ Tape or media (disc or flash drive) number

▶ Scene number

▶ Take number

▶ Time code in- and out-numbers of each shot

▶ Whether the shot is OK or NG (if you don't have a designated OK/NG column, you can simply circle the good takes in the third column)

▶ Prominent sounds

▶ Remarks (brief description of the scene or event)

▶ Vector type and direction

You will probably not find a vectors column in commercially available editing log forms or computer displays, but vectors provide extremely important logging information. As discussed in chapter 6, they depict lines and something pointing or moving in a particular direction. (We elaborate on vectors further in chapter 13.) The advantage of a vector designation is that you can identify a particular screen direction quickly and easily without having to run the source footage again.

If, for example, you need a shot that has objects moving in the opposite direction from the previous shot, all you need to do is glance down the vectors column and look for shots whose *m* symbol (indicating a motion vector) has arrows pointing in an opposing direction. As you can see, the vector notations in the following figure use arrows for the main direction of *g* (graphic), *i* (index), and *m* (motion) vectors. **SEE 12.19** A circled dot ⊙ indicates somebody looking at or moving toward the camera; a single dot ● indicates somebody looking or moving away from the camera. Don't worry too much about the vectors column right now, but after you have read chapter 13, you should revisit figure 12.19 and study the vectors column once more. See whether it helps you visualize the shot sequence listed on this editing log. `ZVL3 CUE 10 ▶`

EDITING→ Postproduction guidelines→ VTR log

A variety of computer programs are available for logging source tapes. Instead of filling out the log by hand, you enter the information on a computer form. Some software allows you to enter actual pictures of the first and last frames of each shot, which is a great help when locating certain shots. In this case, you can skip the vectors column because you can clearly see the principal main vectors of the beginning and end frames of the various shots.

The advantage of a computerized log is that you can quickly find a particular scene by entering either the filename or the time code number. You can then automatically transfer it to the EDL, which will guide the final sequencing of the edit master tape or disc.

12.19 VTR (Editing) Log

The VTR log, or editing log, contains the necessary specifications about all video and audio information recorded on the source tapes. Notice the notations in the vectors column: g, i, and m refer to graphic, index, and motion vectors. The arrows show the principal directions of the index and motion vectors. Z-axis index and motion vectors are labeled with ⊙ (toward the camera) or • (away from the camera).

PRODUCTION TITLE: Traffic Safety					PRODUCTION NO: 114		OFF-LINE DATE: 07/15	
PRODUCER: Hamid Khani			DIRECTOR: Elan Frank				ON-LINE DATE: 07/21	

TAPE NO.	SCENE/ SHOT	TAKE NO.	IN	OUT	OK/ NG	SOUND	REMARKS	VECTORS
4	2	1	04 44 21 14	04 44 23 12	NG		mic problem	m ←
		②	04 44 42 06	04 47 41 29	OK	car sound	car A moving through stop sign	m ←
		③	04 48 01 29	04 50 49 17	OK	brakes	car B putting on brakes (toward camera)	⊙ m
		④	04 51 02 13	04 51 42 08	OK	reaction	pedestrian reaction	→ i
5	5	1	05 03 49 18	05 04 02 07	NG	car brakes ped. yelling	ball not in front of car	⊙ m ← m ball
		2	05 05 02 29	05 06 51 11	NG	"	Again, ball problem	⊙ m ← m ball
		③	05 07 40 02	05 09 12 13	OK	car brakes ped. yelling	car swerves to avoid ball	⊙ m → ← m ball
	6	①	05 12 03 28	05 14 12 01	OK	ped. yelling	kid running into street	→ i m child
		②	05 17 08 16	05 21 11 19	OK	car	cutaways car moving	⊙ · m ↓ ↙
		3	05 22 15 03	05 26 28 00	NG	street	lines of sidewalk	← → g

Transcribe the audio text   Transcribing all speech to typed pages is another time-consuming but important pre-editing chore. Once accomplished, it definitely speeds up the editing. If, for example, you need to edit a long interview, or cut a speech so that it fits an allotted time slot, the printed page gives you a much quicker overview than repeatedly listening to the audio track of the videotape. Because a printed page is much less linear than tape, it allows you to jump around in the text with great speed. Of course, in news coverage you have no time for such transcriptions; all you can do is run the tape and take notes about which portions you would like to keep and where in the tape you have to make the cuts. **ZVL3 CUE 11** EDITING→ Postproduction guidelines→ audio transcript

Lay a control track   Recall that you must record a black signal on the tape that is to become the edit master if you are working with an analog editing system. By recording black you also record a continuous control track whose sync pulses are an essential reference for precise insert editing. Of course, in nonlinear editing you don't have to worry about a control track or whether to do assemble or insert editing; you just capture the clips to the hard drive and give them logical filenames for easy retrieval.

OFF-LINE AND ON-LINE EDITING

When you ask about "off-line" and "on-line" editing, you most likely get conflicting information. One editor might tell you that off-line and on-line has nothing to do with quality and that on-line editing is done even when cutting a low-quality amateur video to fit the assigned time for an extraordinary news story. Another editor tells you that she digitizes the source footage first in low resolution (low-quality video) for off-line editing and then redigitizes the same footage in high resolution (high-quality video) for on-line editing. Who is right? Both are. You got different answers because the first editor was speaking about linear editing and the second about nonlinear editing.

Essentially, *off-line editing* serves as a guide for the people who are doing the final edit. *On-line editing* produces the final edit master that is intended for broadcast or distribution. Off-line editing is usually done as a rough-cut, a preliminary, low-quality editing version intended for critical review.

Linear off- and on-line editing   In linear editing *off-line* refers to an editing process that will produce a low-quality rough-cut or an EDL for the on-line process. `ZVL3 CUE 12` EDITING→ Linear editing→ off-line edit It is the *intent* of the edited version and not the equipment quality that distinguishes the two editing processes. The off-line edit is intended as a guide for the on-line version. The on-line edit produces the edit master tape for broadcast or duplication. `ZVL3 CUE 13` EDITING→ Linear editing→ on-line edit

> ▶**KEY CONCEPT**
>
> In linear editing *off-line* means that the intent is to produce an EDL or a rough-cut. *On-line* means that the editing produces the edit master tape.

Nonlinear off- and on-line editing   After just telling you that it is how the final edit master is used rather than the quality of the equipment that distinguishes off-line from on-line, in nonlinear editing we are back to quality. *Off-line* in nonlinear editing means that you capture the source footage at low resolution. This way you can capture on the hard disk all or most of the source footage needed for the project or at least for the particular scene you are editing.

You now have all the source footage you need on the hard drive of your NLE. From there you can select and sequence clips at low resolution. When you have finished editing, you don't export the final edit to a videotape recorder but rather save the resulting EDL as a text file or a printed hard copy. This EDL now serves as a guide for redigitizing the selected clips, this time in high-resolution, on-line-quality video. The EDL now serves as a guide for the final on-line sequencing. You can then export this on-line editing version to the edit master. `ZVL3 CUE 14` EDITING→ Nonlinear editing→ off-line & on-line

> ▶**KEY CONCEPT**
>
> In nonlinear editing *off-line* means that the capturing and the editing are done in low-resolution video, intended to produce an EDL. *On-line* means that the edited footage is recaptured in high-resolution video for the edit master.

Off-line Editing Procedures

Although off-line procedures differ considerably between linear and nonlinear editing, you can apply some of the initial steps of off-line editing regardless of which system you use for the actual edit. In fact, watching the VHS window dubs a few times and thinking about what you really what to show will speed up either process. You can use the editing log and the window dubs to create a tentative EDL that includes all the source material you might use. More important, it will give you a chance to eliminate the takes that you definitely won't use. (But don't throw them away just yet—you may decide to use them after all.) A simple way of creating this first tentative EDL is by *paper-and-pencil editing,* or *paper editing* for short.

Paper-and-pencil editing   This is how paper-and-pencil editing works:

1. Think again about what it is you want to tell the viewer. This means going back to the basic program objective and the angle (communication intent) that you originally stated. After all, how can you select and assemble event essences if you don't know what the story is all about? The actual videotaped material may suggest a slight variation or a restatement of the original objective, but don't let spectacular shots render the original approach obsolete.

2. Watch, once again, all of the window-dubbed source tapes and see which shots strike you as especially relevant and effective. This review will not only refresh your memory of what you shot but may also suggest, however indirectly, a tentative sequence.

3. Now think more seriously about sequencing the shots. While recalling the program objective and the available footage, prepare a rough storyboard. This is the time to take a good look at the editing log and locate the various key shots. If several clips would be equally effective for a particular scene, list them all. Identify the selected shots with the time code in- and out-numbers and add them to your handwritten EDL. **SEE 12.20** `ZVL3 CUE 15` EDITING→ Linear editing→ paper edit

> **KEY CONCEPT**
> Paper-and-pencil editing is a good way to create a preliminary editing guide.

12.20 Handwritten Edit Decision List

The EDL is the road map for on-line editing. It lists the tape number, the scene and take numbers, the in- and out-numbers for each selected shot, and major audio information. This handwritten EDL contains information for the first, tentative edit.

PRODUCTION TITLE: Traffic Safety					PRODUCTION NO: 114		OFF-LINE DATE: 07/15
PRODUCER: Hamid Khani			DIRECTOR: Elan Frank				ON-LINE DATE: 07/21

TAPE NO.	SCENE/ SHOT	TAKE NO.	IN	OUT	TRANSITION	SOUND	REMARKS
1	2	2	01 46 13 14	01 46 15 02	cut	car	
		3	01 51 10 29	01 51 11 21	cut	car	
	3	4	02 05 55 17	02 05 56 02	cut	ped. yelling—brakes	
		5	02 07 43 17	02 08 46 01	cut	brakes	
		6	02 51 40 02	02 51 41 07	cut	ped. yelling—brakes	

Preliminary rough-cut   If you have time, you could use this preliminary EDL to copy the selected portions of the window dubs from one VHS machine to another. Don't worry about the accuracy of in- and out-points or breakups at the edit points. All you want to get at this point is some feel for the event flow. If you're working on a nonlinear system, you can use the preliminary EDL as a guide for doing a rough edit of the clips listed on your handwritten EDL. Never mind about the audio—you can fix that later when you do the more precise editing from your actual EDL. This is where the nonlinear editing system shines: you can edit a few preliminary versions in a fraction of the time it would take you to do even the simple VCR-to-VCR edit. If you don't like one version, just rearrange the clips. Once you are satisfied with the general sequence of shots, you can think about transitions and effects and the audio requirements for the final on-line version.

On-line Editing Procedures

Regardless of whether you use a linear or a nonlinear editing system, on-line editing will produce the final edit master tape or disc. In a way, on-line editing is easier than off-line editing because the editing decisions have already been made in the off-line process and listed on the EDL. From this point on, the EDL guides the on-line editing procedures.

In linear editing the edit controller will read the in- and out-numbers and help you set up the source and record VTRs for the final edits. In nonlinear editing, the EDL will tell you or the computer which files to play in which order and which transitions and effects to use during sequencing. **SEE 12.21** Although it is still possible to make last-minute changes at this point, try to avoid arbitrary ones. More often than not, such hasty decisions make the edit less effective than the previous version.

Just two more points: Editing is always more time-consuming than you initially thought and budgeted for; and despite the great assistance from edit controllers and nonlinear computing power, it is still you who has to make the decisions about which shot goes where. **ZVL3 CUE 16** EDITING→ Linear editing→ online edit How to make the right aesthetic decisions is the subject of chapter 13.

12.21 Final EDL

The final EDL usually lists the names of the shots (or of the clips in nonlinear editing), their time code in- and out-numbers, the length of each shot, the major transitions and effects, the location of video and audio track numbers, and some other technical information.

```
TITLE: TRAFFIC SAFETY
                              Header
001    003     V    C        00:00:03:12   00:00:05:14   01:00:20:01   01:00:22:03
001    004     V    W001 204  00:00:06:24  00:00:12:23   01:00:08:12   01:00:14:11
EFFECTS NAME IS SWING IN

002    004     V    C        01:16:22:03   01:16:29:02   01:00:06:24   01:00:13:25
002    001     V    W003 204  01:18:27:15  01:18:34:09   01:00:06:24   01:00:13:18
EFFECTS NAME IS SWING IN

003    004     V    C        01:18:33:15   01:00:25:14   01:00:13:18   01:00:20:12
003    001     V    W000 204  01:18:38:02  01:18:44:26   01:00:13:18   01:00:20:12
EFFECTS NAME IS SWING IN

004    004     V    C        01:19:10:02   01:19:15:03   01:19:20:12   01:19:25:12
004    001     V    W002 204  01:19:23:19  01:19:30:13   01:00:20:12   01:00:27:06
EFFECTS NAME IS SWING IN

005    004     V    C        01:34:12:02   01:34:16:04   01:00:22:05   01:00:26:06
005    001     V    W011 203  01:50:15:29  01:50:22:22   01:00:27:06   01:00:33:29
EFFECTS NAME IS ZOOM

006    003     V    C        01:52:14:25   01:52:16:05   01:00:33:29   01:00:35:15

007    001     V    C        01:39:08:00   01:39:14:24   01:00:58:15   01:01:05:09
```

| Event number | Source reel ID | Edit mode | Transition type | Source in | Source out | Record in | Record out |

M A I N   P O I N T S

▶ **Linear Editing**

The use of VTRs designates linear editing, whether the recording is analog or digital. The basic principle of linear editing is copying sections of the source tapes in the desired sequence to the edit master, which contains the final version of the edited program. Subsequent copies are struck from the edit master.

▶ **Single- and Multiple-source Systems**

Typically, single-source VTR editing systems are limited to cuts-only transitions. Dissolves, wipes, and other special-effects transitions are possible with multiple-source editing systems.

▶ **Edit Controller**

The edit controller, also called the editing control unit, is used in linear editing to assist in various functions, such as marking edit-in and edit-out points, backspacing, rolling source and record VTRs in sync, and integrating effects.

▶ **Address or Time Code**

The address code, such as the SMPTE time code, marks each frame with a specific number. The pulse-count system is not a true address code because it counts pulses but does not give each frame a unique address.

▶ **Linear Assemble and Insert Editing**

In assemble editing everything that is recorded on the selected portions of the source tape is transferred to the edit master tape. Insert editing requires the prior laying of a control track (by recording black) on the edit master tape. The continuous control track makes the edits highly stable and tear-free. Insert editing allows the separate editing of audio and video tracks.

▶ **Nonlinear Editing**

The basic principle of nonlinear editing is file management. The nonlinear editing system (NLE) uses computers and high-capacity hard drives for the storage, retrieval, and sequencing of video and audio files. The final edit is exported to the edit master.

▶ **Postproduction Preparations**

The most important preparations for efficient postproduction editing include shooting for continuity, making protection copies, adding time code, making a window dub, reviewing and logging the source footage, transcribing the audio text, and, for linear analog editing, laying a control track on the edit master tape.

▶ **Off-line and On-line Editing**

Off-line linear editing produces a rough-cut and an edit decision list (EDL). It is not intended for an audience. On-line linear editing produces the final edit master tape. In nonlinear editing, off-line refers to the capture of source footage and file manipulation at low picture resolution. On-line refers to recapturing the off-line footage at a higher resolution according to the off-line EDL. The resulting footage is exported to a VTR or DVD for recording the edit master.

Z E T T L ' S   V I D E O L A B   3 . 0

For your reference, or to track your work, the Zettl's VideoLab 3.0 program cues in this chapter are listed here with their corresponding page numbers.

complexity editing Building an intensified screen event from carefully selected and juxtaposed shots. Does not have to adhere to the continuity principles.

continuity editing Preserving visual continuity from shot to shot.

converging vectors Index and motion vectors that point toward each other.

cutaway A shot of an object or event that is peripherally connected with the overall event and that is relatively static. Commonly used between two shots that do not provide good continuity.

continuing vectors Graphic vectors that extend each other, or index and motion vectors that point and move in the same direction.

diverging vectors Index and motion vectors that point away from each other.

jogging Frame-by-frame advancement of a recorded shot sequence, resulting in a jerking motion.

jump cut An image that jumps slightly from one screen position to another during a cut. Also, any gross visual discontinuity from shot to shot.

mental map Tells us where things are or are supposed to be in on- and off-screen space.

vector line An imaginary line created by extending converging index vectors or the direction of a motion vector. Also called *the line of conversation and action, the hundredeighty* (for 180 degrees), or, simply, *the line.*

Editing Principles

Now that you are familiar with the basics of linear and nonlinear editing systems and their use in postproduction editing, you will discover that the real challenge of editing is not necessarily in mastering the equipment but in telling a story effectively and, especially, in selecting shots that bring about a smooth and effective shot sequence. A master editor must know *aesthetics,* not just machines. But what does this mean? This chapter will acquaint you with some of the basic aesthetic editing principles.

▶ **EDITING PURPOSE**
  Why we edit

▶ **EDITING FUNCTIONS**
  Combining, condensing, correcting, and building

▶ **AESTHETIC PRINCIPLES OF CONTINUITY EDITING**
  The mental map, vectors, and on- and off-screen positions

▶ **AESTHETIC PRINCIPLES OF COMPLEXITY EDITING**
  Intensifying the event and supplying meaning

EDITING PURPOSE

Editing means selecting certain portions of an event or events and putting them into a meaningful sequence. The nature of such sequencing depends on the specific editing purpose: to cut a twenty-minute videotape of an important news story to twenty seconds to make it fit the format; to join a series of close-up details so that they make sense and flow without any visual bumps; or to juxtapose certain shots so that they take on added meaning.

Basically, we edit to tell a story with clarity and impact. All editing equipment is designed to make the selection of shots, and their joining through transitions, as easy and efficient as possible. But whether you work with simple cuts-only videotape-editing equipment or a highly sophisticated nonlinear editing system, the functions and the basic aesthetic principles of editing remain the same.

> **KEY CONCEPT**
>
> Editing means selecting significant event details and putting them into a specific sequence to tell a story with clarity and impact.

EDITING FUNCTIONS

The specific editing functions are *combining, condensing, correcting,* and *building*. Although these functions frequently overlap, there is always a predominant one that determines the editing approach and style—the selection of shots, their length and sequence, and the transitions with which they are joined.

Combine

The simplest kind of editing is combining program portions. For instance, you may want to combine the segments you videotaped during your vacation so that they are in chronological sequence on a single tape. Your carefully kept field log will aid you greatly in locating the source tapes and the various shots. Because you simply hook the various videotaped pieces together, there is no need for transitions; it can be "cuts only." The more aware you are of the desired sequence during the actual shooting, the easier it will be to combine the various shots in this postproduction phase.

Condense

Often you edit simply to condense the material—to reduce the overall length of the program or program portion. The most drastic condensing is done in television news. As an editor of news footage, you are often called upon to cut extraordinary stories to unreasonably brief segments. It is not unusual to have to shorten a 30-minute speech to 10 seconds, the 20 hours of a rescue operation to a mere 20 seconds, or the 50 minutes of graphic war footage, videotaped by a daring camera crew, to a mere 5 seconds. The infamous "sound bites" are a direct outgrowth of such drastic editing. Statements by public officials are tailored to a series of brief and memorable catch phrases rather than sensible narrative, very much in the spirit of advertising slogans.

> **▶ KEY CONCEPT**
>
> The condensing function of editing requires recognizing the essence of an event and selecting shots that best express that essence.

But even in less drastic editing, you will find that it is often hard to part with some of the footage, especially if it took extra effort to record. As an editor, try to detach yourself as much as possible from the preproduction and production efforts and concentrate simply on what you need to show and say, rather than what you have available. Don't use three shots if you can communicate the same message with one. Such editing requires that you identify the essence of an event and use only those shots that best communicate that essence.

Correct

Editing to fix production mistakes can be one of the most difficult, time-consuming, and costly postproduction activities. Even simple mistakes, such as the company president's misreading a word during his monthly address, can present a formidable problem when trying to match the body positions and the voice levels of the old (before the mistake) and new (after the mistake) takes. A good director will not pick up the speech exactly where the mistake was made but go back to where a new idea is introduced in the speech so that a change in shots is properly motivated. Starting the "pickup" (new shot) from a different point of view (a tighter or looser shot or a different angle) will make the cut and a slight shift in voice level appear deliberate and ensure continuity.

More-serious production problems, such as trying to match uneven colors and sound, can be a real headache for the editor. White-balancing the camera in each new lighting environment and watching the VU meter while listening carefully to the sound pickup is certainly easier than trying to "fix them in post."

Such seemingly minor oversights as the talent's wearing her coat buttoned while standing up but unbuttoned when sitting cannot be fixed in post even by the most experienced editor; they call for costly retakes. Again, meticulous attention to all preproduction details and keeping a close watch on every aspect of production can reduce many of the costly "fixing in post" activities.

Build

The most satisfying editing is done when you can build a show from a great many carefully recorded shots. Some postproduction people think—not without cause—that the video recording during the production provides merely the bricks and mortar and that it is up to the editor to construct the building—to give the raw material shape and meaning. Regardless of whether editing is done to show an event as clearly as possible or to reveal its intensity and complexity—or a combination of the two—you need to apply one or both of the major aesthetic editing principles: *continuity* and *complexity*. **ZVL3 CUE 1** ›EDITING→ Functions→ select | combine | correct | try it

AESTHETIC PRINCIPLES OF CONTINUITY EDITING

Continuity editing means creating seamless transitions from one event detail to the next so that the story flows even though a great deal of information is purposely omitted. The aesthetic principles of continuity editing are concerned not so much with the logic of the story line and the narrative flow but with how the pictures and the sound from one shot carry over to the next.

Unlike the painter or still photographer, who is concerned merely with the effective composition of a single image, as a video editor you must compare the aesthetic elements of one picture with those of another and see whether they lead smoothly from one to the other when seen in succession. Over the years of filmmaking, certain ways of achieving visual continuity became so firmly established that they matured from conventions to principles and now apply equally to video production.

The major principles of continuity editing are the mental map, vectors, and on- and off-screen positions.

Mental Map

Every time we watch television or a film, we automatically try to make sense of where things are and in what direction they move on and off the screen. In effect, we construct a ***mental map*** of such on- and off-screen positions and directions. For example, if you see somebody looking screen-left in a two-shot, he should also be looking screen-left in a close-up. **SEE 13.1**

If you see a person in a close-up looking screen-right during a two-way conversation, your mental map suggests that the other person is located somewhere in the right off-screen space. **SEE 13.2** According to the established mental map, the next

▶ **KEY CONCEPT**

Careful attention to preproduction and production details can obviate most corrective editing.

13.1 Mental Map

To help establish the mental map of where things are in off-screen space, you need to be consistent with where people look.

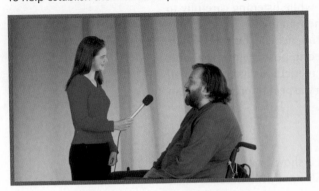

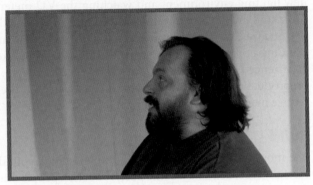

A When someone looks screen-left in a medium shot…

B …he should look in approximately the same direction in a close-up.

13.2 Mental Map of Right Off-screen Position

If you show person A looking and talking screen-right in a close-up, we assume person B to be located in the right off-screen space, looking screen-left.

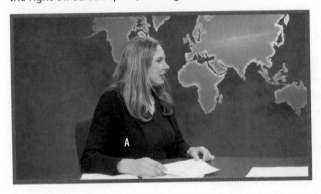

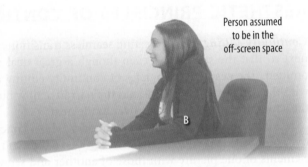

Person assumed to be in the off-screen space

13.3 Mental Map of Left Off-screen Position

When we now see person B in a close-up looking and talking screen-left, we assume person A to be in the left off-screen space.

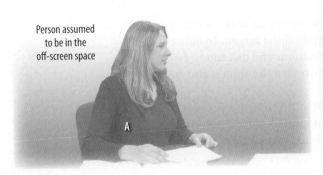

Person assumed to be in the off-screen space

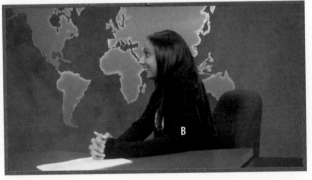

shot must show a close-up of the partner looking screen-left, with the first person having moved into the left off-screen space. **SEE 13.3** To show both persons looking in the same direction in subsequent shots would go against the mental map and suggest that both are talking to a third person. **SEE 13.4**

If, during a three-way conversation, you see a single person in a close-up first looking screen-right and then screen-left, you expect somebody to be sitting on both sides of her rather than two people on one side or the other. **SEE 13.5** But if you see the anchor in a close-up consistently looking screen-right during the three-way conversation, you expect the two other people to be sitting screen-right of her, although we cannot actually see them. **SEE 13.6** A three-shot of all the speakers shows that your mental map was accurate. **SEE 13.7**

13.4 Different Mental Map of Off-screen Position

Showing persons A and B looking in the same direction in subsequent close-ups would suggest that both are talking to a third person.

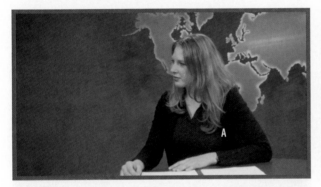

Shot 1

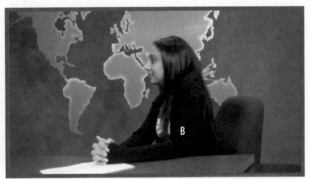

Shot 2

13.5 Person Looking Screen-right and Screen-left

When a person in a close-up looks screen-right in shot 1, then screen-left in shot 2, we expect the other people to be sitting on both sides of her.

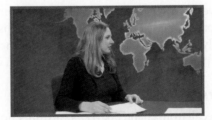

Shot 1

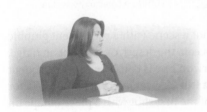

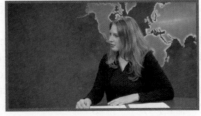

Shot 2

13.6 Screen-right Position of Partners

When someone continues to look screen-right during a three-way conversation, we expect her two partners to be sitting in the right off-screen space.

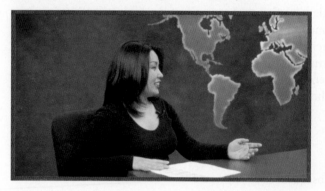

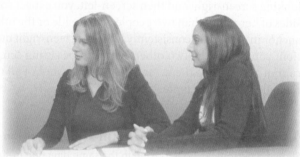

13.7 Actual Screen Positions

When seen in a long shot, the mental map of off-screen space coincides with the actual positions of the three people.

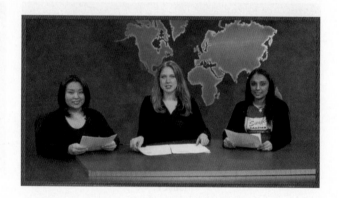

As you can see, the mental map covers not only on-screen space but also off-screen space. Once such a mental map is established, you must adhere to it unless you purposely want to shake the viewers out of their perceptual expectations. Applying continuity principles will keep the map intact. **ZVL3 CUE 2** EDITING→ Continuity→ mental map

Vectors

As you recall from chapter 6, *vectors* are directional forces that lead our eyes from one point to another on the screen and even off of it. They can be strong or weak, depending on how forcefully they suggest or move in a specific direction. Keeping the mental map intact requires proper vector continuity. **ZVL3 CUE 3** EDITING→ Continuity→ vectors

Continuity of graphic vectors   If you shoot a scene with a prominent graphic vector as the horizon line, such as a skyline, the ocean, the desert, or a mountain range, you need to make sure that the height of the horizon line is consistent in subsequent shots and that it does not jump up or down. **SEE 13.8** You can accomplish this vector continuity simply by marking the horizon line of the first shot with a piece of tape on the viewfinder and aligning all subsequent shots according to the tape.

13.8 **Graphic Vector Continuity**

To prevent the horizon line from jumping up and down during subsequent shots, you need to make sure that it forms a continuous graphic vector from shot to shot.

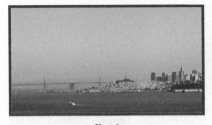
Shot 1

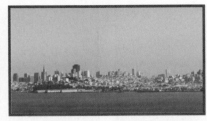
Shot 2

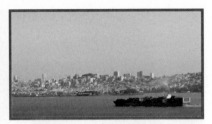
Shot 3

Directions of index and motion vectors   Index and motion vectors can be continuing, converging, or diverging.

Continuing vectors follow each other or move or point in the same direction. **SEE 13.9** They must "continue"—point in the same screen direction—even if shown in separate shots.   **SEE 13.10** If you show one of the people looking in the opposite direction in the close-up, you will jolt the established continuity. Instead of the two

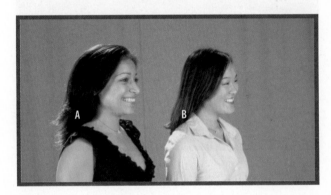

13.9 **Continuing Index Vectors in a Single Shot**

Continuing vectors point or move in the same direction. The continuous index vectors of these two people suggest that they are looking at the same target object.

13.10 **Continuing Index Vectors in Successive Shots**

Even when seen in two successive close-ups (shots 1 and 2), these continuing index vectors suggest that the two persons (A and B) are looking at a common target object.

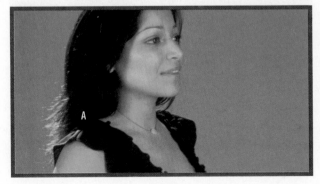
Shot 1

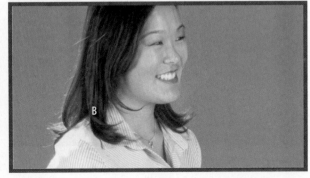
Shot 2

13.11 Index Vector Reversal in Successive Shots

By reversing one of the index vectors (shot 2), we assume that the two persons (A and B) are looking at each other instead of at a common target object.

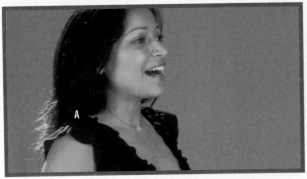
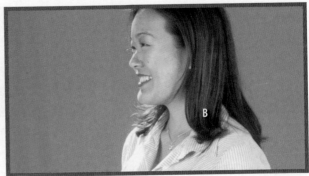

Shot 1   Shot 2

13.12 Converging Index Vectors in a Single Shot

Converging vectors must point or move toward each other. The index vectors of the two people (A and B) looking at each other converge.

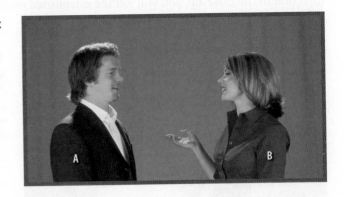

13.13 Converging Index Vectors in Successive Shots

When seen in successive close-ups (shots 1 and 2), the index vector of person A must converge with that of person B.

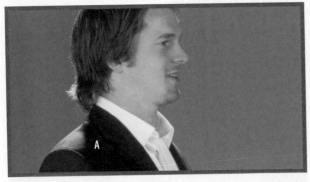
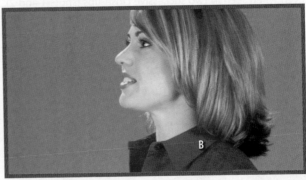

Shot 1   Shot 2

people looking in the same direction, the mental map now tells us that they must be looking at each other. **SEE 13.11**

Converging vectors move or point toward each other. **SEE 13.12** To maintain the mental map, you must maintain their direction in subsequent single shots. **SEE 13.13**

Diverging vectors move or point away from each other. **SEE 13.14** Again, subsequent close-ups must maintain the diverging vector direction. **SEE 13.15**

Vectors, of course, can change their directions in a single shot. In that case, the follow-up shot must continue the index or motion vector as seen just before the cut. For instance, if you show somebody running screen-left who then turns midscreen and runs screen-right, the subsequent shot must show the person continuing to run screen-right.

Someone looking directly into the camera or walking toward or away from it constitutes a *z-axis* index or motion vector. As you recall, the z-axis is the depth dimension or the imaginary line that stretches from the camera to the horizon. Whether we perceive a series of z-axis shots as continuing, converging, or diverging depends on the event context. If you follow a two-shot that shows two people looking at each other

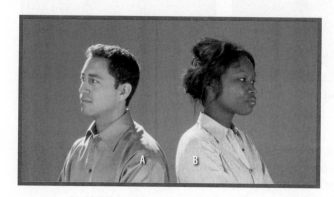

13.14 Diverging Index Vectors in a Single Shot

When two persons (A and B) look away from each other in a two-shot, their index vectors diverge.

13.15 Diverging Index Vectors in Successive Shots

To show that the index vectors are diverging in successive close-ups (shots 1 and 2), the index vector of person A must lead away from that of person B.

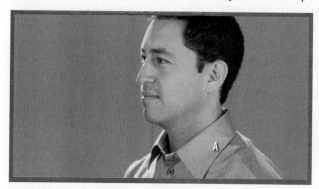

Shot 1

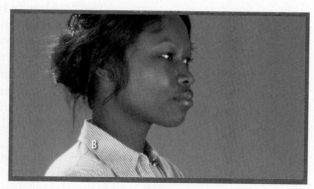

Shot 2

13.16 Converging Z-axis Index Vectors

Shot 1 establishes the index vectors of persons A and B as converging. By establishing that the vectors converge (shot 1), we perceive the subsequent z-axis close-ups of A and B in shots 2 and 3 also as converging.

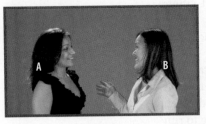
Shot 1

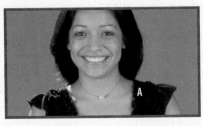
Shot 2

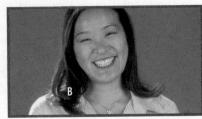
Shot 3

13.17 Two-shot with Diverging Index Vectors

If the context in shot 1 establishes the two people (A and B) as looking away from each other, the subsequent z-axis shots (2 and 3) are also perceived as diverging vectors.

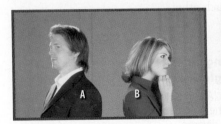
Shot 1

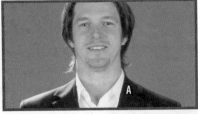
Shot 2

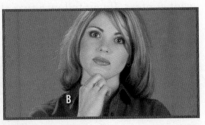
Shot 3

> **▶ KEY CONCEPT**
>
> Graphic, index, and motion vectors play an important part in establishing and maintaining continuity from shot to shot.

with successive close-ups of each person looking into the camera, we perceive their successive z-axis vectors as converging: they are still looking at each other. **SEE 13.16**

If the context (two-shot) shows that they are looking away from each other, we perceive the identical z-axis close-ups as diverging index vectors. **SEE 13.17**

On- and Off-screen Positions

As shown in figures 13.1 through 13.7, we tend to create a mental map that helps us tell where people are located even if we can't see them. Such an off-screen map helps preserve visual continuity and ultimately stabilize the environment. In vector terms, we place a person off-screen wherever the on-screen index vector points. The same is true for on-screen positions: once we establish person A on screen-left and person B on screen-right, we expect them to remain there even if we cut to a different point of view. Such position continuity is especially important in over-the-shoulder and cross-shots. **SEE 13.18** In shots 1 and 2, person A remains screen-left and person B remains screen-right. Our mental map would be greatly disturbed if we saw A and B change places in shot 3—we would perceive them as playing musical chairs. **SEE 13.19**

Vector line   The navigation device that helps maintain on-screen positions and motion continuity is called the ***vector line***, the *line of conversation and action*, the *hundredeighty* (for 180 degrees), or, simply, the *line*. The vector line is an extension of converging index vectors or of a motion vector in the direction of travel. **SEE 13.20**

13.18 Preserving On-screen Positions

When person B is first seen screen-right (shot 1), we expect her to remain there even when cutting to a different point of view, as in this over-the-shoulder sequence (shot 2).

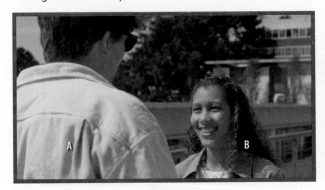
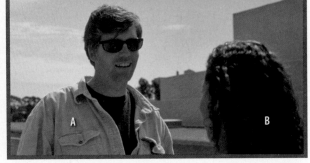

Shot 1   Shot 2

13.19 Reversing On-screen Positions

Our mental map is disturbed when person B appears screen-left in the over-the-shoulder shot (shot 3).

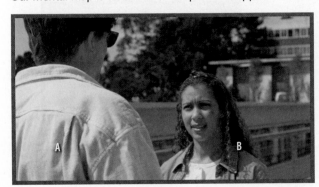
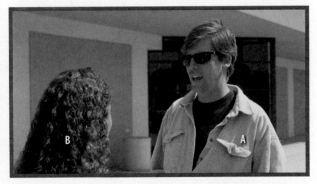

Shot 1   Shot 3

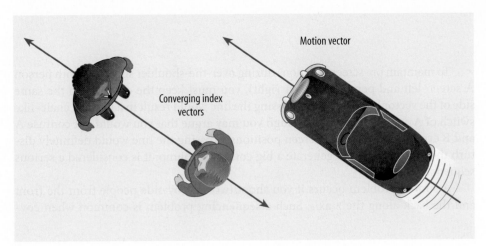

Motion vector

Converging index vectors

13.20 Forming the Vector Line

The vector line is formed by extending converging index vectors or by extending a motion vector.

13.21 **Vector Line and Proper Camera Positions**

To maintain the screen positions of persons A and B in over-the-shoulder shooting, the cameras must be on the same side of the vector line.

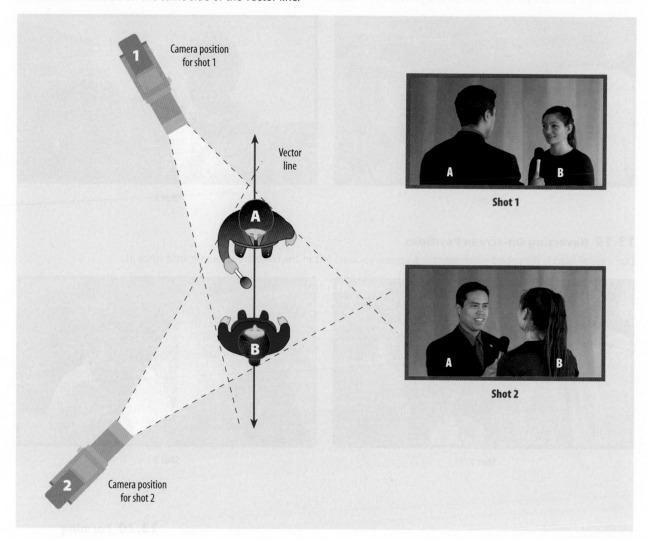

Camera position
for shot 1

Vector
line

Shot 1

Shot 2

Camera position
for shot 2

To maintain on-screen positions during over-the-shoulder shooting (with person A screen-left and person B screen-right), you must keep the cameras on the same side of the vector line. **SEE 13.21** Crossing the line would result in a musical chair–like switch of A and B. **SEE 13.22** Although you may argue that you would not confuse A and B even if they switched screen positions, crossing the line would definitely disturb the mental map and generate a big continuity bump; it is considered a serious sequencing mistake.

A similar problem occurs if you shoot two side-by-side people from the front and the back along the z-axis. Such a sequencing problem is common when cov-

13.22 Crossing the Vector Line

Crossing the vector line with one of the two cameras will result in a position switch of persons A and B. They will seem to play musical chairs.

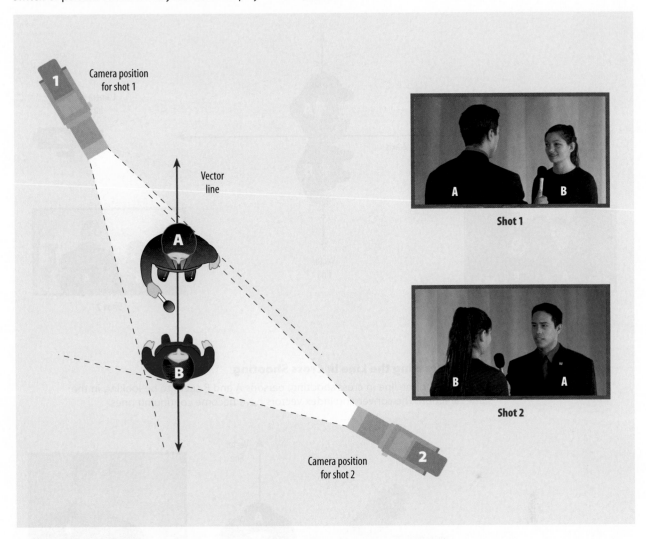

Camera position for shot 1

Vector line

Shot 1

Shot 2

Camera position for shot 2

ering a wedding, when you shoot the bride and groom first from the front and then from the back. When cutting the two shots together, the two people switch positions. **SEE 13.23**

To get around this "wedding switch," you can move to the side with the camera when the couple walks by and see them change positions within the shot. When cutting to the shot from behind, they have already switched positions.

When *cross shooting,* crossing the line will change the properly converging index vectors to improperly continuing vectors. Instead of having two people look at and talk with each other, they seem to be talking to a third person. **SEE 13.24**

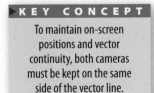

▶**KEY CONCEPT**

To maintain on-screen positions and vector continuity, both cameras must be kept on the same side of the vector line.

13.23 **Z-axis Position Switch**

When shooting two people side-by-side (A and B) from the front and from the back along the z-axis, they will switch positions when the shots are edited together.

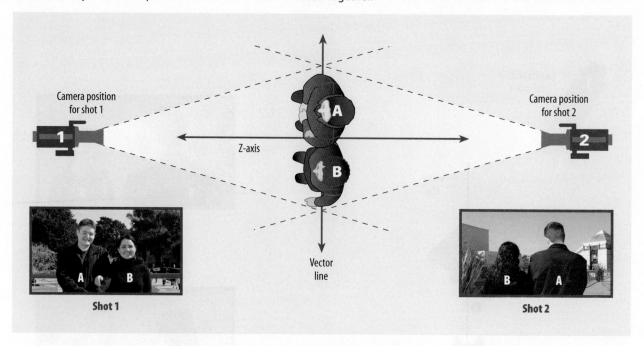

Shot 1

Shot 2

13.24 **Crossing the Line in Cross Shooting**

When crossing the line in cross shooting, persons A and B seem to be looking in the same direction. The converging index vectors have become continuing ones.

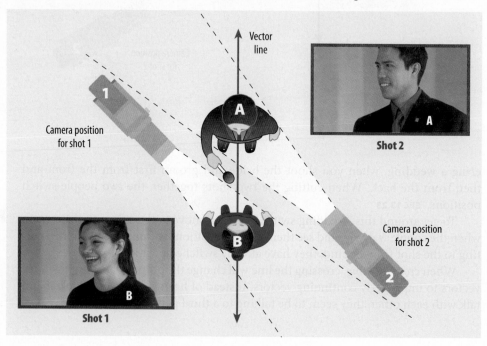

Shot 2

Shot 1

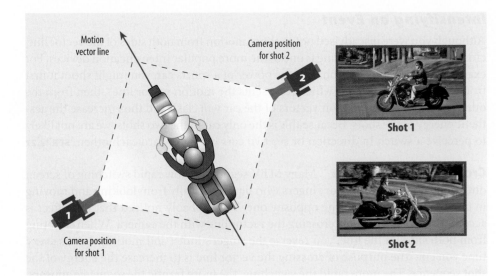

13.25 Crossing the Motion Vector Line

When crossing the motion vector line, the object motion will be reversed with each cut.

13.26 Cutaway

If you want to show that a subject continues to move in the same direction although the successive shots show it moving in the opposite direction (shots 1 and 3), you can establish a continuing motion vector by inserting a neutral cutaway (shot 2).

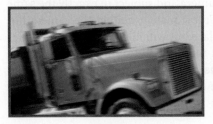

Shot 1

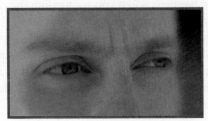

Shot 2

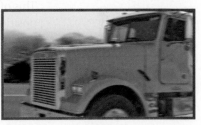

Shot 3

When placing cameras on both sides of the *motion vector line,* the object motion will be reversed with each cut. **SEE 13.25** To preserve the direction of the object motion, you need to position both cameras on the same side of the motion vector line. (Covering a football game from both sides of the field is not a good idea.)

If you need to pretend that an object moves in a single direction although two successive shots show the object moving in opposite directions, you can insert a *cutaway*—a thematically related, usually nonmoving, shot that separates the two opposing motion vectors. **SEE 13.26 ZVL3 CUE 4** EDITING→ Production guidelines→ cutaways

AESTHETIC PRINCIPLES OF COMPLEXITY EDITING

Complexity editing is done primarily to intensify an event and to give it meaning—to help us gain deeper insight into the event. In this sort of editing, you may not always follow the rules of continuity editing but instead opt to edit for heightened emotional impact, even at the risk of jarring the viewer's mental map.

Intensifying an Event

Although you were just advised not to shoot motion from both sides of the vector line, crossing the motion vector line is one of the more popular intensification devices. For example, if you want to emphasize the power of a sports car, you might shoot it first from one side of the street (which represents the motion vector line), then from the other. The converging motion vectors of the car will clash and thus increase the aesthetic energy of the shots. Because this is the only car in the two shots, we are not likely to perceive a switch in direction or see two cars racing toward each other. **SEE 13.27**

Crossing the vector line   Many MTV segments show rapid switching of screen directions, such as dancers or singers who flip frenetically from looking and moving in one screen direction to the opposite one. You probably noticed that this effect is accomplished by purposely crossing the vector line with the camera. When shooting from both sides of the line, you reverse the singer's index and motion vectors every time you cut. The purpose of crossing the vector line is to increase the energy of the shot sequence. The more rapid the switching, the more frantic the sequence appears.

Jump cut   If you first frame a person standing next to the left screen edge, then in the succeeding shot near the right screen edge, the subject seems to vault magically from screen-left to screen-right. Such a drastic position change is aptly called a *jump cut*. You may inadvertently get a jump cut with a very slight position change. This often happens when you try to align the camera and subject in exactly the same positions when setting up subsequent shots. Unfortunately, neither the camera nor the subject will remain in precisely the same place but will inevitably shift positions ever so slightly. When two such shots are cut together, the subtle shift appears as a sudden and highly noticeable jump. **SEE 13.28** To prevent jump cuts, you should always change the angle and/or the field of view, getting a looser or tighter shot, or insert a cutaway (see figure 13.26).

13.27 Intensification Through Converging Motion Vectors

Juxtaposing two converging motion vectors of a single prominent object, such as a powerful sports car, will intensify the object motion without destroying its vector continuity. Note that here the pictures of the car create index rather than motion vectors.

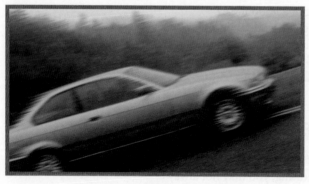
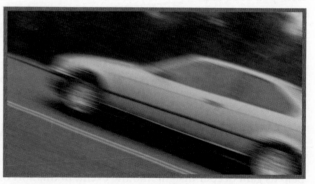

Shot 1   Shot 2

13.28 **Jump Cut**

A The jump cut is caused by an extreme position change from shot 1 to shot 2.

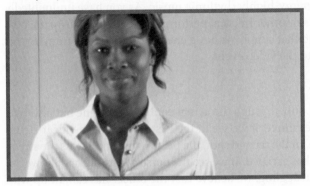

Shot 1

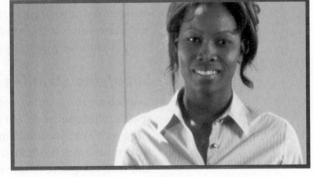

Shot 2

B A relatively subtle position change from shot 3 to shot 4 results in an equally obvious jump cut.

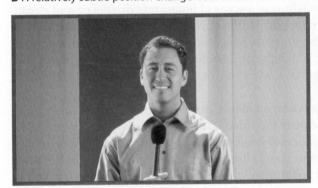

Shot 1

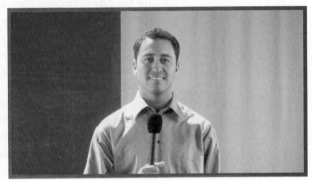

Shot 2

Although the jump cut is undesirable in continuity editing, it has now become fashionable through newscasts. When video editors of news footage did not have time to insert appropriate cutaways when editing interviews, they simply took a few interesting spots on the sound track and cut them together regardless of the video. Because most news interviews are shot with a single camera that is focused on the guest throughout, the final edited version of the interview shows a series of jump cuts. Traditionally considered an aesthetic offense, jump cuts were eventually accepted by viewers because they gave some indication of where the interview had been trimmed. The jump cut is now used in commercials and even dramatic situations—not so much as an indicator of condensing time but rather as a prodding device. Like crossing the line, the jump cut jolts us out of our perceptual complacency.

Jogging   Producing a similar jolt to visual continuity, *jogging* consists of a sloweddown frame-by-frame advance of a motion, which is normally used to locate a specific frame for editing. When shown within a high-intensity scene, it draws attention to the motion itself and can heighten the drama of the shot.

Sound track   The sound track is, of course, one of the most effective and widely used intensifiers. There is hardly a car chase that—besides the squealing tires—is not accompanied by high-energy, highly rhythmic music. As you have undoubtedly experienced at rock concerts or other musical performances, it is primarily the beat and the volume of the music that supply its basic energy. We mentally transfer this basic sound energy readily to the video event.

Supplying Meaning

You can create meaning not only through the actual content of a scene but also by a specific shot sequence. For example, if we see in the first shot a police officer struggling with a person and then, in the second shot, the person running across the street, we presume that the culprit has escaped. If we see the person running first, however, and then the police officer struggling, we believe that the officer has caught up with the culprit. **ZVL3 CUE 5** EDITING→ Functions→ quiz

You can supply additional meaning by juxtaposing the primary event with either related or contrasting events. For example, by showing how the homeless seek shelter in the city plaza and then switching to a scene of limousines driving up and elegant people entering the opera house across the street, you will not only intensify the plight of the homeless but also imply the idea of social injustice. Such a juxtaposition is called a *collision montage*. A *montage* is a carefully calculated juxtaposition of two or more separate event images that, when shown together, combine into a larger and more intense whole.[1]

You can also create audio/video montages, in which the audio event either parallels or counters the basic theme of the video, such as a slow-motion battle scene accompanied by symphonic music as though it were an elegantly choreographed ballet.

Complexity editing does not imply that there are no sequencing rules. Ignoring the conventions of continuity editing will not automatically lead to event intensification but more likely to viewer confusion. Exactly when and how to break the rules of continuity for effective complexity editing requires, first and foremost, a thorough knowledge of the rules, plus your deliberate judgment.

With a firm grasp of the vector concept, you will be ahead of many editors who do their editing more or less intuitively. There is nothing wrong with this so long as everything goes right. But when something goes wrong, intuition might not be sufficient to fix the problem. In any case, knowledge of basic editing aesthetics will give you confidence in making optimal shot selections and sequencing choices the first time around.

---

1. See Herbert Zettl, *Sight Sound Motion: Applied Media Aesthetics,* 4d ed. (Belmont, Calif.: Thomson Wadsworth, 2005), pp. 319–323. See also Steven D. Katz, *Film Directing Shot by Shot* (Studio City, Calif.: Michael Wiese Productions, 1991).

M A I N   P O I N T S

▶ **Editing Purpose and Functions**

Editing means selecting significant event details and putting them into a specific sequence to tell a story with clarity and impact. The basic editing functions are to combine various shots, condense footage, correct production mistakes, and build a show from selected shots.

▶ **Continuity Editing**

Continuity editing means to create seamless transitions from one event detail (shot) to the next. You do this by preserving the location and the motion of objects over a series of shots to help the viewer establish and maintain a mental map of where things are or should be in on- and off-screen space.

▶ **Mental Map**

Editing must help the viewer construct and maintain a mental map of where things are, where they should be, and where they are going, even though only certain parts of the scene are shown in successive shots.

▶ **Vectors**

Graphic, index, and motion vectors play an important part in establishing and maintaining continuity from shot to shot. Index and motion vectors can be continuing (pointing or moving in the same direction), converging (pointing or moving toward each other), or diverging (pointing or moving away from each other).

▶ **Vector Line**

The vector line is established by extending converging index vectors or a motion vector. To maintain position and directional continuity, the camera must shoot from only one side of the vector line. In multicamera productions all cameras must shoot from the same side of the vector line.

▶ **Complexity Editing**

Complexity editing frequently violates the principles of continuity, such as crossing the vector line, to intensify the screen event. The jump cut and jogging are employed as energizing devices.

Z E T T L ' S   V I D E O L A B   3 . 0

For your reference, or to track your work, the Zettl's VideoLab 3.0 *program cues in this chapter are listed here with their corresponding page numbers.*

V

Production Environment: Studio, Field, and Synthetic

When you see a news team covering an event in your hometown and look at some of the footage you shot in your home with your camcorder, you probably wonder why we still use studios. After all, the highly portable camcorders and lights and the wireless microphones make it possible to originate a video program anywhere, indoors or out. In tandem with portable transmission equipment and satellite uplinks, you don't need to re-create a street corner in the studio—you can go to the actual street corner as background for your shoot. So why do we still need studios? The answer is quite simple: because they afford optimal production control.

The next two chapters explain the relative advantages of the studio and field production environments.

Production Environment:

Studio, Field, and Synthetic

KEY TERMS

cyclorama A U-shaped continuous piece of canvas or muslin for backing of scenery and action. Hardwall cycs are permanently installed in front of one or two of the studio walls. Also called *cyc*.

flat A piece of standing scenery used as background or to simulate the walls of a room. There are hardwall and softwall flats.

floor plan A diagram of scenery, properties, and set dressings drawn on a grid.

I.F.B. Stands for *interruptible foldback* or *feedback*. A prompting system that allows communication with the talent while on the air. A small earpiece worn by on-the-air talent that carries program sound (including the talent's voice) or instructions from the producer or director.

intercom Short for *intercommunication system*. Used for all production and engineering personnel involved in a show. The most widely used system has telephone headsets to facilitate voice communication on several wired or wireless channels. Includes other systems, such as I.F.B. and cellular telephones.

master control Controls the program input, storage, and retrieval for on-the-air telecasts. Also oversees the technical quality of all program material.

monitor High-quality video receiver used in the video studio and control rooms. Cannot receive broadcast signals.

P.L. Stands for *private line* or *phone line*. Major intercommunication device in video studios. Also called *party line*.

props Short for *properties*. Furniture and other objects used by talent and for set decoration.

S.A. Stands for *studio address system*. A public address loudspeaker system from the control room to the studio. Also called *studio talkback* or *P.A.* (public address) system.

studio control room A room adjacent to the studio in which the director, producer, various production assistants, technical director, audio engineer, and sometimes the lighting director perform their various production functions.

Production Environment: The Studio

Affording optimal production control, the video production studio provides an environment that is independent of the weather and the restrictions of an outdoor location. The studio also facilitates the coordination and the optimal use of all major production elements—cameras, lighting, sound, scenery, and the actions of production personnel and performers—making video production highly efficient.

After visiting a few studios in television stations, independent production houses, and colleges, you will soon discover that despite their differences in size and layout they all contain similar installations and equipment. Television studios are designed to facilitate the interaction of the various installations and team members for a great variety of production activities. Knowing about how a studio and its facilities function will help you make optimal use of it.

▶ **VIDEO PRODUCTION STUDIO**
Physical layout and major installations

▶ **STUDIO CONTROL ROOM**
Image control and sound control

▶ **MASTER CONTROL**
Overseeing technical quality and controlling program input, storage, and retrieval

▶ **STUDIO SUPPORT AREAS**
Scenery and property storage, and makeup and dressing rooms

▶ **SCENERY, PROPERTIES, AND SET DRESSINGS**
Softwall and hardwall flats; modules, drops, and set pieces; set and hand props; and set dressings

▶ **SET DESIGN**
Program objective, floor plan, prop list, setup, and evaluating the floor plan

VIDEO PRODUCTION STUDIO

Video production studios are designed not only for multicamera productions and teamwork but also to provide an optimal environment for single-camera video productions. Most studios are fairly large rectangular rooms with smooth floors and high ceilings from which the lighting instruments are suspended. They have a number of other technical installations that facilitate a great variety of productions and help make them highly efficient. **SEE 14.1**

Physical Layout

When evaluating a production studio, you should look not only at the electronic equipment it houses but also at its physical layout—its size, floor and ceiling, doors and walls, and air-conditioning.

Size   If you do a simple interview or have a single performer talk to the audience on a close-up, you can get by with amazingly little studio space. But if you plan a more ambitious project, such as a large panel discussion or the videotaping of a music show or drama, you need a larger studio. In general, it is easier to produce a small show in a large studio than a large show in a small one. But you will quickly learn that large studios are usually harder to manage than small ones. Somehow large studios require more energy to get a production started than do smaller ones; they necessitate longer camera and audio cables, more lighting instruments, and usually more crew. If you have a choice, use a studio that fits your production needs.

Floor and ceiling   A good studio must have a hard, level floor so that cameras can travel freely and smoothly. Most studio floors are concrete that is polished or covered with hard plastic or seamless linoleum.

14.1 Video Production Studio

A well-designed studio provides optimal control for multicamera and single-camera video productions. It facilitates teamwork and the coordination of all major production elements.

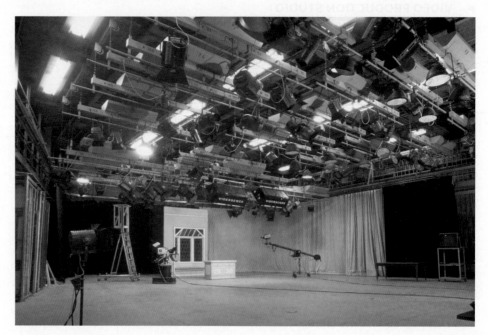

One of the most important design features of a good studio is adequate ceiling height. The ceiling must be high enough to accommodate normal 10-foot scenery and to provide enough space for the lighting grid or battens. Although you may get by with a minimum ceiling height of 14 feet for a very small studio, most professional studios have ceilings that are 30 or more feet above the studio floor. Such a high ceiling makes it possible to suspend the lighting instruments above even tall scenery and leaves adequate space above them for the heat to dissipate.

Doors and walls   Studio doors seem rather unimportant until you have to move scenery, furniture, and large equipment in and out. Undersized studio doors can cause a great deal of frustration for the production crew and frequently damage to equipment and scenery. Good studio doors must also be soundproof enough to keep all but the loudest noises from leaking into the studio.

The studio walls and ceiling are normally treated with sound-absorbing material to "deaden" the studio. A fairly "dead" studio minimizes reverberation, which means that it keeps the sounds from bouncing indiscriminately off the walls.

At least two or three sides of the studio are normally covered with a *cyclorama*, or *cyc*—a continuous piece of muslin or canvas suspended from a pipe or heavy curtain track. The light-gray or light-beige cyc serves as a convenient neutral background for a variety of setups. A *ground row*, which is a curved piece of scenery placed on the studio floor in front of the cyc, helps blend the vertical cyc into the studio floor to form a seamless background. **SEE 14.2**

Some cycloramas are suspended from a double track, with the front track holding a variety of additional curtains, called *drops*. The most frequently used drops are the chroma-key backdrop, which consists of a large piece of chroma-key blue or green cloth, and the black drop, used for special lighting effects.

Some studios have a built-in *hardwall cyc*, which is erected directly in front of a studio wall. The ground row is part of the hardwall cyc. **SEE 14.3** The advantages of a hardwall cyc are that it does not wrinkle or tear even after longtime use and it can be easily repainted. The disadvantages are that it has a high degree of sound reflectance, often causing unwanted echoes, and it takes up considerable studio space.

Air-conditioning   Many studios suffer from air-conditioning problems. Because the lighting instruments generate so much heat, the air-conditioning system must work overtime. When operating at full capacity, all but the most expensive systems create air noise, which is inevitably picked up by the sensitive studio mics and duly amplified in the audio console. You must then decide whether to keep the air-conditioning going despite the noise it makes or to turn it off and expose talent, crew, and equipment to uncomfortably high temperatures. There are quiet systems that transport a great amount of cool air at low velocity, but they are prohibitively expensive for most video studios.

14.2 Ground Row

The ground row is a curved piece of scenery that is placed on the studio floor in front of the cyclorama to blend the two into a seamless background.

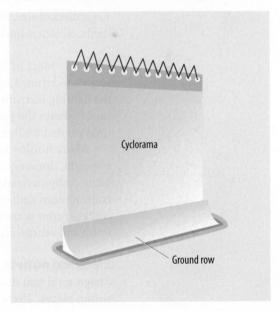

Cyclorama

Ground row

14.3 **Hardwall Cyc**

The hardwall cyc is constructed of fiberboard and placed in front of one of the studio walls. The ground row is built-in.

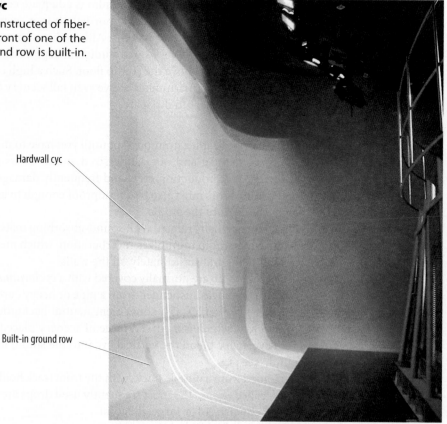

Hardwall cyc

Built-in ground row

Major Installations

Regardless of size, all studios have similar basic technical installations, which include lights, electrical outlets, intercommunication systems, monitors, and studio speakers.

Lights   Most of the lighting instruments used in a video production studio are suspended from a lighting grid or movable battens, as shown in figure 14.1. Hanging the lighting instruments above the scenery and action keeps the lights out of camera range, allows the cameras and the people to move about freely, and minimizes the time needed for lighting a scene.

Many studios have a physical lighting *patchboard* (which routes various lights to a specific dimmer) and even the actual dimmer controls in the studio itself. When using computerized lighting control units, you may find the main control unit in the control room and an additional remote lighting control in the studio. The one in the control room is used for the actual studio production; the one in the studio is for setup and rehearsals. All of the patching is done by computer.

Electrical outlets   You may not consider wall outlets an important factor in studio design until you discover that there are not enough of them or that they are in the wrong places. There should be several groups of outlets for cameras, microphones, monitor lines, intercommunication headsets, and regular AC power distributed along all four walls. If all the outlets are concentrated on only one wall, you will have to string long power cables and extension cords throughout the studio to get the equipment into the desired positions around the scenery.

All outlets must be clearly marked so that you will not plug a certain piece of equipment into the wrong outlet. This labeling is especially important when the outlets are behind the cyc, where it is usually dark and there is little space to maneuver.

Intercommunication systems Reliable *intercom* systems are one of the most important technical installations. Normal studio intercoms use P.L. and I.F.B. systems. The *P.L.* (*private line* or *phone line*) system, also known as the *party line,* allows all production and engineering personnel to be in constant voice contact with one another. Each member of the production team and the technical crew wears a headset with a microphone for talkback. Such systems can be wired (through the camera cables or separate intercom cables) or, in larger studios, wireless. Most P.L. systems operate on at least two channels so that different groups can be addressed separately.

Producers and directors make frequent use of the **I.F.B.** (*interruptible foldback* or *feedback*) system, which allows them to communicate directly with the talent, who wear tiny earpieces instead of telephone headsets while on the air. Such instant communication from the control room to the talent is especially important during news and interviews.

Monitors As you recall, a *monitor* is a high-quality video receiver that cannot receive broadcast signals. You need at least one fairly large monitor in the studio that shows the line-out pictures (the video that goes to the videotape recorder or transmitter) to everyone on the floor. By viewing the line-out picture, the crew can anticipate a number of production tasks. For example, the camera that is not on the air can vary its shot so that it does not duplicate that of the on-the-air camera; and the floor manager can see how close he or she can be to the talent for the necessary hand signals without getting into camera range; and the microphone boom operator can test how far the mic can be lowered before it gets into the camera shot.

News- and weathercasters often work with several studio monitors that carry not only the line-out pictures but also the remote feeds and the videotape playbacks. Because the weathercaster actually stands in front of a plain chroma-key backdrop when pointing to the (nonexistent) weather map, the monitor, which shows the complete key including the map, is essential for guiding the talent's gestures. For audience participation shows, you need several monitors to show the audience how the event looks on-screen.

Studio speakers The studio speakers do for the program sound what video monitors do for the video portion. The studio speakers can feed the program sound or any other sounds—music, telephone rings, crashing noises—into the studio to be synchronized with the action. They can also be used for the **S.A.** (*studio address* system, also called *P.A.,* for *public address* system), which allows the control room personnel (usually the director) to talk to the studio personnel who are not on headsets. The S.A. is obviously not used on the air, but it is helpful for calling the crew back to rehearsal, reminding them of the time remaining, or advising them to put on their P.L. headsets.

STUDIO CONTROL ROOM

The **studio control room,** housed in a separate area adjacent to the studio, is designed to accommodate the people who make the decisions while production is under way as well as the equipment necessary to control the video and audio portions of the production.

The people normally working in the control room are the director, the producer, and their associates; the technical director (TD); the C.G. operator; the audio engineer; and sometimes the lighting director (LD).

The control room equipment is designed and arranged to coordinate the total production process. Specifically, it facilitates the instantaneous editing (selection and sequencing) of available video images, the selection and the mixing of various sound inputs, and the lighting control. Some control rooms have windows that let the control room personnel see what is going on in the studio. More often, however, you will find that the only way you can see what's going on in the studio is by watching the monitors that show the various camera points of view.

Image Control

The *image control* section contains the equipment necessary to select and sequence the various video inputs, to coordinate the video with the audio, and to communicate with the production people, technical crew, and talent.

Monitors   Recall for a moment the video switcher (explored in chapter 10). Each of the buttons on the program bus represents a separate video input. But how can you tell which pictures to choose from all the inputs? Wouldn't you need a separate monitor for each major video input? Yes, indeed. This is why even a rather modest control room requires a large bank of monitors. **SEE 14.4**

Even a small control room requires a surprising number of monitors. Let's count them and identify their functions. **SEE 14.5**

Preview	1	
Line	1	
Air	1	If an on-the-air or cable station studio, this monitor will show what the home viewer sees
Camera preview	4	One for each camera; camera 4 can also be switched to remote
VTRs	3	One for each playback VTR
C.G.	1	
Electronic still store system	1	
Special effects	1	
Remote	1	Remote feeds; can also be used for additional camera
Total	14	Monitors

These monitors are stacked in a variety of configurations in front of the director and the TD. The preview (or preset), line, and air monitors are generally large color monitors placed side-by-side. They usually have the wide-screen 16 × 9 HDTV aspect ratio. All other preview monitors have the traditional 4 × 3 STV aspect ratio and are

14.4 Control Room Monitor Stack

The control room monitors show all available video sources, such as the studio cameras, remote video, VTRs, C.G., ESS, and special effects. The large color monitors show the preview video (the upcoming shots) and the line-out (what is being sent to the videotape recorder and/or the transmitter).

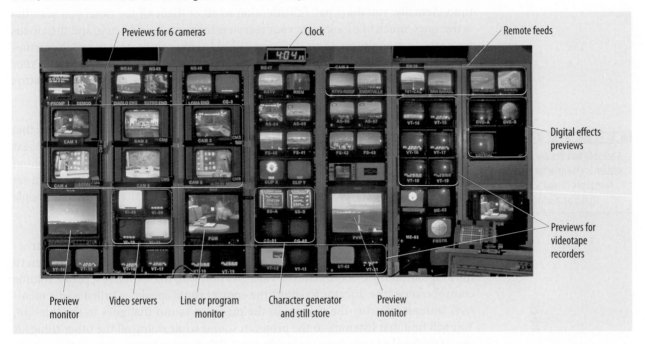

Previews for 6 cameras   Clock   Remote feeds

Digital effects previews

Previews for videotape recorders

Preview monitor   Video servers   Line or program monitor   Character generator and still store   Preview monitor

14.5 Simple Monitor Stack

Even this simple control room display requires fourteen monitors: three large 16 × 9 color monitors for preview, line, and air; four camera previews, one of which is switchable to remote; three for VTRs; and one each for C.G., ESS, special effects, and remote. Except for the 16 × 9 preview, line, and air monitors, all others are 4 × 3 monochrome displays.

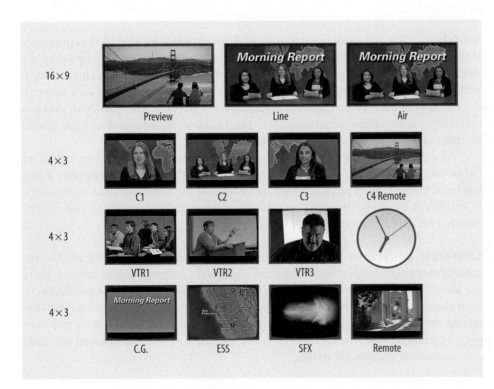

16 × 9   Preview   Line   Air

4 × 3   C1   C2   C3   C4 Remote

4 × 3   VTR1   VTR2   VTR3

4 × 3   C.G.   ESS   SFX   Remote

smaller and black-and-white. The C.G. operator often has a separate color monitor for composing the text. The text or title is then sent to the preview monitor or to a separate color C.G. monitor.

You may wonder how anybody can ever watch all of these monitors at the same time. Actually, you don't pay full attention to all of them all the time; you scan the active ones, much like looking at your rearview mirrors while driving, and then focus your attention on the monitors that carry the video most important to you. Nevertheless, you must always be aware of what the rest of the monitors are showing. After some practice you will be able to see more and more monitors, much like a maestro's reading a complex score while conducting an orchestra.

Intercom   The director also has easy access to a variety of intercom switches that control the P.L., S.A., and I.F.B. systems. The associate director (AD), who sits next to the director, uses the same switches. The producer, who may sit next to or behind the director, will normally have a duplicate set of intercom switches; this extra set enables the producer to communicate with the talent and the production people without interfering with the director.

Program sound   In addition to watching the preview monitors, giving instructions to production people, and listening to the P.L., the director must also listen to the program audio to coordinate the video portion with the sound. A separate volume control enables the director to adjust the control room speakers, called *audio monitors,* without affecting the volume of the program sound that goes to the line-out. You will find that listening to the program sound while doing all the other things is one of the hardest tasks for a rookie director. (We discuss directing more thoroughly in chapter 17.)

Switcher   You already learned that the video switcher is located next to the director's position. But why? This proximity enables the TD (who is normally doing the switching) to use the same monitor stack as the director and remain in close contact. Sitting close together helps the director and the TD communicate not only through the P.L. system but also through hand gestures. For instance, by moving an arm at a certain speed, the director can indicate to the TD how fast a dissolve or wipe should be.   **SEE 14.6** `ZVL3 CUE 1` SWITCHING→ Switching introduction

When fast cutting is required, some directors prefer to do their own switching (labor unions permitting) or snap their fingers, rather than call for a take once a shot has been readied. Such physical cues are faster and more precise than verbal ones. In smaller productions directors may do their own switching, a practice not recommended for complex shows.

Character generator   The C.G. and the C.G. operator are also located in the control room. Although most of the titles are usually prepared ahead of time, there are always changes to be made. Especially during live or live-on-tape productions, such as sports, the C.G. operator must update the scores and prepare various statistics during the game. Or the producer or director may call for titles that have not been preprogrammed. With the C.G. operator in the control room, such changes are easily communicated and quickly made.

►**KEY CONCEPT**

A reliable and flexible intercom system is essential for effective teamwork in multicamera studio productions.

►**KEY CONCEPT**

The director and the TD must sit next to each other in the control room.

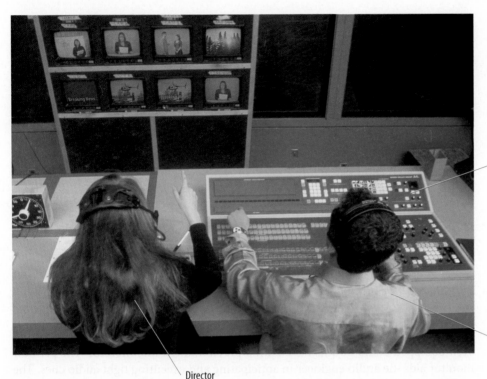

14.6 Production Switcher in Control Room

The production switcher is located next to the director's position.

Production switcher

TD operating switcher

Director

Clocks and stopwatches   These timing tools are essential in broadcast operations, where programs are aired according to a second-by-second schedule. But even if your productions are video-recorded for postproduction, the clock will tell you whether the recording session is going according to the production schedule, and the stopwatch will guide you when inserting other recorded material. Digital stopwatches—actually little clocks—give you a choice of running forward from the start of the program or backward from the end-time. When running backward the stopwatch will display the time actually left in the program. Some directors prefer the analog clock and stopwatch because they can "look ahead" by watching the hands of the clock moving and thus pace the remaining program more accurately.

Lighting control and CCUs   Some control rooms house the *lighting control* (dimmers) and/or the CCUs (camera control units) for each camera. The advantage of having this additional equipment in the control room is that all image control is in a single location, facilitating communication among the various technicians. The disadvantage is that the control room gets quite crowded with additional equipment and people.

Sound Control

The *sound control* is the audio booth attached to the video control room. It is usually isolated from the video control room so that the audio engineer is not disturbed by all the talk. Most audio booths have a window that allows the audio engineer to see the activities in the control room and perhaps even the director's preview monitors.

14.7 Audio Control Booth

The television audio control booth contains a variety of audio control equipment, such as the control console, a patchbay, a CD player, DAT machines, loudspeakers, intercom systems, and a video line monitor.

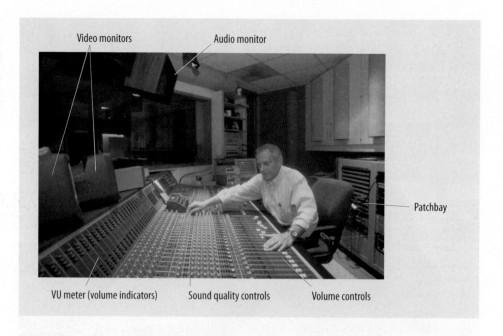

Video monitors   Audio monitor

Patchbay

VU meter (volume indicators)   Sound quality controls   Volume controls

Well-equipped audio booths have both a preview and a line monitor. The preview monitor aids the audio engineer in anticipating and executing tight audio cues. The audio engineer is further aided by a marked script or show format. The various cue lines prepare the engineer for upcoming audio and help him or her react more quickly to the director's cues.

The audio booth normally contains an audio console, a patchbay, various DAT machines, digital carts and other recording devices, and CD players. The audio engineer can listen to the director via P.L. headsets or a small cue speaker and can talk to the control room and the studio through the P.L. and S.A. systems. The program sound is monitored by high-quality program speakers. **SEE 14.7**

MASTER CONTROL

If you use the studio strictly for producing video-recorded programs, you don't need a master control room, assuming that the CCUs are located somewhere in the studio control room. But most larger nonbroadcast production houses have an equipment and communication center called ***master control***. If you are in the business of telecasting programs over the air or via cable, master control becomes an essential electronic nerve center.

Master control normally houses the studio CCUs, on-line VTRs, and computer-controlled digital video cart machines, video servers, electronic still store (ESS) systems, and various routing switchers and installations that monitor the technical quality of every second of programming that is sent to the transmitter or cable. In nonbroadcast operations master control may contain CCUs, C.G.s, VTRs and other video- and audio-recording devices, and various monitors and intercom systems.

The basic functions of master control in broadcast operations are overseeing the technical quality of all program material and controlling program input, storage, and retrieval. *Program input* means that master control keeps track of all incoming programs, regardless of whether they arrive via satellite, cable, or mail. Videotaped material is stored in bins in the master control area, in designated storage rooms, or in large video servers. To aid retrieval, each program, however long or short, is given an identification code, often called the *house number*. *Program retrieval* refers to the selection, ordering, and distribution (on-the-air, cable, or satellite transmission) of the program material.

The *program log* is a document that dictates program retrieval and determines which program goes on the air at what time. It lists every second of programming aired on a particular day as well as other important information, such as the title and the type of each program and its origin (local live, videotape, server, or network or satellite feed). The log is distributed throughout the station by computer display and sometimes also as hard copy. **SEE 14.8**

The actual switching from program to program is mostly done by computer. In case the computer system goes down, however, an operator monitors the automatic switching and is ready to press into service the manual master control switcher. **SEE 14.9**

14.8 Program Log

The program log is a second-by-second list of all programs telecast during a broadcast day. It shows the scheduled (start) times, program title and type, video and audio origin (tape, live, or feed), house number, and other pertinent broadcast information.

HSE NUMBER	SCH TIME	PGM	LENGTH	ORIGIN VID	AUD
N 3349	10 59 40	NEWS CLOSE	015	VT4	VT4
S11	10 59 55	STATION BR	005	ESS	CART20
E 1009	11 00 00	GOING PLACES 1	030	VT5	VT5
C5590	11 00 30	FED EX	010	VT2	VT2
C 9930-0	11 00 40	HAYDEN PUBLISHING	010	VT18	VT18
C 10004	11 00 50	SPORTS HILIGHTS	005	ESS	CART21
PP 99	11 00 55	STATION PROMO SPORTS	005	VT22	VT22
E 1009	11 01 00	GOING PLACES CONT 2	1100	VT5	VT5
C 9990-34	11 12 00	HYDE PRODUCTS	030	VT34	VT34
C 774-55	11 12 30	COMPESI FISHING	010	VT35	VT35
C 993-48	11 12 40	KIPPER COMPUTERS	010	VT78	VT78
PS	11 12 50	RED CROSS	005	ESS	CART22
PP 1003	11 12 55	STATION PROMO GOOD MRNG	005	VT23	VT23
E 1009	11 13 00	GOING PLACES CONT 3	1025	VT5	VT5
C 222-99	11 23 25	WHITNEY MOTORCYCLE	020	VT33	VT33
C 00995-45	11 23 45	IDEAS TO IMAGES	010	VT91	VT91
PS	11 23 55	AIDS AWARENESS	005	ESS	CART02
E 1009	11 24 00	GOING PLACES CONT 4	100	VT5	VT5
N 01125	11 25 00	NEWSBREAK ***LIVE	010	ST1LV	ST1
C 00944-11	11 25 10	ALL SEASONS GNRL FOODS	030	VT27	VT27
N 01125	11 25 40	NEWS CONT***LIVE	200	ST1LV	ST1
C 995-89	11 27 40	BLOSSER FOR PRESIDENT	020	VT24	VT24
PP 77	11 28 00	NEXT DAY	010	VT19	VT19

14.9 Master Control Switching Area

Master control serves as the final video and audio control for all program material before it is broadcast or distributed by other means (satellite or cable). Computers run all master control functions, with the master control technician overseeing the automated functions and, if necessary, taking over control manually in case of emergency.

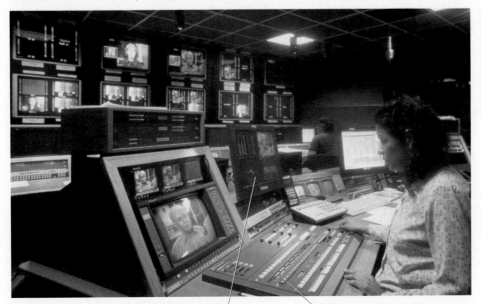

Computer log display   Manual master control switcher

> **KEY CONCEPT**
>
> Master control checks the technical quality of all programs and facilitates program input, storage, and retrieval.

STUDIO SUPPORT AREAS

No studio can function properly without support areas that house scenery, properties, and makeup and dressing rooms. Unfortunately, even large and relatively new studios usually lack sufficient support areas. As a consequence the studios themselves become partial storage areas for scenery and even serve as makeup and dressing rooms.

Scenery and Property Storage

One of the most important features of scenery and property storage is ease of retrieval. The floor crew must be able to find and pull each piece of scenery without having to dig it out from under all the others. The prop areas and the storage boxes must be clearly labeled, especially if they contain small hand props.

Makeup

Wherever you apply makeup, it must be done in lighting conditions that are identical to those in the studio. Most makeup rooms have two types of illumination: indoor lighting (with a color temperature standard of 3,200K) and outdoor lighting (with a color temperature standard of 5,600K). Because the indoor standard has a warmer, more reddish light than the cooler, more bluish light of outdoors, you should always check your makeup on-camera in the actual performance area before the dress rehearsal and again before the performance. (Color temperature is explained in depth in chapter 8.)

SCENERY, PROPERTIES, AND SET DRESSINGS

You may wonder why the networks have such gigantic news sets for the single-person anchor, who usually appears on a loose close-up throughout the show. Although you see the whole set for only a few seconds during the opening and closing, it is supposed to signal that the news department is large, well equipped, and high-tech. Yes, you could certainly do the same newscast just as successfully on a much smaller set.

Be that as it may, scenery and properties are used primarily to create a specific environment in which the action takes place, but they also reflect the nature of the event. The bookcases filled with matching volumes in an interview set may be a cliché, but they communicate instantly a lawyer's office. When dealing with scenery and properties in video production, you must always keep in mind that it is the camera that looks at the scenic environment, not the crew or the casual studio visitor. The set must be detailed enough to withstand the close-up scrutiny of an HD (high-definition) camera yet plain enough to avoid clutter that can detract from the performers. Careful attention to set detail is especially important when using high-definition television (HDTV) cameras. The high resolution of HDTV increases the illusion of depth and makes even background detail more visible. The set must also allow for optimal camera movement and angles, microphone placement and mobility, appropriate lighting, and maximum action by the talent. It is a major factor in setting style.

> ►**KEY CONCEPT**
>
> Scenery must create a certain environment and allow for optimal lighting, audio pickup, and camera movement.

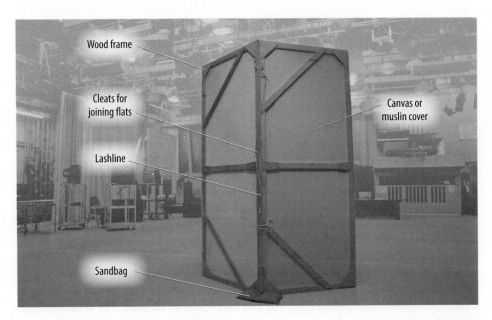

Wood frame

Cleats for joining flats

Lashline

Sandbag

Canvas or muslin cover

14.10 Softwall Flats

Softwall flats are made of 1 × 3 lumber and covered with muslin. They are supported by a wood brace, called a jack, which is weighted down with a sandbag or metal weights.

Scenery

Although the design and construction of scenery requires specific training and skills, you should know what standard set units are and how to use them for creating simple environments. Here we discuss softwall flats; hardwall flats; set modules; seamless paper and painted drops; and set pieces, platforms, and wagons.

Softwall flats   A *flat* is a freestanding piece of scenery used as a background or to simulate the walls of a room. *Softwall flats* are background units constructed of a lightweight wood frame covered with muslin. The wood frame consists of 1 × 3 lumber that is glued together and reinforced at the corners by ¼-inch plywood pieces. To keep the frame from twisting, it is further strengthened by two diagonal braces and a toggle rail. If the studio floor is hard, you can put metal or plastic gliders on the bottom rail of the flat so you can push it around without damaging the flat or the floor. **SEE 14.10**

The traditional, and still most practical, way to tie softwall flats together is by using *lashlines*. When joining flats, you actually lash two pieces of scenery together with a clothesline that is attached to the right top rail of each flat and pulled through cleats, similar to lacing the hooks of a boot. **SEE 14.11** Flats are supported by *jacks*—wood braces that are hinged, tied, or fastened to the flats with C-clamps—and are weighted down and held in place by sandbags or metal weights.

Standard softwall flats have a uniform height but various widths. The height is usually 10 feet, or 8 feet for small sets or studios with

14.11 Flats Joined by Lashline

Softwall flats are connected by lashing them together with a clothesline, called a lashline. The lashline is woven around alternating metal cleats and secured with a slip knot.

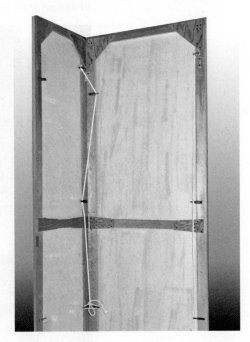

low ceilings; width ranges from 1 to 5 feet. When two flats are permanently hinged together, they are called *twofolds* or *books* (because they open like a book); three flats hinged together constitute a *threefold*.

Softwall flats are easy to move, assemble, and store, but their simple construction is also a disadvantage: they tend to shake when you close a door or window on the set or if someone or something brushes against them. They are ideal for rehearsal and for less demanding productions.

Hardwall flats   Most professional video production sets are constructed with *hardwall flats.* They are usually built for a specific set and do not always conform to the standard dimensions of softwall scenery. Although there is no standard way to build hardwall scenery, most flats are constructed with a sturdy wood or slotted-steel frame (which looks like a big erector set) and covered with plywood or pressed fiber-board. Most hardwall scenery is moved with the help of built-in casters and joined with bolts or C-clamps. **SEE 14.12**

The advantage of hardwall scenery is that it is extremely sturdy; if a scene calls for slamming the door, you can do so without fear of shaking the whole set. You can also attach pictures or posters the way you would on a real wall. The disadvantages of hardwall flats are that they are expensive to build, difficult to move and set up, and even harder to store. Hardwall scenery is also apt to reflect sound and cause unwanted reverberations.

14.12 Hardwall Scenery

Hardwall scenery is built with a sturdy wood or metal frame that is covered with plywood or fiberboard. Most hardwall scenery has built-in casters or is placed on small wagons for mobility. This is the back of a window seat.

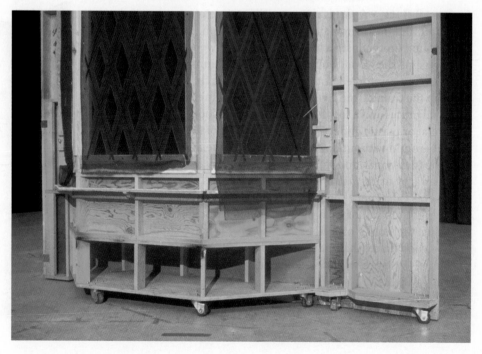

Set modules   Smaller video production companies, whose scenery demands are usually limited to news, interviews, office sets, or environments in which various products are displayed and demonstrated, often use set modules. A *set module* is a series of hardwall flats and three-dimensional set pieces whose dimensions match whether they are used vertically (right-side up) or horizontally (on their sides). They can be assembled in different combinations, similar to building blocks. For example, you might use a modular hardwall set piece as a hardwall flat in one production and as a platform in the next. Or you might dismantle a modular desk and use the boxes (representing the drawers) and the top as display units. A variety of set modules are commercially available.

Seamless paper and painted drops   As you recall, the cyclorama is a large, plain, seamless drop that serves as a neutral background (see figure 14.3). In the absence of a cyc, you can construct a limited neutral area with a roll of seamless paper (usually 9 feet wide by 36 feet long) simply by unrolling it and stapling it horizontally on softwall flats. Seamless paper rolls come in a variety of colors and are relatively inexpensive. Painted drops, on the other hand, usually refer to rolls of paper or canvas with realistic or, more often, stylized background scenes painted on them. You can also create believable backgrounds electronically. (Synthetic environments are discussed in chapter 15.)

Set pieces, platforms, and wagons   *Set pieces* consist of freestanding three-dimensional objects, such as pillars, pylons (which look like three-sided pillars), sweeps (large, curved pieces of scenery), folding screens, steps, and periaktoi (plural of *periaktos*). A periaktos is a three-sided standing unit that looks like a large pylon; it moves and swivels on casters. **SEE 14.13** Set pieces are often constructed in modular

14.13 Set Pieces

Set pieces are freestanding three-dimensional scenic objects used as background or foreground pieces.

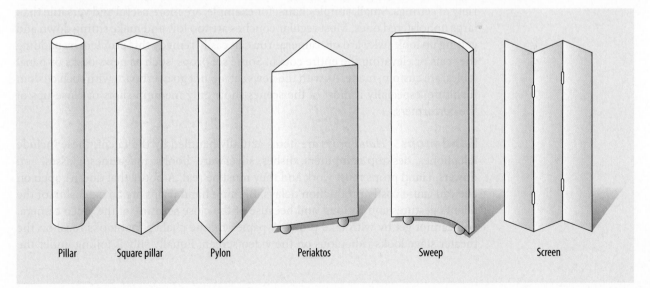

Pillar   Square pillar   Pylon   Periaktos   Sweep   Screen

dimensions so that they can be fitted together in different combinations. Some set pieces, such as pillars and pylons, are somewhat unstable and must be secured so that they do not tip over when bumped by crew, talent, or equipment. It is always better to overbrace than underbrace a set. You may have to tie them to the lighting grid in addition to bracing them with sandbags.

Platforms are elevation devices. Normal platforms are 6 inches, 8 inches, or 12 inches high and can be stacked. Sometimes the whole platform is called a *riser,* although technically a riser is only the elevation part of the platform without its top. Platforms are often used for interview and panel discussion sets so that the cameras see the participants straight-on rather than look down on them. When used for interviews, the entire platform should be covered with carpeting. As well as making the set attractive, the carpeting absorbs the hollow sounds from people moving on the platform. You can further deaden such sounds by filling the platform interior with foam rubber or foam spray.

Some 6-inch platforms have four heavy casters, converting the platforms into wagons that can support scenery and set pieces. When mounted on a series of wagons, a heavy set becomes quite mobile and can be repositioned with relative ease. Once in place, secure the wagons with wood wedges and/or sandbags so they can't move unexpectedly.

Properties

In video production *properties*—**props** for short—and set dressings are often more important than the background scenery for signifying a particular environment. You will work with two kinds of properties: set props and hand props.

Set props   *Set props* include the furniture you use on a set, such as the chairs for an interview, the table for a panel discussion, the desk from which the corporate manager delivers her weekly address, the bookcase and file cabinet for the office set, and the inevitable couch in situation comedies.

When choosing set props, look for functional furniture that can be used in a variety of settings. Small, simple chairs, for example, are more useful and versatile than large upholstered ones. Most regular couches are too low and make sitting down and getting up look awkward on-camera. You can easily remedy this problem by padding the seats or elevating the entire couch. Some set props, such as news desks or panel tables, are custom-made. As with the news set, do not go overboard with such custom furniture, especially if most of the scenes show only medium shots or close-ups of the performers.

Hand props   *Hand props* are items actually handled by the talent; these include telephones, desktop computers, dishes, silverware, books, magazines, glasses, and flowers. Hand props must work and they must be real. A bottle that doesn't open on cue can cause costly production delays. Because hand props are an extension of the talent's gestures and actions, and because of the close scrutiny of the video camera, you cannot get by with fake props. A papier-mâché chalice that looks regal on the theater stage looks ridiculous on the video screen. Equally silly is toiling under the weight of an empty suitcase. Whereas the theater audience may have some sympathy for your toil, the television viewer will more likely consider it a comic routine or a production mistake.

If you have to use food, make certain that it is fresh and that the dishes and silverware are meticulously clean. Liquor is generally replaced with water (for clear spirits), tea (for whiskey), or soft drinks (for white and red wine). With all due respect for realism, such substitutions are perfectly appropriate.

Set Dressings

Set dressings include things that you would place in your own living quarters to make them look attractive and to express your taste and personal style. Although the flats may remain the same from one type of show to another, the dressing gives each set its distinguishing characteristics and helps establish the style of the environment. Set dressings include such items as curtains, pictures, sculptures, posters, lamps, plants, decorative items for a desk and bookshelves, or a favorite toy that survived childhood. Secondhand stores and flea markets provide an unlimited source for such things. In case of emergency, you can always raid your own living quarters or office. As with props, set dressings must be realistic so that they can withstand even the probing eye of an HD camera.

> ▶**KEY CONCEPT**
>
> Properties and set dressings determine the character and the style of the environment.

SET DESIGN

Although you may never be called upon to design a set, you will certainly have to tell the set designer what environment you envision and why. You will also have to know how to interpret a set design so that you can evaluate the set relative to the program objective and the technical requirements, such as lighting, audio pickup, and camera and talent movement.

Program Objective

Once again, a clear statement of the program objective will guide you in designing the appropriate environment. For example, if the objective of an interview is to have the viewer get to know the guest as intimately as possible and probe her feelings and attitudes, what kind of set do you need? Because you should show the guest in intimate close-ups throughout most of the show, you don't need an elaborate interview set. Two simple chairs in front of an uncluttered background will do just fine.

On the other hand, if the objective is to have the viewer see how the guest uses the physical environment of her office to reflect her power, you had better conduct the interview on-location from the guest's actual office or on a studio set that closely resembles it.

As with all other medium requirements, in designing or evaluating a set you must have a pretty good idea of what it is you want the viewer to see, hear, and feel. Once you have interpreted the program objective as to scenic requirements, you need to evaluate and translate the scene design—the floor plan—into an actual studio set.

Floor Plan

The *floor plan* is a diagram of scenery and set properties drawn on a grid that resembles the usable floor space in the studio. To help you locate a certain spot on the studio floor, the lighting grid is normally superimposed over the floor plan, or a grid is drawn over the floor area similar to the orientation squares of a map. By using the lighting grid, the floor plan can also be used for drawing a light plot.

Elaborate set designs are always drawn to scale, such as the common ¼ inch = 1 foot. There are templates with in-scale cutouts for typical set pieces, such as tables, sofas, chairs, beds, and dressers. You can also use one of the many computer programs on the market for architectural layouts or interior design.

If the setup is relatively simple, the art director may make only a rough sketch that shows the background scenery, set props, and approximate location of the set, leaving it up to the floor manager to place the set in the most advantageous spot in the studio. **SEE 14.14** The floor plan should indicate all scenery, including doors and windows, as well as the type and the location of set props and major hand props. **SEE 14.15**

When drawing a floor plan, keep in mind that the set must be workable for the cameras—it must provide adequate backing for a variety of camera angles. A common mistake of inexperienced set designers is to show inadequate backing for the set props and the talent action. Somehow the furniture on the set always seems to take up more room than anticipated. This problem is especially apparent when the floor plan is not drawn to scale.

14.14 Simple Floor Plan

The floor plan grid (often the lighting grid) helps locate
the positions of scenery and set props.

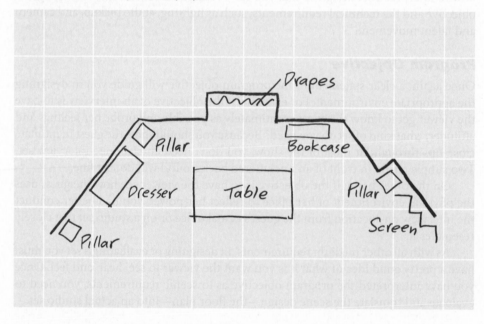

Another frequent mistake is a set design that exceeds the available floor space. As mentioned earlier, the cyc and the items stored in the studio can radically reduce the usable floor area. The floor plan must show the space that is actually available. To help the lighting people direct the back lights at the performance areas at not too steep an angle and avoid unwanted shadows on the background flats, all active furniture (furniture actually used by the talent) must be placed at least 6 to 8 feet from the background flats, as shown in figure 14.15.

Some floor plans indicate a generic set. **SEE 14.16** This set design has all the typical ingredients of a situation comedy: a living area with the inevitable couch in the middle of the room, a door to a second active set area (in this case, the kitchen), another door to an imaginary area (hallway or front yard), and a staircase in the back, leading to yet another imaginary room—usually a bedroom. In a generic set, the basic setup remains the same but can be individualized by different props and set dressings. Note the "escape" behind the stairs, which helps the actors get back down to the studio floor, and the two backdrops on either side that display the imaginary extended space, such as a hallway or front yard on the right and a patio on the left.

14.15 Floor Plan with Set and Hand Props

More-elaborate floor plans indicate the type and the position of set props (furniture, lamp, sculpture, and paintings) and major hand props (newspaper, tea set, and magazines).

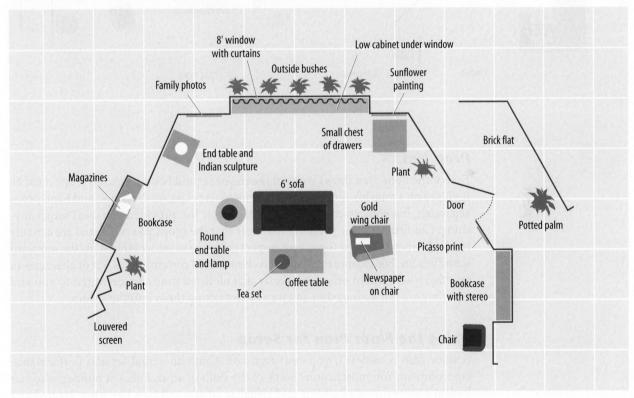

14.16 **Generic Sitcom Residence**

This set is designed so that four cameras, situated side-by-side in front, can pick up the action.
It can be easily changed to other environments by using different set props.

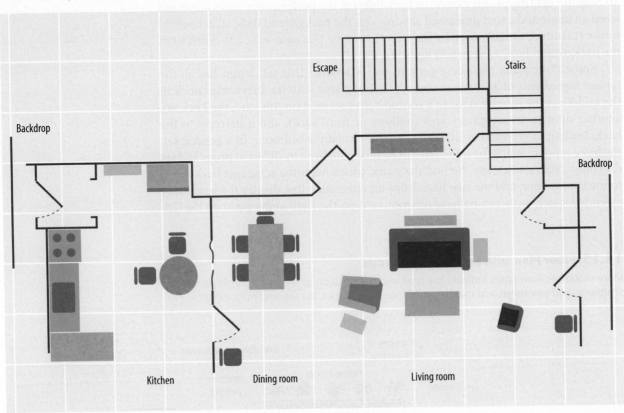

Backdrop

Escape   Stairs

Backdrop

Backdrop

Kitchen   Dining room   Living room

Prop List

Even if the floor plan shows some of the major set and hand props, all props must be
itemized on a *prop list*. Some prop lists itemize set props, set dressings, and hand props
separately, but you can combine them on a single list, provided you don't forget anything. Confirm with the property manager that the props you requested are actually
available when you need them, and inspect each one to see whether it fits the intended
scene design. For example, a Victorian chair would certainly look out of character in
an otherwise modern office set. Verify that all listed props are delivered to you and
that they are not damaged in any way before taking them into the studio.

Using the Floor Plan for Setup

A floor plan is useless if you can't translate it into an actual set and performance
environment. You must acquire some of the skills of an architect or builder, who can
look at a blueprint of a building and visualize what it will look like when erected and
how people will move through and function in it. Figure 14.17 shows how a simple
floor plan (floor plan 1) translates into the corresponding setup. **SEE 14.17**

14.17 Floor Plan 1 and Setup

The floor plan shown on the left translates into the simple set in the photo on the right.

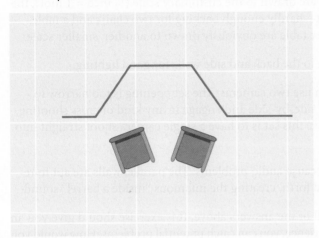

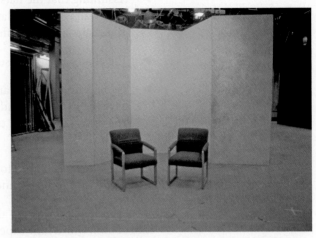

The ability to read a floor plan is a necessary skill for all production personnel. A good floor plan helps the floor manager and crew put up and dress the set fairly accurately, independent of the designer. The director can map out the major talent positions and *blocking* and also design the principal camera shots, positions, and movements before setting foot in the studio. The lighting director can lay out the basic light plot, and the audio engineer can determine mic placement. Also, by knowing how to read a floor plan, you can catch and often solve production problems before they occur. Because the floor plan is such a critical factor in production efficiency, you should insist on having one drawn even if the setup and the production are relatively simple.

Evaluating the Floor Plan

Floor plan 2 below shows a set for a two-camera live interview. Take a close look at it and list all the potential production problems you can find. **SEE 14.18**

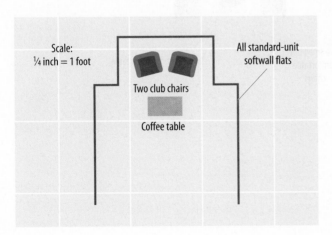

14.18 Floor Plan 2

Interview set

Now let's compare our lists:

▶ Assuming that the flats are drawn to the customary scale (¼ inch = 1 foot), the back wall is a 4-foot flat—hardly enough backing for two chairs and a table. The chairs and the coffee table are obviously drawn to another, smaller scale.

▶ The chairs are too close to the back and side walls for good lighting.

▶ There is no way you can use two cameras. The set opening is too narrow to have the cameras stand side-by-side and engage in any kind of cross shooting. The only way you can use this set is to have a single camera shoot straight into the box.

▶ The box set is bound to cause audio problems. The parallel walls are apt to reflect the sound back and forth, creating the infamous "inside a barrel" sound.

Even if you didn't get all of the answers above, this exercise should give you an idea of how, with a little experience, you can catch potential problems. How would you fix the floor plan? You should be able to come up with several solutions. In keeping with the simple idea of using two chairs, floor plan 3 suggests placing them opposite each other and putting the small table between them. **SEE 14.19**

14.19 Floor Plan 3
Interview set corrected

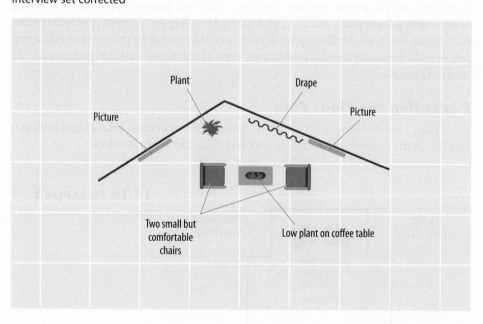

As you can see, two cameras can now get over-the-shoulder shots and cross-shots without any problem. If you have a third camera, you can use it for straight-on shots of the two chairs and the center table. When working in the wide-screen 16 × 9 aspect ratio, this shot should be especially easy to frame.

Floor plan 4, an office set, is an example of a workable production environment for a simulated job interview. **SEE 14.20** The set allows the cameras to get good shots of the interviewer (behind the desk) and the interviewee (in the chair on the right), and the props indicate a creative environment.

You probably have a better idea now about how a studio provides an optimal production environment. First and foremost, it is independent of the weather and the time of day. Rain or shine, morning or midnight—it makes no difference when doing studio productions. The physical layout and the major installations, the control room equipment, the makeup, scenery, and property areas—all are designed to facilitate a great variety of video productions. Although studio operations require a relatively large and highly coordinated production team, the studio makes video production extremely efficient.

> **►KEY CONCEPT**
>
> The floor plan—a diagram of scenery and set props—shows the setup requirements and facilitates preproduction planning.

14.20 Floor Plan 4

Office set

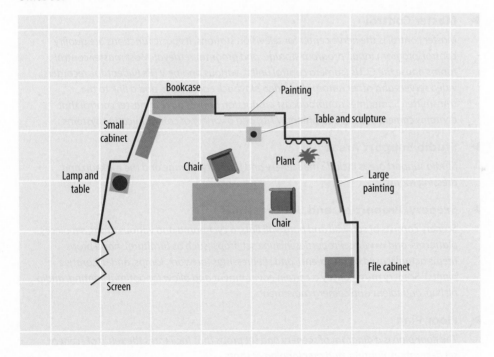

MAIN POINTS

▶ **Video Production Studio**

Video production studios are designed for multicamera productions and teamwork. Important features include sufficient floor space, a smooth floor for camera travel, adequate ceiling height so that the lights can be suspended, large doors, acoustically treated walls, and relatively quiet air-conditioning.

▶ **Major Studio Installations**

The major studio installations include a lighting grid or movable battens, adequate electrical outlets, intercommunication system between the studio and the control room, studio video monitors, and studio speakers.

▶ **Studio Control Room**

The control room is designed and arranged to coordinate the total production process. It usually comprises the image control, with the switcher, C.G., monitor banks, various intercom lines, and sometimes the lighting control board; and the sound control, which contains an audio console and various recording and playback equipment.

▶ **Director and TD**

The director and technical director (TD) must sit next to each other to share the monitors and react quickly to physical signals.

▶ **Master Control**

Master control is the nerve center for television stations. Its basic functions are quality control, program input, program storage, and program retrieval. Most master control rooms house the CCUs (camera control units), various on-line VTRs (videotape recorders), video servers and other automated video playback equipment, and a link to the transmitter. Sometimes nonbroadcast production houses have a master control that contains camera control equipment, VTRs, and a variety of communication systems.

▶ **Studio Support Areas**

Studio support areas include the scenery and property storage and the makeup and dressing rooms.

▶ **Scenery, Properties, and Set Dressings**

Scenery consists of softwall and hardwall flats, a cyclorama and various drops, set pieces, platforms, and wagons. Properties include set props (such as furniture), hand props (items actually used by the talent), and set dressings (artwork, lamps, and decorative plants). Scenery must convey a certain environment and allow for optimal lighting, audio pickup, and talent and camera movement.

▶ **Floor Plan**

The floor plan is a diagram of scenery and set props that facilitates the setup of scenery, set decoration, lighting, and preplanning of shots.

Z E T T L ' S   V I D E O L A B   3 . 0

 For your reference, or to track your work, the Zettl's VideoLab 3.0 *program cue in this chapter is listed here with its corresponding page numbers.*

ZVL3 CUE 1 ▶   SWITCHING→ Switching introduction   **298**

CHAPTER 15

KEY TERMS

big remote A production outside the studio to televise live and/or record live-on-tape a large scheduled event that has not been staged specifically for television. Examples include sporting events, parades, political gatherings, and trials or government hearings.

contact person A person who is familiar with, and who can facilitate access to, the remote location and the key people. Also called *contact*.

electronic field production (EFP) Video production done outside the studio that is usually shot for postproduction (not live).

electronic news gathering (ENG) The use of portable camcorders, lights, and sound equipment for the production of mostly unscheduled daily news events. ENG is usually done for live transmission or immediate postproduction.

field production Production activities that take place away from the studio.

remote survey An inspection of the remote location by key production and engineering personnel so that they can plan for the setup and the use of production equipment. Also called *site survey*.

remote truck The vehicle that carries the control room, audio control, video-recording section, video control section, and transmission equipment.

synthetic environment Electronically generated settings, either through chroma key or computer.

uplink truck Truck that sends video and audio signals to a satellite.

virtual reality Computer-simulated environment with which the user can interact and that can change to the preprogrammed extent.

Production Environment: Field and Computer-generated

Field production does not mean that you have to move your production to an actual field; rather, it refers to any video production that happens outside the studio. Field production includes documentaries that are shot on location, as well as the elaborate remotes for sporting events and the Thanksgiving Day parade.

When taking video equipment outside the studio, the whole world is your stage. The tradeoff for moving outside the studio and into the field is control. In field productions you cannot create and control a specific production environment but must adapt to one. If a shoot takes place outdoors, the weather is always a potential hazard; if you are indoors, the room may not be to your liking or conducive to effective video and audio pickup. Still, you can make the environment work for you instead of against you.

This chapter gives you some guidance about how to work effectively in the field, including *electronic news gathering* (ENG), *electronic field production* (EFP), and *big remotes*. From the field we move to synthetic environments that are partially or entirely created by computer.

▶ **ELECTRONIC NEWS GATHERING**
  News gathering and transmission

▶ **ELECTRONIC FIELD PRODUCTION**
  Preproduction, including the remote survey, survey team, and location sketch; production, including the equipment checklist and shooting outdoors and indoors; and the postproduction wrap-up

▶ **BIG REMOTES**
  The remote truck and remote transmission

▶ **SYNTHETIC ENVIRONMENTS**
  Computer-generated settings, virtual reality, and computer-controlled environments

ELECTRONIC NEWS GATHERING

By their very nature, the time, specifics, and location of most news events cannot be planned. Neither can the coverage of such events, called *electronic news gathering* (*ENG*). All you can do is run after the breaking story and do your best to cover it. This does not mean that you give up all control over production procedures. Preproduction in ENG entails having your equipment ready to go at any time and functioning properly regardless of where you are and under what conditions you are working.

News Gathering

As a news *videographer,* also called a *shooter,* you are responsible not only for videotaping the story but also for making the decisions on just how to tell it. In a breaking story, you must be able to assess the situation, operate the equipment, and capture the essence of the event—all in a matter of minutes. You rarely have time to consult your producer or anyone else about what is going on or how to shoot it. But even in intense situations, good videographers are able to deliver well-composed shots that can be edited into a smooth sequence.

If you are covering a story with a reporter, the news-gathering process is slightly less hectic. You usually have some flexibility in placing the field reporter for his or her "standup" report in a location that tells part of the story (city hall, college campus, county hospital), and in selecting the most effective shots.

Whenever possible have the reporter stand in a shaded area rather than in direct sunlight or, worse, in front of a brightly lit building. As explained in chapter 8, bright sunlight will cause unflattering fast falloff and dense shadows, and the bright background will cause the reporter to be seen in silhouette. Even if you have a reflector handy to slow down the falloff, it is usually easier to place the reporter in a shaded area than to fight excessive sunlight. **ZVL3 CUE 1** ▶ LIGHTS→ Field→ outdoor | use of reflectors Do not forget to white-balance the camera for every new lighting situation. Watch what is behind the reporter so that you do not have street signs, trees, or telephone poles appear to be growing out of the reporter's head.

Be mindful of all audio requirements. Don't have the reporter deliver his or her report on the windiest corner of the street; find a location that is relatively protected. Small rooms or corridors with bare walls have a tendency to produce unwanted echoes and make reporters sound as though they are speaking from inside a barrel. Take an audio level before each video recording. Always have the camera mic on to record ambient sound on a second sound track of the videotape or other recording medium. At the end of the report, record at least one minute of ambient sound to help the editor bridge the sound shifts at the edit points.

Transmission

When a live transmission of the news story is required, you need a production van that has the proper transmission equipment to relay the video and audio signals back to the station and ultimately to the station transmitter or satellite. **SEE 15.1**

The signal can be sent from the camera to the van by ordinary camera cable or via a small microwave transmitter attached to the camera. The more reliable way is to connect the camera to a tripod-mounted dish. From the van the signal can be further

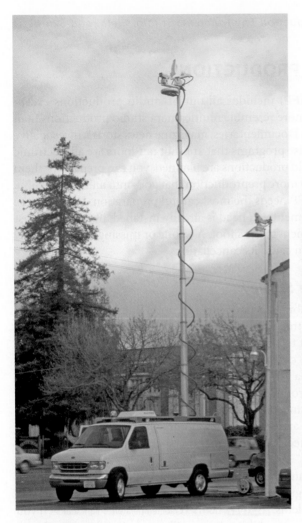

15.1 ENG Van

For ENG and routine productions, a large car or station wagon can serve as a production van. If the signal must be relayed to the station for live transmission or video recording, a van that contains VTRs or other video-recording equipment, generators, and microwave transmission equipment is used.

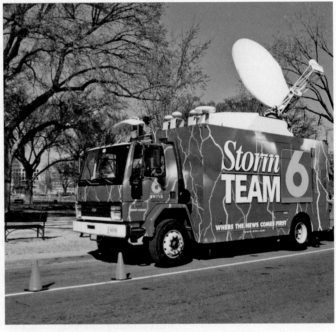

15.2 Satellite Uplink Truck

The satellite uplink truck is a portable station that sends the video and audio signals to a specific satellite.

relayed by microwave to the transmitter. If the signal must be directly *uplinked* to a communications satellite (positioned 23,300 miles above the earth), an ***uplink truck*** that contains the satellite transmitting equipment is used. **SEE 15.2** The satellite then amplifies the signal and sends it back to the receiving earth station or stations, called *downlinking*.

Although signal transmission is always done by qualified engineers, you should at least know what is needed to get the live signal from the camera to the station transmitter. Broadcasting the casual chitchat among the host in the studio and the various guests located in different corners of the world requires a great amount of technical equipment and know-how.

ELECTRONIC FIELD PRODUCTION

Electronic field production (***EFP***) includes all out-of-studio productions except news and the big remotes that more resemble multicamera studio productions than single-camera field productions. Documentaries, magazine news stories, investigative reports, travel shows, and exercise programs that are shot outdoors are all electronic field productions. Because all field productions are planned, you can prepare for them in the preproduction phase. The more preproduction that goes into an EFP, the more likely it is to succeed. In fact, EFP needs the most careful preparation. Unlike in the studio, where most of the equipment you need is already installed, in EFP you must take every single piece of equipment to the shoot. A wrong or missing cable can delay the production for hours or even cause its cancellation.

Preproduction: Remote Survey

In ENG you may be sent at a moment's notice to a location you have never seen in your life; field productions, on the other hand, require careful and extensive planning. Because you need to adapt to a specific environment, it makes sense to look at it before going there with talent, crew, and production gear.

A field inspection is called a ***remote survey*** or *site survey*. You should do a remote survey even if the field production is relatively simple, such as interviewing someone in a hotel room. Looking at the hotel room beforehand will help you decide where to position the guest and the interviewer and where to place the camera. It will also give you important technical information, such as specific lighting and sound requirements.

For example, the small table and the two chairs may be adequate for getting optimal shots of the interviewer and the guest, but the large picture window behind the table will certainly cause lighting problems. **ZVL3 CUE 2** ▶ LIGHTS→ Color temperature→ light sources If you shoot against the window, the guest and interviewer will appear in silhouette. Drawing the curtains would require lighting the interview area with portable instruments.

Are there enough electrical outlets for the lighting instruments? Are they convenient? Perhaps you can move the table and chairs away from the window or use the window as fill or even side-back light. Will the new setup still be workable for the interviewer and the guest and, most important, the camera? Will the background be reasonably interesting, or will it interfere with the shots? Now listen to the room. Is it relatively quiet, or do you hear noises through the door or window or from the air-conditioning? Can you disconnect the telephone so that it won't ring during the interview? Even this relatively simple field production will benefit a great deal from such a preproduction survey.

Survey team   For more-complex productions, careful remote surveys are an essential preproduction activity. You need to find out what the event is all about, where it is to take place, how to adapt the environment to the medium requirements, and what technical facilities are necessary for videotaping or telecasting the event. For a relatively simple field production, the director and/or the producer usually make up the survey team. For complex productions, you need to add a technical expert—the TD or the engineering supervisor. If possible, have a contact person accompany you on the initial survey.

Contact person The *contact person*, or *contact*, is someone familiar with the remote location who can help you adapt the environment to the production requirements. For the hotel room interview, for example, the contact person should not be the guest you are about to interview but rather someone who has the knowledge and the authority to get certain things done in the hotel. If you overload a circuit with the lighting instruments, the contact should be able to call the hotel engineering or maintenance department immediately and have the circuit breaker reset. To prevent the telephone from ringing during the interview, the contact should be able to have the hotel operator hold all calls or a maintenance person disconnect the phone line temporarily. The contact might even find you an empty hotel room that is better suited for videotaping the interview than the one the guest actually occupies.

If the field production involves the coverage of a scheduled event over which you have no real control, such as a parade or a sporting event, the contact person must be thoroughly familiar with the event and supply you with vital information, such as names and the order of the parade entries. Most important, the contact should help you gain access to restricted areas or to facilities at times when they are ordinarily locked. Always get the contact's full name, title, postal and e-mail addresses, and pager, cell, fax, business, and home phone numbers. Also establish an alternate contact and have one or the other accompany you on the initial remote survey. This is especially important if the EFP is scheduled during off-hours or on a weekend.

Conducting the survey Whenever possible, try to conduct the survey at the same time of day as the scheduled field production so that you can see just where the sun will be. The position of the sun will ultimately determine camera placement when shooting outdoors—as well as indoors when large windows are in camera view.

Be sure to prepare a location sketch, which is similar to a studio floor plan. The *location sketch* should show the major streets and structures of the outdoor production environment as well as the main features of the indoor production space, such as hallways, doors, windows, and principal furnishings. Even if the field production happens in an actual field, make a sketch that indicates the approximate size of the production area, the major crossroads, and the location of the sun. Include such details as parking areas, location of the EFP vehicle or remote truck, and the closest toilet facilities. **SEE 15.3 AND 15.4** The following table lists the major survey items and the key questions you should ask. **SEE 15.5**

If you have scheduled a field production outdoors, what will you do if it rains or snows? Obviously, it is a good idea to have alternate dates for a field production, unless the event is going on regardless of weather conditions, such as a football game or the Thanksgiving Day parade.

> ►**KEY CONCEPT**
> The remote survey is an important preproduction activity for all field productions except ENG.

Production: Shooting

Each field production has its own requirements and challenges. Although your careful preproduction survey should have eliminated most of the potential problems, here are a few considerations that are not part of the remote survey: equipment checklist, shooting outdoors, shooting indoors, and general production reminders.

Equipment checklist The success of the production depends a great deal on thorough preproduction and how well you have prepared the production schedule.

15.3 Outdoor Location Sketch

An outdoor location sketch should show the main streets, buildings, and facilities of the immediate production area. It should also indicate the location of the EFP vehicle and the nearest toilet facilities. Also note the position of the sun during the scheduled production period.

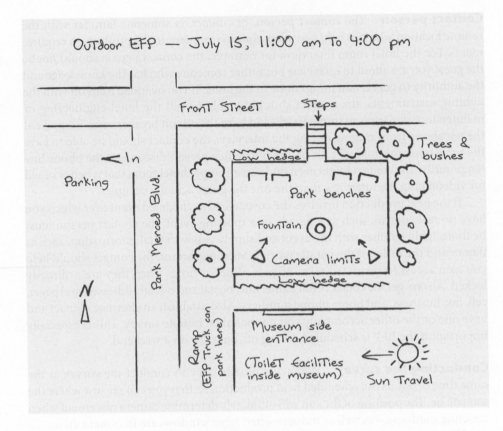

15.4 Indoor Location Sketch

The indoor location sketch should show the principal production areas (room and hallway), windows and doors, and major furnishings, such as desks, chairs, plants, and file cabinets.

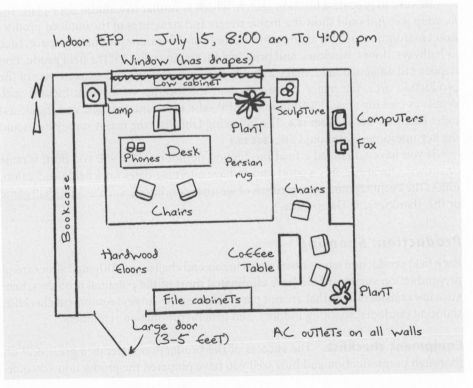

15.5 Remote Survey

SURVEY ITEM	KEY QUESTIONS
Contact	Who is the principal contact? Title; postal and e-mail addresses; and business, cell, home, pager, and fax numbers. Who is the alternate contact? Title; postal and e-mail addresses; business, cell, home, pager, and fax numbers.
Place	What is the exact location of the telecast? Street address, telephone number. Where can cast and crew park and eat? Where are the closest toilet facilities?
Time	When is the remote telecast? Where is the sun at the beginning and the end of the telecast?
Event	What type of action can you expect? Where does the action take place?
Cameras (stationary)	Where are the major positions of the camcorder? When doing a multicamera remote, how many cameras do you need to cover the event? Try to use as few as possible. What are the locations of the cameras? Do not shoot from, or place the cameras on, opposite sides of the action. In general, the closer together the cameras are, the easier and less confusing the cutting will be. Shoot with the sun, not against it. Try to keep the sun behind or to the side of the cameras for the entire telecast. Are there any large objects blocking the camera view, such as trees, telephone poles, or billboards? Will you have the same field of view during the actual time of the telecast? Spectators may block a camera's field of view, although at the time of the survey the view was unobstructed. Do you need camera platforms? How high? Where? Can the platforms be erected at this particular point? If a camera is connected to a power outlet or CCU, what is its action radius? How long a cable run do you need? What camera mounts do you need? For which cameras?
Lighting	If you need additional lighting, what kind, and where? Can you use reflectors? Can the lighting instruments be conveniently placed? Can you place back lights so that they are out of camera range? Are there windows that let in a large amount of daylight? Can they be covered or filtered so that they do not cause silhouette or color temperature problems? How many watts can each circuit handle?
Audio	What type of audio pickup do you need? Where do you need to place the microphones? Which mics are appropriate? What is the exact action radius so far as audio is concerned? Which are stationary mics and which are handled by the talent? Do you need wireless microphones? Otherwise, how long must the mic cables be? Do you need special audio arrangements, such as audio foldback or a speaker system that carries the program audio to the location? Do you need long-distance mics for sound pickup over a great distance? Where should the mics be located?
Power	What is the power source? Even if you run the camcorders by battery, what about the lights? Does the contact person have access to the power outlets? If not, who does? Make sure that the contact is available at the times of the remote setup and the actual production. Do you need extension cords or power cables? Do the extension cords fit the power outlets at the remote location?
Intercommunications	What type of intercom system do you need? In a multicamera production, you need to set up a system that is similar to the studio intercom. How many I.F.B. channels and/or stations do you need, and where should they go? Do you need walkie-talkies to coordinate the crew efforts? Do you need a cellular phone hookup?
Location of production vehicle	If you need a large production vehicle, such as a remote truck, where can you park it? Is it close enough to the event location? Does the production vehicle block traffic? Make sure that parking is reserved for the production vehicle and the cars of talent and crew.
Miscellaneous	Will you need the assistance of the local police or other security service to control vehicle and pedestrian traffic or to secure parking?

Contrary to the studio, where all major installations and equipment are readily available, you need to transport every single piece of equipment to the field production site.

Prepare a checklist that includes all of the equipment and verify every item that is loaded onto the EFP vehicle. Use the same list when reloading the equipment for the return trip. The type and the amount of equipment you need depends on the production requirements and, specifically, on the preproduction survey. Check the following list of equipment items you need to consider for EFP.

CHECKLIST: FIELD PRODUCTION EQUIPMENT

☑ *Camcorders* How many do you need? If a spare camera is available, take it along, even if it is of lower quality. In case of emergency, a properly lighted interview shot with a digital consumer camcorder will certainly be better than having no camcorder at all.

☑ *Camera mounts* Always take along a tripod, even if you intend to work the camera from your shoulder. Do you need special camera mounts, such as tripod dollies, jib arms, or beanbags?

☑ *Recording media* Do you have the proper videotape cassettes for the camcorders and the VTRs? Not all ¼-inch digital cassettes fit all digital camcorders. Check whether the actual length of the tape matches the label on the box. If the cassette has tape on its supply reel, you can be sure that it will not give you the recording time stated on the box. Note that some DVCAM and DVCPRO camcorders will not accept mini-cassettes. If you use a flash memory device, hard drive cassettes, or optical discs, do you have enough of them for extended recording periods? Some flash drives, such as the P2 card, can record only relatively brief shots. You need several to get you through a shoot.

☑ *Power supply* How will you power the camcorder? Are the batteries fully charged? Take several along. If you use an AC/DC power supply, do you have enough AC extension cords to reach the AC outlet? You also need extension cords for portable lighting instruments and a field monitor. If the monitor or external light is battery-powered, do you have the right battery? Is it fully charged? Do you have a spare battery?

☑ *Audio* In addition to lavaliere microphones, bring at least one shotgun and one hand mic. For a more ambitious EFP, you need to match the mics to the acoustics of the location. Are the mic cables long enough to reach the camcorders or audio mixer? All remote mics, including lavalieres, need windscreens. Shotgun mics need additional windsocks. If you intend to use wireless mics, do the transmitter and the receivers work properly? Test them before leaving for the remote location and again before the video recording. Do you need mounting equipment, such as clamps, stands, or fishpoles? Do you need a mixer or an additional ATR (audiotape recorder)? Take along plenty of audiocassettes or audiotape. Test the DAT (digital audiotape) recorder before taking it on location. Don't forget headsets for the mic operator and the audio-recording technician.

☑ *Cables and connectors* Do you have the appropriate cables and connectors? Most professional equipment operates with BNC connectors for the video coaxial cables and XLR connectors for audio cables, as shown in figure 7.26. Consumer-type equipment and some small camcorders often use RCA phono and mini connectors, also shown in figure 7.26. Bring along some adapters for video and audio cables. Double-check all connectors and adapters. If you need to connect the camera to an RCU (remote control unit), do you have enough camera cable with the proper connectors (usually BNC)?

☑ *Monitor and test equipment* Be sure to take along a monitor for playback. If you do a multicamera EFP with a switcher, each camera input needs a separate preview monitor. If a narrator is describing the action, you must provide a separate monitor for him or her. In field productions that require high-quality pictures, you need an RCU for each camera as well as test equipment such as a waveform monitor and a vector scope. Ordinarily, the TD is responsible for such items, but you should still see to it that they are part of the equipment package.

☑ *Lighting* More often than not, you will need at least one or two portable lighting kits, each containing several lighting instruments, barn doors, diffusers, light stands, and spare bulbs. Use floodlights (softlights) or diffusion tents and umbrellas for large-area lighting. Do the spare bulbs actually fit the lighting instruments? Do they burn with the desired color temperature (3,200K or 5,600K)? Use light-blue and amber or pale-orange gels on the lighting instruments if you need to raise or lower the color temperature, unless the lights come with color temperature filters. White diffusion material is always needed to soften key lights. You may also need sheets of pale-orange or amber (warm) color media for windows to change the high outdoor color temperature to the lower indoor one, or sheets of ND (neutral density) filters that lower the light intensity without changing the color temperature. Reflectors (white cards, foam core, aluminum foil, or professional collapsible reflectors) are essential for outdoor productions. Even when shooting indoors, reflectors are often much easier to manipulate than additional lights.

The lighting package should also include: a piece of muslin to cover an off-camera window; a piece of black cloth to cut down on unwanted reflections; diffusion umbrellas; a light meter; extra light stands; and clamps and sandbags for securing the light stands. Unless you have access to sophisticated expandable battens, take along some 1 × 3 lumber for constructing supports for small lighting instruments. Pack a roll of aluminum foil for making reflectors, heat shields, or makeshift barn doors. You will also need a few wooden clothespins to attach the diffusion material or gels to the barn doors of the lighting instruments. Take enough AC extension cords and adapters that fit household outlets. `ZVL3 CUE 3` LIGHTS→ Field→ indoor

☑ *Intercom* In small field productions, you do not need elaborate intercom setups, but you should always leave a telephone number at home base where you can be reached in case of an emergency. A cellular phone is a must if you do primarily EFP. For larger field productions, you need a small power megaphone or walkie-talkies to reach a spread-out crew. If you use a multicamera and switcher system, you need to set up a regular P.L. intercom.

☑ *Miscellaneous* Here is what you should also take along on every EFP: extra scripts and production schedules; field (VTR) log forms; a slate and a water-based marker; several large rain umbrellas and "raincoats" (plastic covers) to protect equipment and crew in case of rain; a white card for white-balancing; a large newsprint pad and markers for writing cue cards or other information for the talent while on the air or recording; if necessary, a remote teleprompter with batteries and all necessary cables; several rolls of gaffer's tape and masking tape; white chalk; several wooden clothespins to hold things in place, even if you don't use any lighting instruments; a makeup kit; a large bottle of water; a small plastic bowl; paper towels; a broom and trash bags; and lots of sandbags.

Test all equipment before loading it onto the EFP vehicle. At the very least, do a brief recording with the camcorder to see whether video and audio portions can be properly recorded. If you don't have a battery tester, attach the batteries one by one to the camera to see that they are properly charged. Test each mic and each lighting instrument before loading it. All this checking may seem like a waste of time—until you get stuck far from your production facility with a malfunctioning camcorder, mic, or light that you neglected to test.

> ► **KEY CONCEPT**
>
> Prepare a checklist of all equipment needed, and test all equipment before taking it to the remote location.

Shooting outdoors

When shooting outdoors, the production environment is determined by the specific EFP location. All you can do is decide which portions of the environment you want to show.

WEATHER When outdoors you are at the mercy of the elements. Always be prepared for bad weather. As mentioned previously, take raincoats along for the cameras (a plastic tarp will do in a pinch) and rain gear for the crew. As old-fashioned as it may seem, a large umbrella is still one of the most effective means of keeping rain off of people and equipment.

If you move from a chilly outside location to indoors, let the camcorder or VTR warm up a bit. The extreme temperature change could cause condensation in the recording section, shutting down its operation automatically. Such a shutdown will certainly put a crimp in the production schedule. In extremely cold weather, zoom lenses and even the video-recording transport in camcorders have a tendency to stick. Keep the camera in a vehicle and run the camcorder for a while when it is exposed to the cold temperature to prevent the lens and the recording mechanism from sticking. If possible, take a car-battery-powered hair dryer along to speed up the defrosting. Some mics refuse to work properly in extremely low temperatures unless protected by a windscreen and/or windsock. Always have a backup plan in case it rains or snows.

Most important, watch the weather for shot continuity. If video-recording a brief scene of two people talking to each other requires several takes that stretch over an hour or so, you may have a cloudless sky as the background for the first few takes and a cloudy one for the last takes. The sudden appearance of clouds or rain between question and answer does not exactly contribute to good continuity. So long as you are aware of the problem, you can try to choose a background that does not show the time progression, or arrange the shooting schedule so that the time change does not jeopardize postproduction editing.

FOREGROUND   With a prominent foreground piece in the shot—a tree, fence post, mailbox, or traffic sign—you can dramatically improve the scene, make the composition more dynamic, and give it depth. If there is no natural foreground piece, you can often plant one. Instead of looking for a convenient foreground tree, you can simply handhold and dip a tree branch into the shot. The viewer's mind will fill in the rest and perceive the whole tree.

BACKGROUND   Always look beyond the main action to the background to avoid odd juxtapositions between foreground and background. You must also be careful to maintain background continuity in postproduction editing. For instance, if you show a prominent tree in the background of shot 1 but not in the following shot with the same background, the tree will seem to have mysteriously disappeared when the two shots are edited together. An alert editor will probably rule against such an edit.

Jump cuts can be caused not only by slight position changes of the foreground pieces but also by a background shift. To avoid background jump cuts, try to keep a prominent horizon line or an especially conspicuous background object, such as the single tree on a distant hill, in the same screen portion in subsequent shots. ZVL3 CUE 4 ▸
CAMERA→ Composition→ background

> ▶ **KEY CONCEPT**
>
> Watch the weather and the background for shot continuity when shooting outdoors.

Shooting indoors   When shooting indoors you may have to rearrange the furnishings and (more often) the pictures on the wall to get optimal shots. Always make a record of what the room looks like (by drawing a sketch, photographing the scene with a digital still camera, or videotaping the room with a camcorder) before you start moving things around. Such a record will greatly assist you in putting things back where they belong.

LIGHTING   Be especially aware of the specific lighting requirements. Again, check the available outlets. Be careful when placing lights inside a room. Do not overload the circuits. Turn off the lights whenever you don't need them. Sandbag all light stands and make a heat shield out of aluminum foil, especially when a lighting instrument is close to curtains, upholstered furniture, books, or other combustible materials.

Even on a cloudy or foggy day, the color temperature of the light coming through an outside window is considerably higher than that of indoor light. ZVL3 CUE 5 ▸LIGHTS→ Field→ indoor In this case, you must decide whether to boost the color temperature of the indoor light or lower the color temperature of the daylight coming through the window. It is usually simpler to gel the indoor lights than the window. ZVL3 CUE 6 ▸LIGHTS→ Color temperature→ white balance

AUDIO   Except for simple interviews, good audio always seems to be a bigger problem than good video. This is because the microphones are often placed at the last minute without adequate consideration of the acoustics of the room or the specific sound pickup requirements. You should include a brief audio rehearsal in the EFP production schedule so you can listen to the sound pickup before beginning the video recording. If you have brought along several types of mics, you can choose the one that sounds best in that environment.

As you recall, it is better to record the principal sounds and the ambient sounds on separate videotape tracks (or other media) rather than mix them in the field. You may find, however, that this separation is difficult, if not impossible, in most EFP situations. In this case, try to record a good portion of the background sounds without the principal sounds after the scenes have been recorded. If necessary, you can then mix the background sounds into the scene during postproduction. If careful mixing between foreground and background sounds is required, you can do it much better in the postproduction studio. If you mix the sounds in the field, you pretty much eliminate the option of further adjustment in postproduction.

General production reminders   Very much like certain routines developed for the studio—striking the sets, rolling up the cables, putting the cameras back in their regular parking places, and sweeping the floor—there are some general guidelines for EFP.

RESPECTING PROPERTY   Whenever you are on someone else's property, be mindful that you are a guest and are actually intruding with your video gear and production people. Working in video does not give you a special license to invade people's homes, upset their routines, or make unreasonable demands on them. When you shoot a documentary in somebody's well-kept garden, don't trample on carefully tended flowers or other plants just to get a good camera position. Dragging equipment dollies or camera cases along polished floors or valuable rugs is not appreciated by the owner. Even if pressed for time, do not get so caught up in the production activities that you lose your common sense.

SAFETY   As in studio productions, you need to be constantly aware of proper safety precautions. Don't be careless with extension cords, especially if you string them outside in damp weather. Tape all connections so that they become waterproof and don't pull apart. If you have to lay cables across corridors or doorways, tape them down with gaffer's tape and put a rug or rubber mat over them. Better yet, try to string them above so that people can walk below them unhindered. Ask the police to assist you when shooting along a freeway or in downtown traffic.

LOGGING   During the shoot keep an accurate field log of all takes, good or bad. Label all recording media and boxes and put them in a container used solely for transporting the video-recorded material. Activate the cassette protection devices so that the source tapes cannot be accidentally erased. Keep the hard drive cassettes and flash drives away from magnetic fields.

PUTTING THINGS BACK AND CLEANING UP   Put everything back the way you found it. As mentioned earlier, consult the record you made (digital still camera shot) of where things were before you rearranged them. When you are finished, verify that everything is back where you found it. Remove all gaffer's tape that you may have used to tape down cables, pick up all extension cords, sandbags, and especially empty soft drink cans and other lunch remnants. An EFP team that had finally gained access to an old and venerable family ranch after weeks of pleading by the show's producer was invited back with a smile for the follow-up show because one of the production people had brought along a broom and swept the area clean.

LOADING THE EQUIPMENT   When loading the equipment onto the remote vehicle after the shoot, pull out the checklist again. Check off every item that is loaded up for the return trip. Look for missing items right away; it is usually easier to find them right after the production than days or weeks later. Check that all source tapes or other recording media are properly labeled and that the field logs match the labels. Keep them close to you until you return to home base.

Postproduction: Wrap-up

The first order of business is to make protection copies of all source material. If necessary, you can combine this dubbing with making VHS window dubs. You now need to review the copies of the source footage and prepare an accurate editing log. Recall that such a log must list all shots by in- and out-numbers, identify good and bad takes, indicate predominant vectors, and list the principal audio for each shot. Then it is up to the postproduction people to put it all together into a comprehensive message that ideally will convey the intended program objective.

BIG REMOTES

While learning basic video production, you will probably not be called upon to participate in a big remote, but you should have at least some idea of what a remote is all about and what equipment it requires. A *big remote* is the field production of a large, scheduled event done for live transmission or the uninterrupted recording of the live event.

Big remotes are devoted to the coverage of major events that are not staged specifically for video (at least not obviously); these include parades, sporting events, significant international occasions, and political gatherings. Big remotes resemble multicamera studio productions in every respect, except that the "studio" is now a remote location: the plaza in front of city hall, the sports stadium, or the Senate chambers.

All big remotes use high-quality field cameras (studio cameras with lenses that can zoom from an extreme long shot to a tight close-up) and EFP cameras, which are normally connected to the remote truck by cable. The *remote truck* represents a compact studio control room and equipment room. It contains an image control center with preview and line monitors; a switcher with special effects; a character generator (C.G.); various intercom systems (P.L., P.A., and elaborate I.F.B. systems); an audio control center with a fairly large audio console, digital audio-recording and playback equipment, monitor speakers, and an intercom; a video-recording center with several high-quality VTRs or other recording media that can handle regular recordings as well as instant replays, slow-motion, and freeze-frames; and a technical center with CCUs (camera control units), technical setup equipment, and patchbays for camera, audio, intercom, and light cables. **SEE 15.6**

Although remote trucks can draw power from available high-capacity electrical sources, most engineers prefer to use portable generators. Because big remotes

15.6 Remote Truck

The remote truck is a studio control center on wheels. It contains the program, audio, and video control centers; a number of VTRs; and transmission equipment.

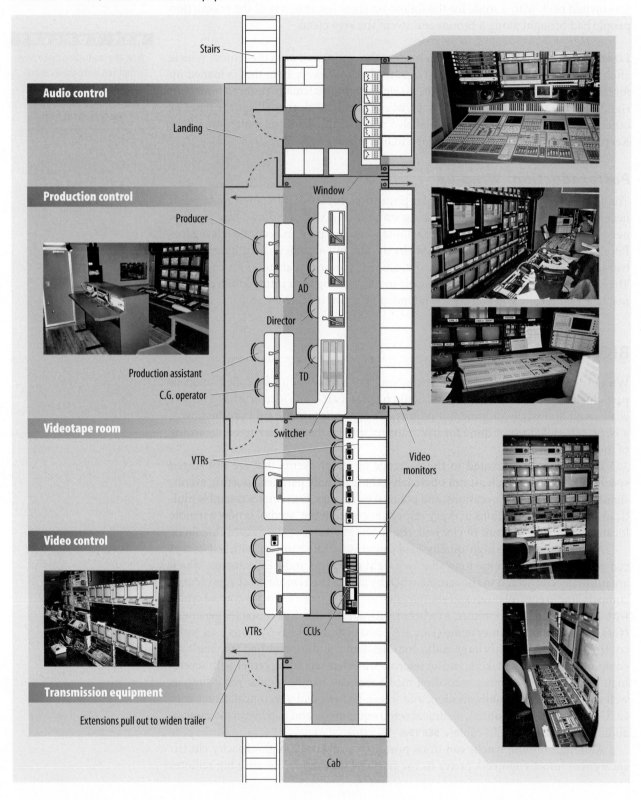

Stairs

Audio control

Landing

Production control

Window

Producer

AD

Director

Production assistant

TD

C.G. operator

Videotape room

Switcher

VTRs

Video monitors

Video control

VTRs

CCUs

Transmission equipment

Extensions pull out to widen trailer

Cab

are often done live, remote trucks have microwave transmission facilities that range from small links from camera to truck, to larger ones that transmit the signal from truck to transmitter. Some large remote trucks have their own satellite uplink; others connect to an uplink truck if a direct satellite feed is necessary. In very big remotes, one or more additional trailers may be used for supplemental production and control equipment, such as instant-replay facilities.

SYNTHETIC ENVIRONMENTS

Not all environments are lens-generated (photographed by the video camera); they can be synthetic as well. ***Synthetic environments*** are generated electronically.

You can create a great variety of backgrounds with a chroma key, which you recall uses a specific color (usually blue or green) for the backdrop into which various still or moving images can be keyed. The actual foreground action then appears to be playing in the keyed environment. Because you can use any photograph, video recording, or computer-generated effect as a chroma-key source, your choices of background are unlimited.   **SEE 15.7**

15.7 **Chroma Key**

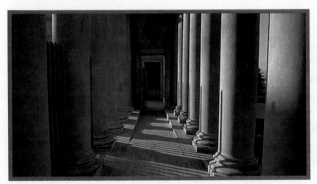

A The source for this background image is a video frame of the museum exterior from the ESS file.

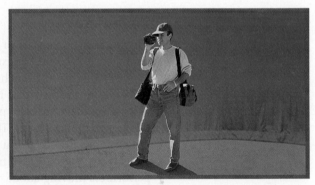

B The studio camera focuses on the actor playing a tourist in front of the blue chroma-key backdrop. The lighting must match the environment of the background.

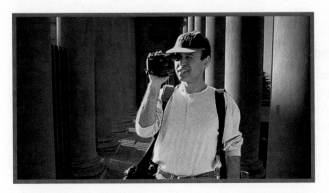

C All blue areas are replaced by the background image; the tourist appears to be in front of the museum.

Computer-generated Settings

Despite all the skills you may have acquired in adapting a real environment to your video needs, the computer offers novel alternatives. Indoor sets, or at least parts of sets, can be keyed in through various blue-screen techniques or computer-generated in postproduction. As you can see in figure 15.8, the two chairs that were photographed in front of some softwall flats in a television studio have now been transported through the skills of a computer artist into an elegant interior setting. You can, of course, use the same technique to put a real desk and chair into a computer-generated office. A favorite use of computer-generated sets is to "lay in" the ceilings and floor coverings of studio sets in postproduction. That way the camera travel and the lighting remain unrestricted during the production. **SEE 15.8**

If all this is possible, couldn't we generate the whole set, with the actors moving about in front of a chroma-key backdrop? Yes, this is certainly possible. You would, of course, need real set props (such as tables and chairs) for the actors to sit on and lean against. There is also the problem of a changing perspective when the real foreground figures (the actors) move against the static background, although sophisticated computer programs can compensate for such a perspective shift. The real problem with such a setup is not technical but human: it is extremely difficult for even experienced actors to operate in a horizonless, undefined space. You can get easily disoriented simply by stepping into such a limitless blue-screen environment.

Virtual Reality

Virtual reality consists of computer-generated environments and events that are animated. You could, for example, change the peaceful scene of vacationers traveling happily along a sun-drenched country road into a frightening event by replacing the fluffy white clouds with a huge computer-generated twister. You can also generate objects, animals, or even people and place them in, or have them move through, this virtual environment. There are synthetic environments that appear to be three-dimensional, provided you wear 3-D glasses when viewing the video screen.

Whenever you combine a blue-screen or virtual reality environment with real performers moving about, you must pay particular attention to the lighting so that the shadows of the synthetic environment correspond to the ones in the actual scene. The size and motion relationships between foreground and background are also a major concern. Unless you want to achieve a special effect, the synthetic environment should fit the dimensions of the people keyed into it and change according to the camera angles.

Computer-controlled Environments

There are programs that produce from a floor plan an actual scenic environment. Once the virtual scenery is set up, you can try out a number of color schemes and textures for the walls, doors, windows, and floor. For example, you can try out a blue rug, change it to red or beige, and take it out again—all with the click of a mouse. You can also put virtual furniture into the set and dress it with properties of your choice. You use the mouse to select the items from a menu and drag them into the desired positions. If you don't like what you selected, simply delete the images and try new ones.

15.8 **Computer-generated Set**

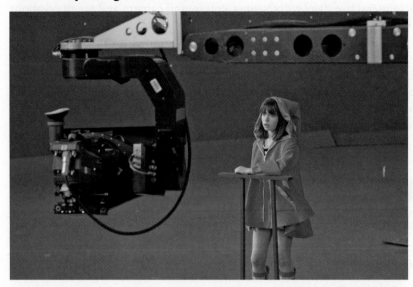

A The blue areas of this actual set, including the armrest, will be keyed out and replaced by a computer-generated set. The electronic cinema camera is on a computer-controlled mount to exactly match the moves of the virtual camera.

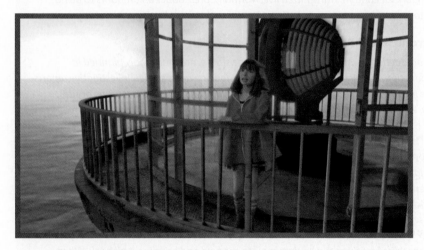

B The finished effect places the actor in a convincingly realistic location while the camera pans across the scene.

Other such programs let you light the set, with a menu offering an assortment of lighting instruments that you can drag onto the set and aim at the elements of the virtual production environment. You can test different lighting setups until you are satisfied. Finally, you can have a virtual camera move through this virtual space to show you what shots you can get from various angles and lens settings. Some sophisticated programs let you generate virtual performers and move them through the synthetic space.

Even if you do not use the virtual sets as the "actual" environment for your production, such interactive displays of setups, colors, and camera and talent positions are an invaluable preproduction aid.

When combined with live action, the virtual environments can create startling effects. The availability of high-speed desktop computers and hard drives brings virtual reality environments into your nonlinear editing system. The marriage of television and computers yields a wealth of picture and sound information that you can use in your productions. All you need now is a thorough knowledge of video basics and plenty of imagination.

MAIN POINTS

▶ **Field Production**

A field production is any production that happens outside the studio, including ENG (electronic news gathering), EFP (electronic field production), and big-remote telecasts.

▶ **Electronic News Gathering**

This process involves newspeople and equipment for reacting quickly to a developing news event. The event is either videotaped and edited for a regularly scheduled broadcast or, if important enough, transmitted live. Normally, preproduction amounts to being ready to go anywhere at a moment's notice rather than conducting a remote survey.

▶ **Electronic Field Production**

These productions, which occur away from the studio, are thoroughly planned in preproduction. EFPs include documentaries, magazine news stories, investigative reports, on-site interviews, and so on. One of the most important steps is the remote, or site, survey. When in the field, you must adapt to the environment.

▶ **Preproduction**

A remote survey is necessary for all field productions except ENG. It supplies important information about such technical aspects as power availability, lighting, and sound requirements, and it gives the director an idea of where to place the camera or cameras. Establishing a reliable contact person is an important part of preproduction.

▶ **Production**

Use a checklist for taking the equipment into the field and bringing it all back. When shooting outdoors, changing weather conditions and random sounds are a constant hazard and must be carefully monitored. Be aware of changing lighting conditions, which may seriously influence your editing continuity. Be careful not to place lighting instruments too close to combustible materials. Respect people's property and take safety precautions at all times. Carefully monitor the audio pickup.

► **Big Remotes**

Big remotes are devoted to the live coverage or the video-recording of large scheduled events, such as parades, sports, and significant international occasions. Big remotes resemble multicamera studio setups and are coordinated from the remote truck. The remote truck houses a complete production control room, primarily devoted to image control, audio control, elaborate intercom facilities, video-recording and video control sections, various other technical facilities, and transmission equipment.

► **Synthetic Environments**

Environments can be electronically generated through chroma keys of computer-generated backgrounds. Interactive virtual reality programs can create entirely synthetic, computer-generated environments. Some programs can also simulate certain production situations (camera positions, scenery colors, or lighting), which can be manipulated to find the most effective combinations. Such a simulation is a valuable preproduction aid.

Z E T T L ' S   V I D E O L A B   3 . 0

For your reference, or to track your work, the Zettl's VideoLab 3.0 program cues in this chapter are listed here with their corresponding page numbers.

ZVL3 CUE 1 LIGHTS→ Field→ outdoor | use of reflectors   **318**

ZVL3 CUE 2 LIGHTS→ Color temperature→ light sources   **320**

ZVL3 CUE 3 LIGHTS→ Field→ indoor   **325**

ZVL3 CUE 4 CAMERA→ Composition→ background   **327**

ZVL3 CUE 5 LIGHTS→ Field→ indoor   **327**

ZVL3 CUE 6 LIGHTS→ Color temperature→ white balance   **327**

Production Control:
Talent and Directing

Now that you have acquired the basics of video production, you need to learn more about the people who work in *front* of the camera—the *talent*—and what they must do to convey the intended message. It is, after all, the people who appear on-camera who do the communicating with the viewers, not the ones who work behind the scenes to make this communication possible. Even if you don't intend to become a television performer or actor, you need to know what performing in front of the camera is all about. Once you are in video production, you are bound to be asked to appear on-camera from time to time, as either a guest or a host. And as a director, before you can tell the talent what to do, you must have some idea of what to expect from a good performer or actor. The last two chapters prepare you for the culminating experience of multicamera directing from the control room and for single-camera film-style directing.

KEY TERMS

actor A person who appears on-camera in dramatic roles. The actor always portrays someone else.

blocking Carefully worked-out positioning, movement, and actions by the talent and for all mobile video equipment used in a scene.

cue card A large hand-lettered card that contains copy, usually held next to the camera lens by floor personnel.

foundation A makeup base, normally done with water-soluble pancake makeup, that is applied with a sponge to the face and sometimes to all exposed skin areas. Pancake foundation reduces unwanted light reflection.

I.F.B. Stands for *interruptible foldback* or *feedback*. A prompting system that allows communication with the talent while on the air. A small earpiece worn by on-the-air talent that carries program sound (including the talent's voice) or instructions from the producer or director.

moiré effect Color vibrations that occur when narrow, contrasting stripes of a design interfere with the scanning lines of the video system.

performer A person who appears on-camera in nondramatic shows. The performer does not assume someone else's character.

talent Collective name for all performers and actors who appear regularly in video.

teleprompter A prompting device that projects moving copy over the lens so that the talent can read it without losing eye contact with the viewer.

Talent, Clothing, and Makeup

The incredible amount of equipment and effort that goes into making even a relatively simple production, such as somebody's announcing on-camera the latest company news, is generally lost on viewers. All they judge the show by is whether the person on-screen is likable and whether he or she is doing a credible job. Similarly, viewers attribute the success of a talk show primarily to the host, not to how it is lighted, how the cameras are handled, or whether the director shows a reaction shot at the right moment.

Video *talent* refers (not always accurately) to all people performing in front of the camera. We divide talent into two groups: performers and actors. **Performers** are primarily engaged in nondramatic activities. They portray themselves and do not assume the role of other characters; they are aware of the viewers and usually communicate directly with them by addressing the camera lens. **Actors**, on the other hand, always portray someone else; they assume a character role, even if the role is close to their own personality. They normally do not acknowledge the presence of the viewers but interact with other actors. Because performance and acting requirements differ in several major ways, they are discussed separately here. Specifically, this chapter focuses on the techniques of appearing in front of the camera, what to wear, and how to do basic makeup for the television camera.

> ►**KEY CONCEPT**
>
> *Talent* refers to video performers and actors. Performers portray themselves; actors portray someone else.

▶ **PERFORMING TECHNIQUES**
Performer and camera, audio and lighting, and timing and prompting

▶ **ACTING TECHNIQUES**
Environment and audience, close-ups, and repeating action

▶ **AUDITIONS**
How to prepare

▶ **CLOTHING**
Texture, detail, and color

▶ **MAKEUP**
Technical requirements and materials

PERFORMING TECHNIQUES

As a performer you are always aware of the viewers. Your goal is to establish as much rapport as possible with them and to have them share in what you do and say. Because video is normally watched by individuals or small groups of people who know one another, your performance techniques must be adjusted to this kind of communication intimacy. Always imagine that you are looking at and talking with someone you know, seated comfortably a short distance from you. Some performers prefer to imagine that they are talking to a small group or family; in any case, don't envision yourself at a mass rally, addressing "millions of people out there in videoland." When viewers watch you at home, it is you who is "out there"—not they. They are not visiting you; you are visiting them.

To help you establish this intimate viewer contact and perform effectively in front of the camera, you need to familiarize yourself with some production aspects of performer and camera, audio and lighting, and timing and prompting.

Performer and Camera

As a performer you have a communication partner: the video camera. It represents the viewer with whom you are talking. You may find it difficult at first to consider the camera your communication partner, especially when all you actually see while talking is the camera or the screen of the prompting device, some lights shining in your eyes, and perhaps the dim outlines of a few production people who are more interested in operating the equipment than in what you have to say.

Eye contact   To establish eye contact with the viewer, you need to look at the *lens*, not at the camera operator or the floor manager. In fact, good performers keep constant eye contact with the lens and seem to look *through* it, rather than merely at it. When pretending to look through the lens, you will more readily extend your glance through the screen—toward the viewer—than if you simply stare at the camera. Also, you must maintain eye contact with the lens much more directly and constantly than when engaged in a real interpersonal conversation. Even a small glance away from the lens will be highly distracting for the viewer; it will not be seen as a polite relief from your stare but as an impolite loss of concentration or interest on your part.

If two or more cameras are used while you demonstrate a product, you need to know which of the two will remain on you and which will take the close-up of the product. Keep looking at the camera (or, rather, through the camera lens) that is focused on you, even when the director switches to the close-up camera that is focused on the product. This way you will not get caught looking in the wrong direction when your camera is switched back on the air.

If both cameras are on you and switched according to the director's cues, you must shift your view from one camera to the other to maintain eye contact. A good floor manager will assist you greatly in this task. He or she will warn you that a switch is coming up by pointing on the director's "ready" cue to the camera you are addressing and then motioning you over to the other camera on the "take" cue. On the floor manager's cue, shift your glance quickly but smoothly in the new direction. Unless told otherwise, always follow the floor manager's cues (shown in figure 16.1) and not the tally light that indicates the hot camera.

If you discover that you are talking to the wrong camera, look down as if to collect your thoughts, then look up into the on-the-air camera. Such a shift works especially well if you use notes or a script as part of your on-camera performance. You can simply pretend that you are consulting your notes while changing your view from the wrong camera to the correct one.

Close-ups   On video you will be shown more often in a close-up than a medium or long shot. The camera scrutinizes and magnifies your expressions and your every move. It does not politely look away when you scratch your ear or touch your nose; it reveals faithfully the nervous twitch or mild panic when you have forgotten a line. The close-up also does not give you much room to maneuver. In a tight close-up, a slight wiggle of the product you are holding will look as though an earthquake has struck. The close-up also accelerates your actions. If you lift up a book at normal speed to show its cover, you will most certainly yank it out of the close-up camera's view. Here are a few important rules for working with close-ups:

▶ When on a close-up, do not wiggle—remain as steady as possible.

▶ Keep your hands away from your face, even if you feel your nose itching or perspiration collecting on your forehead.

▶ Slow down all movements.

▶ When demonstrating small objects, keep them as steady as possible in one position. Better yet, keep them on a display table.

▶ If they are arranged on a table, do not pick them up. You can point to them or tilt them a little to give the camera a better view.

There is nothing more frustrating for the camera operator, the director, and especially the viewer than a performer who snatches the object off the table just as the camera gets a good close-up of it. A quick look at the studio monitor will tell you whether you are holding or tilting the object for maximum visibility.

Also, don't ask the camera to come a little closer to get a better look at what you are demonstrating. As you well know, the camera operator can get a close-up not just by dollying in with the camera but much more quickly and easily by zooming in. You will not make the director very happy by asking for specific shots when the shot is already on the air or when there are technical problems that prevent the director from calling up the desired material. Talent—however eager they may be to look good on the air—should not try to outdirect the director.

Audio and Lighting

A clear, resonant voice alone will not make you a good performer. Besides having something to say and saying it clearly and convincingly, you need to be aware of the audio requirements.

Microphone techniques   At this point you should briefly review the use of microphones in chapter 7. Here is a short recap of the basic microphone techniques of concern to you as a performer:

▶ Treat all microphones gently. They are not props but highly sensitive electronic devices that respond to minute vibrations of air.

▶ If you work with a *lavaliere microphone,* don't forget to put it on. If not assisted by the floor manager, run the cable underneath your jacket or shirt and fasten the mic to the outside of your clothing. Unless you are wearing a wireless lavaliere, once "wired" you have a highly limited action radius. Don't forget to remove the mic and lay it gently on the chair before walking off the set. When using a wireless mic, check the power switch on the transmitter belt pack. It should be on when going on the air but off whenever you are on a break.

▶ When using a *hand mic,* see how far the mic cable will let you move. In normal situations hold the hand mic chest high and speak *across* it, not into it. In noisy surroundings hold it closer to your mouth. When interviewing a guest with a hand mic, hold it near you when speaking and toward the guest when he or she responds. Gently pull the mic cable with your free hand when moving around. If you need both hands for something else, tuck the mic under your arm. A wireless hand mic will make your movements less restricted but will add some liabilities of losing the mic signal on its way to the receiving station. Unless you are in a controlled environment, such as a television or recording studio, stay away from wireless hand mics.

▶ Once a *desk mic* has been placed by the audio engineer, don't move it. Check with the engineer if you think it should be closer to you or pointing more toward you. Talk toward it, not away from it.

▶ When using a *stand mic,* adjust the height of the stand so that the mic is a little below your chin, pointing toward your mouth.

▶ When a *fishpole* or *boom mic* is used, be aware of where the mic is when you are moving, but don't look at it. Move slowly and avoid fast turns. If you see that the boom operator can't follow you with the mic, stop, then move on when the problem is fixed.

Taking a level   When asked to test the mic or to take a level, don't blow into it; say your opening remarks at the volume you will use when on the air. Performers who rapidly count to ten or speak with a low voice off the air and then blast their opening remarks when on the air will not win points with the audio engineer.

Do not speak louder simply because the camera moves farther away from you. Although you correctly assume that the camera is the viewer with whom you are communicating, the camera distance has nothing to do with how close the shot actually is. More important, the distance of the camera has nothing to do with how close the mic is. If you wear a lavaliere, you are heard at the same level and with the same presence regardless of whether the camera is 2 or 200 feet away from you.

Checking lighting   Although as a performer you need not be concerned with lighting, it doesn't hurt to quickly check the lighting before going on the air. When outdoors, don't stand against a brightly lighted background unless you want to be seen in silhouette. When in the studio and there is no light hitting your eyes, you are not in the lighted area. Ask the director where you should stand so that you will be

> ▶ **KEY CONCEPT**
>
> When taking a level, speak at the volume you will actually use during the performance, and speak long enough to set the optimal level on the audio console.

properly lighted. In a play, when you happen to get off the rehearsed blocking into a dark area, move a little until you feel the heat of the lights or see the lights hitting you. Such concern for lighting should not encourage you to take over the director's function. Always check with the director if you have any questions about the technical setup and your activities within it.

Timing and Prompting

As a performer you need to be acutely aware of time, whether or not you're on the air. Even nonbroadcast video programs are packaged according to a rigid time frame. Because the audience has no idea about your time restrictions, you need to appear relaxed and unhurried even if you have only 2 seconds left or you have to fill unexpectedly for an additional 15 seconds. Experienced performers can accurately judge a 10-second or 30-second duration without looking at a clock or stopwatch. Radio professionals can teach you a lot in this respect. They seem to be totally relaxed and never hurried, even when working up to the last second of the segment. Such timing skills are not inborn but acquired through practice. Don't put too much trust in your instincts; use a clock or stopwatch for precise timing. In any case, respond immediately to the floor manager's time cues.

I.F.B. system   As a performer you must rely on—or put up with—a variety of *prompting devices*. The most direct prompting device is the ***I.F.B.***—*interruptible foldback* or, as it is also called, *interruptible feedback*—system. You have probably seen performers or interview guests in remote locations touch their ear as though they were adjusting a hearing aid. That is exactly what they are doing.

When using interruptible foldback, you wear a small earpiece that carries the total program sound, including your own remarks, unless the producer or director (or some other production member connected to the I.F.B. system) interrupts the program sound with specific instructions. For example, if you interview the CEO of a new Internet company, the producer may cut in and tell you what question to ask next, to slow down, to speed up, or to tell the guest that she has only 15 seconds to explain the latest multiplatform software. The trick is to not let the viewer know that you are listening to somebody other than the guest.

If you conduct an interview long-distance, with the guest in a remote location, he or she may also wear an I.F.B. earpiece that transmits your questions on a separate I.F.B. channel. You may find that many guests experience some problem with the I.F.B. system, especially when the location is relatively noisy. Try to test the I.F.B. system in advance to make sure the guest is comfortable using it.

Floor manager's cues   Normal *time, directional,* and *audio cues* are usually given by the floor manager. As a performer you will quickly learn that the floor manager is your best friend during the production. A good floor manager will always be in your vicinity, telling you whether you are too slow or fast, whether you are holding the product correctly for the close-up camera, and whether you are doing a good job. Unlike other prompting devices, the floor manager can react immediately to your needs and to unforeseen performance problems. Normally, the floor manager cues you through a variety of hand signals. **SEE 16.1**

16.1 Floor Manager's Cues

Because the microphone is live during production, the talent must rely on visual time, directional, and audio cues from the floor manager.

CUE	SIGNAL	MEANING	SIGNAL DESCRIPTION
TIME CUES			
Standby		Show about to start.	Extends hand above head.
Cue		Show goes on the air.	Points to performer or live camera.
On time		Go ahead as planned (on the nose).	Touches nose with forefinger.
Speed up		Accelerate what you are doing. You are going too slowly.	Rotates hand clockwise with extended forefinger. Urgency of speed-up is indicated by fast or slow rotation.
Stretch		Slow down. Too much time left. Fill until emergency is over.	Stretches imaginary rubber band between hands.

16.1 **Floor Manager's Cues** (continued)

CUE	SIGNAL	MEANING	SIGNAL DESCRIPTION
TIME CUES			
Wind up		Finish up what you are doing. Come to an end.	Similar motion to speed-up, but usually with arm extended above head. Sometimes expressed with raised fist, good-bye wave, or hands rolling over each other as if wrapping a package.
Cut		Stop speech or action immediately.	Pulls index finger in knifelike motion across throat.
5 (4, 3, 2, 1) minute(s)		5 (4, 3, 2, 1) minute(s) left until end of show.	Holds up five (four, three, two, one) finger(s) or small card with number on it.
Half minute		30 seconds left in show.	Forms a cross with two index fingers or arms. Or holds card with number.
15 seconds		15 seconds left in show.	Shows fist (which can also mean wind up). Or holds card with number.
Roll VTR (and countdown) 2, 1, take VTR		VTR is rolling. Tape is coming up.	Holds extended left hand in front of face, moves right hand in cranking motion. Extends two, one finger(s); clenches fist or gives cut signal.

16.1 **Floor Manager's Cues** (continued)

CUE	SIGNAL	MEANING	SIGNAL DESCRIPTION
DIRECTIONAL CUES			
Closer		Performer must come closer or bring object closer to camera.	Moves both hands toward self, palms in.
Back		Performer must step back or move object away from camera.	Uses both hands in pushing motion, palms out.
Walk		Performer must move to next performance area.	Makes a walking motion with index and middle fingers in direction of movement.
Stop		Stop right here. Do not move anymore.	Extends both hands in front of body, palms out.
OK		Very well done. Stay right there. Do what you are doing.	Forms an *O* with thumb and forefinger, other fingers extended, motioning toward talent.

16.1 Floor Manager's Cues *(continued)*

CUE	SIGNAL	MEANING	SIGNAL DESCRIPTION
AUDIO CUES			
Speak up		Performer is talking too softly for current conditions.	Cups both hands behind ears or moves hand upward, palm up.
Tone down		Performer is too loud or too enthusiastic for the occasion.	Moves both hands toward studio floor, palms down, or puts extended forefinger over mouth in *shhh*-like motion.
Closer to mic		Performer is too far away from mic for good audio pickup.	Moves hand toward face.
Keep talking		Keep on talking until further cues.	Extends thumb and forefinger horizontally, moving them like a bird's beak.

As a performer you must react to the floor manager's cues immediately, even if you think that the cue is inappropriate. Good performers don't try to run the show all by themselves: they react to the floor manager's cues quickly and smoothly.

Don't look around for the floor manager when you think that you should have received a time cue; he or she will make sure that you see the signal without having to break eye contact with the lens. As you just learned, even a brief glance away from the lens will tend to interrupt the contact you have established with the viewer. Once you have seen a cue, don't acknowledge it in any way. The floor manager can tell by your subsequent actions whether you received the cue.

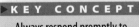

► KEY CONCEPT

Always respond promptly to the floor manager's cues.

16.2 Teleprompter

The teleprompter consists of a small video monitor that reflects the copy onto a slanted glass plate directly in front of the lens. The talent can see the copy clearly while it remains invisible to the camera.

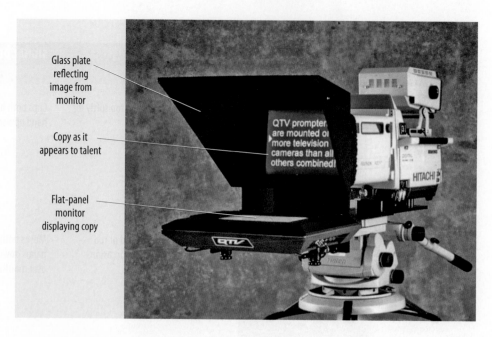

Glass plate reflecting image from monitor

Copy as it appears to talent

Flat-panel monitor displaying copy

Teleprompter   The *teleprompter* makes it possible for you to read copy without taking your eyes off the lens. The teleprompter projects the copy off a small, usually flat-panel monitor onto a glass plate mounted directly in front of the lens. **SEE 16.2** While you read the copy on the glass plate, the lens can view the scene through the plate without seeing the lettering. All newscasters and hosts of shows with a newslike format use teleprompters, as do people who deliver on-camera speeches. The copy itself is normally generated by a word-processing program and sent by a desktop computer to the teleprompter monitor on each camera that focuses on you. The computer scrolls the copy from the bottom of the teleprompter screen to the top exactly at your reading speed. If you have to change your pace to stay within the allotted time, the scrolling speed can be adjusted accordingly.

When you are using a teleprompter, the camera should be far enough away that the viewers don't see your eyes moving back and forth while reading yet close enough that you can clearly see the copy. Experienced performers still manage to look through the lens and make eye contact with the viewer even while reading the copy in front of the lens.

For the small teleprompters that can be used in the field, the copy originates from a laptop computer that also controls the speed of the scroll. Simple field prompters use a paper roll that projects hand-lettered copy over a glass plate in front of the lens. On some field prompters, paper roll is mounted below or to the side of the lens. The roll is battery-powered and can be adjusted to various speeds. If nothing else is available, use white sheets of posterboard for the copy and hold them low enough that you can read the copy just out of camera range.

Cue cards   One of the simplest yet most highly effective cueing devices is *cue cards*—sheets of paper or posterboard on which the copy is hand-lettered with a marker. The size of the cards depends on how well you can see and how far away the

16.3 **Handling Cue Cards**

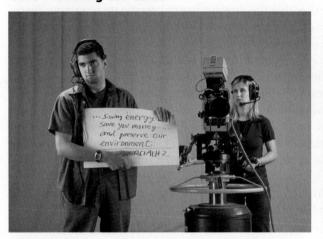

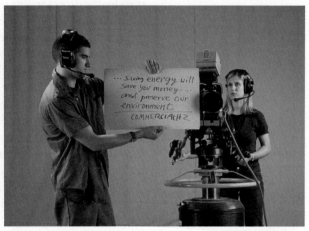

A This is the wrong way to hold cue cards. The card is too far away from the lens. The floor person is also covering part of the copy, is not reading along with the talent, and is therefore unable to change cards when necessary.

B This is the correct way to hold cue cards. The cards are as close to the lens as possible, and the floor person reads along with the talent to facilitate smooth card changes.

camera is when you're reading the copy. A floor person must hold the cards as close to the lens as possible so that you don't have to glance too far away and thereby lose eye contact with the viewer. You must read the copy out of the corner of your eye while looking at the lens. Decide on an optimal distance, then check that the cards are in the right order and that the floor person holds them close to the lens without covering the copy. **SEE 16.3** Ask the floor person to practice changing cards with you. A good floor person will change the card while you are reading the last few words and have the new card up while you are still delivering the last word from the previous card. He or she will not dump the used cards on the floor, but put them quickly and quietly on a nearby chair.

ACTING TECHNIQUES

To become a good video or television actor, you must first learn the art of acting. Whereas performers always portray themselves, actors assume somebody else's character and personality. Even the best stage and film actors must adjust their acting style and methods to the specific requirements of the video medium. Some of the major requirements are working in a technical environment without an audience, adjusting to the small video screen and the frequent use of close-ups, and repeating the action.

Environment and Audience

As a video actor, you will be surrounded by much more technical equipment than if you were on-stage. Worse, you do not have an audience whose reaction you can see or feel. Unless there is a studio audience, all you see are lights, cameras, and production people who do not pay much attention to you. In fact, you will often feel neglected even by the director. But realize that the director has to coordinate numerous pieces of production equipment and a great many personnel and that some of the technical operations may need more of the director's attention than you do.

You may feel even more abandoned because of the lack of a live audience. Unlike in the theater, where the audience remains in a fixed place and gives you direct and indirect feedback, the camera does not respond to your performance but stares at you impassively and moves quietly all around you. It may look at your eyes, your back, your feet, your hands, or whatever the director chooses for the viewer to see. It is a little like acting for theater-in-the-round, except that in video all viewers, as represented by the cameras, sit at arm's length and even join you on-stage to get a better look at you.

Because the viewer is in such close virtual proximity, you need not, and should not, project your actions and emotions to somebody sitting in the last row. The camera, which is doing the projecting for you, can make a small gesture into a grand act. When on a close-up, there is no need for you to act out your role; instead you must *feel* it. Internalizing your role is a key factor in acting for video.

The intimacy of video also influences the way you speak. You must reduce the customary stage declamation and voice projection to clear but normal speech. Good writers help you in this task. Instead of having you, as Oedipus, dramatically request, "Who planned the crime, aye, and performed it, too?" on video you would simply ask, "Who did it?" Getting rid of exaggerated voice projection is one of the hardest things for stage actors to learn when switching over to the video medium. Precise enunciation is often more important than volume and projection.

Most important, you must be able to memorize your lines quickly and accurately. Although there may be a variety of prompting devices available (mainly cue cards), you cannot and should not rely on them if you want to be convincing in your role. Because many of your lines serve as important video and audio cues that trigger all sorts of production activity, you cannot afford to ad-lib. Ad-libbing a cue line will inevitably cause chaos in the control room and prompt a retake of the scene.

► **KEY CONCEPT**

When acting for the video medium, you must feel the role rather than act it out.

Close-ups

The frequent use of close-ups does not give you much wiggle room. Sometimes you must stand uncomfortably close to other actors or move much more slowly than normal without appearing to do so to stay within camera range. The close-up also limits your gestures. If, when seated, you lean back or move forward unexpectedly, you may fall out of focus, and weaving sideways just a little may take you right out of the frame.

The close-up shots require that you be extremely exact in following the rehearsed **blocking**—the carefully worked-out stage positions, movements, and actions relative to other actors and the camera. If you stray even a few inches from the rehearsed blocking, you may be out of camera range or obstructed by another actor. To help you remember the critical blocking positions, the floor manager will usually mark the floor with chalk or masking tape.

If you or the other actor is off the mark in an over-the-shoulder shot, you may be obstructed from camera view by the other actor. You can tell whether the camera sees you simply by looking for the camera lens. If you see the lens, the camera can see you; if you don't see the lens, you aren't being seen. If you can't see the lens, inch to one side or the other without obviously searching for it. Although the camera can be adjusted to get the proper over-the-shoulder shot, it is usually easier to adjust your position than the camera's.

To remember blocking, you may want to establish a mental road map that has prominent landmarks, for example: "First stop, the left corner of the table. Second landmark, couch. Move to the couch and sit on the right. Third landmark, telephone. Get up and move behind the telephone table facing the center camera. Pick up the phone with the left hand."

Although good directors will block you as much as possible so that your movements are natural, you will occasionally be in a position that seems entirely wrong to you. Do not try to correct this position until you have consulted the director. A special shot or effect may very well warrant such blocking.

► KEY CONCEPT

Meticulously follow the rehearsed blocking during each take. If you can't see the camera lens, you won't be in the shot.

Repeating Action

Unlike the theater, where your performance is continuous and according to plot progression, video acting—like acting for film—is usually done piecemeal. You may have to switch from the happy opening scene to the intensely sad closing scene, merely because both play in the friend's living room. By remembering the exact blocking, you also help preserve continuity. For instance, if you held the telephone receiver in your right hand during the medium shots, don't switch it to your left hand for the close-ups.

In single-camera productions, it is normal to repeat the same scene over and over again. Such repetitions are done to get a variety of camera angles or close-ups or to correct major or minor technical problems. In repeats not only must you duplicate exactly the lines and the blocking for each take, you must also maintain the same energy level throughout. You cannot be "on" during the first takes and "off" during the later close-ups.

AUDITIONS

Auditions are a test of your ability as a performer—and of your self-confidence. Not getting the part does not mean that you gave an inferior performance but that somebody else was thought to be more suitable. Take all auditions equally seriously, whether you are trying out for a starring role in a big television drama or for a one-line off-camera utterance for a product demonstration; but don't take them so seriously that you begin to suffer from depression because you didn't get the part.

Although you may not know beforehand what will be asked of you in the audition, you can still prepare for it. Wear something that's appropriate and that looks good on-camera. Be properly groomed. Arrive on time and don't be intimidated by either the number or the caliber of people auditioning with you. You all have an equal chance; otherwise you would not have been called to try out for the part. Have a brief monologue ready that shows your range of ability. Keep your energy up even if you have to wait half a day before being asked to perform.

If you get a script beforehand, study it carefully. If the script calls for you to talk about or demonstrate a specific product, such as a new computer, familiarize yourself with the product ahead of time. The more you know about the product, the more confidence shows in your delivery. Ask the person conducting the audition what shots the camera will take. If close-ups predominate, slow down your actions and avoid excessive movements. Remember that you are not addressing a large audience but an individual or a small family seated near you.

As an actor be sure that you understand the character you are to portray. If you are not sure what the segment you are to read or the character you are to portray is all about, ask the person conducting the audition (casting director or producer)—but don't ask for the proper motivation. As a professional actor, you are expected to motivate yourself. Be inventive but don't overdo it. When working in video, little mannerisms, such as a specific way of keeping your eyeglasses from slipping down your nose, playing with keys, or using a slightly rusty fingernail clipper while engaged in a serious conversation, tend to sharpen your character more readily than simply working up to a high emotional pitch.

CLOTHING

What you wear depends not only on your preference and taste but also on how the camera sees your clothing. Because the camera can look at you from extremely close range or from a distance, you need to consider the overall line of your clothes as well as the texture and the details.

The video camera has a tendency to add a few extra pounds. Clothing that is cut to a slim silhouette usually looks more favorable than something loose and baggy. Avoid horizontal stripes; they emphasize width instead of length and make you look wider around the middle.

Texture and Detail

Because of the frequent close-ups in video, you need to pay special attention to texture and detail. Textured material and ties look better than plain so long as the texture is not too busy or contrasting. Even the best video cameras have a difficult time handling closely spaced and highly contrasting patterns, such as black-and-white herringbone weaves or checks. The electronic scanning of the video image can't accommodate the frequency of the high-contrast pattern, causing the camera to create a new, highly distracting frequency that shows up on-screen as vibrating rainbow colors and patterns, called a *moiré effect*.

Prominent, high-contrast horizontal stripes may also extend beyond the clothing fabric and bleed through surrounding sets and objects as though you were superimposing venetian blinds. On the other hand, extremely fine detail in a pattern will either look busy or, more likely, show up on-screen as smudges.

You can always provide the necessary texture by adding such details as jewelry or a prominent tie or scarf. Although you will undoubtedly prefer wearing jewelry that you like, refrain from overly large or too many pieces. Too much tends to look gaudy on a close-up, even if the jewelry is of high quality.

Color

Again, the colors you select are not entirely up to you but must fulfill certain technical requirements. If the set you work in is primarily beige, a beige dress or suit will certainly get lost in it. Avoid wearing blue if you are part of a chroma-key effect that uses blue as the backdrop. The chroma-key process renders transparent everything blue and lets the background show through. If you wear a blue tie or suit, you will see the keyed background image in place of the blue clothing. Of course, if the chroma-key color is green, you can wear blue but not green.

Although you may like red, most video cameras—and especially home television sets—don't. Except for top-of-the-line models, video cameras show highly saturated reds as vibrating and bleeding into other areas. Such video problems, called *artifacts,* are especially noticeable in low-light conditions. But even if the camera can handle the brilliant red of your dress or sweater, your home receiver will most likely display vibration or bleeding effects.

You should also avoid wearing colors of high-contrast brightness, such as dark blue and white, or black and white. If you wear a black jacket over a reflecting white shirt, the camera, or the video operator (VO), does not know whether to adjust for the high brightness values of the white or the low values of the black. If the VO tries to lighten the black areas to see some shadow detail, the white areas become overexposed and begin to "bloom." If the VO tries to control the overly bright areas to show more picture detail, the shadows become uniformly dense. Your skin tones will also get a few shades darker. Obviously, if you are a dark-skinned performer, you should not wear a starched white shirt or blouse. If you wear a dark suit, reduce the brightness contrast by wearing a pastel shirt rather than a white one.

This contrast problem is especially noticeable when the camcorder is on automatic iris. The auto-iris will seek out the brightest spot in the picture and close down the aperture to bring this excess light under control. As a consequence all other picture areas darken accordingly. If, for example, you wear a brilliantly white blouse while standing in front of a relatively dark restaurant set, the auto-iris will close to darken the brightness of your blouse and, unfortunately, the already dark set as well. What you will get is a properly exposed blouse in front of an underlighted set.

Most high-quality cameras, especially HDTV cameras, can tolerate a relatively high brightness contrast. But again, you will make the lives of the lighting director and the VO much easier if you reduce the contrast of your clothing.

MAKEUP

All makeup is used for three reasons: to enhance appearance, to correct appearance, and to change appearance.

Most video productions require makeup that accentuates the features rather than changes them. For female performers, normal makeup does just fine on-camera; male performers may need some makeup primarily to reduce the light reflections off the forehead or bald spots and perhaps to cover some wrinkles and skin blemishes. In both cases, makeup must be adjusted to the technical requirements of the camera and the scrutiny of the close-up.

> ►**KEY CONCEPT**
> Makeup is used to enhance, correct, or change appearance.

Technical Requirements

The video camera prefers warmer (more reddish) makeup colors over cooler (more bluish) ones. Especially under high-color-temperature lighting (outdoor or fluorescent lighting, which is bluish), bluish red lipsticks and eye shadow look unnaturally blue. Warm makeup colors, with their reddish tint, look more natural and provide sparkle, especially on dark skin.

Regardless of whether you are a dark-skinned or light-skinned performer, you should use *foundation* makeup that matches your natural skin color. This foundation is available in various types of *pancake* makeup. If you perspire readily, you should use a generous amount of foundation; although it won't prevent your perspiration, it will make it less visible to the camera.

Because you will be seen on a close-up, your makeup must be smooth and subtle. This requirement is the reverse of theatrical makeup, which you need to exaggerate as much as possible for good effect for the spectators sitting some distance from the stage. Good video makeup should accentuate your features but remain invisible, even on a close-up.

If possible, check your makeup on-camera: have the camera take a close-up of you in the performance area. You may consider this method a frivolously expensive mirror, but it will benefit you during the performance.

Always apply makeup under the lighting conditions of the performance area. If you apply your makeup in a room that has bluish fluorescent (high-color-temperature 5,600K) lights and then perform under normal studio lights (with a lower color temperature of 3,200K), your makeup will be excessively reddish and your face will look pink. The opposite is true if you apply your makeup under lights with the indoor standard of 3,200K and then move into a location that is illuminated with the outdoor standard of 5,600K: your makeup will look unnaturally bluish.

If you need to use makeup to change your appearance, enlist the services of a professional makeup artist.

Materials

You can easily find a great variety of excellent makeup materials for video. Most large drugstores carry the basics for improving a performer's appearance. Women performers are generally experienced in using cosmetic materials and techniques; men may, at least initially, need some advice.

The most basic makeup item is the foundation that covers minor skin blemishes and cuts down light reflections from oily skin. Water-based pancake makeup foundations are preferred over the more cumbersome grease-based foundations. The Kryolan CTV-1W through CTV-12W pancake series is probably all you need for most makeup jobs. The colors range from a warm light ivory for light-skinned performers to a very dark tone for dark-skinned performers.

Women can use their own lipsticks or rouge, so long as the reds do not contain too much blue. Other materials, such as eyebrow pencils, mascara, and eye shadow, are generally part of every performer's makeup kit. Additional materials, such as hairpieces or even latex masks, are part of the professional makeup artist's inventory. They are of little use in most nondramatic productions.

A solid knowledge of basic video production techniques will aid you greatly not only when working behind the camera but also when working in front of it. In fact, talent who know basic production techniques seem more relaxed in front of the camera and more prepared to cope gracefully with the technical commotion and the unexpected problems while on the air than performers who know little or nothing about video production. On the other hand, knowing how to perform and act in front of the camera will make you a better behind-the-camera production person. As a director, such knowledge is essential.

M A I N   P O I N T S

▶ **Talent**

Talent are people who work in front of the camera. Talent includes performers, who are primarily engaged in nondramatic activities, and actors, who portray someone else.

▶ **Performing Techniques**

The performer must imagine the video camera as his or her communication partner, keep eye contact with the lens when addressing the viewer directly, handle the various microphones for optimal sound pickup, and use prompting devices discreetly, without making the viewer aware of it.

▶ **Close-ups**

When on a close-up, move slowly and keep all gestures small.

▶ **Prompting Devices**

In addition to the floor manager's cues, the major prompting devices are the I.F.B. (interruptible foldback or feedback) system, the studio or field teleprompter, and cue cards.

▶ **Cues**

Always respond promptly to the floor manager's cues.

▶ **Acting Techniques**

Good video actors learn how to work well within a highly technical environment, adjust to the frequent use of close-ups, and repeat certain actions in the same way and with the same intensity.

▶ **Blocking**

Meticulously follow the rehearsed blocking during each take. If you can't see the camera lens, you won't be in the shot.

▶ **Clothing**

On-camera clothing should have a slim silhouette, with textures and colors that are not too busy or contrasting. The camera does not like closely spaced, high-contrast herringbone weaves or checks and highly saturated reds.

▶ **Makeup**

Makeup is used to enhance, correct, and change appearance. Always apply makeup under lights that have the same color temperature as those in the performance area.

angle The particular approach to a story—its central theme.

blocking Carefully worked-out positioning, movement, and actions by the talent and for all mobile video equipment used in a scene.

camera rehearsal Full rehearsal with cameras and other pieces of production equipment. Often identical to the dress rehearsal.

dry run Rehearsal without equipment, during which the basic actions of the talent are worked out. Also called *blocking rehearsal.*

fact sheet Script format that lists the items to be shown on-camera and their main features. May contain suggestions of what to say about the product. Also called *rundown* sheet.

multicamera directing Simultaneous coordination of two or more cameras for instantaneous editing (switching). Also called *control room directing* and *live-switched directing.*

program objective The desired effect of the program on the viewer.

script Written document that tells what the program is about, who says what, what is supposed to happen, and what and how the audience shall see and hear the event.

shot sheet A list of every shot a particular camera has to get. It is attached to the camera to help the camera operator remember a shot sequence.

single-camera directing Directing a single camera (usually a camcorder) in the studio or field for takes that are recorded separately for postproduction.

single-column drama script Traditional script format for television plays. All dialogue and action cues are written in a single column.

standard two-column script Traditional script format with video information on page-left and audio information on page-right for a variety of television scripts, such as for documentaries or commercials. Also called *two-column documentary script.*

time line A schedule that shows the time allotments for various activities during a single production day. Often prepared by the director. Also (but erroneously) called *production schedule.*

trim handles Recording additional footage before and after the major shot content for more-precise editing. Also called *pads.*

two-column news script Traditional script format with video information on page-left and news copy on page-right for news presentations.

visualization The mental image of a shot. May also include the imagining of verbal and nonverbal sounds. Mentally converting a scene into a number of key video images and their sequencing.

walkthrough/camera rehearsal A combination of an orientation session for talent and crew and a follow-up rehearsal with full equipment. This combination rehearsal is generally conducted from the studio floor.

Putting It All Together: Directing

Directing is where everything you have learned so far in television directing all comes together. The job description is relatively simple: all you need to do is tell people behind and in front of the camera what to do and how to do it. The difficulty is that you must know exactly what you want them to do before you can direct them to do it.

Of course, reading about directing or listening to somebody explain it can take you only so far. The real test is when you sit in the control room and literally call the shots. Once you feel comfortable with directing multiple cameras from the control room, you can adjust relatively easily to single-camera directing—from the studio control room or in the field.

Before you learn the finer points of directing, you may want to revisit in earlier chapters the sections on program objective and angle, review and practice visualization, and read about how to prepare for directing a multicamera production.

▶ **REVISITING THE PROGRAM OBJECTIVE**
   Program objective and script formats

▶ **VISUALIZATION**
   Visualization of image, sound, context, and sequencing

▶ **PREPARING FOR A MULTICAMERA STUDIO PRODUCTION**
   Floor plan, talent blocking, camera positions, and script marking

▶ **CONTROL ROOM DIRECTING**
   Terminology, time line, rehearsals, and directing the show

▶ **SINGLE-CAMERA DIRECTING**
   Differences from multicamera, single-camera studio directing, and single-camera field production

REVISITING THE PROGRAM OBJECTIVE

Before you dash into directing by reserving cameras, drawing a storyboard, and marking up a script, you must ask yourself what the intended program is all about. Recall the discussion from chapter 1 about the *production model:* moving from the idea to the desired effect on the viewer, then backing up to the specific medium requirements to achieve the program objective.

Program Objective and Angle

Most scripts and program proposals state the **program objective**—the desired effect of the program on the viewer—as the "goal" or "purpose" on the cover page or in the general introduction to the project. You should also be clear about the angle with which the topic is approached. The **angle** of the program, that is, its central theme and major storytelling approach or framework, is often buried in the script itself. The angle is sometimes given to you by the producer, but most often it's established by you, the director.

Script Formats

The **script** interprets the show idea into what the viewers should actually see and hear when watching the program. It is similar to a recipe in that it lists the major ingredients of the program and how they must be mixed to get the desired result. In the language of the *production model,* the script helps you translate the program objective into specific medium requirements. Although you may not aspire to be a scriptwriter, as a director you must be familiar with the basic script formats used in video production so you can make this translation process as efficient and effective as possible.

Despite considerable variations, there are four basic script formats for video productions: the fact, or rundown, sheet; the two-column news script; the standard two-column script; and the single-column drama script.

Fact, or rundown, sheet   The *fact sheet* format is used for simple demonstrations by a show host. Also called a *rundown sheet,* it normally lists the major features of a product that the host should mention, although the presentation itself is ad-libbed. The director may write in the cameras used for the demonstration, but the cutting from one to the other depends on the host's actions. **SEE 17.1**

Two-column news script   The only thing the news scripts from different newsrooms have in common is that they are, more or less, two-column. In a **two-column news script** format, the right column contains the spoken news copy plus the out-cues of the words of prerecorded news segments. The left column contains cues to who is talking; the name, number, and length of the prerecorded news clips, C.G. copy, and effects; some shot designations; and whether the prerecorded insert is to be played with a *voice-over (VO)* of the anchor describing what is happening on the video insert or with *SOT (sound on tape)*—the actual sounds that are recorded on the recorded news package. **SEE 17.2** In case you use a recording medium other than videotape, you might want to call it *SOS (sound on source).*[1]

---

1. The term *sound on source* was suggested by television producer Phil Sigmund to adapt to a tapeless video operation.

17.1 Fact, or Rundown, Sheet

The fact, or rundown, sheet lists the major points of what the talent is to do and show. The talent ad-libs the demonstration, and the director follows the talent's actions. No specific audio or video cues are listed.

```
Zettl's VideoLab 3.0 DVD-ROM COMMERCIAL
SHOW:
DATE:


PROPS:
Desktop computer running Zettl's VideoLab 3.0.
VideoLab package with disc as hand props.

1.   New multimedia product by Thomson Wadsworth.

2.   Sensational success.

3.   Was nominated for prestigious Codie Award.

4.   Designed for both the production novice and the video
     professional.

5.   Truly interactive. Provides you with a video studio in your
     home. Easy to use.

6.   You can proceed at your own speed and test your progress at
     any time.

7.   Will operate on Windows or Macintosh platform.

8.   Special introductory offer. Expires Oct. 20. Hurry. Available
     from all major software and bookstores. For more information
     or the dealer nearest you, visit www.thomsonedu.com.
```

A *news package* is a brief, prerecorded, self-contained story by the field reporter that is inserted into the newscast after the news anchor's lead-in. There are usually several packages in a newscast.

What news writers don't seem to agree on is just how to format the audio column. Many use capital letters for the spoken words, but some prefer upper/lowercase letters; others use a combination of both. Although it is actually harder to read words written in all-caps, the all-cap format is faster to type. Because of the ease with which word processors can change the fonts of news copy, however, and the clarity with which high-quality teleprompters can display it, more and more copy is written in the traditional upper/lowercase format.

Standard two-column script   This script is also called the *two-column documentary script* or, simply, *documentary format,* although it may be used for a variety

17.2 Two-column News Script

In the two-column news script format, the left column contains such production information as who is on-camera, the type and the length of the videotape inserts, and special effects. The right column shows every word to be spoken by the newscaster as well as the audio in- and out-cues of the videotape inserts.

```
Larkfield Evening News 4/16


SFX bumper

JODEE O/C (on-camera)      Is Silicon Valley in trouble? Yesterday,
CU                         Professor Joseph Alexander of the University
                           of California at Berkeley unveiled his
                           supercomputer in his physics lab. Instead
                           of silicon chips, its processor is built
                           entirely of nanotubes. Nonotubes will make
                           our fastest computers seem like dinosaurs,
                           says Alexander.


Server 04                  Ten years of intensive research have finally
File 147  (1:02)           paid off for the Alexander research team at
JODEE VO                   Berkeley. Their new supercomputer is about the
                           size of a matchbox and a thousand times faster
                           than the best that Silicon Valley can muster.
_____

Package 1                  IN-CUE: "The secret is nanotubes . . ."
Sound on source
Server 02                  OUT-CUE: ". . . will make silicon chips
File 12    (0:27)          totally obsolete."
_____

JODEE O/C                  Professor Alexander thinks that this is only
                           the beginning . . .


                           MORE--MORE--MORE
```

of nondramatic shows, such as interviews, cooking shows, or commercials. In a ***standard two-column script***, the left column contains all the video information, and the right column lists all the audio information. **SEE 17.3** Review the content of this script as well; it is the basis of your control-room directing assignment later in this chapter. **ZVL3 CUE 1** PROCESS→ Ideas→ scripts

17.3 Standard Two-column Script

In the two-column documentary script format, the left column contains all the video information, and the right column shows all the audio information. The dialogue or narration is fully scripted.

```
LIGHT AND SHADOWS Series
Program No. 4: High- and Low-key Lighting


VIDEO                        AUDIO

VTR standard opening         SOT

Mary on camera               MARY

                             Hi, I'm Mary, your LD. Today I will
                             show the differences between high-key
                             and low-key lighting. No, high-key and
                             low-key has nothing to do with how
                             high or low the key light hangs but
                             rather with how much light is on the
                             scene. High-key has plenty of light on
                             the scene. Low-key uses only a few
                             instruments to illuminate specific
                             areas. But high- and low-key make us
                             feel differently about a situation.
                             Let's watch.


Susan sitting on bench       OPEN MICS. SFX: DISTANT TRAFFIC SOUNDS.
waiting for bus              OCCASIONAL CARS GOING BY.

Key titles

John walks to telephone

Freeze-frame                 SFX OUT - MARY (VO)

                             This is a high-key scene. It is obviously
                             daylight. There is plenty of light on
                             the set with fairly prominent shadows.
                             But the faces of the people have enough
                             fill light to slow down the falloff and
                             make the attached shadows transparent.
                             Now let's see what John and Susan are
                             up to.
```

17.3 Standard Two-column Script *(continued)*

VIDEO   AUDIO

John by the phone,   SFX: DISTANT TRAFFIC SOUNDS.
looking for change   OCCASIONAL CARS GOING BY.

John approaches bench   JOHN
                               Excuse me. Could you please change a
                               five-dollar bill? I need to make a
                               call and . . .

Susan gets up and walks   SUSAN
toward curb   No!

Freeze-frame   MARY (VO)
                               Oops. They don't seem to be hitting it
                               off too well. In the meantime, note
                               that the high light level helps to
                               give the scene a great depth of field.
                               Although Susan and John are relatively
                               far apart on the z-axis, they are both
                               in sharp focus. Sorry about the
                               interruption. Let's see how this plot
                               develops.

CU John   JOHN
                               I didn't mean to startle you. But I
                               really need to make this call. You
                               wouldn't have a cell phone I could
                               borrow?

Susan studies the bus   SUSAN
schedule; she looks   No, I am sorry.
through her purse

17.3 **Standard Two-column Script** *(continued)*

```
VIDEO                        AUDIO

CU John                      JOHN
                             You wouldn't use pepper spray on me,
                             would you?


Susan moves to the lamp
post; John steps closer
                             SFX: BUS APPROACHES AND STOPS
                             POLICE SIREN COMING CLOSER

                             SUSAN
                             I'm not so sure . . .

Susan boards the bus         SFX: BUS PULLS AWAY


                             JOHN
                             Thanks a lot.
```

The scene will be repeated under low-key lighting. Mary now comments over the freeze-frames on the specifics of low-key lighting. She emphasizes the change in how we feel about the situation under high-key and low-key lighting.

```
Mary O/C                     MARY
                             I would certainly prefer to have John
                             ask me for change in the high-key scene
                             than in this low-key scene. Wouldn't
                             you? With all those ominous cast shadows
                             around and such sparse street lighting,
                             I wouldn't have taken a chance with him
                             either. Poor John!


Freeze-frame of              MUSIC
low-key scene

Closing credits

Fade to black
```

17.4 **Two-column Partial Script**

The two-column partial script shows all the video information in the left column but only partial dialogue or narration in the right column. The questions are usually fully scripted, but the answers are only partially described.

VIDEO   AUDIO

CU of Katy   KATY
                               But the debate about forest fires is
                               still going on. If we let the fire
                               burn itself out, we lose valuable
                               timber and kill countless animals, not
                               to speak of the danger to property and
                               the people who live there. Where do
                               you stand, Dr. Hough?

Cut to CU of Dr. Hough   DR. HOUGH
                               (SAYS THAT THIS IS TRUE BUT THAT
                               THE ANIMALS USUALLY GET OUT UNHARMED
                               AND THAT THE BURNED UNDERBRUSH
                               STIMULATES NEW GROWTH.)

Cut to two-shot   KATY
                               Couldn't this be done through
                               controlled burning?

                               DR. HOUGH
                               (SAYS YES BUT THAT IT WOULD COST TOO
                               MUCH AND THAT THERE WOULD STILL BE
                               FOREST FIRES TO CONTEND WITH.)

Note that all audio cues in the audio column, including the names of the talent speaking the lines, are in uppercase letters. All spoken words are in upper/lowercase style. The instructions in the video column use both upper- and lowercase. Some scriptwriters maintain the all-caps convention because these words are not spoken. Because upper/lowercase lettering is much easier to read, however, you will find that most scripts use that style for the video column. If there is considerable ad-libbing to be done by the talent, the audio column indicates only who is speaking and the general topic; such a script is generally called a *two-column partial script*. **SEE 17.4**

This partial script format is often used for instructional shows, even if they contain some dramatic scenes.

Single-column drama script   The *single-column drama script* format contains the complete dialogue, narration over video, and all major action cues in one column. **SEE 17.5** As you can see, all names of characters ("ALAN" and "VICKY") and audio cues ("THEME #2") are in capital letters. All spoken dialogue (or narration over a scene) is in upper/lowercase. Specific delivery cues ("surprised") and directions ("getting an extra chair for Alan") are also in upper/lowercase but are clearly isolated from the dialogue either by double-spacing or by parentheses or brackets. You will, however, find scripts in which these instructions are in all-caps. The specific descriptions of shots are omitted and usually left for the director to add in the visualization and script preparation phases.

> ▶ **KEY CONCEPT**
>
> The four basic script formats are the fact, or rundown, sheet; the two-column news script; the standard two-column script; and the single-column drama script.

VISUALIZATION

Take just a moment and pretend that you see your mother on television. Just how do you picture her? In a CU or an MS? Seated or moving around? Where is she? Indoors or out? What is she wearing? What is she doing? Reading? Getting ready for work? Cooking? Sweeping the front steps? Now imagine your dream car. What color is it? Is it parked in your garage or tearing up a winding country road? What sounds do you hear in these scenes?

What you just did is called visualization. In video production *visualization* means creating a mental image of a shot or a sequence of shots. In a wider sense, visualization also includes imagining the sounds that go with the pictures. For the director visualization is an indispensable preproduction tool.

Image   If the script gives you only general visualization cues such as "young woman waiting at the bus stop " or "bus stop in an isolated part of town," you need to fill in the details to make a specific person out of the "young woman" and to give the bus stop a certain look (refer to the script in figure 17.3). You would certainly have different visualizations if the scene were to take place at midday than if it were played on a deserted street at night. Providing such details is an important part of the director's job.

Sound   Though you may find it difficult at first, you should always try to "hear" the sounds simultaneously with the pictures you are visualizing. For example, what sounds do you imagine at a brightly lit bus stop scene and at a dimly lit one? You probably think of different sounds in the two scenes. Assuming that you will support the lighting shifts with audio, we should probably hear more traffic sounds in the daytime scene than in the nighttime one. But the few traffic sounds in the low-key scene should be more penetrating. Similarly, we should hear the steps of the person approaching the young woman much more distinctly (higher volume) in the nighttime scene than in the daytime one. If music is used, the nighttime scene should have more-ominous music than the daytime scene and, for good measure, be mixed with a faint police siren. It is usually easier to establish the emotional context of a shot or scene with the sound track than with the video.

17.5 Single-column Drama Script

The single-column drama script contains every word of characters'
dialogue and occasional descriptions of their major actions.

SCENE 6

SKY ROOM. TABLE BY THE BANDSTAND.

THEME #2

We hear the last bars of dance music. The band is taking a break.
ALAN and YOLANDA are coming back to their table to join STUART, who
has been watching them dance. During their dance, VICKY joined STUART
and is now sitting in ALAN'S chair.

                    ALAN
                 (surprised)
            You're sitting in my chair.

                    VICKY
      Oh, it's YOUR chair? No wonder it felt so good.
      But I didn't see any name on it. You know--reserved
              for . . . what's your name again?

                    ALAN
                    Alan.

                    VICKY
                  Alan who?

                    ALAN
            Alan Frank . . . like in frank!

                    VICKY
          Reserved for Mr. Alan Frank!

                   STUART
               Dr. Alan Frank.

                    VICKY
      Oh, DOCTOR! What are you a doctor of?

                   STUART
         (getting an extra chair for Alan)
            He's a doctor of philosophy.

                    VICKY
                  (laughing)
        A doctor of philosophy? You look like one!

Context   Besides the program objective and the angle, your visualization is ultimately determined by the prevailing context in which a scene plays. For example, in the nighttime scene you would probably work with more tight close-ups of the young woman and have the man approach her more aggressively. But even if you kept the shots pretty much the same for both lighting scenes, the sound tracks could readily establish their different contexts.

Sequencing   Your visualization must include not only the key shots but also a shot sequence. Unless you are dealing with a static setup and little camera movement, such as in news or studio interviews, your visualization must include how to get from one shot to the next. This is where your knowledge of vectors and the mental map comes in handy. A good storyboard can also be of great help in planning shots and sequencing. As you recall from chapter 12, the storyboard shows a number of carefully framed shots and their sequence (see figure 12.17). Such a sequence illustration is especially important for maintaining shot continuity when shooting out of sequence for postproduction editing.

> **KEY CONCEPT**
> A storyboard helps translate the director's key visualizations into effective shots and shot sequences.

But even in seemingly simple directing assignments, such as videotaping the monthly campus report by the college president, shot continuity must be foremost in your mind. Recall from chapter 13 how to preserve continuity when somebody misreads a word during a taping session. This advice is important enough to be repeated here. If, for example, the college president mispronounces a name, stop the tape and inform her of the problem. Do not resume the taping just before the mistake was made; ask her to go back to a point where a new idea—a new paragraph—is introduced. You can then start with a different camera angle or a tighter or looser shot, or have her look up from her notes, thus making the edit look natural and properly motivated.

A good rule is to keep your visualization simple. Don't be afraid to use conventional approaches; they are conventions because they have proved effective. As pointed out earlier, there is nothing wrong with a steady close-up of a "talking head" so long as the head talks well and has something worthwhile to say. This is different from stereotyping, which deliberately seeks out event details that reinforce prejudices. Creativity in directing does not mean doing everything differently from all other directors; it means adding subtle touches that intensify your message and give your visualization personality.

PREPARING FOR A MULTICAMERA STUDIO PRODUCTION

With your understanding of the program objective and the angle, you must now interpret the script for its medium requirements. This implies visualizing the shots, *blocking* the talent and the cameras (working out major talent and equipment positions and moves), and marking the script with cues to the talent and the crew.

Unless you are directing soap operas or dramatic specials right away, most of your initial directing assignments will not involve complicated shots or the blocking of complex scenes. More often you will have to coordinate where the set should be located for optimal lighting, making sure that the audio is functioning properly and that the cameras are positioned for the best shots. Revisit the lighting-show script's

17.6 Bus Stop Floor Plan

This floor plan shows the principal scenery and props for simulating a bus stop.

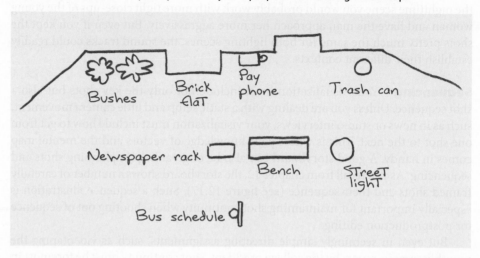

bus stop scene with the two different lighting requirements (figure 17.3); it is a bit more complicated, but it can introduce you to reading a floor plan, blocking talent and cameras, and marking a script.

Reading the floor plan   A floor plan will greatly assist you in visualizing key shots, determining the lighting and audio requirements, and blocking the talent and the cameras. Let's take a brief look at the floor plan sketch for the bus stop scenes. **SEE 17.6**

This bus stop floor plan will make your job relatively easy. You have four major action areas: (1) Susan's bench, (2) John's telephone, (3) the bus stop sign and schedule, and (4) the streetlight. Both cameras can be positioned for z-axis blocking of John and Susan in the bench and streetlight areas. The four areas offer a good opportunity for demonstrating selective low-key lighting. The audio is best handled by two wireless lavalieres, which eliminates any problems with unwanted shadows during the low-key scene.

Blocking the talent   Although the script has already given you basic visualization and action cues, such as "Susan sitting on bench" and "John walks to telephone," you need to be specific about exactly where on the bench Susan will sit and just where John will be at the phone booth. You can probably come up with some other blocking ideas, but try to keep it simple. According to the program objective, you are not demonstrating clever blocking but the difference between high-key and low-key lighting. **SEE 17.7**

Positioning the cameras   Note that whenever possible you should block the talent first, then place the available cameras in optimal shooting positions. This will achieve a more natural flow than if you move the talent to accommodate the camera.

17.7 Talent Blocking and Camera Positions

With a floor plan, the director can block the major moves of the talent and the cameras.

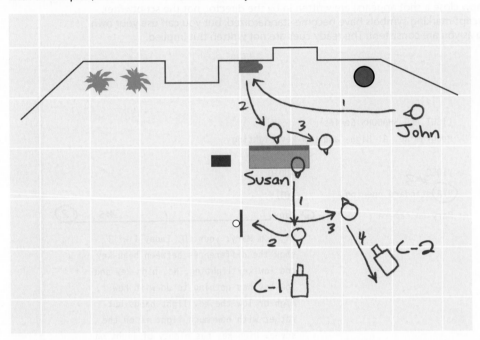

Of course, there are many circumstances in which camera positions are established before you can do any talent blocking. Don't ever forget that you are essentially blocking for the cameras, not for a stage performance. In your current directing assignment, two cameras should be sufficient. Both are positioned to cover z-axis blocking and effective over-the-shoulder shots (see figure 17.7). With minor reblocking you could even do this scene with a single camera.

Marking the script   Unless you have a photographic memory, you need to mark your script for multicamera directing. Although there is no universal standard for marking a script, over the years certain conventions have been developed that make the job easier. The key to good script marking is to keep it consistent and to a minimum. Because every command should have a *ready* or *standby* cue preceding it, you don't need to mark the ready cues. A circled number 2 not only designates camera 2 but also implies the "Ready 2" cue. The worst thing you can do is over-mark your script: while you are trying to read all your scribbles, you won't be able to watch the preview monitors or listen to the audio. Before you know it, the talent is a page or two ahead of you. As you can see in the next figure, some of the cues that were included in the script are reinforced, but most of the other essential cues are marked by the director. **SEE 17.8**

Make the markings big enough that you can see them clearly in the dark control room. Try to keep all the camera markings in one row so you can easily grasp the sequencing cues without having to read all the lines. If there are many shots, you should

17.8 Marked Script

This script has been marked by the director. Note that the markings for the field of view (how close a shot appears) are written in by the director, not the scriptwriter. Many script-marking symbols have become standardized, but you can use your own so long as you are consistent. The ready cues are not written but implied.

LIGHT AND SHADOWS Series
Program No. 4: High- and Low-key Lighting

VIDEO #3
(VTR) standard opening

Mary on camera

AUDIO
SOT

Q MARY |_____ / MS (2)

Hi, I'm Mary, your LD. Today I will show the differences between high-key and low-key lighting. No, high-key and low-key has nothing to do with how high or low the key light hangs but rather with how much light is on the scene. High-key has plenty of light on the scene. Low-key uses only a few instruments to illuminate specific areas. But high- and low-key make us feel differently about a situation. Let's watch. Z Susan CU (1)

Susan sitting on bench
waiting for bus

OPEN MICS. SFX: DISTANT TRAFFIC SOUNDS.
OCCASIONAL CARS GOING BY. ZOOM OUT

(Key titles)

John walks to telephone |_____ Q John walk

(Freeze-frame)

Q
SFX OUT - (MARY (VO))

This is a high-key scene. It is obviously daylight. There is plenty of light on the set with fairly prominent shadows. But the faces of the people have enough fill light to slow down the falloff and make the attached shadows transparent. Now let's see what John and Susan are up to.

17.8 Marked Script *(continued)*

VIDEO	AUDIO
John by the phone, looking for change	(SFX:) DISTANT TRAFFIC SOUNDS. OCCASIONAL CARS GOING BY. *3 John CU ②*
John approaches bench	JOHN *4 z-axis ①* Excuse me. Could you please change a five-dollar bill? I need to make a call and . . .
Susan gets up and walks toward curb	SUSAN No!
⟨Freeze-frame⟩	*Q* MARY (VO) Oops. They don't seem to be hitting it off too well. In the meantime, note that the high light level helps to give the scene a great depth of field. Although Susan and John are relatively far apart on the z-axis, they are both in sharp focus. Sorry about the interruption. Let's see how this plot develops. *5 John CU ②*
CU John	JOHN I didn't mean to startle you. But I really need to make this call. You wouldn't have a cell phone I could borrow? *6 follow ①* *Susan*
Susan studies the bus schedule; she looks through her purse.	SUSAN No, I am sorry. *7 CU Purse ②* *8 John CU ①*

17.8 Marked Script *(continued)*

VIDEO   AUDIO

CU John   JOHN
                               You wouldn't use pepper spray on me,
                               would you?

Susan moves to the lamp
post; John steps closer

                               (SFX:) BUS APPROACHES AND STOPS
                               POLICE SIREN COMING CLOSER
                               SUSAN _____ 9 _____ (2)
                               I'm not so sure . . .

Susan boards the bus   (SFX:) BUS PULLS AWAY ⌐ 10 _____ (1)
Walks past C-2

                               JOHN
                               Thanks a lot. ⌐ 11   *Zoom out*
                                                       FREEZE

> The scene will be repeated under low-key lighting. Mary now comments over the
> freeze-frames on the specifics of low-key lighting. She emphasizes the change in how
> we feel about the situation under high-key and low-key lighting.

Mary O/C   Q MARY ⌐   12   *Mary Ms* (2)
                               I would certainly prefer to have John
                               ask me for change in the high-key scene
                               than in this low-key scene. Wouldn't
                               you? With all those ominous cast shadows
                               around and such sparse street lighting,
                               I wouldn't have taken a chance with him
                               either. Poor John! *13   DISS* (1) *FREEZE*

                               (MUSIC)

Freeze-frame of
low-key scene

(Closing credits)

(Fade to black)

17.9 Shot Sheet
This shot sheet shows the shot sequence for camera 2.

number them in ascending order as they occur in the script. You can then prepare a *shot sheet* for each camera. **SEE 17.9** Don't number the shots for each camera with 1, 2, 3, etc. Rather, copy the shot number that you assigned each camera in the script.

CONTROL ROOM DIRECTING

Now you are ready to step into the studio to rehearse before going into the control room and video-recording the show. To communicate effectively with talent and crew and to make efficient use of your assigned time, you now must learn about the director's terminology, the time line, directing rehearsals, standby procedures, and on-the-air procedures.

Terminology

Most of the director's commands and cues have become pretty well standardized. The following five tables introduce you to the basic visualization, sequencing, special-effects, audio, and video-recording cues. **SEE 17.10–17.14**

Time Line

All studio productions must be done within a tight time frame. The overall *production schedule,* which lists the major deadlines for the production, is usually prepared by the producer. The *time line* for the single production day is your—the director's—responsibility; it assigns each production activity a block of time in which the specific job must be accomplished. Initially, you will feel that the allotted time is much too

17.10 Director's Visualization Cues

The visualization cues are directions for the camera to achieve certain shots. Some of these visualizations can be achieved in postproduction (such as an electronic zoom through digital magnification), but they are much more easily done with proper camera handling.

ACTION	DIRECTOR'S CUE
To reveal what is in the upper off-screen space or to increase headroom.	**Tilt up.**
To reveal what is in the lower off-screen space or to decrease headroom.	**Tilt down.**
To center an object.	**Center it.**
To reveal right off-screen space.	**Pan right.**
To reveal left off-screen space.	**Pan left.**
To raise the camera height.	**Pedestal up.** *or:* **Boom up.** [with a jib or crane]
To lower the camera height.	**Pedestal down.** *or:* **Boom down.** [with a jib or crane]
To move the camera closer.	**Dolly in.**
To move the camera farther away.	**Dolly out.**
To move the camera in a slight left curve.	**Arc left.**
To move the camera in a slight right curve.	**Arc right.**
To zoom to a tighter shot.	**Zoom in.** *or:* **Push in.**
To zoom to a looser shot.	**Zoom out.** *or:* **Pull out.**
To move the camera to the left with the lens pointing at the scene.	**Truck left.**
To move the camera to the right with the lens pointing at the scene.	**Truck right.**
To tilt the camera sideways to the left.	**Cant left.**
To tilt the camera sideways to the right.	**Cant right.**

17.11 Director's Sequencing Cues

The sequencing cues help get from one shot to the next. They include the major transitions.

ACTION	DIRECTOR'S CUE
Cut from camera 1 to camera 2.	**Ready two — take two.**
Dissolve from camera 3 to camera 1.	**Ready one for dissolve—dissolve.**
Horizontal wipe from camera 1 to camera 3.	**Ready three for horizontal wipe** [over 1] **— wipe.** *or:* **Ready effects number x** [the number being specified by the switcher program] **— effects.**
Fade in camera 1 from black.	**Ready fade in one — fade in one.** *or:* **Ready up on one — up on one.**
Fade out camera 2 to black.	**Ready black — go to black.**
Short fade to black between cameras 1 and 2.	**Ready cross-fade to two — cross-fade.**
Cut between camera 1 and VTR 2 (assuming that VTR 2 is already rolling and "locked" or in a "parked" position).	**Ready VTR two** [assuming the videotape is coming from VTR 2] **— take VTR two.** [Sometimes you simply call the VTR number as it appears on the switcher. If, for example, the VTR is labeled 6, you say: **Ready six — take six.**]
Cut between VTR and C.G.	**Ready C.G. — take C.G.** *or:* **Ready effects on C.G. — take effects.**
Cut between C.G. titles.	**Ready change page — change page.**

17.12 Director's Special-effects Cues

Special-effects cues are not always uniform, and, depending on the complexity of the effect, directors may invent their own verbal "shorthand." Whatever cues are used, they need to be standardized among the production team.

ACTION	DIRECTOR'S CUE
To super camera 1 over 2.	**Ready super one over two — super.**
To return to camera 2.	**Ready to lose super— lose super.** *or:* **Ready to take out one — take out one.**
To go to camera 1 from the super.	**Ready to go through to one— through to one.**
To key the C.G. over the base picture on camera 1.	**Ready key C.G.** [over 1] **— key.**
To key the studio card title on camera 1 over the base picture on camera 2.	**Ready key one over two — key.**
To have a wipe pattern appear over a picture, such as a scene on camera 2, and replace a scene on camera 1.	**Ready wipe two over one — wipe.**

Many of the more-complicated effects are preset and stored in the computer program. The retrieval goes by numbers. All you do to activate a whole effects sequence is call for the number: **Ready effects eighty-seven — take effects.**

17.13 Director's Audio Cues

Audio cues involve cues for microphones, starting and stopping various audio sources, such as CD players, and integrating or mixing those sources.

ACTION	DIRECTOR'S CUE
To activate a microphone in the studio.	**Ready to cue talent.** [Or something more specific, like **Mary — cue her.** The audio engineer will automatically open her mic.] *or:* **Ready to cue Mary — open mic, cue her.**
To start music.	**Ready music — music.**
To bring the music under for an announcer.	**Ready to fade music under — music under, cue announcer.**
To take the music out.	**Ready music out — music out.** *or:* **Fade music out.**
To close the microphone in the studio (announcer's mic) and switch over to the sound on videotape.	**Ready SOT** [sound on tape] **— close mic, track up.** *or:* **Ready SOT — SOT.**
To roll audio recording.	**Ready audiotape — roll audiotape.** [Do not just say, "Roll tape," because the TD may start the VTR.] *or:* **Ready Zip** *x* **— play.**
To fade one sound source under and out while simultaneously fading another in (similar to a dissolve).	**Ready cross-fade from** [*source*] **to** [*other source*] **— cross-fade.**
To go from one sound source to another without interruption (usually two pieces of music).	**Ready segue from** [*source*] **to** [*other source*] **— segue.**
To increase program speaker volume for the director.	**Monitor up, please.**
To play a sound effect from a CD or other recording device.	**Ready CD** [*or other source*] **cut** *x* **— play.** *or:* **Ready sound effect** *x* **— play.**
To put slate information on videotape (either open floor manager's mic or talkback patched to VTR).	**Ready to read slate — read slate.**

17.14 Director's Video-recording Cues

These cues are used to stop or start the recording mechanism (VTR, hard drive, video server, optical disc), to slate a video recording, and to switch to the recording output.

ACTION	DIRECTOR'S CUE
To start videotape or other recording device for recording a program.	**Ready to roll VTR one [*or other recording device*] — roll VTR one.** [Now you have to wait for the "in-record" or "speed" confirmation from the VTR operator.]
To "slate" the program after the VTR is in the record mode. The slate is on camera 2 or on the C.G.; the opening scene is on camera 1. (We are assuming that the color bars and the reference level audio tone are already on the tape.)	**Ready two [or C.G.], ready to read slate — take two [or C.G.], read slate.**
To put the opening 10-second beeper on the audio track and fade in on camera 1. (Do not forget to start your stopwatch as soon as camera 1 fades in.)	**Ready black, ready beeper — black, beeper.** **Ten — nine — eight — seven — six — five — four — three — two — cue Mary — up on one.** [Start your stopwatch.]
To roll a VTR as a program insert while you are on camera 2; sound is on tape. Assuming a 2-second roll.	**Ready to roll VTR three, SOT — roll VTR three.** **Two — one, take VTR three, SOT.** If you are using another recording device, say **SOS** — sound on source. If you do not use a countdown because of instant start, simply say: **Ready VTR three, roll and take VTR three.** [Start your stopwatch for timing the VTR insert.]
To return from VTR to camera and Mary on camera 1. (Stop your watch and reset it for the next insert.)	**Ten seconds to one, five seconds to one.** **Ready one, ready cue Mary — cue Mary, take one.**

short to even get through the basic rehearsals, or you may allocate too much time for one activity and too little for another. With some experience, however, you will quickly learn how long the individual production activities take and what you can accomplish in a certain period of time. The time line in the following figure allows generous time blocks for your lighting-show assignment. **SEE 17.15**

Once you have a realistic production schedule, you must stick to it. Novice directors tend to spend an inordinate amount of time polishing the first takes and then have to rush through the better part of the show before having to clear the studio. When rehearsing, good directors move on to the next activity according to schedule, even if they are not quite done with the current one. They usually gain enough time to pick up the skipped part at the end of the rehearsal.

7.15 Time Line

The time line shows when the major production phases are to take place.

6:45 a.m.	Crew call
7:00–10:00 a.m.	Setup and lighting; dry blocking in rehearsal room
10:00–10:30 a.m.	Talent and crew meeting; trim lighting
10:30–11:30 a.m.	Camera and talent blocking in studio
11:30–11:45 a.m.	Notes and reset (correction of minor problems)
11:45 a.m.–12:15 p.m.	Lunch
12:15–1:15 p.m.	Camera (dress) rehearsal
1:15–1:30 p.m.	Notes and reset
1:30–1:35 p.m.	Break
1:35–3:00 p.m.	Recording
3:00–3:30 p.m.	Spill (grace period to fix whatever needs fixing)
3:30–4:00 p.m.	Strike

Rehearsals

For most nondramatic shows, you probably need only two rehearsal methods: the *dry run* and the *walkthrough/camera rehearsal.* The best way to explain these two methods is to apply them to your lighting-show assignment.

Dry run   You use the **dry run**, or *blocking rehearsal,* to work out the basic actions of the talent—where they stand and walk and what they do. If you have worked out such blocking on the floor plan, you simply test your blocking schematic in a real situation. Any room will do because you don't need an actual set. You can use masking tape on the floor to indicate the sidewalk and use chairs for the bench. For the dry run of your lighting show, you could use three chairs for the bus stop bench, another chair for the public phone, a trashcan for the streetlight, and a fifth chair for the sign with the bus schedule. Your eyes will substitute for the cameras.

Watch the blocking first from camera 1's *PoV* (*point of view*), then from camera 2's PoV. In a complicated scene, you may want to use a director's viewfinder (an optical device that is similar to a monocular with which you can set various aspect ratios and zoom lens positions) or a small camcorder to check the approximate shot framing. Effective dry runs usually include all or some of the following points:

▶ Start with the more complicated blocking, but don't get hung up on details at this point. In the lighting show, you can block Susan first, then John, then both of them. If your time is limited, you can block both talent simultaneously. Have Susan seated on the bench, anxiously looking for the bus. Enter John from camera-right and have him go to the telephone and look for change. Susan gets up and walks toward camera 1, and so forth. Check especially the z-axis positions so that the camera can get good over-the-shoulder shots.

▶ Be as precise with your cues as possible. Don't just say, "Susan, sit on the bench," but, "Susan, sit on the left side—your left—of the bench." Your cue to the floor manager would be: "Have Susan sit on the camera-right side of the bench."

▶ Whenever possible, run through the scenes in the order they will be taped. This will help the talent prepare for the sequence. More often than not, the scene sequence is dictated by location rather than narrative development.

▶ Call out the cues, such as, "Ready two, cue John—take two," and so on. This will enable you to get used to the major cues and will help the talent anticipate them.

▶ If the timing is critical, do a rough timing for each scene.

Walkthrough/camera rehearsal   A form of dress rehearsal or orientation, the *walkthrough/camera rehearsal* combination is conducted from the studio floor and involves crew, talent, cameras, audio, and other necessary production equipment.

To rehearse a routine show, such as a standard interview in a permanent set, you can go straight to the control room. From there you (1) ask the cameras to line up their shots, (2) ask the audio engineer to check the audio levels of host and guest, (3) have the video-record (VR) operator calibrate the VTR or other recording device with the audio console, and (4) ask the C.G. operator to run through the titles and the credits for a final check of proper sequence and correct spelling of names.

If the show is a special event, you need to do a walkthrough and a separate camera rehearsal. If you have enough time (a rare occurrence), you can do one after the other. In a *walkthrough* you have the talent repeat the rehearsed blocking on the actual set, and you give the technical people some idea of what you expect them to do during the show. Then you go to the control room and conduct a **camera rehearsal**, which should approximate the on-the-air or recording sessions as closely as possible except that the signal goes only as far as the line-out monitor.

More often than not, you won't have time for separate walkthroughs and camera rehearsals, so you must combine them to stay within the allotted rehearsal time. Even then you won't have time to rehearse the entire show but only the most important parts of it, such as the talent entrances and exits and the camera positions for over-the-shoulder and cross-shots. Once in position, you move on to the next part.

Here are some recommendations for conducting a walkthrough/camera rehearsal combination:

▶ Always conduct such a rehearsal from the studio floor, not the control room. To change some minor blocking or camera positions, you can simply walk to the spot where you want the talent or camera to be. Explaining such corrections over the intercom would take up too much valuable rehearsal time. Use a headset or a wireless lavaliere to communicate with the control room.

▶ If possible, have the TD show a split feed of all cameras used. (You may have to discuss such a split-screen display with the TD prior to the rehearsal.) This way you can preview the cameras from the studio floor. If this is not practical, have the TD switch as usual and feed the line-out signal to the studio monitor.

▶ Have all talent and crew who are actively involved in the rehearsal take their positions. On the studio floor, this includes the floor manager and the floor persons, all camera operators, and the fishpole mic operator. In the control room, you should have the TD, the audio engineer, and, if necessary, the LD, standing by to adjust the lighting.

▶ Give all cues as you would in the control room. The TD will execute your switching calls and feed them to the studio monitor (assuming you don't have a split-screen setup).

▶ Have the floor manager do all the cueing, as though you were giving the instructions from the control room. The more you involve the floor manager in the walkthrough/camera rehearsal, the better prepared he or she will be when you give the cues from the control room during the actual taping.

▶ Once the talent has moved into a new position or you are satisfied with an especially demanding camera maneuver, skip to the next section. Do not get hung up on a minor detail while neglecting to rehearse more important parts. For example, in your lighting show, don't waste time rehearsing John standing at the telephone, looking for change. Instead, rehearse his walk from the phone to the bench while Susan walks to the curb.

▶ If you encounter some minor problems, don't stop the rehearsal. Have the AD (associate director) or the PA (production assistant) take notes. Your time line should have notes and reset time scheduled at least twice for this rehearsal (see chapter 2).

▶ Allow some time for yourself in the control room to rehearse the most critical parts of the show. At least go through the opening of the show and the opening cues to the talent.

▶ Stay calm and be courteous to everyone, even if things don't go as well as expected. Give the talent and the crew a brief break before the video recording. Rehearsing right up to airtime rarely contributes to a better performance.

Directing the Multicamera Show

You are finally ready to undertake **multicamera directing**, also known as *control room directing* and *live-switched directing;* that is, to use switching to coordinate two or more cameras from the control room while directing your live-on-tape show. *Live-on-tape* does not necessarily mean that you must do the entire show in a single take but that you videotape fairly long, uninterrupted sequences that require no, or only minor, postproduction editing. Normally, such editing consists of joining the videotaped segments in their correct sequence.

Once in the control room, your directing job becomes largely a matter of coordinating and cueing the production crew to instantly execute their assigned tasks. The following lists give some pointers on the major standby and on-the-air procedures. Of course, such lists are no substitute for actual control room experience, but they can help you avoid common mistakes and speed up your learning.

Standby procedures   Use these procedures immediately preceding your on-the-air or live-on-tape show. We assume here that the program is videotaped rather than recorded on another recording medium.

▶ Use the S.A. (studio address) system and have every crewmember put on a P.L. headset. Call on each crewmember and ask whether he or she is ready. This includes the TD, audio technician, VR operator, C.G. operator, teleprompter operator (if necessary), floor manager, camera operators, audio boom or fishpole operator, and lighting technician (if light changes occur during the segment).

▶ Ask the floor manager whether the talent and the rest of the floor crew are ready. Tell the floor manager who gets the opening cue and which camera will be on first. The floor manager is the essential link between the control room and the studio.

▶ You can save time by having the TD and the VR operator prepare the video leader. Have the VR operator do a test recording, including a brief audio feed of the talent's opening remarks.

▶ Announce periodically the time remaining until the telecast or taping.

▶ Alert everyone to the first cues and shot sequence. Ready the VR operator to roll tape, the C.G. operator to bring up the opening titles, the audio engineer to fade in the opening music, and the TD to fade in the opening shot.

▶ Have the floor manager get the talent into position.

On-the-air procedures   You now need to use the director's terminology as explained in figures 17.10 through 17.14. When giving standby and on-the-air cues, speak clearly and precisely. Do not chatter on the intercom to show how relaxed you are; you will only encourage the crew to do the same. Don't shout, even if something goes terribly wrong. Keep your cool and pay particular attention to these matters:

▶ Call for the VTR roll and wait for the "speed" or "in-record" confirmation.

▶ Unless done by the AD or TD, start the recording with the leader information.

▶ Fade in the camera that has the opening shot and key the opening titles.

▶ Cue talent by name. Don't just say, "Cue her"; say, "Cue Susan."

▶ Cue the talent *before* you fade in the camera. By the time the floor manager has relayed your cue to the talent and the talent begins to speak, the TD will have faded in the picture.

▶ Talk to the cameras by number, not by the name of the operator.

▶ First call the camera before you give the instructions: "Three, dolly in. One, stay on the close-up."

▶ Do not pause too long between your ready and take cues. The TD may no longer be ready by the time you get to the action cue.

▶ Do not pause between the "take" and the number of the camera. Do not say, "Take [pause] one." The TD may punch up your camera at the take cue.

▶ If you change your mind after your ready cue, cancel the cue by saying, "No" or "Cancel" or "Change that." Then give the correct ready cue.

▶ Try to watch the camera preview monitors as much as possible while reading the script. Clear script markings make this juggling act easier.

▶ Do not do one take after another to get the first scene right at the expense of the rest of the show. Realize that the crew and the talent may lose energy and interest if you require too many takes.

▶ If you must stop the tape because of a technical problem, ask the floor manager to inform the studio crew and the talent of the nature of the problem. If solving the problem takes more than a few minutes, have the crew and talent relax until you call for the taping to resume.

▶ If timing is critical, keep an eye on the clock and the stopwatch.

▶ After fading to black at the end of the show, call for a "Stop VTR" and give the all-clear signal. Have the VR operator spot-check the recording before dismissing the talent and calling for a scenery strike. But we are not there yet.

It's time to go into the control room and do the show. Again, we are assuming that the program is recorded on a VTR.

Standby. Ten seconds to VTR one roll. Ready VTR. Roll VTR [wait for the in-record confirmation]. Bars and tone. Ready slate. Take slate. Read slate [done by the AD or audio technician; this will give you an additional audio slate]. Black. Countdown [done by the AD or audio technician; the numbers from 10 to 2 flash by each second]. Ready VTR three. Roll VTR three, take it, sound up. Two on Mary. One on Susan. Ready two. Cue Mary. Take two. Ready one. Take one. Cue Susan [this is strictly an action cue]. Traffic sounds. Open mics. Ready key. Key. Change page [new title from C.G.]. Lose key. Cue John [action cue for John to walk]. Ready freeze-frame. Ready to cue Mary voice-over . . .

You are on your way. Don't bury your face in the script; by now you are pretty familiar with it. As much as possible, keep your head up and watch the preview monitors. Listen to what is being said, but especially to the cue lines. Unless something went wrong, stop the tape only after the daylight segment is finished. You can use this break for a brief notes session, and the lighting people can use the opportunity to fine-tune the nighttime lighting. Give everyone a short break before taping the nighttime scene but tell them the exact time to be back in the studio.

This time around you don't need any tape leader. But before you start the videotape again, make sure that Mary's VO script now contains the low-key commentary. You don't need a new tape leader, but you should have a new slate that indicates you are now doing the low-key scene. Fade in camera 1 (with Susan sitting on the bench), key the low-key scene titles, cue John to walk to the phone, freeze the long-shot frame, and cue Mary for her low-key voice-over.

When you have about one minute left, get ready for the closing (two-shot on C2):

> Thirty seconds. Ready bus effect [this is a sound effect of the bus pulling up]. Ready to cue Susan. Bus effect one [sound effect of bus pulling up]. Cue Susan [she delivers her last line, turns, and walks past C2]. SFX (audio) police siren low under. Bus effect two [sound effect of bus closing door and driving off]. Ready one on John. Take one. Cue John. Zoom out. Slowly. Freeze. Ready two on Mary. Cue Mary. Take two. Ready dissolve to one. Ready C.G. credits and music. Dissolve. Music. Roll credits. Key. Lose key. Fade music. Fade to black. Stop tape. Hold everything. Check tape. All clear. Thank you all. Good job.

If everything goes that smoothly, you have indeed done a superior job. But don't be discouraged if you need to stop down to repeat a portion of the scene or even to reblock a certain shot. Just don't spend an inordinate amount of time polishing a specific shot while the clock ticks right into the next time line segment.

> ▶ **KEY CONCEPT**
> When in the control room, give all your calls with clarity and precision.

SINGLE-CAMERA DIRECTING

In *single-camera directing*, you need to observe all the continuity principles of multicamera directing except that you are videotaping the shots piecemeal and not necessarily in the order of the script. Let's first look at some of the more obvious differences between single-camera (film-style) and multicamera directing, and then demonstrate these differences briefly with the lighting-show example.

Major Differences

Rehearsals Single-camera scenes are easier to rehearse than multicamera scenes because you can walk through and rehearse the talent and crew immediately before the actual video recording. The performers can quickly review their lines, and you can give detailed instructions to the crew as to the nature of the upcoming shot and the specific lighting and audio requirements. Because of the short time lapse between rehearsal and recording, your directions will be fresh in the minds of talent and crew for each take.

Rehearsing single-camera scenes can also be more difficult, however, because you need to reconstruct the preceding and following shots for each take to maintain continuity of action, emotion, and aesthetic energy. This is why many movie directors like to work from carefully worked-out storyboards. The storyboard helps them recall what happens before and after the specific shot they are rehearsing.

Performing and Acting   Single-camera production puts an added strain on the performers. Because the video-recording sequence is not governed by the narrative continuity of the script, the talent cannot build or maintain a specific emotional level but must often switch from one extreme to another. Also, many repetitions of a single take to get a variety of camera angles and close-ups require the performers to deliver identical performances each time. As a director you need to make sure that the talent not only repeat the same blocking and actions but also maintain the same energy level and rhythm during each subsequent take.

Continuity   One of the major challenges for the director in single-camera shooting is maintaining continuity from shot to shot. Because the shots are almost always video-recorded out of sequence, you need to maintain a mental map of how they will cut together for good continuity. This is where your record of the principal vectors comes in handy (see chapter 13).

In the absence of a detailed storyboard, marking the field log with principal vector symbols can greatly facilitate your lining up shots for proper continuity. For example, if in the lighting show you want to imply in a CU that Susan is watching John walk to the phone, Susan's index vector must converge with John's screen-left motion vector. The field log would simply show $i[->]$ (for Susan's CU) and $[<-]m$ (for John's walk). This notation will be enough for you to remember John's shot even if the actual takes are fairly far apart.

An experienced DP (director of photography) or the AD can greatly assist you in continuity matters, such as vector continuity, continuity of sound, and continuity of the general aesthetic energy level. Don't be afraid to ask. To make the editor's job a little easier, ask the camera operator to start the camera before you call for action and to let it run for a few seconds after the action is finished. These *trim handles* (ample "leaders" and "tails") will give the editor some wiggle room to cut precisely on action and dialogue. At this point it might be worthwhile for you to revisit the discussion of field production in chapter 15.

Single-camera Studio Directing

Most directors do single-camera directing from the studio floor, similar to a walk-through/camera rehearsal. If you direct the single-camera production from the studio floor, you can have the AD in the control room, handling all the operational activities such as rolling the VTR, putting on the leader, calling for the slate, and keying the titles. The AD or the PA can also keep the field log. You, as the director, are then free to watch the line monitor on the studio floor and call for action to get the first take recorded.

For practice, let's direct the first three "scenes" of the lighting program. Strictly defined, they are actually shots, but for logging they count as scenes. Your first scene in the lighting program is Mary's intro: "Hi, I'm Mary . . ."

The AD rolls the VTR and calls for the slate: *Scene 1, take 1 (Mary)*. After Mary says, "Let's watch," have her stand there quietly for a moment before calling "cut"—to stop the action. This will make it easier for the editor to locate the exact edit-out point. "Cut" in this context means to stop the action and the camera.

Because Mary did such a good job, you can now move on to the next scene, John's walk to the telephone. The slate should now read: *Scene 2, take 1 (J walk)*. On your "action" call, John walks to the phone and the camera pans with him. John stops at the phone and waits for your "cut." Both John and the camera operator did a great job, but you must call for another take. Why? Because your cut to a CU of John looking for change would not allow the editor to *cut on action*—a fundamental aspect of postproduction editing. John must start to reach into his pocket while still on the wide or medium shot and then repeat the action on the close-up. The editor can now cut from an LS to a CU *during the action*, not before or after it. This way the cut will remain virtually invisible to the audience. For the second take of John's walk, the slate now reads: *Scene 2, take 2 (J walk)*.

Now you can have the camera line up on the z-axis shot that includes Susan in the foreground and rehearse John's approach to the bench. Now the slate should read: *Scene 3, take 1 (J and S)*. Again, start the scene with John looking for coins before approaching Susan, to give the editor the necessary trim handles and the opportunity to cut on action. Susan blocks John while he's walking to the curb, so you need to retake the scene. The slate now reads: *Scene 3, take 2 (J and S)*.

Although not in the script, an essential shot would be a CU of Susan watching John walk to the phone. You decide to do this reaction shot, so the slate reads: *Scene 3, take 3 (S CU)*.

What happened to the traffic sounds, the occasional cars going by, and the police siren? Shouldn't the AD have cued the sound engineer to mix John's walking sounds and the brief dialogue between John and Susan with the traffic sounds? No. That audio will be laid in later in postproduction mixing. That way you can keep the sounds continuous through John's walk, fishing for coins, and talking to Susan.

Single-camera Field Production

Your single-camera production changes radically if you were to take the lighting show on location—to an actual bus stop. In effect, you would now be directing a single-camera EFP (electronic field production). The major change would be in the script breakdown, that is, how the scenes are arranged for video recording.

The order of the shooting script is no longer determined by narrative progression (Susan waiting for the bus and John walking to the telephone) but by location. Location here refers to the action areas of the bus stop. All shots are exterior—outdoors and, in this case, at a real bus stop.

Daytime Shot Breakdown

1. Bus pulls up. Susan boards bus. Bus drives off. (This shot is listed first because you need to adhere to the bus schedule to get a variety of angles. The timing of all the other shots is under your control.)

2. *Location:* John. Show him walking to the phone and to the bench from several angles. Get CUs of him looking for change and glancing at Susan. Ordinarily, you would do a pickup of close-ups after shooting most of the long shots and medium shots. In this case, however, the continuity of lighting is crucial. You should therefore get the close-ups right away.

3. *Location:* Susan sitting on the bench. Moves 1 through 4 in combination with John's blocking and, depending on the angle, without John (seated on the bench, looking for the bus, and watching John; walking toward the curb and looking back at John; looking at the bus schedule, looking through her purse, moving to the lamp post, and talking to John; moving toward the curb to board the bus).

4. *Cutaways:* Bus pulling up and departing, the bus schedule, the telephone, the newspaper rack, and the bench—or whatever event details that would serve as transitions and intensifiers.

5. *Audio:* You will have ample background sounds of traffic and cars going by whether you like it or not. But this can also be a disadvantage, especially if the street noise overpowers the talent's lines. Wind noise is always a potential hazard. Be sure to audiotape a generous amount of such sounds after you are done with the actual production. This will help the postproduction editor establish shot continuity through ambient sound. The police siren can be supplied by the sound-effects (SFX) library.

The real problem is that all these shots must now be repeated as closely as possible for the nighttime scene. Night shooting is always difficult because of the additional lighting requirements. Also, as pointed out earlier, the audio requirements change. In this case, the postproduction sound manipulation is becoming more difficult.

As you can see, the single-camera EFP of the lighting show is getting more and more complicated. What at first glance seemed to be the easier aspect of the production assignment turns out to be a much more formidable job than the multicamera studio production.

Isn't shooting on location a rather clumsy way of doing the lighting show, especially if it can be done more efficiently with multiple cameras in the studio? Yes, in a way it is. This is where the producer's judgment comes in. A relatively simple production, such as the lighting program, is much more efficiently done as a multicamera studio production than a single-camera EFP. But more-ambitious projects are more effectively done film-style with a single camera. Fortunately, neither video production nor filmmaking is locked into one or the other approach.

Many film productions use multiple cameras simultaneously, not just for spectacular one-time-only shots but even for ordinary scenes. Video too uses both approaches, depending on the nature of the production. ENG and most EFP are done with a single camera. Discussions, game shows, and daytime dramas are all shot with multiple cameras in the studio. All sports and special events require a multicamera approach not unlike that of a studio production.

That said, there are two program formats that undoubtedly are directed with a single-camera setup: the interview with a single guest, and various forms of documentary.

Interview

The standard formula for setting up an interview for a host and a guest is to position the camera next to the host (interviewer), pointed at the guest (interviewee), who is sitting or standing opposite the host. **SEE 17.16** Ask the camera operator to get a fairly tight close-up and keep the camera rolling throughout the interview. At the end of the

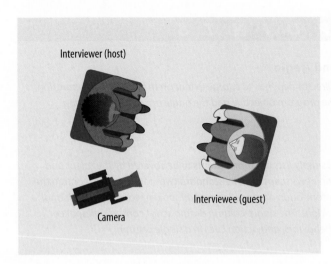

17.16 Standard Single-camera Interview Setup

In the standard single-camera interview setup, the interviewer (host) sits opposite the interviewee (guest). The camera is placed next to the interviewer.

interview, place the camera next to the guest's chair or where the guest was standing and get some reaction shots of the host.

In this postshow pickup session, watch that you don't cross the vector line with the camera in the new setup. If the host sports an automatic smile when on-camera, be careful that he or she doesn't smile in all reaction shots, especially when the interview had some serious moments. To show the host asking some of the questions, you can have him or her repeat them. Try to match the CU sizes of guest and host—don't make one or the other CU noticeably larger. The editor will insert the reaction and question shots in the spots you designate.

Documentary

When shooting a documentary, you cannot and should not direct the event itself but simply the coverage of it. Although you usually have a basic objective or angle in mind before you start recording, don't try to predetermine shots before you see the actual event. Directors who draw up detailed scripts and storyboards before they have seen the subject of the documentary often fail to document the actual event and instead seek shots that fit their preconception of what the event should look like. Ultimately, they document their prejudices rather than the true event.

A good initial approach is to "take notes" with the camera. If you are open-minded and sensitive to what is going on, you may not only refine your initial objective but also develop an idea for an effective angle.

In any case, get some shots that best express the essence of the event; then get some environmental shots that establish the location and the atmosphere, as well as plenty of cutaways. Remind the camera operator to shoot tight: inductive sequencing with plenty of close-ups packs a more powerful punch than a series of medium and long shots. Note that every person you interview must sign a talent release form.

Your real directing skills may have to come into play during postproduction, when you work with the video and sound editors. If you have a specific idea of what the show should look like, do a paper-and-pencil rough-cut for the editor that will quickly communicate your idea.

> **KEY CONCEPT**
>
> In single-camera directing of out-of-sequence shots, watch for continuity of vectors, action, sound, and aesthetic energy.

M A I N   P O I N T S

▶ **Program Objective and Angle**

The success or failure of a director depends to a large extent on the degree of preparation. A clear understanding of the program objective and the angle are essential starting points for the director.

▶ **Script Formats**

The fact, or rundown, sheet simply lists the major points to be covered by the talent and the director. The two-column news script and the standard two-column script contain the video and some directing information on page-left and all spoken words and additional audio information on page-right. The single-column drama script contains all spoken dialogue, major character behaviors, and action cues in a single column.

▶ **Visualization**

A principal task of the director is translating the script into video images and sound. Visualization is one of the techniques employed. It means creating a mental image of a shot or a series of shots. It also includes the mental imaging of sound, context, and sequencing.

▶ **Floor Plan**

A floor plan can help the director visualize key shots, determine lighting and audio requirements, and decide on blocking for talent and cameras.

▶ **Script Marking, Director's Terminology, and Time Line**

Easy-to-read script markings, consistent terminology, and a realistic time line are essential to successful multicamera directing.

▶ **Rehearsals**

A dry run, or blocking rehearsal, is used to block the movements of the talent—where they stand and walk and what they do. In a walkthrough/camera rehearsal combination, the director explains to talent and crew what is happening on the set before doing a run-through with full equipment. The initial walkthrough/camera rehearsal should be conducted from the studio floor.

▶ **Multicamera Directing**

When directing from the control room, the director communicates all major cues to the crew via P.L. headset. The director's cues and procedures must be consistent.

▶ **Single-camera Directing**

In single-camera directing, production efficiency rather than script narrative dictates the order of shots. Utmost care must be taken that the out-of-order shots will enable seamless continuity in postproduction editing. Always provide the editor with usable trim handles.

Z E T T L ' S   V I D E O L A B   3 . 0

For your reference, or to track your work, the Zettl's VideoLab 3.0 program cue in this chapter is listed here with its corresponding page number.

ZVL3 CUE 1   PROCESS→ Ideas→ scripts   **360**

Epilogue

Enough of my preaching! It's now up to you to apply these techniques and principles effectively and efficiently. But I cannot help but give you one more bit of advice: You are now in command of a powerful means of communication and persuasion. Use it wisely and responsibly. Treat your viewers with respect and compassion, regardless of whether they are third-graders, the local university alumni association, corporate employees, or a worldwide audience. Whatever role you play in the production process—pulling cables or directing a complex show—do the very best you can muster. Ultimately, your video accomplishments, however modest they may seem, will make a difference and help us all see the world with heightened awareness and joy.

Glossary

480p A scanning system of digital television. The *p* stands for *progressive,* which means that each complete television frame consists of 480 visible lines that are scanned one after the other.

720p A scanning system of digital television. The *p* stands for *progressive,* which means that each complete television frame consists of 720 visible lines that are scanned one after the other. Generally considered high-definition television. *See* **progressive scanning**.

1080i A scanning system of high-definition television. The *i* stands for *interlaced,* which means that a complete frame is formed from two interlaced scanning fields. Generally considered the high-end HDTV system.

above-the-line Category for nontechnical personnel, such as producers, directors, and talent. Also used as a budget category.

AB-roll editing Creating an edit master tape from two source VTRs, one containing the A-roll, and the other the B-roll. Transitions other than cuts, such as dissolves and wipes, are possible.

academy leader *See* **video leader**

actor A person who appears on-camera in dramatic roles. The actor always portrays someone else.

AD Stands for *associate* or *assistant director.* Assists the director in all production phases.

additive primary colors Red, green, and blue. Ordinary white light (sunlight) can be separated into the three primary light colors. When these three colored lights are combined in various proportions, all other colors can be reproduced.

address code An electronic signal that marks each frame with a specific address. *See* **SMPTE time code**.

AGC Stands for *automatic gain control.* Regulates the volume of the audio or video levels automatically, without using pots.

ambience Background sounds.

analog A signal that fluctuates exactly like the original stimulus.

angle The particular approach to a story—its central theme.

aperture Iris opening of a lens; usually measured in *f*-stops.

arc To move the camera in a slightly curved dolly or truck.

aspect ratio The ratio of the width of the television screen to its height. In STV (standard television), it is 4 × 3 (4 units wide by 3 units high); for HDTV (high-definition television), it is 16 × 9 (16 units wide by 9 units high).

assemble editing Adding shots on videotape in a consecutive order without first recording a control track on the edit master tape.

ATR Stands for audiotape recorder.

attached shadow Shadow that is on the object itself. It cannot be seen independent of (detached from) the object.

ATV Stands for advanced television. *See* **DTV**.

audio track The area of the videotape used for recording the audio information.

auto-focus Automatic focusing system on most consumer camcorders and some ENG/EFP cameras.

auto-iris Automatic control of the aperture (lens opening).

background light Illumination of the set pieces and the backdrop. Also called *set light.*

back light Illumination from behind the subject and opposite the camera; usually a spotlight.

barn doors Metal flaps in front of a lighting instrument that control the spread of the light beam.

baselight Even, nondirectional (diffused) light necessary for the camera to operate optimally. Refers to the overall light intensity.

beam *See* **electron beam**

beam splitter Optical device within the camera that splits the white light into the three additive primary light colors: red, green, and blue.

below-the-line Category for technical personnel, including camera operators, floor persons, and video and audio engineers. Also used as a budget category.

bidirectional The microphone can hear best from two opposite sides.

big remote A production outside the studio to televise live and/or record live-on-tape a large scheduled event that has not been staged specifically for television. Examples include sporting events, parades, political gatherings, and trials or government hearings. Also called *remote*.

binary digit (bit) The smallest amount of information a computer can hold and process. A charge is either present, represented by a *1*, or absent, represented by a *0*. One bit can describe two levels, such as on/off or black/white. Two bits can describe four levels (2^2 bits); three bits, eight levels (2^3 bits); four bits, sixteen (2^4 bits); and so on. A group of eight bits (2^8) is called a *byte*.

blocking Carefully worked-out positioning, movement, and actions by the talent and for all mobile video equipment used in a scene.

blocking rehearsal *See* **dry run**

book *See* **twofold**

boom (1) *Audio:* microphone support. (2) *Video:* part of a camera crane. (3) To move the boom of the camera crane up or down; also called *crane*.

bump-down Copying a videotape to a lower-quality tape format. Also called *dub-down*.

bump-up Copying a videotape to a higher-quality tape format. Also called *dub-up*.

calibrate the zoom lens To preset a zoom lens to keep in focus throughout the zoom.

camcorder A portable camera with the VTR or other recording device built into it.

camera chain The television camera and associated electronic equipment, consisting of the power supply, sync generator, and camera control unit.

camera control unit (CCU) Equipment, separate from the actual camera, that allows the video operator to adjust the color and brightness balance before and during the production.

camera rehearsal Full rehearsal with cameras and other pieces of production equipment. Often identical to the dress rehearsal.

cam head A camera mounting head that permits extremely smooth tilts and pans.

cant To tilt the camera sideways.

cap (1) Lens cap: a rubber or metal cap placed in front of the lens to protect it from light, dust, and physical damage. (2) Electronic device that eliminates the picture from the camera CCD.

capture Moving video and audio from an analog or digital videotape to the hard drive of a computer with a nonlinear editing program. Analog signals must be converted to digital before they can be imported by the computer.

cardioid Heart-shaped pickup pattern of a unidirectional microphone.

cast shadow Shadow that is produced by an object and thrown (cast) onto another surface. It can be seen independent of the object.

C channel *See* **chrominance channel**

C-clamp A metal clamp with which lighting instruments are attached to the lighting batten.

CCU *See* **camera control unit**

CD Stands for *compact disc*. A small, shiny disc that contains audio and/or video information in digital form.

C.G. *See* **character generator**

character generator (C.G.) A computer dedicated to the creation of letters and numbers in various fonts. Its output can be directly integrated into video images.

charge-coupled device (CCD) An imaging device that translates the optical image into a video signal. Also called *chip*.

chip *See* **charge-coupled device (CCD)**

chroma key Special key effect that uses a color (usually blue or green) for the key source backdrop. All blue or green areas are replaced by the base picture during the key.

chrominance channel Contains the RGB video signals or some combination thereof. Also called *color*, or *C, channel*.

close-up (CU) Object or any part of it seen at close range and framed tightly. The close-up can be extreme (extreme or big close-up) or rather loose (medium close-up).

closure *See* **psychological closure**

codec Stands for *compression-decompression*. Can be one of several compression systems of digital video, graphics, and audio files.

coding To change the quantized values into a binary code, represented by 0's and 1's. Also called *encoding*.

color bars A color standard used in video production for the alignment of cameras and videotape recordings. Color bars can be generated by most professional portable cameras.

color channel *See* **chrominance channel**

color media *See* **gel**

color temperature Relative reddishness or bluishness of white light, as measured on the Kelvin (K) scale. The norm for indoor video lighting is 3,200K; for outdoors, 5,600K.

complexity editing Building an intensified screen event from carefully selected and juxtaposed shots. Does not have to adhere to the continuity principles.

component system *See* **Y/C component video**, **RGB component video**, and **Y/color difference component video**

composite video A system that combines the Y (luminance, or black-and-white) and C (color—red, green, and blue) video information into a single signal. Also called *NTSC*.

compression The temporary rearrangement or elimination of redundant picture information for easier storage and signal transport.

condenser microphone High-quality, sensitive microphone for critical sound pickup.

contact person A person who is familiar with, and who can facilitate access to, the remote location and the key people. Also called *contact*.

continuing vectors Graphic vectors that extend each other, or index and motion vectors that point and move in the same direction.

continuity editing Preserving visual continuity from shot to shot.

contrast The difference between the brightest and the darkest spots in a video picture.

control room directing *See* **multicamera directing**

control track The area of the videotape used for recording synchronizing information.

control track system *See* **pulse-count system**

converging vectors Index and motion vectors that point toward each other.

crane To move the boom of the camera crane up or down. Also called *boom*.

cross-shot (X/S) Similar to the over-the-shoulder shot except that the camera-near person is completely out of the shot.

CU *See* **close-up**

cue card A large hand-lettered card that contains copy, usually held next to the camera lens by floor personnel.

cut (1) The instantaneous change from one shot (image) to another. (2) Director's signal to interrupt action (used during rehearsal).

cutaway A shot of an object or event that is peripherally connected with the overall event and that is relatively static. Commonly used between two shots that do not provide good continuity.

cyc *See* **cyclorama**

cyc light *See* **strip light**

cyclorama A U-shaped continuous piece of canvas or muslin for backing of scenery and action. Hardwall cycs are permanently installed in front of one or two of the studio walls. Also called *cyc*.

DAT Stands for digital audiotape.

delegation controls Controls that assign a specific function to a bus on a switcher.

depth of field The area in which all objects, located at different distances from the camera, appear in focus. Depends primarily on the focal length of the lens, its *f*-stop, and the distance from the camera to the object.

diffused light Light that illuminates a relatively large area with an indistinct light beam. Diffused light, created by floodlights, produces soft shadows.

digital Pertaining to data in the form of digits (on/off pulses).

digital television (DTV) Digital systems that generally have a higher image resolution than standard television. Sometimes called *advanced television (ATV)*.

digital versatile disc (DVD) The standard DVD can store 4.7 gigabytes of video and/or audio information.

digital video effects (DVE) Video effects generated by a computer with high-capacity hard drives and graphics software. The computer system dedicated to DVE is called a *graphics generator*.

digitizing Similar to capturing analog audio and video. The analog signals of a videotape are converted to digital signals for storage on the computer hard drive.

dimmer A device that controls the intensity of light by throttling the electric current flowing to the lamp.

directional light Light that illuminates a relatively small area with a distinct light beam. Directional light, produced by spotlights, creates harsh, clearly defined shadows.

diverging vectors Index and motion vectors that point away from each other.

documentary script *See* **standard two-column script**

dolly To move the camera toward (dolly in) or away from (dolly out) the object.

downstream keyer (DSK) A control that allows a title to be keyed (cut in) over the picture (line-out signal) as it leaves the switcher.

dress (1) What people wear on-camera. (2) Dress rehearsal: final rehearsal with all facilities operating. The dress rehearsal is often videotaped. (3) Decorating a set with set properties. (4) Set dressing: set properties.

drop Heavy curtain suspended from a track (usually in front of the cyc). A painted drop is a large piece of canvas with a background scene painted on it.

dry run Rehearsal without equipment, during which the basic actions of the talent are worked out. Also called *blocking rehearsal*.

DSK *See* **downstream keyer**

DTV *See* **digital television**

dub The duplication of an electronic recording. The dub is always one generation away from the recording used for dubbing. In analog systems, each dub shows increased deterioration.

dub-down *See* **bump-down**

dub-up *See* **bump-up**

DVD *See* **digital versatile disc**

DVE *See* **digital video effects**

dynamic microphone A relatively rugged microphone. Good for outdoor use.

edit controller A machine that assists in various editing functions, such as marking edit-in and edit-out points, rolling source and record VTRs, and integrating effects. It can be a desktop computer with a specific software program. Also called *editing control unit.*

edit decision list (EDL) Consists of edit-in and edit-out points, expressed in time code numbers, and the nature of transitions between shots.

editing control unit *See* **edit controller**

editing log *See* **VTR log**

edit master The videotape or disc that contains the final version of an edited program. Subsequent copies are struck from the edit master.

EDL *See* **edit decision list**

effects bus Rows of buttons on the switcher that can select the video sources for a specific effect. Usually the same as a mix bus that has been switched to an effects function.

effect-to-cause model Moving from idea to desired effect on the viewer and then backing up to the specific medium requirements to produce such an effect.

EFP *See* **electronic field production**

EFP team Usually a three-person team, consisting of the talent; a camcorder operator; and a utility person who handles lighting, audio, and/or video recording, and, if necessary, the microwave transmission back to the studio.

electron beam A thin stream of electrons, generated by the electron gun in back of the video tube, which strikes the photosensitive color dots at the face of the tube.

electronic field production (EFP) Video production done outside the studio that is usually shot for postproduction (not live).

electronic news gathering (ENG) The use of portable camcorders, lights, and sound equipment for the production of mostly unscheduled daily news events. ENG is usually done for live transmission or immediate postproduction.

electronic still store (ESS) system Stores many still video frames in digital form for easy access.

encoding *See* **coding**

ENG *See* **electronic news gathering**

ENG/EFP camera Highly portable, high-end self-contained camera for electronic field production.

ESS *See* **electronic still store (ESS) system**

essential area The section of the television picture that is seen by the home viewer, regardless of minor misalignments of the receiver. Also called *safe title area.*

establishing shot *See* **long shot**

facilities request Written communication that lists all facilities needed for a specific production.

fact sheet Script format that lists the items to be shown on-camera and their main features. May contain suggestions of what to say about the product. Also called *rundown sheet.*

fade The gradual appearance of a picture from black (fade-in) or disappearance to black (fade-out).

fader A volume control that works by sliding a button horizontally along a specific scale. Identical in function to a pot. Also called *slide fader.*

fader bar A lever on the switcher that activates buses and can produce superimpositions, dissolves, fades, keys, and wipes of different speeds.

falloff The speed (degree) with which a light picture portion turns into shadow areas. *Fast falloff* means that the light areas turn abruptly into shadow areas and there is a great difference in brightness between light and shadow areas. *Slow falloff* indicates a very gradual change from light to dark and a minimal brightness difference between light and shadow areas.

fast lens A lens that permits a relatively great amount of light to pass through at its largest aperture (lowest f-stop number). Can be used in low-light conditions.

field One-half of a complete scanning cycle, with two fields necessary for one television picture frame. In standard (NTSC) television, there are 60 fields, or 30 frames, per second.

field dolly A plywood platform supported by four wheels with pneumatic tires. Used for moving a tripod-mounted camera on a rough surface.

field log A record of each take during the videotaping.

field of view The portion of a scene visible through a particular lens; its vista. Expressed in symbols, such as *CU* for close-up.

field production Production activities that take place away from the studio.

fill light Additional light on the opposite side of the camera from the key light to illuminate shadow areas and thereby reduce falloff; usually done with floodlights.

film-style *See* **single-camera production**

fishpole A suspension device for a microphone; the mic is attached to a pole and held over the scene for brief periods.

flash drive *See* **flash memory device**

flash memory device A read/write portable storage device that can download, store, and upload a limited amount of digital audio and video information. Also called *flash drive* or *memory card*.

flat A piece of standing scenery used as background or to simulate the walls of a room. There are hardwall and softwall flats.

floodlight A lighting instrument that produces diffused light.

floor director *See* **floor manager**

floor manager In charge of all activities on the studio floor, such as setting up scenery, getting talent into place, and relaying the director's cues to the talent. In the field, basically responsible for preparing the location for the shoot and for cueing all talent. Also called *floor director* or *stage manager.*

floor plan A diagram of scenery, properties, and set dressings drawn on a grid.

focal length With the lens set at infinity, the distance from the iris to the plane where the picture is in focus. Normally measured in millimeters or inches.

foldback The return of the total or partial audio mix to the talent through headsets or I.F.B. channels. *See* **I.F.B.**

foot-candle (fc) The unit of measurement of illumination, or the amount of light that falls on an object. One foot-candle is 1 candlepower of light (1 lumen) that falls on a 1-square-foot area located 1 foot away from the light source. *See also* **lux**.

foundation A makeup base, normally done with water-soluble pancake makeup, that is applied with a sponge to the face and sometimes to all exposed skin areas. Pancake foundation reduces unwanted light reflection.

frame A complete scanning cycle of the electron beam. In interlaced scanning, two partial scanning cycles (fields) are necessary for one frame. In progressive scanning, each scanning cycle produces one complete frame. *See* **interlaced scanning** and **progressive scanning**.

frame rate The time it takes to scan a complete frame; usually expressed in frames per second (fps). In standard (NTSC) television, there are 60 fields, or 30 frames, per second. In DTV the frame rate is flexible (ranging from 15 fps to 60 fps). HDTV cinema cameras have adopted the film standard of 24 fps, but you can change their frame rate.

frame store synchronizer Image stabilization and synchronization system that has a memory large enough to store and read out one complete video frame. Used to synchronize signals from a variety of video sources that are not locked to a common sync signal. Can also produce a limited number of digital effects.

Fresnel spotlight One of the most common spots, named after the inventor of its lens, which has steplike concentric rings.

f-stop The scale on the lens, indicating the aperture. The larger the f-stop number, the smaller the aperture; the smaller the f-stop number, the larger the aperture.

gel Generic name for color filter put in front of spotlights or floodlights to give the light beam a specific hue. *Gel* comes from *gelatin*, the filter material used before the invention of much more heat- and moisture-resistant plastic material. Also called *color media*.

generation The number of dubs away from the original recording. A first-generation dub is struck directly from the source tape. A second-generation tape is a dub of the first-generation dub (two steps away from the original tape), and so forth. The greater the number of nondigital generations, the greater the loss of quality.

graphics generator A computer specially designed for creating a variety of images and colors. Also called *paint box*. *See also* **digital video effects**.

hand props Objects, called *properties*, that are handled by the performer or actor.

HDTV *See* **high-definition television**

HDV *See* **high-definition video**

headroom The space between the top of the head and the upper screen edge.

high-definition television (HDTV) Includes the 720p, 1080i, and 1080p scanning systems. Because the 480p system produces high-quality video, it is sometimes included in the HDTV category.

high-definition video (HDV) A recording system that produces images of the same resolution as HDTV (720p and 1080i). The images are much more compressed than those of HDTV, resulting in a slightly lower image quality.

high-key lighting Light background and ample light on the scene. Has nothing to do with the vertical positioning of the key light.

hypercardioid A very narrow pickup pattern with a long reach. The mic can also hear sounds coming directly from the back.

I.F.B. Stands for *interruptible foldback* or *feedback*. A prompting system that allows communication with the talent while on the air. A small earpiece worn by on-the-air talent that carries program sound (including the talent's voice) or instructions from the producer or director.

imaging device *See* **pickup device**

incident light Light that strikes the object directly from its source. To measure incident light, point the light meter at the camera lens or into the lighting instruments.

insert editing Produces highly stable edits. Requires the prior laying of a continuous control track by recording black on the edit master tape.

instantaneous editing *See* **switching**

interactive video A computer-driven program that gives the viewer some control over what to see and how to see it. It is often used as a training device.

intercom Short for *intercommunication system.* Used for all production and engineering personnel involved in a show. The most widely used system has telephone headsets to facilitate voice communication on several wired or wireless channels. Includes other systems, such as I.F.B. and cellular telephones.

interlaced scanning The scanning of all the odd-numbered lines (first field) and the subsequent scanning of all the even-numbered lines (second field). The two fields make up a complete television frame. *See also* **frame**.

iris Adjustable lens-opening mechanism. Also called *lens diaphragm.*

jack (1) *Audio:* a socket or receptacle for a connector. (2) *Scenery:* a brace for a flat.

jib arm A small camera crane that can be operated by the cameraperson.

jogging Frame-by-frame advancement of a recorded shot sequence, resulting in a jerking motion.

jump cut An image that jumps slightly from one screen position to another during a cut. Also, any gross visual discontinuity from shot to shot.

Kelvin (K) The standard scale for measuring color temperature, or the relative reddishness or bluishness of white light.

key An electronic effect in which the keyed image (figure—usually letters) blocks out portions of the base picture (background) and therefore appears to be layered on top of it.

key bus Row of buttons on the switcher used to select the video source to be inserted into the background image.

key light Principal source of illumination; usually a spotlight.

lavaliere A small microphone that is clipped to clothing. Also called *lav.*

leadroom The space in front of a laterally moving object or person.

lens Optical lens, essential for projecting an optical image of the scene onto the front surface of the camera imaging device. Lenses come in various fixed focal lengths or in a variable focal length (zoom lenses) and with various maximum apertures (lens openings).

lens diaphragm *See* **iris**

level (1) *Audio:* sound volume. (2) *Video:* video signal strength.

light intensity The amount of light falling on an object that is seen by the lens. Measured in lux or foot-candles. Also called *light level. See* **foot-candle** and **lux**.

light level *See* **light intensity**

light plot A plan, similar to a floor plan, that shows the type, size (wattage), and location of the lighting instruments relative to the scene to be illuminated and the general direction of the light beams.

lighting triangle *See* **photographic principle**

line *See* **vector line**

line monitor The monitor that shows only the line-out pictures that go on the air or on videotape.

linear editing system Uses videotape as the editing medium. It does not allow random access of shots.

line-level input Input channel on a mixer or an audio console for relatively high-level audio sources. *See also* **mic-level input**.

line-out The line that carries the final video or audio output.

live-on-tape The uninterrupted videotape recording of a live show for later unedited playback.

live-switched directing *See* **multicamera directing**

location sketch A rough, hand-drawn map of the locale for a remote telecast. For an indoor remote, the sketch shows the dimensions of the room and the locations of furniture and windows. For an outdoor remote, the sketch indicates the buildings and the location of the remote truck, power source, and the sun during the time of the telecast.

location survey Written assessment, usually in the form of a checklist, of the production requirements for a remote.

long-focal-length lens *See* **telephoto lens**

long shot (LS) Object seen from far away or framed very loosely. The extreme long shot shows the object from a great distance. Also called *establishing shot.*

lossless compression Rearranging but not eliminating pixels during digital storage and transport.

lossy compression Throwing away redundant pixels during digital compression. Most compression is the lossy kind.

low-key lighting Fast-falloff lighting with dark background and selectively illuminated areas. Has nothing to do with the vertical positioning of the key light.

LS *See* **long shot**

luma *See* **luminance**

luma channel *See* **luminance channel**

lumen The light intensity power of one candle (light source radiating in all directions).

luminance The brightness (black-and-white) information of a video signal. Also called *luma* to include the grayscale information.

luminance channel Contains the black-and-white part of a video signal. It is mainly responsible for the sharpness of the picture. Also called *luma,* or *Y, channel.*

lux European standard unit for measuring light intensity. One lux is 1 lumen (1 candlepower) of light that falls on a surface of 1 square meter located 1 meter away from the light source. 10.75 lux = 1 foot-candle. Most lighting people figure roughly 10 lux = 1 foot-candle. *See also* **foot-candle**.

M/E bus Row of buttons on the switcher that can serve mix or effects functions.

master control Controls the program input, storage, and retrieval for on-the-air telecasts. Also oversees the technical quality of all program material.

matte key The key (usually letters) is filled with gray or a color.

MD *See* **mini disc**

medium requirements All personnel, equipment, and facilities needed for a production, as well as budgets, schedules, and the various production phases.

medium shot (MS) Object seen from a medium distance. Covers any framing between a long shot and a close-up.

memory card *See* **flash drive**

mental map Tells us where things are or are supposed to be in on- and off-screen space.

mic Short for *microphone.*

mic-level input Input channel on a mixer or an audio console for relatively low-level audio sources, such as microphones. *See also* **line-level input**.

mini disc (MD) A small optical disc that can store one hour of CD-quality audio.

mini plug Connector used for some consumer audio equipment.

mix bus Rows of buttons on the switcher that permit the mixing of video sources, as in a dissolve or a super. Mix buses are fundamental for on-the-air switching.

mixing (1) *Audio:* combining two or more sounds in specific proportions (volume variations) as determined by the event (show) context. (2) *Video:* combining two shots as a dissolve or superimposition via the switcher.

moiré effect Color vibrations that occur when narrow, contrasting stripes of a design interfere with the scanning lines of the video system.

monitor High-quality video receiver used in the video studio and control rooms. Cannot receive broadcast signals.

monochrome One color. In video it refers to a camera or monitor that produces a black-and-white picture.

mounting head A device that connects the camera to its support. Also called *pan-and-tilt head.*

MPEG A digital compression technique developed by the Moving Picture Experts Group for moving pictures.

MPEG-2 A digital compression standard for motion video.

MS *See* **medium shot**

multicamera directing Simultaneous coordination of two or more cameras for instantaneous editing (switching). Also called *control room directing* and *live-switched directing.*

multicamera production The use of two or more cameras to capture a scene simultaneously from different points of view. Each camera output can be recorded separately (iso configuration) and/or fed into a switcher for instantaneous editing.

multimedia Computer display of text, sound, and still and moving images. Usually recorded on CD-ROM or DVD.

narrow-angle lens *See* **telephoto lens**

NLE *See* **nonlinear editing system**

noise (1) *Audio:* unwanted sounds that interfere with the intentional sounds, or unwanted hisses or hums inevitably generated by the electronics of the audio equipment. (2) *Video:* electronic interference that shows up as snow.

nonlinear editing system (NLE) Allows random access of shots. The video and audio information is stored in digital form on computer disks. Usually has two external monitors, small loudspeakers, and an audio mixer.

nonlinear storage system Storage of video and audio material in digital form on a hard drive or read/write optical disc. Each single frame can be instantly accessed by the computer.

noseroom The space in front of a person looking or pointing toward the edge of the screen.

NTSC Stands for *National Television System Committee.* Normally refers to the composite video signal, consisting of the Y signal (luminance, or black-and-white information) and the C signal (red, green, and blue color information). *See also* **composite video**.

off-line editing In linear editing it produces an edit decision list or an edit master not intended for broadcast. In nonlinear editing the selected shots are captured in low resolution to save computer storage space.

omnidirectional Pickup pattern with which the microphone can hear equally well from all directions.

on-line editing In linear editing it produces the final high-quality edit master for broadcast or program duplication. In nonlinear editing it requires recapturing the selected shots at a higher resolution.

over-the-shoulder shot (O/S) Camera looks over the camera-near person's shoulder (shoulder and back of head included in shot) at the other person.

P.L. Stands for *private line* or *phone line.* Major intercommunication device in video studios. Also called *party line.*

PA Production assistant.

P.A. system *See* **S.A.**

pads *See* **trim handles**

pan To turn the camera horizontally.

pan-and-tilt head *See* **mounting head**

pancake A makeup base, or foundation makeup, usually water-soluble and applied with a small sponge.

party line *See* **P.L.**

patchbay A device that connects various inputs with specific outputs. Also called *patchboard*.

patchboard *See* **patchbay**

pedestal To move the camera up or down using a studio pedestal.

performer A person who appears on-camera in nondramatic shows. The performer does not assume someone else's character.

photographic principle The triangular arrangement of key, back, and fill lights, with the back light opposite the camera and directly behind the object, and the key and fill lights on opposite sides of the camera and to the front and the side of the object. Also called *triangle,* or *three-point, lighting*.

pickup device In a video camera, converts the optical image into electric energy—the video signal. Also called *imaging device*.

pickup pattern The territory around the microphone within which the mic can hear well.

polar pattern The two-dimensional representation of the microphone pickup pattern.

pop filer A wire-mesh screen attached to the front of a mic that reduces breath pops and sudden air blasts.

postproduction Any production activity that occurs after the production. Usually refers to either video editing and/or audio sweetening.

postproduction editing The assembly of recorded material after the actual production, in contrast to instantaneous editing with the switcher.

postproduction team Normally consists of the director, a video editor, and, for complex productions, a sound designer who remixes the sound track.

pot Short for potentiometer, a sound-volume control. *See* **fader**.

preproduction Preparation of all production details.

preproduction team Comprises the people who plan the production. Normally includes the producer, writer, director, art director, and technical director. Large productions may include a composer and a choreographer. In charge: producer.

preroll To start a videotape and let it roll for a few seconds before it is put in the playback or record mode to give the electronic system time to stabilize.

preset bus *See* **preview bus**

preset the zoom lens *See* **calibrate the zoom lens**

preview bus Row of buttons on the switcher that can direct an input to the preview monitor at the same time another video source is on the air. Also called *preset bus*.

preview monitor Any monitor that shows a video source, except for the line and off-the-air monitors.

producer Creator and organizer of video programs.

production The actual activities in which an event is recorded and/or televised.

production model Moving from idea to the program objective and then backing up to the specific medium requirements to achieve the objective.

production schedule A calendar that shows the preproduction, production, and postproduction dates, and who is doing what, when, and where. *See also* **time line**.

production switcher Switcher designed for instantaneous editing, located in the studio control room or remote truck.

production team Consists of a variety of nontechnical and technical people, such as producer and various assistants (associate producer and production assistant), director and assistant director, and talent and production crew. In charge: director.

program bus Row of buttons on the switcher, with inputs that are directly switched to the line-out.

program objective The desired effect of the program on the viewer.

progressive scanning The consecutive scanning of lines from top to bottom. *See also* **frame**.

properties *See* **props**

props Short for *properties*. Furniture and other objects used by talent and for set decoration.

psychological closure Mentally filling in missing visual information that will lead to a complete and stable configuration. Also called *closure*.

pulse-count system An address code that counts the control track pulses and translates that count into time and frame numbers. Also called *control track system*.

quantizing A step in the digitization of an analog signal. It changes the sampling points into discrete numerical values (0's and 1's). Also called *quantization*.

quick-release plate A mechanism on a tripod that makes it easy to mount and position the camera so that it is perfectly balanced each time.

radio mic *See* **wireless microphone**

RCA phono plug Connector for video and audio equipment.

reflected light Light that is bounced off the illuminated object. To measure reflected light, point the light meter close to the object from the direction of the camera.

refresh rate The number of complete scanning cycles per second. Also expressed in frames per second. *See* **frame**.

remote A production of a large, scheduled event done for live transmission or live-on-tape recording. *See* **big remote**.

remote survey An inspection of the remote location by key production and engineering personnel so that they can plan for the setup and the use of production equipment. Also called *site survey*.

remote truck The vehicle that carries the control room, audio control, video-recording section, video control section, and transmission equipment.

RGB Stands for red, green, and blue—the basic colors of television.

RGB component video A system in which all three color signals are kept separate and recorded separately on videotape. Often called *RGB system*.

RGB system *See* **RGB component video**

ribbon microphone High-quality, highly sensitive microphone for critical sound pickup in the studio, usually for recording string instruments.

rough-cut A preliminary off-line edit.

rundown sheet *See* **fact sheet**

S.A. Stands for *studio address system*. A public address loudspeaker system from the control room to the studio. Also called *studio talkback* or *P.A.* (public address) *system*.

safe title area *See* **essential area**

sampling Taking a number of samples (voltages) of the analog video or audio signal at equally spaced intervals.

scanning The movement of the electron beam from left to right and from top to bottom on the television screen.

scene Event details that form an organic unit, usually in a single place and time. A series of organically related shots that depict these event details.

scenery Background flats and other pieces (windows, doors, pillars) that simulate a specific environment.

scoop A scooplike floodlight.

scrim A heat-resistant spun-glass material that comes in rolls and can be cut with scissors like cloth; it is attached to a scoop to diffuse the light beam.

script Written document that tells what the program is about, who says what, what is supposed to happen, and what and how the audience shall see and hear the event.

sequencing The control and the structuring of a shot sequence.

set light *See* **background light**

shader *See* **video operator (VO)**

shot The video contained between transitions. Also called *take*.

shot sheet A list of every shot a particular camera has to get. It is attached to the camera to help the camera operator remember a shot sequence.

shotgun microphone A highly directional mic with a shotgun-like barrel for picking up sounds over a great distance.

shutter speed A camera control that reduces the blurring of bright, fast-moving objects. The higher the shutter speed, the less blurring occurs but the more light is needed.

signal-to-noise ratio The relation of the strength of the desired signal to the accompanying electronic interference (the noise). A high signal-to-noise ratio is desirable (strong video or audio signal and weak noise).

single-camera directing Directing a single camera (usually a camcorder) in the studio or field for takes that are recorded separately for postproduction.

single-camera production All the video is captured by a single camera or camcorder for postproduction editing. Similar to the traditional film approach. Also called *film-style*.

single-column drama script Traditional script format for television plays. All dialogue and action cues are written in a single column.

site survey *See* **remote survey**

slant track The video track that is recorded on the videotape in a slanted, diagonal way.

slate (1) To identify, verbally or visually, each videotaped take. (2) A blackboard or whiteboard upon which essential production information is written, such as the title of the show, date, and scene and take numbers. It is recorded at the beginning of each videotaped take.

slide fader *See* **fader**

slow lens A lens that permits a relatively small amount of light to pass through (relatively high *f*-stop number at its largest aperture). Requires higher light levels for optimal pictures.

SMPTE Stands for Society of Motion Picture and Television Engineers. This time code is officially called SMPTE/EBU (for European Broadcasting Union).

SMPTE time code A specially generated address code that marks each video frame with a specific number (hour, minute, second, and frame). Named for the Society of Motion Picture and Television Engineers, this time code is officially called SMPTE/EBU (for European Broadcasting Union).

sound perspective People (or other sound-producing sources) sound farther away in long shots than in close-ups.

source VTR The videotape recorder that supplies the program segments to be edited by the record VTR.

spotlight A lighting instrument that produces directional, relatively undiffused light.

stage manager *See* **floor manager**

standard two-column script Traditional script format with video information on page-left and audio information on page-right for a variety of television scripts, such as for documentaries or commercials. Also called *two-column documentary script*.

Steadicam A camera mount that allows the operator to walk and run, with the camera remaining steady.

sticks *See* **tripod**

storyboard A series of sketches of the key visualization points of an event, with the corresponding audio information given below each visualization.

strike To remove certain objects; to remove scenery and equipment from the studio floor after the show.

strip light Several self-contained lamps arranged in a strip. Used mostly for illumination of the cyclorama. Also called *cyc light*.

studio camera Heavy, high-quality camera and zoom lens that cannot be maneuvered properly without the aid of a pedestal or some other type of camera mount.

studio control room A room adjacent to the studio in which the director, producer, various production assistants, technical director, audio engineer, and sometimes the lighting director perform their various production functions.

studio pedestal A heavy camera dolly that permits raising and lowering the camera while on the air.

studio production Production activities that take place in the studio.

studio talkback *See* **S.A.**

super Short for *superimposition*. A double exposure of two images, with the top one letting the bottom one show through.

S-video *See* **Y/C component video**

sweep Curved piece of scenery, similar to a large pillar cut in half.

sweetening The postproduction manipulation of recorded sound.

switcher (1) A panel with rows of buttons that allows the selection and the assembly of various video sources through a variety of transition devices as well as the creation of electronic effects. (2) Production person who is doing the switching.

switching A change from one video source to another and the creation of various transitions and effects during production with the aid of a switcher. Also called *instantaneous editing*.

sync generator Part of the camera chain; produces electronic synchronization pulses.

synthetic environment Electronically generated settings, either through chroma key or computer.

take The video contained between transitions. Also called *shot*.

talent Collective name for all performers and actors who appear regularly in video.

tally light Red light on the camera and inside the camera viewfinder, indicating when the camera is on the air (switched to the line-out).

tapeless systems Refers to the recording, storage, and playback of audio and video information via computer storage devices rather than videotape.

TBC *See* **time base corrector**

TD Stands for *technical director*. The TD usually operates the switcher.

telephoto lens Gives a close-up view of an event relatively far away from the camera. Also called *long-focal-length*, or *narrow-angle, lens*.

teleprompter A prompting device that projects moving copy over the lens so that the talent can read it without losing eye contact with the viewer.

threefold Three flats hinged together.

three-point lighting *See* **photographic principle**

tilt To point the camera up or down.

time base corrector (TBC) An electronic accessory to videotape recorders that helps make videotape playbacks electronically stable. It keeps slightly different scanning cycles in step.

time code *See* **SMPTE time code**

time line A schedule that shows the time allotments for various activities during a single production day. Often prepared by the director. Also (but erroneously) called *production schedule*.

tongue To move the boom with the camera from left to right or from right to left.

track *See* **truck**

triangle lighting The triangular arrangement of key, back, and fill lights. Also called *three-point lighting* or *photographic principle*. *See* **photographic principle**.

triaxial cable Thin camera cable in which one central wire is surrounded by two concentric shields.

trim handles Recording additional footage before and after the major shot content for more-precise editing. Also called *pads*.

tripod A three-legged camera mount. Also called *sticks*.

truck To move the camera laterally by means of a mobile camera mount. Also called *track*.

two-column documentary script *See* **standard two-column script**

two-column news script Traditional script format with video information on page-left and news copy on page-right for news presentations.

twofold Two flats hinged together. Also called a *book*.

two-shot Framing of two people in a single shot.

unidirectional Pickup pattern with which the microphone can hear best from the front.

uplink truck Truck that sends video and audio signals to a satellite.

variable-focal-length lens *See* **zoom lens**

vector A directional screen force. There are graphic, index, and motion vectors.

vector line An imaginary line created by extending converging index vectors or the direction of a motion vector. Also called the *line of conversation and action*, the *hundredeighty* (for 180 degrees), or, simply, the *line*.

video leader Visual and auditory material that precedes any color videotape recording. Also called *academy leader*.

video operator (VO) In charge of the camera setup and picture control during a production. Also called *shader*.

video-record operator In charge of video recording. Also called *VR operator* and *VTR operator*.

video server A large-capacity computer hard drive that can store and play back audio and video information.

video track The area of the videotape used for recording the video information.

viewfinder A small video monitor or flat-panel screen on a camera that displays the black-and-white or color picture the camera generates.

virtual reality Computer-simulated environment with which the user can interact and that can change to the preprogrammed extent.

visualization The mental image of a shot. May also include the imagining of verbal and nonverbal sounds. Mentally converting a scene into a number of key video images and their sequencing.

VO *See* **video operator**

volume-unit (VU) meter Measures volume units, the relative loudness of amplified sound.

VR operator *See* **video-record operator**

VU meter *See* **volume-unit meter**

VTR log A record of each take on the source tapes. Also called *editing log*.

VTR operator *See* **video-record operator**

walk-through/camera rehearsal A combination of an orientation session for talent and crew and a follow-up rehearsal with full equipment. This combination rehearsal is generally conducted from the studio floor.

white balance The adjustments of the color circuits in the camera to produce white color in lighting of various color temperatures (relative reddishness or bluishness of white light).

wide-angle lens A short-focal-length lens that provides a large vista.

window dub A dub of the source tapes to a lower-quality tape format with the address code keyed into each frame.

windscreen Acoustic foam rubber that is put over the entire microphone to cut down wind noise.

windsock A moplike cloth cover that is put over the windscreen to further reduce wind noise in outdoor use.

wipe A transition in which one image seems to "wipe off" (replace) the other from the screen.

wireless microphone A system that sends audio signals over the air, rather than through microphone cables. The mic is attached to a small transmitter, and the signals are sent to a receiver connected to the audio console or recording device. Also called *radio mic*.

XLR connector Professional three-wire connector for audio cables.

X/S *See* **cross-shot**

Y/C component video A system that keeps the Y (luminance, or black-and-white) and C (color—red, green, and blue) signals separate. Y and C are combined again when recorded on tape. Also called *Y/C system* or *S-video*.

Y channel *See* **luminance channel**

Y/color difference component video Video-recording system wherein the three signals—the luminance, or luma (Y) signal, the red signal minus its luminance (R–Y), and the blue signal minus its luminance (B–Y)—are kept separate during the recording and storage process. All three signals are recorded separately on videotape.

Y/C system *See* **Y/C component video**

z-axis Indicates screen depth. Extends from camera lens to horizon.

zoom To change the focal length of the lens through the use of a zoom control while the camera remains stationary.

zoom lens Variable-focal-length lens. All video cameras are equipped with a zoom lens.

zoom range How much the focal length can be changed from a wide shot to a close-up during a zoom. The zoom range is stated as a ratio, such as 20:1. Also called *zoom ratio*.

zoom ratio *See* **zoom range**

Index

PHOTO CREDITS

360 Systems: 7.32

Edward Aiona: author portrait p. xiii, 3.3, 3.4, 4.6, 4.7, 4.16, 4.20, 4.21, 5.1, 5.2, 5.3, 5.4, 5.5, 5.6, 5.7, 5.8, 5.14, 5.25, 5.27, 6.1, 6.2, 6.3, 6.4, 6.6, 6.8, 6.9, 6.10, 6.11, 6.12, 6.13, 6.14, 6.15, 6.16, 6.19, 6.20, 6.22, 6.23, 6.24, 6.26, 6.27, 6.33, 6.34, 7.5, 7.7, 7.9, 7.10, 7.14, 7.15, 7.16, 7.17, 7.25, 7.26, 7.30, 8.8, 8.9, 8.14, 8.20, 8.26, 8.31, 8.32, 8.33, 8.34, 8.35, 8.36, 9.8, 9.9, 9.11, 9.17, 9.19, 9.20, 9.21, 9.22, 9.23, 9.24, 9.25, 9.26, 10.5, 10.6, 10.9, 10.10, 10.11, 10.12, 10.13, 11.11, 12.1, 12.12, 12.18, 13.1, 13.2, 13.3, 13.4, 13.5, 13.6, 13.7, 13.8, 13.9, 13.10, 13.11, 13.12, 13.13, 13.14, 13.15, 13.16, 13.17, 13.21, 13.22, 13.23, 13.24, 13.25, 13.26, 13.28, 14.1, 14.4, 14.5, 14.6, 14.7, 14.9, 14.12, 15.1, 16.1, 16.3

AKG Acoustics, Inc.: 7.6

Avid Technology, Inc.: 7.33

Azden Corporation: 7.20, 7.21

beyerdynamic Inc.: 7.8, 7.21

Bogen Imaging, Inc.: 5.10

Broadcast and Electronic Communication Arts Department at San Francisco State University: 9.29

Buhl Industries: 8.16

Renee Child: 9.28

Chimera: 8.24

Cinekinetic PYT, Ltd., Australia: 5.18

Colortran, Inc.: 8.15

DAZ Productions, Inc.: 9.33

Digidesign, Inc.: 8.34

Dudkowski Patent Properties: 10.2

DykorTech: 5.19

Egripment USA: 5.13

Electro-Voice: 7.5, 7.21

Fujinon, Inc., Broadcast and Communications Products Division: 5.24

Harris Corporation: 9.30

Lowel-Light Manufacturing, Inc.: 8.17, 8.18, 8.22, 8.23, 8.28

Mole-Richardson Co.: 8.19, 8.21, 8.25, 8.27

NewTek: 10.3

Nikon, Inc.: 5.26

Gary Palmatier: 4.11, 11.12, 12.13, 12.14, 15.2

Panasonic Broadcast: 4.12, 12.2, 12.3, 13.4

QTV: 16.2

Selco Products Company: 7.23

Sennheiser Electronic Corporation: 7.19, 7.21

Shure, Inc.: 7.21, 7.22

Sony Electronics, Inc.: 4.10, 4.13, 4.14, 4.15, 4.22, 4.23, 8.21, 11.9

The Tiffen Company, LLC: 5.17

Thomson/Grass Valley: 9.18, 10.1, 10.4

VariZoom Lens Controls: 5.15, 5.16

Vinten, Inc.: 5.9, 5.11, 5.12, 5.20, 5.22, 5.23

Vizrt: 15.8

Herbert Zettl: 4.3, 4.4, 4.5, 4.18, 6.17, 6.18, 6.25, 6.28, 6.29, 6.31, 6.32, 7.11, 7.12, 7.13, 7.29, 8.1, 8.3, 8.4, 8.5, 8.6, 8.7, 8.10, 8.11, 8.13, 8.29, 9.5, 9.10, 9.12, 9.32, 12.8, 13.18, 13.19, 13.27, 14.3, 14.10, 14.11, 14.17, 15.6, 15.7

The storyboard (12.17) is courtesy of Bob and Sharon Forward. The generic sitcom residence (14.16) is based on a floor plan provided by Scott Fishman, Nickelodeon Studios.